The Draft Civil Code for Israel
in Comparative Perspective

The Draft Civil Code for Israel in Comparative Perspective

Edited by

Kurt Siehr and Reinhard Zimmermann

Mohr Siebeck

ISBN 978-3-16-149590-8

Die deutsche Nationalbibliothek lists this publication in the Deutsche Nationalbibliographie; detailed bibliographic data is available in the Internet at *http://dnb.d-nb.de.*

The book was typeset and printed by Gulde-Druck in Tübingen on non-aging paper and bound by Buchbinderei Held in Rottenburg.

Printed in Germany.

Preface

It is commonly accepted today that Israel is a mixed jurisdiction. It has been shaped by influences from the English (and US-American) common law and from the civilian tradition prevailing in Europe. But it does not conform to the usual pattern as we find it in South Africa, Scotland, Québec or Louisiana. For one thing, some aspects of family affairs remain governed be religious law. For another, we do not have here an originally civilian jurisdiction that is subsequently transformed, gradually, by being exposed to common law influence. For when the State of Israel was founded, in 1948, it was essentially a common law jurisdiction. Since then, it has moved towards the civilian world. One of the chief characteristics of a modern civilian legal system is a codification of private law. Israel is now contemplating the introduction of a Civil Code. That does not mean that it will cease to be a mixed jurisdiction. Public law has been, and will probably continue to be, subject to very considerable influence from the United States. The law of procedure remains firmly anchored in its common law origin. None the less, the adoption of a Civil Code may also, to some extent, civilianize legal methodology and the Israeli style of adjudication.

The proposed codification of Israeli private law is part of a remarkable resurgence of the idea of codification in the Western world. *Natalino Irti*'s racy catchword of *decodificazione* no longer adequately describes the modern reality. A broad variety of states (the Netherlands, Québec, Brazil, Russia, and many others) have recodified their private law within the past twenty-five years. The Republic of China also attempts to modernize its law by introducing, step by step, a codification in the civilian mould. In Germany, the most sweeping individual reform ever to have affected the BGB entered into force in 2002. In the course of it, large parts of consumer contract law have been repatriated into the general codification private law. That monument of stability of French legal culture, the *Code civil*, may also be caught up in this movement to reinvigorate the idea of codification by bringing the latter up to date. Even the idea of a European Civil Code has become a hotly contested issue; the "Common Frame of Reference" that has just been published, may one day turn out to be a first step in that direction.

This restoration of the faith in codification appears to be indicative of a widespread belief that the legal material does not constitute an indigestible and arbitrary mass of individual rules and cases, but that it can be reduced to a rational and organized system. For codification promotes the internal coherence of the law and facilitates its comprehensibility. At the same time, it provides both the conceptual framework and the intellectual point of reference for any further doctrinal, judicial and legislative development of the law.

At any rate, a Civil Code is an important document, both being shaped by, and shaping, a legal culture. The symposium that took place in January 2007 in the Hamburg Max Planck Institute for Comparative and International Private Law was designed to inform the community of comparative lawyers about the likely contents of the proposed Code, and to provide Israeli lawyers with a comparative assessment from the point of view of German (and Austrian) law. On the one hand, therefore, it is hoped that this symposium will further stimulate interest in Israeli law; on the other hand, it may still be possible, in the further stages of the legislative process, to take account of some of the suggestions made by the German-speaking contributors to the symposium, both in their papers and in the subsequent discussion. That the symposium took place in Hamburg is testimony to the close and happy links between the Max Planck Institute and legal scholarship in Israel since the days of Konrad Zweigert. Preeminent among those who have fostered these links, is Amos Shapira, and it was an auspicious coincidence that we were able to celebrate his 70th birthday in the *Überseeclub* on the evening of the first day of our conference. The present volume is concluded by Gunther Kühne's after-dinner speech on that occasion, and it therefore constitutes, in its entirety, a token of our esteem and friendship.

I would like to take this opportunity to thank all those who have contributed to this symposium, both from the German (and Austrian) and from the Israeli side. I am especially grateful to Aharon Barak, formerly Dean of the Faculty of Law of the Hebrew University, Attorney General of Israel, President of the Supreme Court, and Chairman of the Commission appointed for the preparation of the Civil Code for having come to Hamburg and for having provided the opening address. Many thanks are due also to Kurt Siehr for co-organizing the symposium, and to Matt Dyson and Ingeborg Stahl for editorial assistance.

A final word has to be said about the Draft Civil Code that has been appended, in an English translation, to the present volume. It is designed to facilitate what Roman lawyers are accustomed to call *Textstufenforschung*. The German (and Austrian) contributors to the symposium had at their disposal the English translation of a Draft from 2004 that had been kindly made available by the Israeli Ministry of Justice (Draft X). At the symposium, it turned out that the contributors from Israel had based their lectures on a more recent Draft from 2006 (Draft Y). For a number of reasons it was impossible to obtain an English translation of Draft Y (which, in turn, may be subject to further change in the course of the legislative process). Eventually, a revised version of Draft X was made available in English translation, by the Israeli Ministry of Justice, to all German-speaking contributors (Draft Z). It is this latter Draft – the latest one available to non-Hebrew speakers – that has been included in this volume; and all German (and Austrian) contributors have revised their papers accordingly. In most cases, the Israeli contributors have also supplied their German-speaking counterparts with a translation of the relevant provisions in Draft Y. Thus, in order to make their papers fit both the papers of their Israeli colleagues and the Draft printed as Appendix I, the German (and Austrian) contributors have usually referred to the numbering of provisions according to Draft Z (= old version) and Draft Y (= new version). The table of concordance printed as Appendix II also relates to Drafts Z and Y. By and large, there are only minor variations between the different versions.

Reinhard Zimmermann *Hamburg, December 2007*

Table of Contents

List of Abbreviations

A.	Atlantic Reporter, US
A.C.	Appeal Cases Reports, UK
ABGB	*Allgemeines Bürgerliches Gesetzbuch* (General Civil Code), Austria
AGBG	*Gesetz zur Regelung des Rechts der Allgemeinen Geschäftsbedingungen* (Standard Contract Terms Act), Germany
All E.R. (D)	All England Law Reports (Digest), UK
ALR	*Allgemeines Landrecht für die Preußischen Staaten* (Prussian Civil Code)
BGB	*Bürgerliches Gesetzbuch* (Civil Code), Germany
BGH	*Bundesgerichtshof* (Federal Supreme Court), Germany
BGHZ	*Entscheidungen des Bundesgerichtshofs in Zivilsachen* (Reports of the Federal Supreme Court in Private Law Matters), Germany
BVerfG	*Bundesverfassungsgericht* (Federal Constitutional Court), Germany
BVerfGE	*Entscheidungen des Bundesverfassungsgerichts* (Reports of the Federal Constitutional Court), Germany
BW	Burgerlijk Wetboek (Dutch Civil Code)
C.A.	Civil Appeal, Israel; Court of Appeal, UK
Ch.	Chancery Reports, UK
COM	European Community Documents
D.	The Digest of Justinian
D.L.R.	Dominion Law Reports, Canada
E.C.R.	European Court Reports, EU
E.R.	English Reports, UK
EC	European Community
ECJ	European Court of Justice
ECT	Treaty Establishing the European Community
ed.	editor, edition
eds.	editors
EEC	European Economic Community
EWCA Civ.	England and Wales Court of Appeal Civil Division neutral citation, UK
F.	Federal Reporter, US
F.H.	Further Hearing, Israel (Supreme Court hears an appeal from one of its own decisions, sitting in a larger panel than when it heard the decision being appealed)
H.C.J.	High Court of Justice, Israel
L.C.A.	Permitted Civil Appeal, Israel
Minn.	Minnesota Reports, US

NoB.	Nomikon Vima (Greek law journal)
N.W.	North Western Reporter, US
N.Y.S.	New York Supplement, US
NIS	New Israeli Schekel
OJ EC L	Official Journal of the European Union (Legislation), EU
P.	Pacific Reporter, US
P.D.	Piskei-Din, Law Reports of the Israeli Supreme Court; Probate Division, UK
P.M.	Pesakim Mehoziim, Law Reports of the Israeli District Courts
PECL	Principles of European Contract Law
PICC	Unidroit Principles of International Commercial Contracts
Q.B.	Queen's Bench Reports, UK
R.C.A.	Request for Civil Appeal, Israel
RG	*Reichsgericht* (Imperial Supreme Court), Germany
RGZ	*Entscheidungen des Reichsgerichts in Zivilsachen* (Reports of the Imperial Supreme Court in Private Law Matters), Germany
s.	section
SCC	Supreme Court of Canada
S.C.R.	Supreme Court Reports, Canada
Slg.	*Sammlung* (Reports of the Cases before the Court of Justice and the Court of First Instance, EU)
ss.	sections
U.S.	United States Supreme Court Reports
W.L.R.	Weekly Law Reports, UK
ZGB	*Zivilgesetzbuch* (Civil Code), Switzerland

List of Contributors

AHARON BARAK is the former President of the Supreme Court of Israel and Professor of Law emeritus at the Hebrew University of Jerusalem

NILI COHEN is Professor of Law at the Tel Aviv University Faculty of Law and a former Rector of Tel Aviv University

HANOCH DAGAN is Professor of Law at, and Dean of, the Tel Aviv University Faculty of Law

JOSEF DREXL is Director of the Max Planck Institute for Intellectual Property, Competition and Tax Law, Munich

IZHAK ENGLARD is a former Justice at the Supreme Court of Israel and Bora Laskin Professor of Law emeritus at the Hebrew University of Jerusalem

DANIEL FRIEDMANN is the Minister of Justice of Israel and Professor of Law emeritus at the Tel Aviv University Faculty of Law

ISRAEL GILEAD is Bora Laskin Professor of Law at the Hebrew University of Jerusalem

HANS CHRISTOPH GRIGOLEIT is Professor of Private Law, Commercial and Corporate Law, and European Private Law at the University of Regensburg

OFER GROSSKOPF is Professor of Law at the Tel Aviv University Faculty of Law

EVA-MARIA KIENINGER is Professor of German and European Private Law, and Private International Law at the University of Würzburg

HELMUT KOZIOL is Director of the European Centre of Tort and Insurance Law, and Professor of Private Law emeritus at the University of Vienna

GUNTHER KÜHNE is Professor of Law and Director of the Institute for German and International Mining and Energy Law at the Technical University of Clausthal, and Honorary Professor at the University of Göttingen

KURT SIEHR is Professor of Private Law, Private International Law and Comparative Law emeritus at the Faculty of Law, University of Zürich

CHRISTIANE WENDEHORST is Professor of Private Law, Medical Law, Private International Law and Comparative Law at the University of Göttingen

REINHARD ZIMMERMANN is Director at the Max Planck Institute for Comparative and International Private Law in Hamburg, and Professor of Private Law, Roman Law, and Comparative Legal History at the University of Regensburg

Introduction to the Israeli Draft Civil Code

By Aharon Barak*

Summary of Contents

I. Historical Background

1) Prior to the Establishment of the State

Until it was conquered by the British, Palestine was part of the Ottoman Empire. The civil law in the country – as well as in other parts of the Ottoman Empire – was comprised of statutes influenced by a number of sources[1]. Thus, for example, as a result of the reforms in the second half of the 19th century, the European influence upon Ottoman statutes increased (e.g. the French influence). However, the central source of the civil law was not influenced by Europe. That

* I would like to thank my research assistant, Yonatan Arbel, for his help in preparing this paper.

[1] *Norman Bentwich*, The Legal System of Israel, (1964) 13 International and Comparative Law Quarterly 236 and *Eliezer Malchi*, The History of the Law in Israel (2nd ed., 1952), 3 (in Hebrew).

was the Mejelle, which constituted the Ottoman Civil Code. It is composed of chapters (books) which were enacted from 1867 to 1877. Its sources are religious – Muslim – and it deals with civil relationships. Each chapter (or book) of the sixteen chapters of the Mejelle is dedicated to a separate legal subject, for example, sale, guarantee, assignment, and pledge[2]. Beside the Mejelle there were special statutes regarding land, whose sources were Muslim. In the areas of family law there was religious autonomy. The law recognised autonomous adjudication by the various religious communities, according to the law of those communities (Jews, Muslims, and different Christian denominations).

In 1917 Palestine was conquered by the British army. At first, martial law was put in place, and in 1922, as a result of the Lausanne Treaty[3], a civil regime was established. The main law of 1922 (the Order in Council 1922) stated (Article 46):

> "The jurisdiction of the Civil Courts shall be exercised in conformity with the Ottoman Law in force in Palestine on November 1st, 1914, and such later Ottoman Laws as have been or may be declared to be in force by Public Notice, and such Orders in Council, Ordinances and Regulations as are in force in Palestine at the date of the commencement of this Order, or may hereafter be applied or enacted; and subject thereto and so far as the same shall not extend or apply, shall be exercised in conformity with the substance of the common law, and the doctrines of equity in force in England, and with the powers vested in and according to the procedure and practice observed by or before Courts of Justice and Justices of the Peace in England, according to their respective jurisdictions and authorities at that date, save in so far as the said powers, procedure and practice may have been or may hereafter be modified, amended, or replaced by any other provisions. Provided always that the said common law and doctrines of equity shall be in force in Palestine so far only as the circumstances of Palestine and its inhabitants and the limits of His Majesty's jurisdiction permit and subject to such qualification as local circumstances render necessary."[4]

Pursuant to that provision, the civil law which had applied in the Ottoman Empire continued to apply in mandatory Palestine, joined by the new mandatory statutes. Where there was a lacuna in the local law, one could turn to the English common law and equity (but not to English statutes)[5]. During the thirty one years of British rule, a deep process of Anglification took place[6]. At first, this was a slow process, but one which steadily intensified. This Anglification

---

[2] For an English translation of the Mejelle, see *Charles A. Hooper*, The Civil Law of Palestine and Transjordan (1933).

[3] For an overview of the Lausanne Treaty, see *Philip Marshall Brown*, The Lausanne Treaty, (1927) 21 American Journal of International Law 503.

[4] The Palastine Order in Council, 1922–1947, Art 46 in: *R.H. Drayton* (ed.), The Laws of Palastine, vol. III, 2569, 2580 (1934).

[5] See H.C.J. 5/48 *Leon v. Acting District Commissioner of Tel-Aviv*, available online at http://elyon1.court.gov.il/files_eng/48/050/000/z01/48000050.z01.pdf; *Gad Tadeski*, The Problem of Lacunae in Law and Article 46 of the Palastine Order in Council, (1952) Mechkarim Be'Mishpat A'artzenu 54 (in Hebrew).

[6] Malchi (n. 1), 127.

was manifest in the replacing of Ottoman statutes by statutes influenced by the English tradition (e.g. in the areas of commercial law[7] and tort law[8] [in 1944]). The Anglification was also manifest in the increasing use of the "substance of the common law, and doctrines of equity," as determined in Article 46 of the Order in Council, 1922. However, these alterations did not bring about the annulment of the Mejelle, which continued to apply in its Turkish version, and in translation into Hebrew[9], Arabic[10] and English[11].

1) The Change at the Time of the Establishment of the State

At the time of the establishment of the State (in 1948) two major legal projects began: one in the field of public law, and the other in the area of private law. In the field of public law, the main undertaking was the enactment of Basic Laws (the *Grundgesetz* if you will). These are separate chapters, which are ultimately supposed to unite into one text – the Constitution of Israel[12]. The first Basic Law was enacted in 1958 and, since then, 10 additional Basic Laws have been enacted[13]. According to the 1995 case law of the Supreme Court of Israel, they constitute supra-statutory constitutional norms, like the German *Grundgesetz*[14]. Every court is authorised to conduct judicial review of the constitutionality of a statute[15].

---

7 See, for example, the Companies Ordinance (1929), Bills of Exchange Ordinance (1929) (Hebrew) and the Bankruptcy Ordinance (1936).

8 Civil Wrongs Ordinance (1944). For the process of integrating the English law of torts, see: *R. Gottschalk*, The Development of the Law of Torts in Israel, (1961) 24 Modern Law Review 345.

9 Mejella, *Kovetz Dinei Mishpat* (2nd edition, 1927) (in Hebrew, translated by Gad Frumkin).

10 *Salim Al-Rastum Baz*, Al Mejelle (1923).

11 *Supra*, n. 2.

12 That decision was made by the Knesset (the Israeli Parliament), and is known as "The Harari Proposal", after the name of the Parliament Member who suggested it. Protocols of the Knesset, 1950, 1743 (in Hebrew); see also *Amnon Rubinstein/Barak Medina*, The Constitutional Law of Israel (2005), 37 (in Hebrew) and *Dorner Dalia*, Does Israel Have a Constitution, (1999) 43 St. Louis University Law Journal 1325, 1326.

13 The Basic Laws, in chronological order, are: Basic Law: The Knesset (1958); Basic Law: Israel Lands as Basic Law: The People's Lands (1960); Basic Law: The President of the State 18 LSI (1964); Basic Law: The State Economy (1975); Basic Law: The Army (1976); Basic Law: Jerusalem, the Capital of Israel (1980); Basic Law: The Judiciary (1984); Basic Law: The State Comptroller (1988); Basic Law: Human Dignity and Liberty (1992); Basic Law: Freedom of Occupation (1994); Basic Law: The Government (2001). All of these are available online at: http://www.knesset.gov.il/description/eng/eng_mimshal_yesod1.htm.

14 C.A. 6821/93 *United Mizrachi Bank Ltd. v Migdal Coop. Vill.*, (1995) 49(4) P.D. 221 extracted in (1997) 31 Israel Law Review, 764, 770. (Other than Cheshin J, all other eight Judges agreed that the Israeli Parliament is capable of constituting a Constitution.)

15 *Aharon Barak*, Judicial Review of the Constitutionality of Laws, (1996) 3 U'Mimshal 403; this is, to some degree, the logical result of the opinions expressed in C.A. Mizrachi, *supra*, n. 14.

The second legal project was in the field of private law. The decision was taken gradually to abolish the Mejelle, and replace each of its chapters with an original Israeli statute. These statutes were drafted as chapters of a codification, as the idea was, in the words of the then Minister of Justice, "in the second phase, to unite these statutes, as well as other special statutes, into one whole and uniform document, which will serve as our comprehensive civil code"[16]. This undertaking did not include the law of marriage and divorce, to which the Ottoman regime continued to apply (religious law and religious courts).

In preparing the various statutes replacing the Mejelle, the Israeli legislature relied upon Israeli legal experience (the existing statutes and the case law), Jewish law, and comparative law (Anglo-American and Continental). Among those three sources, great weight was given to the third one (comparative law). For each statute a public committee was established (usually headed by a judge), including legal experts, which formulated the solution which seemed best for the issue before it. In explaining the statutory planning, Professor U. Yadin, who headed the project in the Ministry of Justice, noted:

> "Whereas the legal planning defined the sources of the new statutes from the beginning, and decided to eclectically draw from all of them, it never stopped to formulate a conceptual basis from which, *prima facie*, the statutory solutions for each issue were supposed to be derived. The Israeli planner could benefit from the Dutch example, by which the father of the reform, the late great Jewish professor Meyers, brought 50 principled questions before parliament and went to work, processing the details of his proposals, only after the legislature responded to them. In Israel as well there have been those who have demanded such prior conceptual clarification; that demand has been made especially by Professor Tadeschi, the head doctrinaire of civil law in the country.
>
> The Ministry of Justice, with the Government and the Knesset following it, have not gone that way. The system employed from the very beginning, and which is employed today, is completely pragmatic. The various solutions to a certain question in the Israeli, Jewish, and foreign law are presented before the legislature, examined on their merits according to what seems most efficient and just on that issue, and it is only according to that test that the choice between them is made.
>
> Thus, I cannot indicate the abstract principles at the foundation of the new statutes, and cannot present this legislation to you as a uniform 'legal system'"[17].

That project continued until 1981. It resulted in the enactment of 23 new statutes, replacing the various chapters of the Mejelle[18]. The Mejelle itself was for-

---

[16] (1965) *Divery Knesset* 41 (in Hebrew).

[17] *Uri Yadin*, The Law of Succession as Part of the New Israeli Civil Legislation, (1973) 3 Eyoney-Mishpat 26, 31 (in Hebrew).

[18] They are as follows: The Civil Wrongs (State Liability) Law, 1952; The Statute of Limitations, 1958; The Legal Capacity and Guardianship Law, 1962; The Amendment of Civil Wrongs (Compensation for Bodily Damage) Law, 1964; The Agency Law, 1965; The Pledges Law, 1967; The Guarantee Law, 1967; The Keepers Law, 1967; The Gift Law, 1968; The Sale Law, 1968; The Debt Assignment Law, 1969; The Land Law, 1969; The Contracts (Remedies) Law, 1971; The Rental and Lending Law, 1971; The Chattels Law, 1971; The Loss Return Law, 1973; The Con-

mally annulled[19]. It was determined, in a special statute, that "The Majelle is annulled" (The Majelle Annulment Law, 1984). The living connection to English law was gradually abolished. At first, a provision regarding "the independence of the statute" was included in the four central Laws of the 23 new statutes, pursuant to which, on the issues dealt with in those statutes, article 46 of the Order in Council 1922–1947 was not to apply[20]. Later, Article 46 itself was abolished[21] (in the Foundations of Law Statute, 1980). There was public debate regarding the question what would replace English law as the source which could fill lacunae in the Israeli statutes. Some wished to turn to Jewish law. Others said that there was no need for any reference provision. Ultimately a compromise was reached, which I proposed as the Attorney General[22], according to which:

> "If the court sees a legal question requiring decision, and does not find the answer in the statute, in case law precedent, or by way of analogy, it shall decide it according to the principles of liberty, justice, equity, and peace of the heritage of Israel"[23].

II. The Civil Statutes which Replaced the Mejelle: Codification by Instalments

As the new civil legislation projects progressed, an argument arose about whether this legislation has the characteristics of a civil code, even though it was being legislated chapter by chapter. My opinion then was – as it is today – that "the new statutes enacted by the Knesset in the areas of civil law are different than legislation in Israel, as they have the character of codification. They constitute a code, each in its subject matter and all of them together."[24] I emphasised the attempt to establish an entire legislative arrangement, with the intent that the answer to each issue could be found within it. I pointed out the attempt to be systematic and to ensure sufficient abstraction, and highlighted the wide scope and novelty in each of the fields. Professor Friedman was of the opinion that this legislation is not to be seen as a code, as it is not systematic, does not have common principles, and is not based on a common ideology[25].

---

tracts (General Part) Law, 1973; The Contracting Contract Law, 1974; The Restitution Law, 1979; The Trust Law, 1979; The Liability for Faulty Products Law, 1980; The Insurance Contract Law, 1981; The Standard Contract Law, 1982.

[19] The Mejelle Annulment Law, 1984.

[20] Art. 150 of the Succession Law, 1965; Art. 150 of the Land Law, 1969; Art. 24 to the Contracts (Remedies) Law, 1971; Art 63 Contracts (General Part) Law, 1973.

[21] Foundations of Law Law, 1980.

[22] See *Aharon Barak*, Foundations of Law and Legacy of Israel Act, (1987) 3 Shnaton Ha'Mishpat Ha'Ivri 265.

[23] Article 1 of the Foundations of Law Statute, 1980.

[24] *Aharon Barak*, Towards Codification of the Civil Law, (1975) 9 Tel Aviv University Studies in Law 10.

[25] *Daniel Friedman*, About the Interpertation of the New Israeli Legislation, (1977) 5 Eyonei

That disagreement is no longer relevant. Suffice it to say that an urgent need was felt in the past to annul the various chapters of the Mejelle and to put in place an original Israeli law instead. Such draft did not exist. Its preparation required a considerable amount of time. The State did not have that time. Thus, the method of "codification in instalments"[26] was chosen. Separate statutes were legislated. Each statute was intended to contain a comprehensive, systematic, and abstract solution, with the understanding that the various statutes would be unified in the future in a single text: a code[27]. Each statute was intended to reach as close to the ideal solution as possible. In most cases it succeeded in doing so. Anglification of the interpretation of the new statutes did not take place. The independent status of each of those statutes from English law was recognised, as well as the close internal link between them. When a lacuna in a legislative arrangement was discovered, it was solved by way of analogy from similar arrangements, and not by adopting the parallel English regime[28].

As time went by, the disadvantages of "codification in instalments" were felt. The various statutes did not have a united ideology. There was disharmony between the various arrangements. The wording was not uniform, and the solutions were not always in line with each other. Over time, amendments were made on particular points in one statute or another. Alongside that, the need to complete the codification project was felt. At the time of their enactment, the statutes were intended to be integrated together into a civil code[29]. There was a feeling that the time had come to complete the project.

III. Preparation of the New Code Proposal

At the time of my appointment as Attorney General (in 1975) I saw the preparation of the new Draft Code as one of my main tasks. I asked the late Professor U. Yadin, who had prepared the first phase, to submit a proposal for the new code. Professor Yadin began to prepare that proposal, but sadly did not have time to complete it. After his passing away, the draft which he had worked on was completed by me and by Ms. T. Spanic. That draft was presented to a public committee appointed by the Minister of Justice. Israeli experts on civil law par-

---

Mishpat 463 (in Hebrew). The reply to this opinion has been put in *Aharon Barak*, Law of Agency, 146 (vol. 1, 1995) (in Hebrew).

[26] This expression was first used by *Uri Yadin*, Realization of the Israeli Codification, (1979) 6 Eyonei Mishpat 506 (in Hebrew).

[27] Barak, Towards Codification of Civil Law (n. 24), 14.

[28] Barak, Law of Agency (n. 25), 153; see also H.C.J. 212/03 Herut – The National Jewish Movement v. Justice Mishael Cheshin, Chairman of the Central Elections Committee for the Sixteenth Knesset, paragraphs 8–11. Available online at: http://elyon1.court.gov.il/files_eng/03/120/002/a04/03002120.a04.HTM.

[29] *Supra*, n. 27; see also *Miguel Deutsch*, The Interpretation of the Civil Code 28–29 (vol.1, 2005) (in Hebrew).

ticipated in the committee[30]. Professor M. Deutsch served as a Committee Member and the primary researcher, and I chaired it. We were aided by employees of the Ministry of Justice, lead by T. Spanic, and when she retired, by S. Dana. The committee met once a month. It operated for approximately twenty years. The Israeli experts on various subjects presented their proposals to it. Considerable weight was given to comparative law. The existing codifications in Europe, and the various proposals to amend them, were examined. The new codifications, such as those in Québec and Holland, were examined[31].

The task assigned to the committee was not to make a new civil code from scratch. No revolution was called for in the new civil legislation. No fundamental change was needed in civil law. The role of the committee – and the role of the new code – was limited. The starting point was the existing law. Amendments and improvements – sometimes of considerable scope – which would allow the unification of the existing statutes into a civil code, were needed; a uniform and modern legislative policy was called for; consistent and uniform terminology was necessary; legislative amendment in cases of faults and lacunae which had been discovered in the existing legislation was required. What was needed, therefore, was improvement and amendment of the *status quo*, while replacing it with a coherent, comprehensive code which would provide modern solutions to the problems of our civil law[32].

The preparation of the proposal was completed. It was made available to the public at large, accompanied by detailed explanatory notes and an index for easy reference. Comments were received. Amendments were made. We have now reached the beginning of the legislative phases. The work will soon be turned into a bill and submitted to the Knesset for the legislative process.

IV. The Scope of the Draft Civil Code

The scope of the Draft Civil Code proposal fits the scope of the civil statutes which it aspires to replace. The chapters on pledges and inheritance are still missing from it. Regarding those two subjects, Israeli statutes exist, and the Ministry of Justice is preparing new proposals which will be added later[33]. The hope is also to add adoption, which a public committee is working on, and private interna-

---

[30] Throughout the different stages of work, the following jurists have participated: Yitzchak Englard, Me'eir Aran, Ricardo Ben-Uliel, Israel Gilead, Miguel Deutsch, Yehoshua Weisman, Ellen Zisbelt, Eyal Zamir, Nili Cohen, Dafna Levinson-Zamir, Birkiyaho Lifshitz, Menachem Mautner, Dani Mor, Rene Senilevits, Daniel Friedman, Mordechai Rabello, Shirley Rener, Gaberiala Shalev and Tana Shepnitz.

[31] *Hanoch Dagan*, Risks in Codification: On Over-Unification and Multiplicity of Remedies, (2007) 36 *Mishpatim* 249, 268, note 53.

[32] *Deutsch* (n. 29), 20–29.

[33] A committee, headed by Justice Tirkel (retired), was appointed to deal with the codification of the law of succession. The committee has handed in its recommendations.

tional law, with regard to which Professor Levontin submitted a proposal[34]. The Draft Code will not include a chapter on marriage and divorce. There is no civil law on those matters; they are regulated by religious laws (Jewish, Muslim, Canon law etc.)[35] in Israel, and the committee did not prepare such a law. The statutes dealing with "particular issues requiring great detail, regular updating, and integration of 'civil' arrangements with administrative arrangements" were removed from the subjects included in the proposal[36]. Thus, for example, the Draft Civil Code contains a chapter on sale, but does not contain the Sale (Apartments) Law, 1973; the Draft contains a new chapter on torts, but does not contain the Compensation for Persons Injured in Automobile Accidents Law, 1975. Nor was consumer legislation included, or the administrative arrangements in the existing law, such as management of the land registry, or administrative provisions regarding the returning of lost assets. On all those subjects, changes may occur during the legislative process in the Knesset.

V. The Structure of the Draft Civil Code

A great deal of thought was put in to the general structure of the Draft Civil Code. We aspired to attain internal integration and a uniform platform for a regime resting on a uniform legal policy. The Draft is composed of three major parts. The first is the general part. It includes the fundamental principles of the proposal, the rights pertaining to persons and the rules on legal acts. In the framework of that part we at first considered including a chapter on human rights, as was done in Québec. We refrained from doing so due to the difficulties which that would raise in the legislative process. At the head of the Draft we placed its objectives and the principle of good faith (*bona fides*). The rights regarding persons are based mainly upon existing law. The part on legal acts is new, excepting the chapter on agency which reflects the existing law. We at first wished to include a definition of "legal act", but after a few attempts we stopped trying. The second major part deals with obligations, and the third with property. The Draft Code closes with the part on limitations of claims and provisions regarding entry into force, application, and transition. In the sections dealing with obligations and property, the proposal's structure leads from the general to the specific. We attempted to ensure a systematic and rational distribution, while using a uniform structure[37].

---

[34] *A. Levontin*, The Choice of Law: A Model Statute with Section-by-Section Commentary (2004).

[35] See the Rabbinical Courts Jurisdiction (Marriage and Divorce) Law (1953), the Dayanim Law (1955), the Qadis Law (1961), The Druze Religious Courts Law (1962) and The Jurisdiction in Matters of Dissolution of Marriages (Special Cases) Law (1969).

[36] Introduction to the Civil Code Bill, 16.8.06, 5 (2004) (in Hebrew).

[37] For an elaboration on this matter, see *Deutsch* (n. 29), 29–55. See also *Miguel Deutsch*, The

VI. The Need for a Civil Code

When the State was established an urgent need was felt to abolish the Mejelle and to replace it with new civil legislation. A similar need is not at the foundation of the code proposal. Some are of the opinion that it would be sufficient to make amendments to particular points in existing statutes, or to pass new legislation on issues on which the existing statutes should be replaced, for example, to annul the Civil Wrongs Ordinance and replace it with a new torts statute. Others believe that all that should be done in the framework of unifying the sporadic statute law and adapting it to a codification structure[38]. That is the approach at the foundation of the code proposal. In the introduction to the proposal, we pointed out the advantages of that way of legislation.

1) The Improvement of Legal Certainty through Ensuring Coherence

The Draft Code will ensure coherence in different areas in which it is lacking today. Thus, for example, there is currently no fitting hierarchy between the regimes in the area of competition between conflicting rights to property. The regime in s. 4 of the Debt Assignment Law is not consistent with the one in s. 12 of the Chattels Law; the regime in s. 14 of the Trust Law is not consistent with the ones in s. 9 of the Land Law and s. 12 of the Chattels Law; and so on. The new law determines a comprehensive and concentrated arrangement in the area of competition between conflicting rights, which will deal with all types of such conflicts, regarding all types of rights.

At times, the lack of coherence is due to the various sources of inspiration in the law, which are not consistent. Thus, s. 5 of the Pledge Law ("market overt" in a pledge) is based upon a view stemming from the glorification of the public dimension in possession of chattels according to French law. That view is foreign to the view of "market overt" in sales, according to s. 34 of the Sale Law. The Code will base the arrangements upon a uniform ideology, annulling s. 5 of the Pledge Law.

Another example from this "family" regards the right to protect property by way of self help. The regime on this issue in the Land Law, s. 18, is based upon a continental view. The regime in the Civil Wrong Ordinance, within the framework of the tort of assault (s. 24(2) of the Civil Wrong Ordinance [new version]) is the product of English law. Both regimes are totally inconsistent, and it is not infrequent that a person is entitled to act, for the purposes of the one, but he is not able to do so according to the other regime, and *vice versa*. These differences

---

Structuring of the Israeli Codification: A Proposal of a Structure, (1999) 29 *Mishpatim* 587 (in Hebrew).

[38] For details on the different approaches, see: *Aharon Barak*, Codification of Civil Law and the Law of Torts, (1990) 24 Israel Law Review 645.

are not based upon any real justifications, rather upon the historical character of the laws. The code will remove this obstacle.

An additional important example is the law of remedies. The code will unify the principles of the remedy regimes in contract and tort law. There is no sufficient justification for the "alienated" development of the regimes in the two areas. Thus, for example, the principle of enforcement of the interest of the party harmed, and the exceptions to that principle, should be common to both areas. The code will create a uniform infrastructure, whereas in certain given contexts, when there is justification for differentiating between tort and contract, such a differentiation will be made.

It is also worth mentioning the law of multiple parties in this context. The law of multiple tortfeasors and the law of multiple debtors are arranged today in separate statutes. Once the common obligation has arisen, its historical source – whether in torts or contracts – should have but slight weight regarding the fate of the obligation afterwards (e.g., whether a waiver on the part of the creditor with regard to one debtor also affects the other debtors). The proposal unifies the rules concerning multiple parties in a single chapter, in the part dealing with the general law of obligations.

2) Adapting the Law to Modern Development

Most of the existing civil law was enacted about 30 years ago. Although that is not a very long time ago, the world of law, in and outside of Israel, has seen important developments over those years. Those developments should be properly expressed in statute law. Thus, for example, modern contract law is marching toward a demand for greater cooperation between the parties to a contract, weakening the confrontational aspects of the contract. This trend, and others, will be reflected in the Draft Code. Thus, for example, the doctrine of comparative fault will be adopted in contract law, and the doctrine of frustration of contract will be comprehensively revised. The elements of contractual liability will be softened, ensuring greater justice between the parties to the contract. The doctrine of frustration, which has today become a dead letter in Israel, will receive its deserved place in the framework of the more cooperative view of a party's liability for new events which alter the basis of the contractual relationship.

3) Establishment of a Comprehensive Jurisprudence

The code will make an important contribution to the establishment of a systematic jurisprudence. Coherence will lead to the crystallisation of a clear outline of the system, and vagueness of legal doctrines is prevented. Beyond this general and important contribution, the code will develop central doctrinal institutions, such as the legal act. A special chapter, which will apply to all types of legal acts, is dedicated to this subject. In addition, the purposes of the code will be determined, serving as a fundamental source for interpretation.

4) "Reinforcing" the Statutory Basis of the Law

Various subjects in the statute law today "suffer" from their overly laconic nature, or from a complete lack of any arrangement, which takes a toll on legal certainty. What the statute law misses is at times completed by case law. Nevertheless, the institutional limitations on the courts in developing the law create a preference to reach a comprehensive arrangement through legislation. The code will "reinforce" these areas of the law. This will be the case especially in the law governing gifts, conclusion of contracts, and liens, whose regimes are no more detailed than a telegram, and subjects like trust law and brokerage contracts, for which there is no systematic regime whatsoever. The code will, in future, govern the law in those areas.

5) General Revision

The code is the result of a comprehensive revision of the existing statutory provisions. As mentioned, more than 30 years have passed since the original Israeli statute law was enacted. Great judicial experience in interpretation and development of the law has been gathered. Faults in wording and failures to realise the purpose of the statutes have been discovered. Now, a revision done in one stroke is clearly preferable to accumulating specific statutory patches at different times. Amendment of a statute on a certain point may upset the balance between it and the law on a different point, in a different area of law. When the revision is done en bloc, it is possible to ensure that the balance will be preserved, as the legislature is aware of the whole picture.

The scope of the revision in the code varies, according to the character of the issue at hand. Regarding subjects upon which the law is acceptable, only minor alterations have been made. That is the case, for example, regarding the general part of contract law. Tort law, however, needs a more comprehensive revision. For example: the property torts, which are today split up on the basis of archaic differentiations, will be unified into one general tort, based on fault-liability; wide immunity will be granted to public servants, whereas the public body will remain liable for the tort; various concrete torts will be abolished, as they offer nothing that the principle of liability for negligence cannot provide. These changes, and others, are called for in order to grant more rationality to the law and to adapt it to the proper policy. Another subject which underwent comprehensive revision, as mentioned above, is the law frustration of contract. The regimes concerning the law of remedies, the law of multiple debtors and creditors, and the law of liens can also be counted among those subjects which underwent comprehensive revision. A new part on limitations of claims has also been written. The existing statute of limitations was promulgated in 1958. The law of limitations is among the most complicated areas in civil law. In the existing law there are conspicuous cases of imprecision, lacuna, and vagueness. The new part is detailed, and it formulates a modern and systematic regime, and thus aspires to add certainty to this complex area. In a wide range of cases, the revision in the draft law is a surgical one, amending certain faults in certain provisions, as required in the light of the case law experience or the literature[39].

Some authors have expressed the concern that the new code will make legal reasoning more formalistic[40]. I hope that this concern will prove to be unfounded. Formalism is one thing; structured thinking is a different matter altogether. The general concept of the code does not mean a uniform approach that does not recognise the uniqueness of each area and subject-matter. The drive for coherence does not mean the abandonment of the values and principles which characterise each area of law[41]. Indeed, the fundamental goal of the Draft Code is not merely one of aesthetics; but rather the desire to express the values of society. The Draft is intended to allow for each area of the law to evolve according to its own values and characteristics, while taking into account the general framework. In this respect it is like an orchestra composed of many players, where each player tries to maximise the effect of his own instrument but all the players together try to optimise the composition. Indeed, the aim of the Draft is not to bring about a new legal thinking, to create a new trend in scholarship, to change the relationship between the Judge and the Legislator, or to enact a new legal environment. The Draft Civil Code is but a tool. It is based upon pre-existing rules, and it is aimed at providing for a better solution, one that is more organic.

VII. The Future of the Draft Civil Code

The question of the "future" primarily arises on three levels: its future in the legislative process; its future in the interpretation it will be given by the courts; and its future in Israeli society in general.

The proposal's future in the legislative process is not clear whatsoever. That is certainly the case regarding the question whether the proposal will turn into law or not. Moreover, it is not at all clear how the legislature (the Knesset) will handle the Draft Code. The concern is that if the Draft is submitted for debate in the

---

[39] Introduction to the Codification Bill (n. 35), 7–10.

[40] *Menachem Mautner*, Codex of the Common Law, (2007) 36 Mishpatim 199 (in Hebrew).

[41] For the importance of coherency in law, see *Aharon Barak*, Judicial Discretion (1989); *Alon Harel*, Coherence Theories of Law, (1994) 18 Tel Aviv University Law Review 387–406 (in Hebrew).

plenum of the Constitution, Statute, and Law Committee, it will take a long time; many amendments are likely to be inserted into it, resulting from political pressure and changing the internal balance within the proposal. In a similar case – the new Companies Law, which was the product of a public committee which I headed and which laboured for fifteen years – a special technique was employed: A small subcommittee of the Constitution, Statute, and Law Committee was established, headed by one of the committee members. Within a short time the proposal was approved by it, and was passed to the plenum of the committee and approved with few alterations. I assume that this system will be considered by the Knesset.

After the codification proposal has passed all phases of legislation, its future will be determined to a large extent by the courts. Its fate will depend upon the interpretation it is given. In the beginning of the Draft Code, its purposes are determined. That is intended to direct the judges toward purposive interpretation. The hope is that the courts will make use of that guidance. It must be remembered that in Israel we do not have experience with the need judicially to interpret a code of wide scope. Our judges are accustomed to interpreting specific statutes, which are surrounded by "common law – Israeli style". The use of the doctrine of lacuna and of filling such lacunae is not frequent. Indeed, Israel is a mixed jurisdiction[42]. It has wide and deep common law influences. However, it also contains influences from the continental legal systems. The existing statutes are an example of that. The hope is that our courts will allow the Civil Code to develop organically; to provide solutions to new problems; and to develop a proper balance between substance and formalism, while preserving and advancing the core values. That will be "Israeli style" interpretation of an "Israeli style" Civil Code.

How will the proposal be received by the population at large, and specifically, among jurists? It is difficult to answer that question. From responses to date, the attitude is generally a positive one. The hope is that it will continue be so after the Draft Code has become law.

[42] See *Aharon Barak*, The Israeli System of Law: its Heritage and Culture, (1992) *Ha'Parklit* 40, 197 (in Hebrew); see also Bentwich (n. 1). For a discussion on mixed jurisdictions, see *Vernon V. Palmer*, Mixed Jurisdictions Worldwide: The Third Legal Family (2001).

Consumer Protection Law under the Israeli Draft Civil Code

By Ofer Grosskopf*

Summary of Contents

I. Introduction

Consumer protection law in Israel is still in its evolutionary stages. Starting in the early days of Israeli law, one can find occurrences of laws based on the theory that efficient and fair exchange between merchants and consumers requires a unique legal environment, divergent from the classical "freedom of contracts" regime[1]. However, only in the 1980s was this theory effectively and consistently assimilated into Israeli private law, a transition achieved through the combined forces of the legislator and the judiciary. The considerable consumer protection legislation of the 1980s and 1990s reshaped the legal relationships between merchants and consumers, mainly through the introduction of mandatory rules (*ius cogens*) in favour of consumers. The courts reinforced this development by de-

---

* I am grateful to Hanoch Dagan, Roy Kreitner, and Barak Medina for their helpful comments and suggestions and to Michal Shnapp for her excellent research assistance.

[1] See, e.g., the Interest Law, 1957, and the Commodities and Service (Control) Law, 1957.

parting from a formalist and non-interventionist position and adopting a value-driven, activist approach that justified the imposition of external standards of fairness on contracting parties in general, and the merchant-consumer relationship in particular. This process is still in motion. In various cases the legal protection provided to consumers in Israel today is still deficient and should be allowed to evolve further. Conversely, in a few contexts, consumer protection is excessive and should be relaxed.

As we stand at the brink of codifying our private law, we need to ask ourselves how the prospects of this ongoing project – the development of consumer protection law – will be affected by the new Civil Code? Will consumer protection law be a part of the new Civil Code? Will the future development of consumer protection law take place within the Civil Code, or only outside of it? The present paper seeks to address these questions in view of the Draft Civil Code that was put forward by the codification committee headed by former Chief Justice Aharon Barak.

The introductory notes to the Draft Civil Code state categorically that "the Civil Code Proposal does not include the various statutes dealing with consumer protection"[2]. As this paper demonstrates, this statement is both inaccurate and misleading. It is inaccurate because several pivotal elements of the consumer protection legislation of the 1980s and 1990s (e.g. the Standard Contracts Law, 1982) were incorporated into the Draft Civil Code. Further, it is misleading because a crucial ingredient of consumer protection in Israel today is based on a tailored application of general contract law principles (e.g. the provisions of the Contracts (General Part) Law, 1973), which naturally forms the core of the Draft Civil Code. Moreover, a few of the most important innovations in the Draft, such as the broad "purpose" clause (on which see below) and the authority to grant exemplary damages, have the potential to reinforce consumer protection law. Therefore, my final conclusion will be that the Draft does allow for the development of consumer protection law within the Code. Whether the courts will follow this lead or not remains, as under current legislation, a matter for their own discretion.

A note of caution as to the scope of this paper is in order. As its title indicates, the inquiry will concentrate on the current state of consumer protection in Israel, on its inclusion within the Draft Civil Code, and on new possibilities that the Draft offers to the courts. The paper will not, therefore, attempt to rationalise consumer protection law nor to evaluate the cases in which it is either still lacking, or overreaches its justification. Particularly, an investigation into the various grounds that may justify such intervention on the part of the law (asymmetric information, tacit collusion among merchants, behavioural biases of consumers, etc.), and thus the proper extent and boundaries of consumer protection law, goes beyond the limits of the present inquiry. In short, the present paper

---

[2] See s. 13 of the introductory notes to the Draft Civil Code.

deals with descriptive and institutional matters, not with substantial normative evaluations of the consumer protection agenda.

This paper contains three parts: the first part provides a brief account of the current status of consumer protection law in Israel; the second part examines the extent to which current consumer protection law was incorporated into the Draft Civil Code; and finally, the third part describes a few of the Draft Civil Code's innovations and suggests ways in which they can be employed by the courts in the context of consumer protection. Short concluding remarks summarise my key findings.

II. The Current Status of Consumer Protection Law in Israel

Consumer protection law, much like any other branch of law, can evolve in many different forms. Change may be the result of an instantaneous, revolutionary transformation or of a gradual, evolutionary process. It may grow out of judicial interpretation, or sprout from legislative efforts; development may incrementally result from numerous statutes or decisions, each dealing with a specific consumer activity (taking out a loan, buying insurance, purchasing commodities, etc.); or it may be jumpstarted by one statute (or maybe even by one groundbreaking legal precedent) that attempts to relate to divergent fields of consumer activity. All of the above developmental tacks can be discerned in the evolution of Israeli consumer protection law, but in general, we can see the following four layers: (1) specific consumer protection legislation; (2) general consumer protection legislation; (3) general legislation that has special relevance to consumer protection; and (4) general contract legislation. Here is a short account of these four layers, arranged from the specific to the general:

1) Specific Consumer Protection Legislation

Beginning in the 1970s, and continuing with vigour during the 1980s and 1990s, a considerable number of statutes were enacted and amended in order to include provisions that protect consumers who engage in specific economic activities[3]. For instance, the Sale (Housing) Law, 1973[4], and the Sale (Apartments) (Assurance of Investment of Persons Acquiring Apartments) Law, 1974, oblige sellers of new buildings and apartments to provide purchasers with warranties for the quality of the construction projects and with assurances for their money[5],

---

[3] For a survey in English, see *Allen Zysblat*, Consumer Protection Legislation in Israel, in: Alfredo Mordechai Rabello (ed.), Essays on European Law and Israel (1996), 643.

[4] The protection provided to purchasers by this act was considerably strengthened by the 1990 amendment.

[5] The Sale (Apartments) (Assurance of Investment of Persons Acquiring Apartments) Law, 1974, contained a serious loophole until the mid-1980s, since one of the types of collateral it al-

respectively. Another example is the second chapter of the Guarantee Law, 1967, which was enacted in 1992 and amended in 1997. That chapter, as it now stands, provides significant defences to a "protected surety" (i.e. most of the non-commercial private sureties) including a requirement that the debtor will exhaust the proceedings against the principle debtor, a reduction of each protected surety's liability to his or her relative part in the debt, and a limitation on the amount of interest that may have to be paid in case of default[6]. Similar statutes exist with respect to other spheres of consumer activities, such as banking[7], insurance[8], non-banking loans[9], and real estate agents[10]. In fact, out of about 20 statutes that are usually considered to constitute the consumer protection legislation, at least 11 can be described as specific consumer protection legislation.

The effect of the special consumer protection legislation has been considerable[11]. In certain instances it changed market norms and provided a much more protective environment for consumers. The two examples mentioned above, housing and guarantees, demonstrate such transformations. Construction projects in Israel are conducted these days with close scrutiny of the financial institutions that guarantee the purchasers' investments, and most of the loans are secured by charges over property and not by personal guarantees of relatives. Obviously, enhanced protection for consumers does have its costs. Buyers are required to pay for the financial guaranties they are compelled to receive[12], and borrowers who cannot provide sufficient collateral are sometimes forced to take out loans in the grey market. Yet, there seems to be a relatively large consensus that the special consumer protection legislation has at least partially succeeded in achieving its goals.

---

lowed was often ineffective. This reality changed when the Supreme Court reinterpreted the legal regime in order to protect consumers who received the problematic collateral. The Court's intervention had a considerable effect on the market, and the main collateral provided today for most of the construction projects is a financial guarantee from a bank. The Court decisions that closed the loophole are discussed in the text to n. 64, *infra.*

[6] Sureties are not consumers in the strict sense of the term. Nevertheless, it is customary to regard the protection of private non-commercial sureties as part of consumer protection law. See also n. 34 *infra.*

[7] See the Banking (Service to Consumers) Law, 1981.

[8] See the Insurance Contract Law, 1981.

[9] See the Non-bank Loans Arrangement Law, 1993.

[10] See the Real Estate Agents Law, 1996.

[11] Apart from private sanctions (usually damages) nearly all of the special consumer protection legislation includes criminal sanctions. In addition, the new Class Actions Law, 2006, opens the door for the submission of class actions according to the special consumer protection legislation, but only for violations against private end-users. See s. 3(a) of the Class Actions Law, 2006, and item 1 in the second appendix.

[12] See C.A. 3190/99 *Shoker v. A.R.M. Ra'anna Building and Renting Ltd* (2000) 54(3) P.D. 127 (the Supreme Court approved the practice of passing-on the costs of financial guarantees to purchasers, noting that the cost will be transferred in any case through the price).

2) General Consumer Protection Legislation

In 1981 the Knesset enacted the Consumer Protection Law, which, as its name proclaims, was destined to serve as the pillar of consumer protection law is Israel[13]. The act, amended 21 times during the past 25 years (13 times since 2000), includes both a substantive part, which specifies different measures of consumer protection, and a procedural part, which establishes several enforcement mechanisms.

The substantive part contains four types of controls: (a) detailed prohibitions against certain practices, such as misleading consumers, exploitation, and false advertisement; (b) extensive duties of disclosure, including detailed provisions as to how products should be marked and which kind of information and documents must be conveyed to the consumer; (c) regulation of specific distribution methods (door-to-door sales and telemarketing) and the sale of holiday units; (d) provisions that delegate power to the Minister of Commerce to regulate certain aspects of consumer deals, including warranties, formalities (e.g. the size of the letters in standard contracts), advertisements directed to minors, credit sales and so on. It is worth noting that while the original act, and its initial amendments, were concerned with the first two types of controls (detailed prohibitions and duties of disclosure), the amendments in the last 10 years or so deal mainly with the last two types (regulating specific activities and delegating power to the minister of commerce).

The procedural part, that deals with the enforcement of the substantial provisions of the act[14], is based on a mixture of public and private enforcement. Public enforcement comprises both criminal sanctions and the establishment of an administrative authority named the Commissioner of Consumer Protection and Fair Trade. Private enforcement was detailed by an elaborate section that allowed the submission of class action suits for violation of the Law. Recently, this section was replaced by the more general Class Actions Law, 2006, which allows private end-users to sue for any violation of their rights[15].

There is very little doubt that those enforcement mechanisms have functioned quite poorly in the past. Public enforcement is almost non-existent due to insufficient funding, while private enforcement, through class actions, encountered considerable difficulties in the courts[16]. It is hoped that with the enactment of the

---

[13] An important difference between most of the special consumer protection legislation and the Consumer Protection Law is that the former usually protects both private and commercial end users, while the latter explicitly defines "consumer" as a private user ("a person who buys a product or receives a service ... mainly for his or her personal use or for his or her home or family").

[14] Most of the enforcement mechanisms in the Consumer Protection Law refer specifically to the substantive provisions of the Law and as such are irrelevant to the enforcement of provisions in the special consumer protection legislation. An exception is the Supervisor Commissioner of Consumer Protection, who can deal with any injury to consumers.

[15] See n. 11, *supra*.

[16] The introduction of class actions into Israeli law was done in a piecemeal fashion, and without a proper legislative framework. Consequently, the implementation of this mechanism raised

new Class Action Law, 2006, this important mechanism will become an effective enforcement tool. Enforcement is thus considered a major problem, which greatly diminishes the efficacy of the Consumer Protection Law.

However, there are at least two other impediments, beside deficient enforcement, that prevent the Consumer Protection Law from providing effective protection to consumers. First, the act deals mainly with the process of contracting, putting a very strong emphasis on the goal of providing maximum information to consumers[17]. In contrast, its regulation of the content of consumer contracts or the ability to break contracts is very limited[18]. Consequently, the act provides consumers with very poor protection against behavioural biases[19]. For instance, it does not regulate the issue of terminating service contracts, thus allowing merchants to take advantage of consumers' present preferences by offering low prices in the short run in exchange for restricting the consumers' ability to opt-out of the relationship in the long run. In addition, the act does not provide significant protection against the reality of tacit collusion among merchants[20]. Recently this problem received considerable public attention when all of the major banks in Israel simultaneously raised their commissions. Yet, the Consumer Protection Law's concentration on the issue of information turns it into a toothless tool for combating such practices. Furthermore, though considerable powers of regulation were delegated to the Minister of Commerce, their implementation by the minister has been rather slow. For instance, it took almost six years to execute the authority to regulate warranties and post-sale services, and even then, the long-awaited regulation covers only one segment (albeit an important one) of the market[21].

Second, the Israeli courts tend to interpret the provisions of the Consumer Protection Law in the light of the general principles of contract and tort law. Consequently, though the rhetoric employed by the courts asserts that the stand-

---

many difficulties, and came to a practical halt with the Supreme Court decision in R. C. A. 3126/00 *The State of Israel v. A. S. T. Project Management and Human Resource Ltd* (2003) 57(3) P. D. 220.

[17] The Law, however, has very little to say about the problem of consumers' information overload.

[18] For example, the 2005 amendment that deals with return policies only obliges merchants to publish their return policy in a clear and comprehensive manner, and to act according to their stated policy. The act imposes a return policy only in case the merchant did not act according to his declared policy or failed to publish his return policy. See s. 4C of the Consumer Protection Law.

[19] Actually, the only worthwhile defence that the act provides against behavioural biases is with respect to well-defined transactions, such as door-to-door sales, sale of vacation units, and telemarketing.

[20] The Anti-trust Law, 1988, prohibits agreements that limit market competition, but does not provide efficient tools to prevent tacit collusion among repeat players. See, e.g., *David Gilo/Ariel Porat*, The Hidden Roles of Boilerplate and Standard-Form Contracts: Strategic Imposition of Transaction Costs, Segmentation of Consumers, and Anticompetitive Effects, (2006) 104 Michigan Law Review 983, 1003–1014.

[21] The authority was given in June 2000, but the regulations were introduced only in February 2006 and came into force 180 days later. The regulations cover only electronic and gas equipment. See Consumer Protection Regulations (Liability and After-sale Service), 2006.

ards set under the Consumer Protection Law are stricter, it is hard to see the practical effects of this strict treatment. The decision of the Supreme Court in the case of *Barzani v. Bezeq the Israel Telecommunication Corp. Ltd*[22] is an important precedent demonstrating this tendency. The case involved an attempt by a consumer to bring a class action suit against the national telephone company, Bezeq, for misleading consumers[23]. Due to its methods of calculation, Bezeq charged its international callers, including the plaintiff, at a slightly higher tariff per minute than the one it published. The plaintiff claimed that these small miscalculations accumulated to considerable sums of money and sought to sue for them in a class action. The Supreme Court majority opinion refused, stating that since the plaintiff was not able to demonstrate that he himself had read the publication and was deceived by it, he had no personal claim, a necessary precondition for submitting a class action. The majority relied heavily on established tort doctrines, such as causation and damage assessment, in reaching its conclusion that the plaintiff must show that he was misled by the publication. In doing so, the Supreme Court refused to follow the minority's suggestion to apply different principles for the interpretation of the Consumer Protection Law, stating that such innovative principles were not set by the legislator, and could not be invented by the Court[24].

The upshot of the above mentioned limitation is that the Consumer Protection Law has not fulfilled its destiny, and did not become the bedrock of consumer protection in Israel. From a theoretical perspective it failed to instigate an independent jurisprudence of consumer protection. As a result, Israeli consumer protection law today is not based on general principles, but on the specific legislation (layer 1 above) or on the application of general principles of contract law (layers 3 & 4). From a practical perspective, the influence of the general provisions of the act (i.e. provisions that do not deal with specific transactions, such as the sale of vacation units) is also quite modest[25]. A very common pattern in the case law is to justify the ruling on general principles, and then to mention that

---

[22] F.H. 5712/01 (2003) 57(6) P.D. 385

[23] See s. 2 of the Consumer Protection Law.

[24] Another example for the same tendency concerns the scope of s. 2 of the Consumer Protection Law (misleading consumers). Following general principles of contract law with respect to the scope of s. 15 of the Contracts (General Part) Law (recession due to deceit), the district courts applied s. 2 of the Consumer Protection Law only to pre-contractual representations, and refused to apply it to representations that became part of the contract or to representations made after the contract was signed. The Supreme Court had not intervened in this practice (see C.A. 3955/04 *Raizel v. Bank Leumi of Israel* [not published, 4/7/2005]), and finally the act had to be amended in order to facilitate such claims under it. See Consumer Protection Law (Amendment No. 18), 2005 (from 22/12/2005).

[25] See *Gabriela Shalev*, Codification of Private Law and Consumer protection, in: *Alfredo Mordechai Rabello* (ed.), European Legal Traditions and Israel (1994), 493, 497 where she writes: "It is interesting to note that the influence of the Consumer Protection Law has been quite limited, and most consumer complaints are currently resolved within the framework of the general contract codification ...".

the same result could have been achieved according to the Consumer Protection Law, or vice-versa[26]. Moreover, in the past, an important practical reason for invoking the Consumer Protection Law has been the relatively exceptional ability to file class actions under it[27]. After the enactment of the Class Actions Law, 2006, which does not limit the class actions of private consumers to causes arising under any specific act[28], the Consumer Protection Law need no longer be invoked solely for this purpose. Consequently the impact of the Consumer Protection Law could decline even further.

3) General Legislation that has Special Relevance to Consumer Protection

Some pivotal safeguards available to consumers under Israeli law are provided through general legislation, which protects at least in theory, merchants as well as consumers[29]. Two key examples are the Defective Products (Liability) Law, 1980 and the Standard Contracts Law, 1982. The Defective Products (Liability) Law imposes strict liability on producers for bodily harm caused by defective products they have manufactured. The Standard Contracts Law authorises the standard contracts tribunal and the general courts to strike down or amend unfair provisions that are included in a standard contract[30]. Obviously, the prime beneficiaries of these statutes are private consumers, but their scope of operation is by no means limited to them. In fact, these acts cover any person who suffers bodily harm caused by a defective product and any party who accepted an offer to contract according to a standard contract[31], respectively. For that reason their provisions may also protect a commercial agent who suffers bodily harm while handling defective merchandise or who attempts to break away from an unfair restriction contained in the supplier's standard contract. Nevertheless, the liti-

---

[26] See, e.g., R.C.A. 8733/96 *Langbert v. The State of Israel – Israel Land Authority*, (1999) 55(1) P.D. 168 (a duty to disclose the full cost of paying in credit was based on s. 2(13) and s. 9 of the Consumer Protection Law, but the Court mentioned that a similar result could be reached based on the general duty to act in good faith according to s. 12 and s. 39 of the Contracts (General Part) Law).

[27] See n. 16, *supra*. For a survey in English, see *Allen Zysblat*, Consumer Class Actions in Israel – Some First Impressions, in: Alfredo Mordechai Rabello/Andrea Zanotti (eds.), Developments in European, Italian and Israeli law (2001), 365.

[28] See n. 11, *supra*.

[29] In this context I use the term consumer in the widest possible sense, i.e. end users, both private and commercial. See also n. 13, *supra*.

[30] For a survey in English, see *Gabriela Shalev*, Standard Contracts under Israeli Law, (1990) 10 Tel Aviv University Studies in Law 229.

[31] The original Standard Contracts Law of 1964 limited its application to a "contract for the supply of a commodity or a service", i.e. to "consumer contracts" in the wide sense of the term. In contrast, the current statute defines a "standard contract" without reference to the nature of the transaction ("the text of a contract all or part of the conditions of which have been determined in advance by one party ...").

gants who employ these statutes are mainly consumers, and these statutes are thus considered to be part and parcel of consumer protection legislation[32].

The implementation of the Standard Contracts Law by the judiciary encountered considerable difficulties. The original act was introduced in 1964, but its operation in the two decades that followed was a complete failure. In most cases, judges limited their intervention to clauses that were invalid as being contrary to public policy as well (e.g. broad exemption clauses), and did not use the authority granted to them to ensure fair treatment of consumers. The courts reluctance to give the Standard Contracts Law its full force moved the legislator to re-enact the statute in 1982, in order to send a clear message to the judiciary that a much more vigorous application was called for. This time the courts grabbed the reigns, and in the last two decades we have witnessed a growing tendency to employ the act in order to protect consumer interests.

However, the application of the Standard Contracts Law still suffers from two main deficiencies: first, the standard contracts tribunal, which was established under the statute in order to decide the legality of standard contract drafts, suffers from acute malfunctioning. One major difficulty (certainly not the only one) is that the organisations that are authorised to set the review process in motion (i.e. the attorney general, consumers' organisations, and suppliers) are either without resources or without incentives to do so. Second, the Supreme Court has yet to establish a clear jurisprudence for the regulation of standard contracts. In particular, it has not yet addressed the question of economic arguments concerning *ex ante* effects of judicial intervention. Consequently, different judges will apply the act in dramatically different ways. Some judges examine the standard condition purely as it stands and do not give any weight to the possible adverse effects of their intervention on future transactions; others are well aware of the flexibility of economic relationships and thus apply a much more cautious approach. Despite these flaws, it seems that the Standard Contracts Law, in its 1982 incarnation, does serve as one of the main pillars of consumer protection law in Israel.

4) General Contract Legislation

The Contracts (General Part) Law, 1973, and the Contract Law (Remedies for Breach of Contract) Law, 1970, form the backbone of Israel's contract law. They were drafted under the assumption that contracting parties have similar market power and sufficient knowledge, and thus the assumptions seem to be at odds with the underlining demands of the consumer protection agenda. Nevertheless, the courts have demonstrated considerable flexibility in applying the general

---

[32] See, e.g., C.A. 825/88 *Israel Football Players Organization v. The Israel Football Association* (1991) 45(5) P.D. 89, 100 ("The Standard Contracts Law is a consumer protection Law in the broad sense of the term").

provisions of these statutes to consumer contracts. Through this flexibility the courts have ruled in favour of consumers in numerous cases, without relying on specific consumer law legislation. The following are three examples of general statutes that have been tailored to the context of consumer contracts.

In *United Mizrahi Bank v. Tzigler*[33], the Supreme Court examined a claim by a surety requesting a release from his obligation towards a bank, due to the fact that he had not been informed that the credit account, which he agreed to secure, was already in considerable deficit when he had assumed his obligation. All five justices ruled in favour of the surety, disagreeing only about the statutory ground that should inform their ruling: two judges, Shamgar CJ, and Strasberg-Cohen J., based their decision on the Banking (Service to Consumer) Law, 1981, which is part of the special consumer protection legislation. Conversely the majority opinion of Or J., Mazza J., and Goldberg J., ruled that this special act, as it stood at that time, did not apply to sureties[34]. Nevertheless the majority had no difficulty reaching the same practical outcome, in favour of the surety, based on a tailored application of s. 15 of the Contracts (General Part) Law, which deals with deceit. According to this section, "deceit" includes "the non-disclosure of facts which according to law, custom or the circumstances the other party should have disclosed." The majority held that the bank was obliged in the given circumstances to provide the surety with full and accurate information about the nature of his obligation, and consequently the surety was allowed to cancel his obligation toward the bank.

In *Lesserson v. Workers' Housing Ltd*[35] the plaintiffs, the owners of 25 new apartments, asked the general contractor who constructed their building to install a generator that was required according to certain regulations concerning buildings of that height. The general contractor refused, claiming that there was no such obligation according to the written contracts. The Court rejected that argument, and ordered the general contractor to supply the generator. Each of the three judges based his or her opinion on a different provision of the Contracts (General Part) Law: Ben-Porat J. relied on s. 25(b) of the act, which states: "Where a contract is capable of different interpretations, an interpretation preserving its validity is preferable to an interpretation according to which it is void"; Bejski J. based his decision on the duty to fulfil a contract in good faith (s. 39 of the Law, and s. 6 of the Sales Law, 1968) and Elon J. relied on the requirement to interpret a contract according to the contract's purpose as understood in the light of the circumstances (s. 25(a) of the Law). Essentially, all three judges

---

[33] C.A. 1570/92 (1995) PD 49(1) 369.

[34] The original definition of a "Customer" in the Banking (Service to Consumer) Law, 1981, was "a person who receive[s] a service from a banking corporation." Since a surety does not receive a service from the lender, the Supreme Court, by a majority, had held in a previous case, C.A. 1304/91 *Tefahot – Mortgage Bank of Israel Ltd v. Lippert* (1993) P.D. 47(3) 309, that a surety was not a customer, and that the act did not apply to her. Following that decision the Banking (Service to Consumer) Law, 1981, was amended in 1994, so as to include sureties within its scope.

[35] C.A. 391/80 (1984) 38(2) P.D. 237.

agreed that some version of a general contract law concept should be adopted to protect the consumer. Their disagreements concerned only which doctrine should be manipulated in order to reach the desired result.

While the previous examples refer to doctrines that regulate contract formation and interpretation, the last example comes from the field of remedies. In *Erbus v. Abraham Rubinstein and Co. – Construction Co. Ltd*[36] the plaintiffs bought two new apartments from the defendant, a building company. The plaintiffs performed their part of the bargain by paying the full contractual price according to the timetable set in the contract. The defendant, in contrast, breached the contract, and delivered the apartments only 13 months after the due date. The plaintiffs did not sue for their additional housing costs, as is common. Instead they asked the Court to award them fair interest on the money they had paid the seller for the period of the delay. Such a remedy is at odds with conventional principles of contract damages, and cannot be founded on any special consumer protection legislation either. Nevertheless, the Court allowed it through the adaptation of general legal principles. Dorner J. held that the purchasers' payment duty and the sellers delivery duty were concurrent obligations and that the plaintiffs were therefore coerced to pay the purchase money before the due date; Tirkel J. agreed with the final outcome but preferred to rely on unjust enrichment principles, claiming that the benefit of holding the money, while not delivering the apartments, was an unjustified benefit. Both justifications are problematic, to say the least[37]. They powerfully demonstrate how far Israeli courts are willing to go in order to provide consumer protection through a tailored application of general legislation.

The aforementioned examples give some indication as to how broadly Israeli courts interpret general doctrines of contract law (contract interpretation, good faith, deceit, damages, etc.) in order to adapt them to consumer contracts. Those examples do not stand alone[38]. Israeli courts are simply accustomed to the idea that consumer protection jurisprudence need not be based on special legislation – it may be developed through the tailored application of the open-texture principles contained in general contract legislation.

To sum up, though consumer protection law in Israel is a mixture of several layers of legislation, actual legal protection, when available, is provided either through narrowly tailored special legislation, or through general legislation. The former is aimed at specific consumer activities, the latter applicable to all contractual settings, and either intended primarily for consumer contracts or applied with due adaptation to this setting. A middle category of legislation – one that sets general consumer protection principles – does exist as well, but its jurispru-

---

[36] C.A. 1632/98 (2001) 55(3) P.D. 913.

[37] For a much more satisfying justification for this kind of remedy, which is not limited to the context of consumer protection, see *Eyal Zamir*, The Missing Interest: Restoration of the Contractual Equivalence, (2007) 93 Virginia Law Review 59.

[38] For additional examples, see *sub* IV. 3) *infra*.

dential significance and practical effects are very limited. Thus, consumer protection in Israel is a hybrid of detailed regulation of specific markets by the legislator and tailored application of general contract legislation by the courts. By and large it is a jurisprudence that develops at specific instances, not through the employment of generalisations.

III. Consumer Protection in the Draft Civil Code

Those who would anticipate a special chapter dedicated to consumer protection in a modern civil code would be disappointed by the Israeli Draft Civil Code. No such chapter exists. In fact, the Consumer Protection Law, 1981, Israel's main, general consumer protection act, was deliberately not included in the Draft.

A superficial glance might suggest that such an omission reflects a conscious decision to limit the Draft Civil Code's scope to commercial matters and to leave consumer contracts out of its ambit. This view is mistaken, as the provisions of the Draft Civil Code are meant to regulate any kind of private legal transaction, including consumer contracts. Furthermore, the Draft Civil Code does include many provisions that are part of the special consumer protection legislation (e.g. those dealing with insurance contracts[39] and "protected guarantees"[40]) as well as elements of general legislation that have special relevance to consumer protection (e.g. the substantive part of the standard contracts law[41]). If the drafters' intent had been to leave consumer contracts out of the Draft Civil Code's sphere of influence, they would not have included such provisions in the Draft Civil Code.

On a more fundamental level, any attempt to create a clear division between commercial contracts and consumer contracts is foreign to Israel's private law jurisprudence. As explained under II., important aspects of Israel's consumer protection law were developed through the tailored application of general principles or through the creation of general legislation that has special relevance to consumer protection. Thus, any endeavour to create separate codes for commercial matters and consumer contracts would represent a major substantive transformation in Israel's private law. The Draft Civil Code, at least in its present form, is not a vehicle for a substantive transformation of Israel's private law[42]. Consumer protection issues are clearly not an exception to the Draft Civil Code's overall status-quo approach.

---

[39] See ss. 288–361 of the Draft Civil Code.

[40] See ss. 272–287 of the Draft Civil Code.

[41] See ss. 143–154 of the Draft Civil Code.

[42] See *Ofer Grosskopf*, The Codification Proposal: Great Expectations – Modest Outcomes, (2006) 36 Mishpatim (The Hebrew University Law Review) 413 (in Hebrew).

What elements of the current consumer protection law are included in the Draft Civil Code? From a quantitative perspective the answer is indeed not much. Most of the special consumer protection legislation and, as mentioned above, the Consumer Protection Law itself, were not included in the Draft. The main explanation for their exclusion is that those are specific and detailed legal arrangements, which are constantly subject to revision. Hence they are not fit to be included in a general and hopefully enduring document such as a civil code.[43] Yet, as mentioned above, parts of the special consumer protection legislation were included in the Draft Civil Code (i.e. those concerning insurance contracts and sureties). Their inclusion raises doubts as to the above explanation, since the specific provisions that were included are no less detailed[44] and have not proven to be more enduring[45] than the absent parts of the special consumer protection legislation. Furthermore it seems that the main reason for the decision to include only these parts in the Draft Civil Code is the fact that these provisions were not enacted as a separate statute, but as part of an act that regulates other aspects of the special contracts mentioned above (i.e. insurance contracts and guarantee contracts). It seems that such a technical test should not serve as the basis of a substantive decision. Instead, a cumulative significance test should perhaps be used, that takes into account both the level of generality of the specific statutes that were included and their practical importance. Indeed, by this test, much of the special consumer protection legislation is too particular and does not have sufficient impact to be included in a civil code. Yet some statutes, such as those dealing with the acquisition of new apartments[46] and with bank-client relationships, may be vital enough to be included in spite of their limited generality.

Be that as it may, a qualitative evaluation of the incorporation of current consumer protection law within the Draft Civil Code may reveal a different picture than one that merely focuses on how many specific consumer protection provisions have been included. The Draft does include the most significant parts of general legislation that pertain to consumer protection (i.e. the substantive part of the Standard Contracts Law and the Defective Products (Liability) Law) and, naturally, all of the general contract law provisions, which the courts have adapted in order to protect consumers (e.g. good faith, public policy, disclosure duties etc.). Given the immense significance of general legislation to the development

[43] Another explanation that was given is that Israel's consumer protection laws typically contain criminal and administrative sanctions that could not be included in a civil code. This is indeed a problem, though obviously not an insoluble one.

[44] For example the second chapter of the Guarantee Law, 1967, (which is part of the Draft Civil Code) is quite detailed and contains 15 sections. In contrast, the Sale (Apartments) (Assurance of Investment of Persons Acquiring Apartments) Law, 1974, (which is not a part of the Draft) is relatively short, and contains only 4 substantive sections.

[45] For example, the Sale (Housing) Law, 1973, (which is not included in the Draft Civil Code) has been amended only 3 times during the last 33 years, while the Insurance Contract Law, 1981, (which is included) has already been amended 4 times during its 25 years of existence.

[46] Cf. *Shalev* (n. 25), 498.

of Israel's consumer protection law in the past, it seems that the ability of the courts to continue this process under the Draft Civil Code is almost unlimited.

In fact, the main ingredient that is absent from the Draft Civil Code – a special chapter that deals with consumer protection principles – is basically missing from our current private law as well. As explained under II., Israel's current consumer protection law has a very limited and relatively insignificant layer of legislation that contains general principles of consumer protection. The drafters of the Draft Civil Code considered the possibility of introducing such a layer into the Draft Civil Code, but for reasons unknown to me did not follow this road in the end. Not knowing their reasoning, I am not in a position to challenge the wisdom of their decision[47]. My modest claim is that even though they chose to leave out a discussion of underlying principles, the Draft Civil Code has not derogated from the protection awarded to consumers under current Israeli law, but simply proposes to re-enact the status quo.

IV. Reinforcing Consumer Protection through the Draft Civil Code's Innovations.

As I mentioned above, the Draft Civil Code, at least in my view, would not cause a major transformation in Israel's private law[48]. Yet it would incorporate a few innovations into our law, some of which might offer new and interesting ways to develop consumer protection in appropriate cases. In the last section of this paper, I would like to review some of these innovations and propose a few possible applications in the context of consumer contracts.

1) The Purpose Clause

The Draft Civil Code starts with a very broad purpose clause (s. 1), which states that

> "[T]he purposes of this Act include the following list:
> (1) Insuring justice, fairness and reasonableness;
> (2) Advancing security, stability and efficiency of the law;
> (3) Achieving consistency between the institutions of civil law;
> (4) Protecting acquired rights;
> (5) Protecting the legitimate expectation and reliance of the parties."

Such an all-encompassing purpose clause allows the courts considerable discretion in implementing the Code's provisions. One possible way to employ this

---

[47] One possible explanation involves political considerations; thus, for instance, such a chapter in the Draft Civil Code would probably raise fierce opposition from business circles, who have a very strong lobby in the Israeli Parliament (the Knesset).

[48] See n. 42, *supra*.

authority is as a justification for giving the Code's provisions different interpretations in divergent social contexts. Thus, the purpose clause may help to create a distinctive interpretive framework for the Code, which would allow due weight to be given to the unique features of commercial relationships on the one hand and consumer-merchant relationships on the other hand. Indeed, as noted above (*sub* II. 4.)), Israeli courts were willing to make considerable adjustments in the application of general principles to the consumer protection context even without such justification. Yet, the fact that they often disagreed about the way to achieve those adjustments, each judge showing willingness to manipulate only one specific doctrine, while strongly refusing to circumvent another[49], suggests that providing for a general justification for developing a divergent jurisprudence of consumer contracts within the Code may help to achieve consensus.

Consider for example how such flexibility would be vital in the case of contract interpretation. The Draft Civil Code has only one provision that states how a contract should be interpreted (s. 123). Yet, in the light of the purpose clause, it is possible to suggest that this provision should be given different meanings in the case of commercial contracts as opposed to the case of consumer contracts. After all, "justice, fairness and reasonableness" can have different meanings in the contexts of commercial and consumer transactions; similarly, the legitimate expectations and reasonable reliance of consumers may diverge from those of commercial parties. If so, trying to devise the same interpretative framework for commercial contracts and for consumer contracts may be possible only at the highest level of generality. When we try to be more specific, we may wish to develop different interpretative frameworks for each setting. For instance, we may choose a scheme that emphasises fairness and objective intentions in the case of consumer contracts but a framework that gives more weight to certainty and subjective intentions in the case of commercial contracts[50].

Another useful example for the potential contribution of the purpose clause concerns the role of custom in contract interpretation. Section 123(c) of the Draft Civil Code, which duplicates s. 25(c) of the Contracts (General Part) Law, states that: "Contractual terms and provisions, which are customarily used in contracts of that kind, shall be interpreted according to the customary meaning in such contracts", while s. 124 of the Draft Civil Code, which is a replica of s. 26 of the Contracts (General Part) Law, states that "[P]articulars not determined by or under the contract shall be in accordance with the accepted practice between the parties; in the absence of such a practice, this particular shall be in accordance with the practice customary in contracts of that kind; such particulars shall be regarded as having been agreed upon by the parties." These sections, which

---

[49] See, e.g., text to n. 35, *supra* (discussing the *Lesserson* case).

[50] Compare *Alan Schwartz/Robert E. Scott*, Contract Theory and the Limits of Contract Law, (2003) 113 Yale Law Journal 541 (supporting a textualist theory as the optimal default position for the interpretation of business contracts).

establish "the customary meaning in such contracts" as an interpretative tool and the "practice customary in contracts of that kind" as a gap-filler, create a considerable threat to consumers. The customary meaning and general practice in any given market is usually known to merchants (who are repeated players), but not necessarily to consumers. Given this asymmetric information, the parties are likely to negotiate only those meanings and practices that are disagreeable to the merchant. For that reason, in the long run the market's general practice and customary meaning are likely to be both hidden from the consumer and in favour of the average merchant's interests. Using custom in the interpretation of consumer contracts may therefore be undesirable and inefficient[51].

A case that well demonstrates this problem concerns the general practice in the banking industry (until 1991)[52] of calculating interest on bank-loans (but not on saving accounts) based on the assumption that there are only 360 days in a year. It is obvious why such a practice would emerge in the banking industry[53]. It is much less clear why courts should enforce it against consumers who, by and large, are completely unaware of it. Indeed when the matter came before the courts, they refused to follow the general practice of the trade and decided that the ordinary meaning of the word "year" – 365 days – should govern the interpretation of the contract[54]. In the light of the above discussion, this result seems justifiable. However, the Supreme Court did not provide any explanation for its refusal to follow the customary meaning of the term "annual interest" in bank-loan contracts or the practice customary to the banking industry in accordance with s. 25(c) and s. 26 of the Contracts (General Part) Law. It seems that if a similar issue were to arise under the Civil Code, the emphasises on "justice, fairness and reasonableness" and "legitimate expectation" in the purpose clause could serve as an appropriate instrument to circumvent s. 123(c) and s. 124 in the context of consumer contracts.

To sum up, the broad purpose clause can serve as the medium through which the unity of the code is unstitched into divergent legal categories. In fact, it may even be an instrument for the creation of a medium level of consumer protection jurisprudence – a level that, as noted above[55], does not exist in the current legal regime and is not explicitly set in the Draft Civil Code either.

---

[51] Compare *Ian Ayres/Robert Gertner*, Filling Gaps in Incomplete Contracts: An Economic Theory of Default Rules, (1989) 99 Yale Law Journal 87.

[52] The practice was brought to an end by a directive from the Bank of Israel, which came into effect on 1/4/1991.

[53] When the interest is calculated according to 360 days, the debtor pays slightly more for the full year (e.g., a 12% interest a year is actually 12% for 360 days and 12.17% for the full 365 days).

[54] See C. A. 7948/96 *Bank Hapoalim Ltd v. Geha Junction Garage Ltd*, (1998) 55(1) P.D. 865, 891–892; C. A. 7085/98 *Tzibiak Jerseys Ltd (in Liquidation) v. Bank Leumi of Israel* (2002) 56(6) P.D. 493, 515–517.

[55] See text to n. 25, text after n. 38, and text to n. 47, *supra*.

2) Exemplary Damages

Deficient public enforcement due to budget constraint, on the one hand, and inadequate private enforcement because of insufficient incentives to sue, on the other hand, make consumer contracts an ideal setting for the implementation of punitive or exemplary damages[56]. Yet, existing consumer protection legislation in Israel makes very little use of such enforcement tools. There is no general provision authorising courts to award punitive damages[57], and specific provisions are not common. Until recently the only example for such provision was s. 28A of the Insurance Contract Law, 1981 which allows the courts, at their discretion, to award additional exemplary interest to the insured, of up to 12% annually[58], in cases where the insurance company does not pay undisputed-in-good-faith personal insurance claims within 30 days of receiving all the appropriate documentation. The very recent Consumer Protection Law (Amendment No. 21), 2007 (from 24/10/2007)), allowing exemplary damages of up to 50,000 NIS for certain infringement of the act, greatly extend the scope of cases in which this tool can be used in order to protect consumer interests. Yet, it does not confer a general power to award exemplary damages to consumers.

The Draft Civil Code offers a potentially important innovation in this area. Section 462 of the Draft Civil Code deals with exemplary damages and states: "[T]he court may award the injured person damages that are unrelated to his harm, if it finds that the infringement was malicious." The scope of this provision is very wide. It covers not only tortious behaviour but breaches of contract as well. Needless to say, exemplary damages are not limited to the consumer protection arena, but may also be applied to other spheres. Yet, in the context of our discussion, this has the potential of providing consumers with a substantial award for taking legal action against businesses, even if their personal harm is relatively small. The main benefit of such an award is that it can provide for ef-

---

[56] Cf. *A. Mitchell Polinsky/Steven Shavell*, Punitive Damages: An Economic Analysis, (1998) 111 Harvard Law Review 869 (advocating the use of punitive damages as a mechanism to solve deficient enforcement problems).

[57] Even the criminal law does not provide for punitive damages to victims (as opposed to fines in favour of the treasury). Indeed, s. 77 of the Criminal Law, 1977, allows courts, in case of a conviction, to award damages to the victim, but sub-section (b) makes clear that such damages should be set according to the victim's actual loss. In any case, the use of this authority in order to compensate consumers is quite scarce (partially because criminal prosecutions for offences against consumers are not very common). I have found only 3 cases in recent years in which such awards were requested: in the first case each of the two complainants received 5,000 NIS (about 1,000 Euros) which was probably restitution of their money; in the second the complainant received 250 NIS (about 50 Euros) and in the third case the judge did not even find it worthwhile to consider the prosecutor's request to award compensation.

[58] The exemplary interest is allowed on top of the statutory interest; that is provided as a matter of right in s. 28 of the Insurance Contract Law. The annual statutory interest in Israel today is 4%, and the exemplary interest is defined as triple statutory interest (i.e. 12%).

fective incentives to sue and thus encourage private enforcement in an area where it is both desirable and needed.

Awarding exemplary damages to consumers who bring just lawsuits can thus serve as an effective vehicle for enforcing consumer protection legislation. This tool is especially viable against small businesses and sporadic infringements by large corporations, since the heavy instrument of class action is ineffective in such cases (the total damage is simply not sufficient to justify the huge expense associated with class action proceedings). For instance, a misleading nationwide advertisement campaign by a big food chain can attract a class action, while publications by a local restaurant or even private initiatives by the local franchiser of a big food chain would not. Hence, as for the latter, exemplary damages may be the only effective way to provide incentives for filing private lawsuits[59].

My main concern about the prospects of exemplary damages serving as an effective tool in the enforcement of consumer protection legislation is that judges may be reluctant to award such damages in contractual settings. Our very limited experience in Israel with exemplary damages suggests that courts are disinclined to award exemplary damages in cases of breach of contract. For instance, the effect of s. 28A of the Insurance Contract Law, 1981, which in theory allows such awards, seems to be very limited. The Supreme Court has determined that, since s. 28A creates a sanction, it should be employed only in rare and exceptional cases, when the insurance company's bad faith is obvious[60]. Given that guidance, it is not surprising that lower courts rarely use this authority. I was able to find only 22 cases in which such interest was awarded in recent years (2000–2006), and even then in only six cases was it applied to the full extent allowed by the legislator (12% per year). Considering the fact that the number of disputed insurance claims in that period is enormous (the inspector on insurance alone receives about 3,000 complaints each year), the effect of this sanction on insurance companies' behaviour must be insignificant. A different approach is needed if we wish to turn exemplary damages into an effective enforcement mechanism. Proving bad faith (or malice) need not be turned into an (almost) impossible mission, but should rather be decided according to the weight of the evidence. Furthermore, once bad faith has been proven, there is no place to show leniency towards the defendant. Overall, Israeli consumer protection legislation is gravely under-enforced. There seems to be no better way to prevent those violations than to severely penalise those violators that can actually be caught (In

[59] In the absence of exemplary damages, judges sometime provide substantial compensation for consumers through s. 13 of the Contracts (Remedies for Breach of Contract) Law, 1970, which allows the court to award damages at the rate it deems appropriate for non-pecuniary loss. This tendency has caused a few sectors to suffer from excessive litigation (e.g., travel agencies) while other sectors have remained practically immune from litigation.

[60] See R.C.A. 2244/04 *R.D. Gourmet Drinks Ltd v. Eliahu Insurance Co. Ltd* (unpublished decision, 1/12/2004); R.C.A. 3121/04 *Evroni v. Clal Insurance Co.* (unpublished decision, 17/5/2005).

fact, are we not using a similar strategy when we employ criminal enforcement of consumer protection law?). As mentioned above, the fact that we can provide consumers with additional incentives to bring lawsuits is, at least as things currently stand, only a blessing.

3) Interpretation Contra Proferentem

Employing the old rule that the words of a written document should be construed against the party putting forward the document (*verba chartarum fortius accipiuntur contra proferentem*) has a long tradition in the context of consumer contracts within the common law world. An implicit example for such application can be found in the classic case of *Carlill v. Carbolic Smoke Ball Co.*[61] The plaintiff (Mrs. Carlill) asked the English Court of Appeal to enforce the payment of £100, which the defendant advertised it would pay to any person who contracted influenza after inhaling its smoke-balls three times a day over a period of at least two weeks. One of the strongest points in the defendant's argument was that it makes no commercial sense for a drug company to promise to compensate any customer who uses its product and still contracts a disease without being able to supervise the customer's actual use of the product. Despite its commercial reasonableness[62], the Court rejected this argument because the advertisement contained no reference to the concern of supervision. As Lindley L.J. bluntly put it, "if they have been so unwary as to expose themselves to a great many actions, so much the worse for them." In fact the Court applied the *contra proferentem* rule in that it interpreted the advertisement according to the reading of an unsophisticated consumer, not of a reasonable merchant. Therefore the Court was able to protect the consumer from any ambiguity that the Smoke Ball Company created by not specifying the way in which one could accept the challenge of the advertisement.

In the past, Israeli courts have pushed the concept of interpretation *contra proferentem* to its limits in the context of consumer contracts. Consider, for example, the case of *Bariah v. Bank Otzar Ha-Hayal Ltd*[63]. The defendant signed a document that was titled "pledge agreement." However, certain provisions within the agreement were drafted to the effect that any person signing the agreement was personally responsible as a surety for the full debt. The Court refused to give those provisions any meaning, stating that since it is unclear whether the contract

---

[61] (1893) 1 Q.B. 256 (C.A.). It is interesting to note that Lindley L.J mentions explicitly "the doctrine of taking language most strongly against the person relying on it," but only in the context of an argument that "would be pushing [it] too far."

[62] Indeed, in a subsequent publication the Carbolic Smoke Ball Co. required that customers who wished to be eligible for the reward should sign and deposit an application document before commencing the treatment. See *A. W. Brian Simpson*, Quackery and Contract Law: The Case of the Carbolic Smoke Ball, (1985) 14 Journal of Legal Studies 345.

[63] C.A. 664/89 (1991) 45(4) P.D. 783.

is in fact a "pledge agreement" or a surety agreement, it must be interpreted against its drafter (the bank) and given the less stringent interpretation.

A crucial implication of the *contra proferentem* rule used to protect consumers can be found in the groundbreaking precedents *Hovny v. Dikla Construction & Investment Co Ltd*[64] and *Nachshon v. Shai*[65]. These cases dealt with the most problematic loophole in the Sale (Apartments) (Assurance of Investments of Persons Acquiring Apartments) Law, 1974. As mentioned above[66], this special consumer protection act is meant to provide purchasers of new apartments with securities. The act allows the seller to choose between 5 possible methods of securing the purchaser's money: bank guarantee, insurance, transferring ownership in the land, charging the land with a first mortgage, or registration of a cautionary note on the transaction[67]. The last method, a cautionary note, is the cheapest and thus became the favourite way of securing a purchaser's money in the 1970s and 1980s.

However, a cautionary note turned out to be ineffective in the context of a very popular land transaction scheme, widely known in Israel as a "combination transaction". In a "combination transaction" a landowner and a contractor enter into an agreement (the combination agreement) according to which the contractor promises to build an apartment building on the landowner's property, and in return the landowner promises to transfer some of the apartments to the contractor after the building project is complete. In order to finance the building project, it is commonplace for the contractor to start selling his apartments (i.e. the apartments allocated to him according to the combination agreement) to private purchasers straight away. Since the Sale (Apartments) (Assurance of Investments of Persons Acquiring Apartments) Law requires the contractor to guarantee the purchaser's money with a security, it was also customary for the landowner and the contractor to include in the combination agreement provisions that allowed those who purchase apartments from the contractor to register cautionary notes, which served in many transactions as the only security provided to the purchasers. This complex legal structure turned out to be unfortunate for the purchasers whenever the contractor failed to perform his part of the combination agreement. In such cases the landowner usually terminated the combination agreement, and asked for the cautionary notes that had been entered according to this agreement (including those in favour of purchasers from the contractor) to be removed.

Until the *Hovany* and *Nachshon* decisions, courts routinely accepted the landowner's request, reasoning that the cautionary notes reflected the landowner's obligations under the combination agreement, and as such depended upon the

---

[64] C.A. 205/83 (1987) 41(3) P.D. 96.

[65] C.A. 813/85 (1988) 42(1) P.D. 340.

[66] See text to n. 5, *supra*.

[67] Section 2 of the Sale (Apartments) (Assurance of Investments of Persons Acquiring Apartments) Law.

agreement remaining in force[68]. Consequently, purchasers could find themselves without any security for their money, in sharp opposition to the clear intent of the legislator. In the *Hovany* and *Nachshon* decisions the Supreme Court closed this loophole by adopting a different interpretation of the combination agreement. According to this novel interpretation the landowner's obligations toward the purchasers were meant to be independent of the combination agreement that created them, and remained in force even after its termination. The Court's reasoning is based on the reasonable expectation that the cautionary note created with the purchasers, and on the argument that "the landowner is free to limit the scope of the cautionary note, and to include conditions, but if he has not done so, one cannot read in an implied term into his obligation according to which the cautionary note should be void once the combination agreement is terminated"[69]. Considering both the statutory background and the precedents, this reasoning might seem tenuous. Yet I consider it to be a strong implementation of consumer protection via the concept of interpretation *contra proferentem* in the broad sense[70].

During the last 15 years, with the establishment of the purposive interpretation in Israeli law in general, and in its contracts law in particular, the doctrine of interpretation *contra proferentem* has been in decline. The Supreme Court has reduced it to a "secondary interpretation rule", which should be employed only as a last resort, after all the efforts to ascertain the (subjective or objective) purpose of the contract have been exhausted, with no clear resolution between two reasonable possibilities[71]. Given this limited scope of application, the *contra proferentem* doctrine was not given any significant weight in the leading precedent concerning contract interpretation, *The State of Israel v. Apropim Housing and Initiatives (1991) Ltd*[72], a case that dealt with a commercial transaction. More disturbing for consumer protection supporters, some judges have sought to extend the marginalisation of the *contra proferentem* doctrine to the sphere of consumer

---

[68] This ruling is in line with s. 37 of the Contracts (General Part) Law, 1973, which states with respect to a contract in favour of a third party (and that is what the combination agreement is with respect to the purchasers) that "any plea available to the debtor against the creditor in connection to the obligation is also available to him against the beneficiary."

[69] C.A. 813/85 *Nachshon v. Shai* (1988) 42(1) P.D. 340, 349 *per* Shamgar C.J. Following this development landowners became very cautious about allowing the registration of cautionary notes in favour of purchasers in the context of combination agreements. Consequently, the main collateral provided today for purchasers by constructors is a financial guarantee from a bank. The extra costs associated with this collateral are, at least partly, transferred to purchasers. See n. 5 and text to n. 12, *supra*.

[70] Obviously, the landowner is not the single drafter of the combination agreement. Yet, the Court's argument is basically that vis-à-vis the purchasers (i.e. beneficiaries that are third parties to the agreement) he should be considered as the party who had put forward the document.

[71] See C.A. 779/89 *Shelev v. Sela Insurance Co. Ltd* (1993) 48(1) P.D. 221; *Aharon Barak*, Interpretation in Law, vol. 4 – The Interpretation of Contracts (2001), 634–643 (in Hebrew).

[72] C.A. 4628/93 (1995) 49(2) P.D. 265. The contract in that case was a standard contract that was drafted by the Israeli government. Notwithstanding these facts, the Court interpreted it according to its objective purpose, and gave no weight to the *contra proferentem* doctrine.

contracts as well[73]. That would mean that a major vehicle for consumer protection would be lost.

In the light of this tendency, it is somewhat surprising to find in the Draft Civil Code a new provision that enacts the interpretation *contra proferentem* rule in the section that deals with contract interpretation. Section 123(d) of the Draft Civil Code states: "It is preferable to interpret a contract that is open to several interpretations against the party who had an advantage in shaping its terms." I doubt whether courts will give this provision much weight with respect to commercial transactions. It is, however, quite possible that courts will use it in order to reinforce decisions such as *Bariah*, *Hovany* and *Nachshon* that employ the interpretation *contra proferentem* with respect to consumer contracts. Indeed, courts may even use this new sub-section in order to reshape the concept altogether. One way of doing so is to give the doctrine a new meaning, one that separates its relatively uncontested application in the consumer protection context from its controversial application in the commercial sphere. For instance the new provision can be understood as protecting only weak parties, who are suffering from a bargaining disadvantage, and not any party who allows the other party to take control over the drafting process[74]. If so, the new provision can help keep the old principle intact with respect to consumer contracts, despite the courts' tendency severely to limit its application in other contexts.

4) Suspending Performance

In many instances a consumer finds herself in a critical dilemma: some payment under the contract is due, but she has doubts as to the merchant's ability to perform his part. If she does not pay, the merchant may blame her for breaching the contract, and the consumer may lose much of any money she has already paid him; if she would keep her part of the contract, the merchant may still not produce the item and she would be throwing away good money after bad money. The consumer's dilemma is even worse in the typical case in which she has no effective guarantees under the contract.

Consider, for example, the case of a consumer who rents a motor-home for August. She pays a deposit of 500 Euro and is required to pay the rest of the money (2,000 Euro) by the end of June. As the due date gets closer, she starts hearing disturbing rumours as to the rental company's financial situation. The

---

[73] See, e.g., Or J., the minority opinion in C.A. 779/89 *Shelev v. Sela Insurance Co. Ltd* (1993) 48(1) P.D. 221 (refusing to apply the doctrine with respect to the interpretation of an insurance contract). This view is still a minority view, at least with respect to insurance contracts. Cf. R.C.A. 3128/94 *The Ramat-Chen Synagogue Association v. Sahar Insurance Co.* (1996) 50(3) P.D. 281 (holding that the *contra proferentem* rule should be employed in order to interpret insurance contracts according to the reasonable expectations of the insured).

[74] Cf. *Barak* (n.71), 644–646 (supporting a purpose presumption that reinforces the weaker party's expectation).

consumer is in a tight spot: if she chooses not to pay the 2,000 Euro, the deposit would be lost, but if she pays, she might lose the further 2,000 Euro. What should she do?

Israel's current specific consumer legislation offers no relief to the distressed consumer. Her remedy must therefore be found in the application of general principles such as good faith[75] and anticipatory breach of contract[76]. In contrast, the Draft Civil Code provides her with a handy solution. Section 128(b) of the Draft Civil Code states that: "[I]f there is a reasonable concern that one party will not perform a fundamental obligation that is not yet due, the other party is entitled to demand adequate assurances for the performance of said obligation, and he is entitled to postpone the performance of his obligation until receiving such assurances"[77]. This section incorporates a precedent that was based on the duty to perform a contract in good faith[78]. As such, s. 128(b) is neither groundbreaking nor aimed especially at protecting consumers. However, it may be crafted into an important shield to protect consumers from their own innocence and inexperience. While courts ought to be suspicious of merchants who ask for relief based on this section, they should not doubt its applicability to consumers. Merchants are expected to evaluate the risks they bear in advance, and to demand either insurance or a premium (through the price of the deal) for these risks. Hence it might be argued that only on rare occasions do courts need to change the order of performance at their request[79]. In contrast, consumers are much more likely to be caught unguarded, i.e. to discover the actual risks they confront only in hindsight. Thus it is not inappropriate for courts to protect consumers through s. 128(b), even at the cost of a retroactive adjustment in the order of performance.

---

[75] See s. 39 of the Contracts (General Part) Law ("An obligation or right arising out of a contract shall be fulfilled or exercised in customary manner and in good faith").

[76] See s. 17 of the Contracts (Remedies for Breach of Contract) Law, 1970 ("Where a party to the contract indicates his intention not to perform it or where it appears from the circumstances that he will be unable or unwilling to perform it, the other party is entitled to the remedies under the law even before the time fixed for performance of the contract ...").

[77] See also s. 497 of the Draft Civil Code ("If the contract was fundamentally breached, the injured party is entitled to postpone the performance of his obligation until the breaching party will perform his obligation") and s. 496 (dealing with anticipatory breach).

[78] See C. A. 701/79 *Shohat v. Lobianiker* (1981) 36(2) P. D. 113 (a case that dealt with the sale of a second hand apartment between two private parties).

[79] Cf. *Scott v. Crown* (1988) 765 P.2d 1043 (Colorado); the Court of Appeals of Colorado refused to allow a seller to rely on s. 2–609 of the Uniform Commercial Code which applies to commercial sales contracts and provides for a "right to adequate assurance of performance." One of the court's reasons for rejecting the seller's claim was that "a demand for performance assurances cannot be used as a means of forcing a modification of the contract".

V. Concluding Remarks

The Draft Civil Code has been criticised by leading Israeli scholars for its inattentive and inconsistent treatment of consumer protection legislation[80]. As these scholars justly point out, it is hard to discern any substantial criterion according to which the decisions were made about whether or not to include any given part of the consumer protection legislation in the Draft Civil Code. I add my voice to their critique, but at the same time believe that, despite those concerns, the prospects of integrating consumer protection law into the Draft Civil Code are rather favourable.

Indeed, it might have been more desirable for the Draft Civil Code to include a special section that deals with the principles of consumer protection. However, since such general principles have not crystallised yet, the reluctance of the drafters to conceive them is quite understandable. Likewise, the Draft could have benefited from the inclusion of additional parts of the specific consumer protection legislation, such as the Sale (Housing) Law, 1973 or the Banking (Service to Consumers) Law, 1981. Yet again, leaving these specific acts outside of the Draft Civil Code is not expected to have considerable effect on their application.

The crucial point, in my view, is that the Draft Civil Code maintains, and to some extent even reinforces, the courts' discretion to develop consumer protection law through the general principles of the private law. Israeli consumer protection law can thus evolve, and even transform into a discipline, within the Civil Code. Obviously, there is no certainty that such evolution will occur. Ultimately the decision whether or not to accept this task depends on the Supreme Court, which, as past experience reveals, has not always been willing to rise to this challenge[81]. Yet, the fastening ties between the business and political communities in Israel, on the one hand, and lack of real consumer awareness within its general population, on the other hand, may drive the Supreme Court to take upon itself the task of developing consumer protection law through the Civil Code. If the courts will choose to do so, it is to be hoped that they are going to construct a sensible and balanced legal regime – one that is built around an adequate substantive normative theory of consumer protection.

---

[80] See *Eyal Zamir*, Special Contracts under the Israeli Civil Code Proposal, (2006) 36 Mishpatim 531 (in Hebrew); *Sinai Deutch*, Consumer Protection and the Israeli Civil Code Proposal, (2006) 36 Mishpatim 499 (in Hebrew).

[81] Cf. text to n. 24 and text after n. 34, *supra*.

Consumer Protection Law under the Israeli Draft Civil Code: A Response from a European and German Perspective

By Josef Drexl

Summary of Contents

I. Introduction

The paper presented by Ofer Grosskopf provides an excellent analysis of the Draft Civil Code and its relevance for consumer protection. The following comments relate to two aspects of his paper, and take into account experiences with the recent reform of German contract law codified in the *Bürgerliches Gesetzbuch* and existing European legislation on consumer contract law.

Firstly, Ofer Grosskopf informs us of the explicit decision that "the Civil Code Proposal does not include the various statutes dealing with consumer protection"[1]. Whereas rules protecting the consumer are not unknown to Israeli private law, the drafters of the new code obviously hold that general private law and consumer law should better be kept separate. Accordingly, the first aspect to be discussed in this response relates to the relationship between general private law and consumer law. The question to be asked is: does consumer law belong to

[1] *Ofer Grosskopf*, Consumer Protection Law under the Israeli Draft Civil Code, *sub* I., in this volume, referring to s. 13 of the Introductory Notes to the Draft Civil Code.

the general private law – and should it therefore be integrated into the general private-law codification – or does it rather constitute an exception to fundamental principles of private law the general recognition of which might be endangered by the inclusion of consumer law in the codification? That question will be discussed in the following section of this response (see section II of this paper).

In the light of the very title of Ofer Grosskopf's paper, the decision not to include consumer law in the Code is certainly disappointing. However, the author very closely scrutinises the code to highlight many rules that can be applied in order to protect consumers[2]. Obviously the author applies a functional concept of consumer law. Not only rules that explicitly address the consumer belong to the body of consumer law, but all rules that effectively protect consumers, even if their scope of application is not limited to that group of persons. Instead of discussing some of the rules and concepts of the Draft Civil Code analysed by Ofer Grosskopf, this response (under III.) will support the author's general proposition of defining all rules protecting consumers as consumer law and will try to sketch a model of consumer law as an integral part of general private law.

II. Consumer Protection as Part of General Private Law

1) Reasons for Omitting Consumer Law in the Draft Civil Code

The introductory statement to the Draft Civil Code does not give any reason for not integrating specific consumer-related legislation into the new codification. According to the account by Ofer Grosskopf, Israeli law has an impressive body of consumer law. He mentions 20 statutes that are "usually considered" as belonging to consumer-protection legislation. Among those 20 statutes 11 are described as "special consumer protection legislation"[3]. A closer look at those statutes provides further insight into the decision not to integrate consumer-protection law into the Code. Israel passed a Consumer Protection Law in 1981 that includes provisions analogous to European consumer legislation. These rules relate to certain distribution methods (doorstep selling, distance selling), misleading advertising and the sale of vacation units (timeshare contracts under EC legislation). This seems to indicate that the framers of the Draft Civil Code maintain a concept of consumer law as forming a separate body of private-law rules that address problems that are specific to the situation of consumers. Although Ofer Grosskopf does not mention whether such laws, like the Consumer Protection Law in particular, are limited in scope to consumer contracts, it seems that this limited scope is considered the criterion for not including these provisions in the new codification. In contrast, the Draft Civil Code integrates the

---

[2] *Grosskopf* (n. 1): "Consumer Protection Law under the Israeli Draft Civil Code".

[3] *Grosskopf* (n. 1), *sub* II. 1).

Standard Contracts Law of 1982 into the Civil Code for the clear reason that this act is not limited to the protection of consumers[4].

This view is confirmed by Ofer Grosskopf's analysis[5]: The Draft Civil Code does not only apply to commercial contracts but covers "any kind of private legal transaction, including consumer contracts". Ofer Grosskopf goes on to hint at the provisions dealing with insurance contracts[6] and the "protected guarantee"[7]. Apparently, these provisions will often apply to consumer contracts, although they do not mention consumers as the only group of protected persons. The provisions on insurance contracts cover all types of insurance, including those for the risks of businesses, but, of course, also apply to health insurance contracts, which typically cover private risks of consumers. The Draft Civil Code even provides for particular rules on life insurance contracts specifically protecting the insured[8]. In the case of the protected guarantee, the provisions are limited to the "protected guarantor"[9], who is defined as a person concluding a contract of guarantee with a creditor for a sum that does not exceed 60,000 NIS, or 500,000 NIS in the case of covering the debt for the creditor's purchase of a private home. This definition does not use the term "consumer". Also, in fact, even a bank that gives such a guarantee as part of its business seems to be covered. However, such rules will typically apply to private guarantors, like family members in particular.

We may conclude: the Draft Civil Code only includes rules that are not explicitly limited to consumers but nevertheless *also* protect consumers. In the light of the new codification, Israeli law seems to distinguish between generally applicable private law codified in the Civil Code and specific consumer law.

2) Consumer Protection and the Concept of Freedom of Contract

Specific consumer contract rules may also be distinguished from general private-law rules in that they provide for strict contract rules from which the parties may not depart to the disadvantage of consumers. In contrast, private-law codifications are generally based on the concept of freedom of contract. However, it is true that modern private-law codifications have already departed from the liberal understanding of unrestricted freedom of contract for some time now. Nowadays, they include a number of rules that are imposed by the legislature restricting the freedom of contract of the parties. The Israeli codification will not form an exception in this regard. Yet even today, the drafters of the Draft Civil Code seem to argue that strict consumer law does not belong to general

[4] Sections 143–154 of the Draft Civil Code.
[5] *Grosskopf* (n. 1), *sub* III.
[6] Sections 288–361 of the Draft Civil Code.
[7] Sections 272–287 of the Draft Civil Code.
[8] Sections 330–338 of the Draft Civil Code.
[9] Section 272 of the Draft Civil Code.

private law – and therefore should not be included in the codification – since it introduces the general idea of protecting the consumer and restricting the freedom of contract of the other party.

Whether such an argument is convincing depends very much on the specific concept of freedom of contract in a given jurisdiction. The argument relies on a formalistic understanding of the concept of freedom of contract. In general, according to this formalistic understanding, whatever the contracting parties agree upon, in whatever situation, will be held to be a valid contract.

This formalistic kind of understanding, however, has been replaced in the legal systems of Germany and the EC by a material concept of freedom of contract. At the same time German and European law rely on different legal principles while nevertheless reaching the same legal end.

Courts in Germany used to defend a formalistic understanding of contractual freedom. Most strikingly, in 1989, the Federal Supreme Court (*Bundesgerichtshof*) still held that a man's 19-year-old daughter would not be protected against granting a private guarantee for her father's debt although she did not possess any business experience and although it was obvious, given her income and level of education, that she would never be able to pay back the debt. Still, the Court expected her, having attained maturity, to know about the risks of a private guarantee[10]. The decision was supported by some authors[11], whereas others criticised the bluster of the icy wind from the 19th century[12]. It was then up to the Federal Constitutional Court (*Bundesverfassungsgericht*) to intervene in this particular case[13]. That Court, in relying on the general protection of individual freedom under Art. 2(1) of the German Fundamental Law (*Grundgesetz*), required the legislature and the private-law courts, in interpreting and applying the law, to intervene in favour of the weaker party to a contract in "specific situations of structural inequality of bargaining power"[14]. The conceptual progress of that judgment consists in explaining such intervention as a consequence of a concept of freedom. The German *Grundgesetz* obliges the legislature and the courts to provide for a legal system that, in principle, provides all individuals with the same possibility of making use of their contractual freedom. Thereby, one might be tempted to say, the Court implements an element of equality into the concept of individual freedom but, still, develops a liberal concept of contractual protection of the weaker party. The Court did not identify the private-law doctrine under which the 19-year-old daughter should be protected against granting a private guarantee for her father. The Federal Supreme Court later held that the contract between the young woman and the bank was void under

---

[10] BGH of 19 January 1989, BGHZ 106, 269.

[11] See Dieter Medicus, Leistungsfähigkeit und Rechtsgeschäft, [1989] Zeitschrift für Wirtschaftsrecht 817, 822 ff.

[12] *Heinrich Honsell*, [1989] Juristen-Zeitung 495.

[13] BVerfG of 19 October 1993, BVerfGE 89, 214.

[14] In German: "in typisierbaren Situationen strukturellen Vertragsungleichgewichts".

the general clause invalidating contracts *contra bonos mores*[15], arguing that the bank, turning from the path of ethical behaviour, took advantage of the father's violation of his legal duty under German family law to take into account the interests of his daughter by imposing emotional pressure on her in requesting the guarantee[16]. Whereas this development of a material concept of the freedom of contract was welcomed by many[17], some authors complained strongly about the Court restricting the concept of freedom of contract in the private-law codification[18]. In fact, however, the Federal Constitutional Court did not question the traditional concept of freedom of contract. It only identified a conflict between the contractual freedoms of the two parties to the contract – as a conflict of constitutional rights – and ordered the private-law courts to balance these rights appropriately in situations in which the fundamental equality of the bargaining power of the parties is affected.

In contrast to the German situation, European law has considerable problems relying either on a traditional concept of freedom of contract, owing to the lack of a European civil code as a comprehensive body of Community contract law, or on constitutional rights protection. Yet a material concept of freedom of contract was developed by the European Court of Justice in the framework of applying the free-movement principles of the Treaty and – quite astonishingly – EC competition law. Already in the 1990s, when academics, initially in Germany, started to think about "Community private law", the idea was voiced that the free-movement principles have to be considered as the legal basis of the concept of freedom of contract[19]. In line with this argument, the European Court of Justice, already by its *GB-Inno* judgment of 1990, postulated a "freedom of consumers" under former Art. 30 ECT (now Art. 28) to "travel ... to the territory of another Member State to shop under the same conditions as the local population."[20] However, the free-movement principles should not be misunderstood as mere principles of liberalisation and, consequently, the basis for a formalistic concept of freedom of contract. In its case law, the ECJ allows application of

[15] § 138 I BGB.

[16] BGH of 24 February 1994, [1994] Wertpapier-Mitteilungen 680. See also the judgment on a similar case of the same day, BGH of 24 February 1994, BGHZ 125, 206. Whereas in the first case, the daughter would have been required to pay 100,000 German marks, the 24-year-old son in the second case was requested to pay 7.7 million German marks for the business debt of his father.

[17] For a detailed analysis of this development, see *Josef Drexl*, Die wirtschaftliche Selbstbestimmung des Verbrauchers (1998), 263ff. (on the decision of the Federal Constitutional Court) and 505ff. (on the subsequent case law on family guarantees).

[18] See *Wolfgang Zöllner*, Regelungsspielräume im Schuldvertragsrecht – Bemerkungen zur Grundrechtsanwendung im Privatrecht und zu den sogenannten Ungleichgewichtslagen, (1996) 196 Archiv für die civilistische Praxis 1.

[19] See *Stefan Grundmann*, EG-Richtlinie und nationales Privatrecht, [1996] Juristen-Zeitung 274, 278 (according to whom the free-movement principles extend contractual freedom across national borders); *Peter von Wilmowsky*, Der internationale Verbrauchervertrag im EG-Binnenmarkt, (1995) 3 Zeitschrift für Europäisches Privatrecht 735, 736ff.

[20] Case C-362/88, *GB-Inno-BM*, [1990] ECR I-667, para 8.

conflicting non-discriminatory domestic rules on consumer protection provided that they are – in the sense of the principle of proportionality – suitable for attaining the objective of consumer protection, and that they do not go beyond what is necessary in order to attain it. Still, quite recently, the ECJ[21] ordered the referring domestic court to consider under certain criteria whether a national ban on doorstep selling of silver jewelry can still be justified in the light of the existence of a right to withdraw from a doorstep contract under the European Doorstep Selling Directive[22], which only provides for minimum harmonisation. In the famous *Courage* judgment of 2001[23], the ECJ came much closer to the material concept of contractual freedom as developed by the German Federal Supreme Court. In this judgment, the ECJ had to answer the question whether national law can deny a right to compensation of a party to a distribution contract in violation of the prohibition of restrictive agreements under Art. 81 EC for the mere reason that this party took part in the illegal conduct. The ECJ, just like the German Federal Constitutional Court, relied on the concept of contractual equality and ordered the referring court

> "to ascertain whether the party who claims to have suffered loss ... found himself in a markedly weaker position than the other party, such as seriously to compromise or even eliminate his freedom to negotiate the terms of the contract and his capacity to avoid the loss or reduce its extent ..."[24]

Hereby the court, from a private-law perspective, highlights two very important principles: Firstly, EC competition law is a most important element for guaranteeing freedom of contract within the internal market. Secondly, this concept of freedom of contract must not be understood in a purely formalistic way. In a material sense, competition law is meant to enable the contracting parties actually to take free decisions. Hence, on different grounds, namely constitutional rights on the one hand and EC competition law on the other hand, the German Federal Constitutional Court and the competition-law decision of the ECJ developed similar material concepts of contractual freedom.

The material concept of freedom of contract is of utmost importance for a modern understanding of the relationship between consumer law and general private law. A fundamental conflict between the two can only be seen to exist on the basis of a merely formalistic concept of freedom of contract. In contrast, the material understanding defines the concept of contractual freedom as a fundamental principle for the whole body of private law and, thereby, regards consumer protection as an integral part of general private law. It is true that when the decision was taken to include specific consumer legislation in the reformed German Civil Code in 2001, the predominant objective was to create a code that

---

[21] Case C-441/04, *A-Punkt Schmuckhandel*, [2006] ECR I-2093.

[22] Council Directive 85/577/EEC of 20 December 1985 to protect the consumer in respect of contracts negotiated away from business premises, OJ EC L 372, 31. 12. 1985, p. 31.

[23] Case C-453/99, *Courage*, [2001] E.C.R. I-6297.

[24] *Courage* (n. 23), para 33.

was to inform all citizens on the existing private law[25]. Still, it is apparent that, based on the modern concept of private law in Germany, the substantive argument according to which consumer protection forms a part of general private law[26] provides a much better justification for what the legislature did.

3) The Limited Scope of Application of Consumer Law

As can be seen from Ofer Grosskopf's analysis, the Israeli Draft Civil Code does not necessarily conflict with the "material" concept of freedom of contract as recognised under German and EC law. The Draft Code contains many rules that respond to situations in which the contractual equality (the balance of bargaining power) is affected. Still, the Draft only seems to include rules that are not limited specifically to consumers but have a general scope of application. Therefore, the question arises whether "specific" consumer law should be excluded from the general codification because of its limited scope of application.

The answer clearly is "no". Modern consumer legislation in the EC and in Germany, the latter being in conformity with EC legislation in this regard, follows a situational concept of consumer protection. According to this concept, the consumer is not considered as a weaker party in principle; the law only interferes in specific situations in which contractual equality is disturbed to the disadvantage of the consumer. As shown in the analysis of German constitutional law above[27], the legislature or the courts are not requested to intervene whenever consumers enter into a contract, but only in specific situations in which there is a lack of equality. Therefore, the primary objective of consumer legislation consists in defining such situations of "market failures" in the economic sense and of "failures of the system of contract law" in the legal sense. Only then does the question arise whether the applicability of rules redressing a specific situation of contractual inequality should be limited to consumer contracts. In fact, the very question of whether certain rules should be limited to consumer contracts should be decided against the background of the question whether such limitation better defines the area of the disparity. Some examples may be given:

---

[25] See *Jürgen Schmidt-Räntsch*, Reintegration der Verbraucherschutzgesetze durch den Entwurf des Schuldrechtsmodernisierungsgesetzes, in: Reiner Schulze/Hans Schulte-Nölke (eds.), Die Schuldrechtsreform vor dem Hintergrund des Gemeinschaftsrechts (2001), 169. On the integration and the pros and cons in general, see *Thomas Pfeiffer*, Die Integration von "Nebengesetzen" in das BGB, in: Wolfgang Ernst/Reinhard Zimmermann (eds.), Zivilrechtswissenschaft und Schuldrechtsreform (2001), 481.

[26] For a more detailed discussion of consumer law as part of general private law in Germany, see *Josef Drexl*, Verbraucherrecht – Allgemeines Privatrecht – Handelsrecht, in: Peter Schlechtriem (ed.), Wandlungen des Schuldrechts (2002) 97,109–117.

[27] *Supra*, at 2).

The first example relates to an area in which German and Israeli law obviously follow the same approach, whereas European Community law seems to be different. With regard to standard contract terms, Israeli law and German law apply rules controlling such terms both to contracts concluded by consumers and to those among businesses. In Germany, at the time of the adoption of the original Standard Contract Terms Act[28] in 1976[29], it was intensively debated whether the new law should be limited to consumer contracts. Quite rightly, this idea was rejected in favour of the general applicability of that Act, even if commercial actors (*Kaufleute* in the sense of the German Commercial Code) were dealt with differently in some respects, so as to take account of the specificities of commercial transactions. Persons other than consumers, so it was held, are not in principle in a better situation to protect themselves against the use of standard contract terms introduced by the other party to the contract[30]. The European Unfair Contract Terms Directive[31], in contrast, is limited to consumer contracts.

The situation is quite different in the case of German and European legislation on consumer credit contracts, and this forms the second example. European law, according to the Directive dating from 1986[32], protects consumers via specific duties to inform, whereas German law adds a right of withdrawal from the contract within a specific "cooling-off" period[33]. In contrast to what one might suspect at first glance, such rules are not only to be explained by the simple reason that consumers are held to have less acumen than do business people. Rather, we can identify specific circumstances which mandate protecting consumers only. Whereas business people can be expected to make appropriate judgments on the necessity and the economic sense of taking up a credit and, maybe much more importantly, will use the credit to make future profit, consumers conclude credit contracts only rarely, are therefore typically inexperienced, and will not necessarily use the credit for financing future and lasting assets, such as a family home, but for consumption. The personal risks involved in a consumer credit are therefore much more serious than for a business credit. These arguments are also convincing with regard to the same individual concluding credit contracts in

---

[28] *Gesetz zur Regelung des Rechts der Allgemeinen Geschäftsbedingungen* (AGBG).

[29] Adopted on 9 December 1976; BGBl. I, p. 3317. The AGBG was integrated in the BGB on the occasion of the fundamental reform of the latter in 2001.

[30] See also *Drexl* (n. 17), 407–412.

[31] Council Directive 93/13/EEC of 5 April 1993 on unfair terms in consumer contracts, OJ EC L 95, 21. 4. 1993, p. 29.

[32] Council Directive 87/102/EEC of 22 December 1986 for the approximation of the laws, regulations and administrative provisions of the Member States concerning consumer credit, OJ L 42, 12. 2. 1987, p. 48.

[33] Such additional protection is now under consideration on the European level; see Amended proposal of 28 October 2004 for a Directive of the European Parliament and of the Council on the harmonisation of the laws, regulations and administrative provisions of the Member States concerning credit for consumers repealing Directive 87/102/EC and modifying Directive 93/13/EC, COM(2004)747 final: http://ec.europa.eu/consumers/cons_int/fina_serv/cons_directive/credit_cons_en.pdf.

different situations: A person who signs a business credit contract after an assessment of the economic risks and benefits involved may well still deserve and need special protection in the situation of a credit meant to finance private consumption. German law deviates from the EC Consumer Credit Directive by also protecting persons who enter into a credit contract in order to start a business[34]. Since that type of credit is meant to finance an economic activity, such persons do not meet the general definition of a consumer. Still, because of their lack of experience, they deserve the same protection as consumers: they will often not be able sufficiently to evaluate in advance the likelihood of making the expected profits with the credit. They are therefore in a very similar situation as consumers[35].

Finally, the approach to protecting consumers only in specific situations of contractual inequality is reflected in the way modern European and German law define the consumer. The definition is not personalised but "role-oriented". The question is not whether an individual "is" a consumer but whether such a person "acts as" a consumer. This definition highlights again that consumer law should be considered to be part of general private law even where rules only apply to consumers. The argument is simple: All individuals may act as consumers. Therefore, rules specifically applicable to consumers are of potential applicability to all individuals as members of the society. There remains only one limitation, namely that the definition is restricted to natural persons. This, however, is not a sufficient argument to exclude specific consumer legislation from the private-law codification.

III. Sketching a System of Consumer Protection as Part of General Private Law

In the light of the preceding analysis, the approach of Ofer Grosskopf generally to include those provisions of the Israeli Draft Civil Code that provide consumer protection, or can be developed so as to provide such protection, in his concept of consumer law merits full support. In contrast, those who are afraid that a codification of general private law may depart too far from the general principle of party autonomy may well oppose the "integrative" approach, which defines consumer law as part of general private law. Still, their concerns are not well founded. By excluding specific consumer legislation from the ambit of the private-law codification, the legislature merely increases the risk that a specific doctrine of consumer law will develop according to which consumer contracts are increasingly separated from general private law, and that would gradually reduce the code's application to commercial and business contracts. Consequently, there would be a real danger that "protectionist" consumer law would de-

[34] § 507 BGB.

[35] See also *Drexl* (n. 26), 131.

velop outside the code, whereas "commercial" contract law would tend to be too formalistic by not taking into account the fact that commercial actors may also be affected by an imbalance of bargaining power in specific situations. It seems that Israeli law is still very much influenced by its legislative history with a specific consumer contact law and, therefore, as the Draft Civil Code suggests, will not implement an integrative approach. Yet it seems very important that legal writers should stress, as Ofer Grosskopf does, that consumer protection may also be found in the private-law codification, that many of the provisions of that codification may be relied upon for developing a sensible consumer protection and, in general, that the borderline between consumer contract law and general private law is not as clear as may be suggested by the separation of legal sources in Israel.

Most importantly, it is to be argued that the integrative approach protects the legal system against exaggerations with regard to the protection of consumers. Implementation in the private-law codification reminds the legislature that a justification for an exception to the general principle of party autonomy is absolutely necessary. Based on the modern "material" concept of freedom of contract, as described above in the context of the analysis of German constitutional law and European Community law[36], the law should only depart from the principle of party autonomy in situations in which contractual equality is affected. Otherwise, consumer law would be degenerated and would be transformed into a paternalistic law that actually limits consumer options and ultimately restricts their freedom.

Therefore, from a perspective of legislative policy, but also when it comes to formulating operational principles of private law with the objective of protecting consumers, a principle of proportionality should be applied[37]. Beyond the need to limit protective private-law measures to situations of disparity, thereby also providing guidance for the definition of the personal scope of application of specific provisions[38], this principle is meant to generate legal doctrines and rules that should be applied to compensate for certain failures of the system of contract law. Hence, according to that principle of proportionality, rules enabling the weaker party to make an informed and conscious decision have to be preferred to rules defining the rights and obligations of a contract. Also, it is clearly required that the law bans certain unfair standard contract terms, since rules of transparency will not sufficiently protect the other party, who had no chance to influence the drafting and the legal evaluation of these terms. Within the group of rules enabling a party to take an informed decision, duties to inform should be preferred to a right to withdraw from the contract. The latter is applied in Europe in particular in situations of doorstep selling and distance selling in

[36] See *supra*, II. 2).

[37] Such a proportionality principle for consumer law, in German "verbraucherschutzrechtlicher Verhältnismäßigkeitsgrundsatz", was proposed and further explained by Drexl (n. 17), 449–452.

[38] See *supra*, II. 3).

which the first step to the conclusion of the contract is not made by the consumer, or in which the consumer cannot test the quality of the goods prior to their delivery. In both situations, duties to inform do not compensate for the existing disparity. Among the rules relating to the rights and duties of the parties, rules invalidating contracts, like under the legislation on unfair contract terms, should be preferred to a strict definition of the rights and duties of the parties by the law. The former leave much larger scope for party autonomy than the latter.

Even in Europe, it is questionable whether consumer contract law is in line with these principles. Whereas it is a continuous challenge to react adequately to situations of disparity that were previously unknown, there are also features of EC law that seem to be the result of the above-mentioned fallacy of keeping consumer law and general private law separate. To a large extent, this fallacy is due to an institutional problem. Within the European Commission, the Directorate General for Health and Consumer Protection (SANCO) can only justify its work and existence by limiting its legislative proposals to consumers, although it might be better to provide for general application. Such an approach has to be criticised in particular with regard to the Unfair Contract Terms Directive[39] and the more recent Unfair Commercial Practices Directive[40]. It makes no sense to protect commercial customers and consumers under different rules when it comes to the marketing of goods and services. In many instances, goods may be equally bought and used by businesses and consumers. More importantly, the justification of strict liability of the seller of consumer goods, including used goods, under the EC Consumer Sales Directive, seems most problematic[41].

IV. Concluding Remarks

Modern consumer law can well be understood as an integral part of general private law. Consumer law is meant to react to specific situations of contractual inequality, or disparity. Whether the scope of specific provisions should be lim-

[39] See *supra* (n. 31).

[40] Directive 2005/23/EC of the European Parliament and of the Council of 11 May 2005 concerning unfair business-to-consumer practices in the internal market, OJ EC L 149, 11. 6. 2005, 22.

[41] For an evaluation of this problem, see *Josef Drexl*, Zwingendes Recht als Strukturprinzip des europäischen Verbraucherschutzrechts, in: Festschrift für Haus J. Sonnenberger (2004), 771; see also *Michael Martinek*, Unsystematische Überregulierung und kontraintentionale Effekte im Europäischen Verbraucherrecht oder: Weniger wäre mehr, in: Stefan Grundmann (ed.), Systembildung und Systemlücken in Kerngebieten des Europäischen Privatrechts (2000), 511, 535–548 (specifically crticising the application to used goods). *Claus-Wilhelm Canaris*, Wandlungen des Schuldvertragsrechts – Tendenzen zu seiner "Materialisierung", (2000) 200 Archiv für die civilistische Praxis 273, 362ff., argues that the Directive, by stipulating strict contract rules, may even violate the Constitution and primary Community law.

ited to consumers depends on the disparity in question. In this regard, even rules of a general scope of application can be considered to be part of consumer law to the extent that such provisions also protect the consumer. General rules of the private-law codification should be used and developed in practice with the objective of providing adequate protection to consumers in situations of such disparity.

There is no reason why specific consumer legislation, i.e. provisions applying to consumer contracts only, should not be integrated into the general private-law codification. On the contrary, such a way of proceeding would have considerable advantages. On the one hand, it would remind the legislature that specific consumer legislation needs to be justified in the light of contractual freedom which would be a safeguard against expansionist and paternalistic consumer legislation. On the other hand, it would help to avoid a too formalistic approach in situations in which commercial actors are in need of protection just like consumers.

For historical reasons, Israel may well be in a situation that makes it difficult to integrate specific consumer legislation into the new law. Therefore, it is all the more important that legal writing should spread an integrated "way of thinking", so as to help to avoid the described fallacies. Ofer Grosskopf's analysis certainly responds to this challenge.

The Four C's: Coherence, Clarification, Continuity, Change – Remedies for Breach of Contract in Israeli Draft Civil Code

By Nili Cohen*

Summary of Contents

I. Prologue – from the Common Law to the Continent

About thirty years ago, in 1972, the faculty of law at Tel-Aviv University held a conference entitled "The Codification of Israeli Law" which was dedicated to the new Israeli legislation being developed. Israel was then a young state, only 24 years old, which had started to pave a new legal road. By that time several specific contract statutes were enacted, among them the Standard Contracts Law, 1964, a world-wide novelty, the Agency Law, 1965, the Guarantee Law, 1967, the Pledges Law, 1967, the Sale Law, 1968, the Gift Law, 1968, and the Hire and Loan Law, 1971. The specific contract statutes preceded the General Contract Statutes. The Contracts (Remedies for Breach of Contract) Law (hereinafter: the Remedies Law) was enacted in 1970. It preceded the Contracts (General Part) Law, which was a bill at the time, and came into force a year later in 1973.

In one of the sessions dedicated to remedies for breach of contract Daniel Friedmann called for the enactment of comprehensive legislation which would provide for general remedies to each and every injured party – be it as a result of a breach of contract or a tort. The injured party would be entitled, as a matter of

* I would like to thank Lilach Naveh-Lurie and Tomer Shoyerman, my research assistants, for their very valuable work in the preparation of this paper.

right, to three remedies: the first, enforcement of the right; the second, a compensatory remedy; the third, a restitutionary remedy. Another remedy, namely self help, would be limited in its scope compared to the other remedies. Included within it are the use of force for the protection of possession, rescission of contract, set-off and reduction of price[1].

That proposal was revolutionary in several respects. First, it put emphasis on the substantive right, and regarded the remedy as secondary to the right. Second, it regarded enforcement of the right as the primary remedy for the infringement of a right. Third, on a more formal level, it called for systematic legislation which should comprehensively organise the field of private law remedies. This was diametrically opposed to the common law tradition which has been nourishing the Israeli legal system since the advent of the British Mandate.

First, relations between right and remedy: English private law sprang from the forms of action and had a strong practical-remedial inclination. Its focus was on the injury, on the accident, which brought the parties to court. Indeed torts and restitution are basically conceived as being remedial in nature, though at times they serve to create new substantive rights[2]. The emphasis English law put on the remedy was a reflection of the maxim taken up by the common law: *ubi remedium ibi ius*. Contract as an offspring of a tort is thus scrutinised at the time of the breach (*ex post*) and not at the time of its creation (*ex ante*).

Second, the primary remedy common both to torts and contracts has been compensatory damages[3]. Only where damages were not adequate, the equitable remedy of specific performance could be granted at the discretion of the court[4]. In modern parlance, the English remedial rule was that of liability rather than property[5].

Third, English Law does not pay too much attention to the systematic and analytical exposition of the law. Its infrastructure does not consist of legal scholarship but rather of an accumulation of cases, the hierarchy of which is determined by virtue of the principle of binding precedent. What counts is law-in-action through the lens of its addressees, namely the public at large and the legal community. A code system under which the applicable rules are to be collated and sifted through several standards of abstraction – juristic act, obligation, contract, specific contract – seems to English lawyers to be costly in operation[6]. The common law as a judge-made law needed accessible rules, easy to act upon, easy

---

[1] *Daniel Friedmann*, Remedies for Breach of Contract, (1973) 3 Tel Aviv University Studies in Law 135.

[2] *Daniel Friedmann*, The Protection of Entitlements via the Law of Restitution – Expectancies and Privacy, (2005) 121 Law Quarterly Review 400.

[3] For criticism, see *Nick Kurwen*, The Remedy in Conversion: Confusing Property and Obligation, (2006) 26 Legal Studies 570.

[4] Guenther Treitel, The Law of Contract (11th ed., 2003), 1019–1049.

[5] *Guido Calabresi/Douglas Melamed*, Property Rules, Liability Rules, and Inalienability: One View of the Cathedral, (1972) 85 Harvard Law Review 1089.

[6] On the distinction between code and judge-made law in historical perspective, concerning the 19th century in the United States, see *Lewis A. Grossman*, Langdell Upside-Down: The Anticlas-

to apply. Indeed the law of contract and the law of torts have not, so far, been the subject of comprehensive legislation in England, let alone of codification.

In fact in the early 1970s, a Contract Code was considered in England[7] but the idea was suspended if not rejected. Guenther Treitel, perhaps the greatest English contract scholar of our time, remarked in his Clarendon lectures in 2001 that the decision to suspend the process was a fortunate one. He stated that in the common law countries that have codes of contract law "the vague language of the relevant codes has done little, if anything, to improve the 'clarity and accessibility' of contract law". 'Clarity and accessibility' were the aims that stood behind the English project[8]. As it stands now, no part of private law in England is covered by comprehensive legislation. One should, however, note that the dividing lines between England and the Continent have become blurred, largely, probably as a result of the European Union. For example, today one can find scholarship in England dealing with obligations[9]. Also some private initiatives, such as UNIDROIT and PECL, try to establish a bridge between the two legal systems[10]. And last but not least, EC Directives obviously contribute to that end.

The move of Israeli law towards Continental concepts was gradual. An important substantive move first took place in 1970. The Remedies Law was enacted and provided in section 3 for enforcement as the primary remedy for breach of contract, replacing a liability rule with a property one. Another substantial move was made with the enactment of the General Contract Law in 1973. It rejected the remedial common law definition of contract as a promise for the breach of which the law gives a remedy[11], and defined contract as the merger of offer and acceptance[12]. The focus, thus, was on the creation of the right and not on the remedy.

The same statute marked a type of formal move towards the Continent. Section 61(b) of the General Contract Law applied the provisions of the law to other legal acts and obligations not stemming from contracts. The Contract Law

sical Jurisprudence of Anticodification, (2007) 19 Yale Journal of Law and the Humanities http://law.bepress.com/cgi/viewcontent.cgi?article=4828&context=expresso.

[7] Law Commission, Seventh Annual Report, Section 7 (1972).

[8] *Guenther Treitel*, Some Landmarks of Twentieth Century Contract Law (2002), 8. For a comprehensive survey on codifications in the common law world, see *Gunther A. Weiss*, The Enchantments of Codification in the Common-Law World, (2000) 25 Yale Journal of International Law 435.

[9] *Andrew M. Tettenborn*, An Introduction to the Law of Obligations (1984); *Joshua Getzler*, Patterns of Fusion, in: Peter Birks (ed.), The Classification of Obligations (1997), 157–92; *David J. Ibbetson*, A Historical Introduction to the Law of Obligations (1999).

[10] UNIDROIT Principles of International Commercial Contracts (2004); *Ole Lando/Hugh Beale* (eds.), Principles of European Contract Law, Parts I and II (2000): Ole Lando/Eric Clive/André Prüm/Reinhard Zimmermann, Principles of European Contract Law, Part III; see also *Reinhard Zimmermann*, Comparative Law and the Europeanization of Private Law, in: Mathias Reimann/Reinhard Zimmermann (eds.), The Oxford Handbook of Comparative Law (2006), 539, 550ff.

[11] Restatement (Second) of Contracts (1981), § 1.

[12] The Contracts (General Part) Law, 5733- 1973, 27 LSI 117 (1969–1970) (Isr.) §§ 1, 2, 5.

thus became the basis for the general law of obligations in Israel. Although the Remedies Law did not include a provision similar to s. 61(b), case law reasoned by analogy in order to apply its provisions to the breach of non-contractual obligations. In one case where the conflict was between a first and second buyer of the same property, the remedy of enforcement was directed against the second buyer – whose contractual right was inferior to that of the first buyer, even though no contractual relations existed between the two[13].

In sum, the primary status of the substantive right, the primary position of the remedy of enforcement, and the enactment of s. 61(b) constituted a significant re-orientation towards the Continental system – both in form and in substance.

Israeli Law, the historical roots of which are based partially on Continental law, i.e., those rules of French Law that had been adopted by the Ottoman law prevailing in Palestine before the British Mandate[14] – returned to the Continental system in some of its basic conceptual respects. This eventually materialised in the codification project, which started in 1984 and yielded a first draft in 2004, and a second one in 2006. Incidentally, this second draft embodies some of the proposals made in 1972, at the time when the ties with the Max Planck Institute in Hamburg began to flourish.

II. The Objects of Codification

The codification project was not intended to create Israeli private law *de novo*, nor did it purport to create a new legal culture. Nobody thought of touching the principle of *stare decisis* and of changing the primary role of courts in shaping the system; nobody thought of substituting the role of judges by academic scholarship. Indeed, the American experience shows that the enactment of a code does not radically change the importance of case law, nor the elevated status of the judges[15]. It is likely that this will also be a characteristic of Israeli law when the Draft Civil Code is adopted.

---

[13] f.H. 21/80 *Wertheimer v Harari* (1981) 35(3) P.D. 253, 270. See also C.A. 2643/97 *Ganz v British Colonial* (2003) 57(2) P.D. 385, 409, where section 3 of the Remedies Law, which deals with enforcement, is regarded as being of general application in the law of obligations. But, alternatively and preferably, the remedy sustaining the prior party's claim to the property is restitution: *Nili Cohen*, The Nature of the Undertaking to Effect a Transaction, (1978–9) 4 Tel-Aviv University Studies in Law 33, 68–70.

[14] *Daniel Friedmann*, The Effect of Foreign Law on the Law of Israel: Remnants of the Ottoman Period, (1975) 10 Israel Law Review 192, 196.

[15] *R. Lee Warthen*, The Non-Emergence of the Anglo-American Law Code, (1986) 6 Legal Reference Services Quarterly 129, 146–155. Louisiana, which was under the influence of French law, is the exception: *Rodolfo Batiza*, Origins of Modern Codification of the Civil law: The French Experience and its Implications for Louisiana Law, (1982) 56 Tulane Law Review 477; see also *Vernon Valentine Palmer*, The Death of a Code – The Birth of a Digest, (1988) 63 Tulane Law Review 221. The same holds true for the Uniform Commercial Code which has been interpreted in each state alongside the principles of the common law: *William D. Hawkland*, The Uniform Com-

As an infrastructure the project had available the various pieces of legislation enacted during the 1960's and 1970's and also a great many court decisions. The idea behind the project was at first quite modest. The current legislative framework and the leading court decisions were to be moulded into a systematic piece of legislation reflecting coherence in style and context. The project was meant to unify concepts and terminology; to avoid repetitions and lacunae; to clarify misunderstandings; and to specify in more detail some vague areas of the current legislation. In sum, the intention was to create a systematic piece of legislation that would cover the relevant areas of private law; that would be accessible; and that would reflect the values of Israeli society. Some change was expected, but nobody suggested major revisions. Over the years, however, the project has become more ambitious and some substantial novelties have been introduced. This is rather conspicuous in the sphere of remedies, the subject of my paper.

The present paper will focus on the four aims behind the codification project: coherence, continuity, clarification, change – each of which will be discussed with reference to some specific points in the law of remedies and to some lingering question marks.

Coherence will be examined with regard to the general framework of remedies; continuity with regard to the doctrine of *cy-près*; for clarification, the problem of enforcement of debt will provide the focal point of discussion; and for change, the punitive measures that have been introduced into the Draft Civil Code.

III. Coherence

The comprehensive arrangement of the remedies chapter is a major novelty, probably the most significant one of the entire project. It provides for remedies for the breach of an obligation, whatever the origin of that obligation. Thus, it applies both to the case of a breach of contract and the commission of a wrong[16].

It is interesting to note that the great historical codifications – the BGB and the *Code civil* – do not have a comprehensive system of remedies at large but that such an arrangement does exist in the more modern codes of Québec[17] and the Netherlands[18].

---

mercial Code and the Civil Codes, (1995) 56 Louisiana Law Review 231. Cf. also *Daphne Barak-Erez*, Israeli Codification in the Perspective of Contract Law, (1999) 22 Tel-Aviv University Law Review 793, 811–815 (in Hebrew).

[16] Section 445 provides that for the purposes of this sub-chapter the duty to abstain from commission of a wrong is deemed to be an obligation. This is to clarify that the remedies section applies both to contracts and torts.

[17] This is a modern codification (it dates from 1994). The first provisions of the code deal with the enjoyment and the operation of rights in private law (§§ 1–9). The following provisions deal with personal rights, property rights and in book 5 with obligations. Book 5 opens with general

Obviously, it may be asked whether a comprehensive arrangement dealing with remedies is substantively warranted and, indeed, needed, if there is a great diversity among the various branches of the law that require separate normative arrangements to different kinds of obligations. This question relates to the very structure of a code. Some differences alongside certain similarities obtain among all branches of private law in the substantive as well as in the remedial sphere. The question is whether to focus on the common features or on the differences.

English law basically chose to disregard the common ground in the formal sense (it did not formulate common remedial rules regarding tort and contracts), but the basic rule – damages as the primary remedy – applies to both areas[19].

Is there a fundamental difference in the principal ideas behind tort liability and contract liability that might justify a different remedial arrangement for each of them? This is not the place to develop fully the distinctions and similarities between liability in tort and contract, yet they share a common remedial feature, namely the idea of corrective justice. This is clear from the perspective of tort law, but it is equally clear from the point of view of contract law. Once a contract is created, it imposes on the debtor a duty to perform. If the contract is not performed, the other party is entitled to the correction of the wrong (i.e., the breach) inasmuch as an injured party in the sphere of tort liability is entitled to. The difference in tort and contract law relates to the ground of the creation of the primary right: in contracts – the will of the parties; in torts – the operation of the law. But the duty to correct the injustice caused by the breach of contract is imposed upon the breaching party as if it had been created by law. We are dealing in both cases with secondary, remedial rights. One also may add that even with regard to the difference between tort and contract concerning primary rights the demarcation line between the two has become blurred. Tort liability may result from contract (products' liability; professional liability), and contract liability is often predicated on a legal or a statutory duty (where the law imposes a duty to contract or sometimes infuses a duty into the contract irrespective of the will of the parties). That justifies a uniform starting point also on the remedial level, certainly with regard to the supremacy of remedies (enforcement or damages)[20].

---

provisions (§§ 1371–1376), then deals with general contract law rules, and finally turns to civil liability (§§ 1457–1481); the latter section includes liability in contracts, in torts and in unjust enrichment. Within the sections dealing with the performance of obligations (§§ 1553–1636) remedies for breach of an obligation are specified.

[18] *Arthur S. Hartkamp*, Law of Obligations, in: *Jeroen M.J. Chorus/Piet-Hein M. Gerver/Ewoud H. Hondius/Alis K. Koekkoek* (eds.), Introduction to Dutch Law (1999), 123, 129–133.

[19] *Supra*, text accompaying n. 3. Cf. also *Andrew Burrows*, Remedies for Torts and Breach of Contract (3rd ed., 2004), 504–05.

[20] I refer briefly to this point as a response to Hanoch Dagan's chapter in this volume: Codification, Coherence and Priority Conflicts. For an expanded, and thorough, response, see *Yehuda Adar*, Why unify Tort and Contract Remedies? A Reply to Professor Dagan, (2006) 36 Mishpatim 357 (in Hebrew).

The Israeli Draft Code does not establish a comprehensive regime of remedies for the whole of private law, but rather a narrower one for the law of obligations. In that sphere there was an attempt to establish a comprehensive regime with regard to enforcement (ss. 448–451) and damages (ss. 455–493), the two major remedies. The other two general remedies, restitution and self-help, for which Friedmann had also suggested a unified arrangement[21], have been left somewhat scattered in the Draft Code, especially in the case of self-help.

Some brief words about the latter. Restitution has a double character: it is a set of principles which generates a cause of action and it also supplies the remedy, i.e., restitution. Within the Draft Civil Code's general heading of involuntary obligations both torts and unjust enrichment are included. While the tort law provisions contain solely substantive causes of action (ss. 387–408), the remedies for which are borrowed from the general chapter on remedies, the unjust enrichment section combines substantive causes of action and the remedy of restitution (ss. 411–420)[22]. Hence, where the law of unjust enrichment creates a new cause of action should there be any relation between the remedies chapter and that of unjust enrichment? For example, is the plaintiff entitled to an injunction to prevent unlawful enrichment? This possibility has already been recognised in the case law[23], but the Draft Code does not mention it. Nevertheless it seems that the general law of remedies might apply *mutatis mutandis* also to obligations arising out of unjust enrichment, so that an injunction to prevent unlawful enrichment could be issued in appropriate cases[24].

In the chapter on remedies for breach, the remedy of restitution has a very limited application. It applies in s. 494 only to the case of rescission of a contract for breach, though it might have been included in s. 413(2)(a) (in the chapter on unjust enrichment)[25] which deals with restitution where the cause is null and void or has been avoided[26]. The explanation for the additional separate section is as follows: in the case of a breach the injured party has the option whether to make restoration *in specie* or whether to receive the performance *in specie*[27]. This option is unavailable to a party who rescinds the contract for a consensual defect. Allowing such an option would serve as an approval of an initially defective contract. Therefore a separate regime was needed. But in all other respects there

---

[21] *Friedmann*, (1973) 3 Tel Aviv University Studies in Law 135.

[22] On the distinction between the substantive and the remedial parts of restitution, see *Peter Birks*, Unjust Enrichment and Wrongful Enrichment, (2001) 79 Texas Law Review 1767. For critical remarks and for the suggestion to distinguish between the substantive and the remedial parts of restitution in the code, see Christiane Wendehorst's chapter in the present volume.

[23] C.A. 347/90 *Soda Gal Ltd v Spilman* (1990) 47(3) P.D. 459; C.A. 5768/94 *A.S.I.R. v Forum* (1998) 52(4) P.D. 289.

[24] Section 444 provides that the possibility of issuing an injunction is included within the remedy of enforcement.

[25] We see here the double function of unjust enrichment as a cause of action and as a remedy.

[26] A duty of mutual restitution is imposed on the contracting parties following rescission for defects in contracting.

[27] Explanation to s. 494, 202.

is a reference in s. 495 to the chapter dealing with unjust enrichment (ss. 411–420).

The section on restitution (in the chapter on remedies) does not deal with the case of disgorgement of benefits the party in breach received as a result of the breach, but rather with the mutual restitution of benefits which both parties conferred and received. However, the restrictive application of restitution in the chapter on remedies is supplemented by the application of the general chapter on unjust enrichment. The latter includes, alongside the general principle (s. 411), a provision imposing a duty to restore the benefit received as a result of a wrongdoing (s. 413(1)). A breach of contract might be conceived as a "wrongdoing", in particular following the influential *Adras* case, in which the party in breach was bound to disgorge the benefits to the injured party[28]. Yet it would have seemed preferable to have included this major point in the chapter on remedies or at least briefly to have acknowledged it.

Self-help remedies include, mainly, the remedies of repossession, reduction, set-off, and rescission of contract. The draft did not formulate a comprehensive concept of self-help remedies presumably due to the variations among these different expressions of the core idea and the high degree of abstraction that would have been needed to build a unified concept. The self-help remedy of rescission of contract[29] was the only one to be included in the chapter on remedies and is obviously limited to contracts[30].

We shall move now to the two paradigmatic remedies with regard to which an attempt has been made to build a coherent regime: enforcement and damages.

It has been pointed out above that the Israeli Remedies Law deviated in 1970 from the common law tradition and provided that enforcement should be the primary remedy for breach of contract[31]. The Civil Wrongs Ordinance is faithful to the English tradition with damages as the primary remedy[32]. The Draft Civil Code solves this divergence in favour of the contractual approach: enforcement is the primary remedy whatever the source of the obligation. Hence, the formal

[28] f.H. 20/82 *Adras v Harlow & Jones* (1988) 42(1) P.D. 221 discussed in *Daniel Friedmann*, Restitution of Benefits Gained Through Breach of Contract, (1988) 104 Law Quarterly Review 383. For a critical approach, see *Hanoch Dagan*, Restitution and Unjust Enrichment: Restitutionary Damages for Breach of Contract: An Exercise in Private Law Theory, (2000) 1 Theoretical Inquiries in Law 115. For support, see *Daphna Lewinsohn-Zamir*, The Impact of Economic Theory on the Israeli Case Law on Property, (2006) 39 Israel Law Review 5, 27–30.

[29] Now dealt with in the Contracts (Remedies for Breach of Contract) Law, 1970, s. 7.

[30] See ss. 452–454. The other remedies of self-help are dealt in the following sections: repossession, currently covered by The Land Law 1969 s. 18, is dealt in s. 506 of the Draft Civil Code; set off, currently in The Contracts (General Part) Law, 1973, s. 53, in s. 62 of the Draft Civil Code in the chapter dedicated to the performance of obligations, and reduction, now in The Sales Law, 1968, s. 28, in s. 498 of the Draft Civil Code.

[31] *Supra*, text accompanying notes 10–11.

[32] But the Land Law 1969, *supra*, n. 30, that applies also to the proprietary torts, has adopted a property rule: ss. 16–19, *infra* n. 57.

incompatibility between the remedy for breach of contract – enforcement – and the remedy for inducing breach of contract[33] – damages – is avoided[34].

The remedy of enforcement is currently subject to four exceptions, the most important of which is the justice exception (s. 3(4) of the Remedies Law). The Draft Code basically adopts these exceptions[35], and adds one more. The fifth new exception to enforcement (448(a)(5)) applies where damages are more adequate given the nature of the particular obligation. It was added mainly in order to adjust the general rule to the field of tort law where usually compensatory damages are the natural remedy[36]. One should hope that this exception does not serve as a point of departure to infuse into contract law the English "inadequacy" test of damages, which is rejected by the supremacy of enforcement in our system.

The Draft tries to build a common infrastructure of damages (s. 455) which aims to put the injured party in the same position she would have been in had the injury or breach not occurred (s. 456). Within this framework are included sections dealing with mitigation, benefits, and some other issues whose relevance is mainly in tort law, such as damages for bodily injury and damages as a result of death. According to the draft, the dependents of the deceased (who died as a result of a breach of contract) would be entitled to damages from the party in breach[37], a remedy that is unavailable for them to date[38]. Yet one may wonder whether a breach of contract case causing death would not almost always be governed also by tort liability[39].

---

[33] The Civil Wrongs Ordinance [New Version], s. 62. The draft relates to inducing a breach of an obligation (not necessarily a contractual one): s. 400. This was proposed in Nili Cohen, Inducing Breach of Contract (1986), 26–33, ss. 13–16 (in Hebrew). – It should be noted though that in many cases dealing with inducing breach an injunction has been issued against the third party inducer in order to guarantee the enforcement of the contractual right: C.A. 123/50 *Baurenfreund v Drezner* [1951] 5 P.D. 1559 (a contract which imposed upon the seller of apartments an obligation to include in the contract with a future buyer of the cellar in that building an undertaking not to use any machines in the cellar. No such undertaking was included in the contract with the person who bought the cellar, knowing about the seller's obligation, and yet used machines in his cellar. The Court issued an injunction against this buyer for knowingly inducing a breach of contract). See also H.C.J. 1683/93 *Yavin Plast v National Labour Tribunal* (1993) 47(4) P.D. 702 (an injunction against an employee for misusing trade secrets and also against his new employer for inducing the breach); C.A. 3668/98 Best Buy Ltd v Fidias (1999) 53(3) P.D. 380 (an injunction against a landlord who granted his lessee an exclusive right to sell electronic products in a shopping-mall and later on broke it by allowing a second lessee to sell similar products. The second lessee was also subject to an injunction for inducing the breach).

[34] The problem is discussed in *Cohen*, Inducing Breach of Contract (n. 33), 288–289, s. 207.

[35] See s. 448(a) (see explanation to the Draft Civil Code, 186).

[36] Explanation to the Draft Civil Code, 186.

[37] Section 471.

[38] The Civil Wrongs Ordinance [New Version], § 78.

[39] And whether a rare possible case justifies special provisions which might be applied by analogy in any case.

The law governing a dependent's claim which originated in tort has been applicable also to contracts, while the provision regarding anticipatory breach, the roots of which are contractual[40], now also applies to torts[41] and rightly so[42].

A significant deviation from the common-denominator theme was made with regard to the test for the remoteness of damages. Israeli law – like the common law – has applied different tests to contract and tort: in contract law the test of foreseeability[43] has been applied, in tort that of natural damage[44]. The draft preserved the common law line of thought, though one may wonder whether a unified test might not have been devised instead.

Also the provisions dealing with damages where no proof of loss is required are mostly applicable to the context of contracts (ss. 489–493).

The final provision of the chapter on remedies is a problematic novelty. It includes the remedies of a deterring order (the French *astreinte*) the application of which is general[45] and that of punitive damages[46]. Both of these novelties are discussed below.

What is the general scheme behind the remedies arrangement? Some provisions formally apply to both contracts and torts; others explicitly apply to either contracts or torts. The provisions dealing with bodily injury, the application of which is general, are likely to be developed mainly in the tort context. The remedies of liquidated damages (ss. 492–493), rescission, and restitution are applicable in the remedies section to contracts only, and so are the additional remedies of postponement (s. 497) and reduction (s. 498).

This raises the question whether the common basis is broad enough to justify the energy that has been invested to establish a unified concept of remedies. Perhaps one might have achieved the desired result by stating that the primary remedy in tort law is also enforcement, by making some additional amendments (e.g., applying anticipatory breach to torts), and by keeping the remedies separate, thereby making the rules more comprehensible. This goes back to the root of the question of whether or not to adopt a code. On balance it seems that the choice in favour of codification naturally leads to an attempt to systematise the rules also in the remedial sphere[47].

---

[40] The Contracts (Remedies for Breach of Contract) Law, 1970, s. 17.

[41] See s. 496.

[42] Frustration and *force majeure*, relevant to contracts, which are part of The Contracts (Remedies for Breach of Contract) Law, 1970, s. 17, were omitted from the remedies section in the Draft, and were transplanted into the substantive part on contracts (§§ 131–137).

[43] The Contracts (Remedies for Breach of Contract) Law, 1970, s. 10.

[44] The Civil Wrongs Ordinance [New Version], s. 76.

[45] See s. 499.

[46] See s. 462.

[47] For a comprehensive survey supporting the codification of remedies, see *Yehuda Adar*, Of the Honey and the Sting – Some Reflections on Remedies and the Draft Civil Code, (2006) 5 Law and Business 347 (in Hebrew).

IV. Clarification

The extension of the remedy of enforcement to tort law, and the elevated position of this remedy in current contract law, has been discussed above. Enforcement is subject to exceptions, the most important of which is that of "justice": the court has a power not to grant enforcement if enforcement in the circumstances of the case is unjust[48]. This exception has raised a series of problems regarding the enforcement of a monetary obligation or the enforcement of a property interest. Both substantive rights are considered to be strong, and the discretion of the court to which they are formally subject is deemed to be too wide. Indeed, s. 448(b) of the Draft Civil Code excludes almost entirely the justice exception with regard to both rights.

I shall deal with the enforcement of a debt. If a seller has delivered the goods and the buyer has failed to pay the price, a claim for the price has accrued. In English law the claim of the seller is not the equitable remedy of specific performance, but rather the common law remedy of debt. This monetary claim differs from both specific performance and damages. It is not subject to the exception of justice (that obtains in specific performance) nor to the duty to mitigate (in damages)[49]. The reason is clear. If the contract is not tainted with any defect, and if no claim of supervening circumstances or breach by the seller is raised, why should the court interfere with the price on the remedial level? Interference by the court is incompatible with basic contractual principles; it would be a gross breach of the principle of freedom upon which the law of contract is predicated[50]. Also, if the seller did what was expected of her under the contract, there is no room for an argument based on the duty to mitigate.

Unlike the common law, the Remedies Law did not keep the claim of debt independent but merged it with the remedy of enforcement[51]. Thus, the claim has become subject to the justice exception. The argument that the claim for debt is unjust and therefore should not be enforced was raised in several Supreme Court cases and failed. In one case Assoulin filed an action against Plateau-Sharon for the payment of 200,000 dollars due to him as consultancy fees. Plateau-Sharon argued that the enforcement of the debt was unjust because the contract had been made under duress. The Court rejected the argument and held that the contract had been made voluntarily. Furthermore, it remarked that even if enforcement were unjust, the seller might claim damages the value of which would

---

[48] The Contracts (Remedies for Breach of Contract) Law, 1970, s. 3(4); s. 448(a)(4) in the Draft Civil Code.

[49] *Treitel*, Contract (n. 4), 1013–1019.

[50] See C.A. 11/87 *The State of Israel v Hiram Landau* (1989) 43(4) P.D. 287, 293: The provision in the Remedies Law which excludes enforcement "does not purport to interfere in the contract and to change its provisions ..."

[51] The Contracts (Remedies for Breach of Contract) Law, 1970, s. 1: "'Enforcement' means enforcement by an order for the discharge of a monetary obligation"; see *Nili Cohen*, Right and Remedy in the Enforcement of Debt, in: Festschrift für Andreas Heldrich (2005), 39.

be the same as the price. But the Court added that cases are conceivable in which enforcement of a debt might be deemed unjust[52]. That was problematic and begged the question: what circumstances make the enforcement of a debt unjust?[53] The drafters of the Draft Civil Code took upon themselves the task to clarify the matter.

Section 448(b)(1) states that the justice exception shall not apply to "a monetary obligation under a contract, provided that the injured party performed his contractual obligations earning him the payment of the debt, and the party in breach did not object to the performance".

The two requirements in the section – performance by the injured party and no objection by the party in breach – allude to the difficulty that was raised in the famous case of *White & Carter v McGregor*[54]. An advertising contractor agreed with a garage proprietor to advertise the garage for three years on plates attached to litterbins. The contract was repudiated by the garage-owner on the very day it was made. But the advertiser – the injured party – fully performed and after three years claimed the price. A majority of the House of Lords upheld the claim. The contract was not terminated by the repudiation; the injured party chose to perform and succeeded (no co-operation with the party in breach was needed). By fully performing the contractor earned the right to the price. But Lord Reid – of the majority – said that if the injured party has "no substantial or legitimate interest"[55] in completing performance his only remedy will be damages, in which case he would be subject to the rules on mitigation. That means that he would have to give up his right to performance and be satisfied with his loss of profits[56].

Section 448(b)(1) of the Draft has adopted the reservation of Lord Reid and even expanded it. The section does not mention the injured party's need of a legitimate interest to justify the performance being forced on the party in breach. But one can read the section as stating the following proposition: the objection of the party in breach to the performance by the injured party opens the gate for

---

[52] C. A. 1894/90 *Plateau-Sharon v Assoulin* (1992) 46(4) P. D. 822. See also C. A. 254/86 *Ninio v Mishcan* (1988) 42(1) P. D. 1.

[53] In one case – C. A. 3437/93 *Adler v Eged* (1998) 54(1) P. D. 817 – there is a clarification which, however, only covers part of the problem: a member in a co-operative society who served as a driver was unable to perform his duties due to a mental injury. For about 16 years he refused to perform any other assignment. The co-operative society decided to expel him from its ranks. The member argued that the expulsion was unlawful and demanded his wages for the whole period. The Court ruled that, though the expulsion was invalid, an enforcement of his wages for the whole period would be unjust. This was found on the conduct of the member who persistently, and with no good cause, refused to carry out any alternative assignment. In other words, the justice exception is combined with the burden of mitigation.

[54] [1962] A. C. 413; see *A. L. Goodhart*, Measure of Damages when a Contract is Repudiated, (1962) 78 Law Quarterly Review 263; *P. Nienaber*, The Effects of Anticipatory Repudiation: Principles and Policy, [1962] Cambridge Law Journal 213.

[55] [1962] A. C. 413, 431.

[56] *Treitel*, Contract (n. 4), claims that the result in the case is consistent with the mitigation rules: 1018–1019.

the justice exception, within which the court may consider whether the injured party had a legitimate interest in performing. On the other hand such a reading might actually neutralise the effect of the section: in order to apply the justice exception all the party in breach needs to do is to object to the performance irrespective of whether she has a reasonable ground to do so. Therefore it seems preferable to interpret the section as stating that only a reasonable objection by the party in breach would open the gate to the argument that the justice exception ought to apply and that enforcement should not be allowed.

The justice exception may also apply to the enforcement of a property right. Section 448(b)(2) expresses the view – compatible with the notions of property in Israeli law – that an infringement of a property right would generally activate a property-enforcement rule and not a liability-for-damages rule[57]. The damages rule is tantamount to a private taking and will be allowed only in exceptional cases.

The Draft which divided the law of property and the law of obligations, also distinguished between the remedies for the protection of property rights[58] and those for the breach of obligations. But property rights are protected also within the sphere of obligations and some adjustment was necessary[59]. Obviously, a legislative draft, in spite of twenty years of preparation (and it may even be because of such a long legislative period) is not immune from difficulties. Thus, for instance, a problem arises as to the meaning of "a right in property". Is a holder of a contractual right to an apartment entitled to a "right in property"? According to Israeli case law such holder is an owner of an equitable right[60], and thus is an owner of a "right in property". The courts applied a vast discretion based on the justice exception with regard to the enforcement of such a right[61]. According to the Draft Civil Code the justice exception would not apply to the case of a conflict between a vendor and purchaser of an apartment. The result is strange. Is it conceivable that the justice exception would be excluded in a paradigmatic type of case to which it has formerly been applied?

The Draft Civil Code created an opportunity to clarify matters but it chose to do so unevenly. An important question relating to enforcement is as follows: Is a buyer of non-specific goods entitled to enforcement or should such a buyer purchase a replacement and claim only her monetary loss? In English law specific performance is not available to a buyer of non-specific goods because this is a

---

57 The Land Law 1969, ss. 16–19.

58 See the proprietary protection in ss. 504–507, replacing ss. 16–19 of the Land Law 1969. – The proprietary remedies in the Civil Wrongs Ordinance [New Version], ss. 49–55, were omitted except for the tort of trespass: ss. 393–394. See also s. 397 which creates a tort of private nuisance by reference to the property rules.

59 Section 448(b)(2) proposes two versions, but for our purposes the difference is irrelevant.

60 C. A. 1559/99 *Zimbler v Turgemann* (2003) 57(5) P. D. 49.

61 For some examples of the application of the justice exception to land transactions, see C. A. 839/90 *Raz v Orenstein* (1991) 45(5) P. D. 739 (conflicting transactions) and C. A. 48/81 *Pomeranz v K. D. S.* (1984) 38(2) P. D. 813, 818–820 (laches and waiver) *per* the minority opinion of President Shamgar.

case where damages are adequate. The reason is clear: the injured party can easily replace non-specific goods in the market place[62], and the loss will be compensated at a later stage. This result puts the burden of mitigation on the buyer who is expected to prevent additional losses to herself. In other words, while the right to enforcement implies that the burden of a replacement is on the party in breach (the seller in our case), the common law puts the replacement burden on the injured party (the buyer in our case).

In Israeli law the injured party is entitled to enforcement but the party in breach might argue that enforcement is unjust because it leads to an inefficient result: losses have increased due to the inaction of the injured party. In other words, the burden to mitigate is a consideration relevant to the question whether enforcement is just or unjust[63]. Furthermore, the burden to mitigate to which the injured party is subject in the claim for damages may result in damages being assessed as the difference between the contract price at the date of rescission and not at the date when judgment is rendered. If all this is correct our distinct remedy of enforcement is likely to become identical with that of specific performance, irrespective of the change the Remedies Law purported to make[64]. Another outcome likely to follow is that the party in breach – and not the injured party – has the power to rescind the contract. This leads to the application of the doctrine of "efficient breach" which was firmly rejected by Israeli courts[65].

All of this raises a difficulty that needs to be cleared up. The elevated position of enforcement should enable the purchaser of non-specific goods to claim enforcement. Consequently the burden of getting a replacement will be imposed on the party in breach and not on the injured party. This is the position of French law: by combining the substantive and the remedial rights, French law imposes on the party in breach the duty to supply the original goods or a suitable substitute[66].

---

[62] Unless replacement for the goods cannot be attained on the market; or the buyer who had already paid the seller does not have the means to enter into another transaction; or the claim of specific performance was rejected but not due to the wrongful conduct of the injured party: *Wroth v Tyler* [1974] Ch. 30; *Treitel*, Contract (n. 4), 961. Similarly: *Semelhago v Paramadevan* [1996] 2 S.C.R. 415; 136 D.L.R. (4th) 1 (SCC), discussed in *Lionel Smith*, Understanding Specific Performance, in: Nili Cohen/Ewan McKendrick (eds.), Comparative Remedies for Breach of Contract (2005), 221, 228–230.

[63] For mitigation as a consideration in enforcement: C.A. 3437/93 *Adler v Eged* (1998) 54(1) P.D. 817. See also *Cohen*, Right and Remedy (n. 51), 49, 50–53.

[64] Indeed, one commentator, Professor Uri Yadin, remarked that theoretically such arguments should not be raised, but practically a prudent injured party will make self-replacement and will claim the remaining loss from the party in breach: *Uri Yadin*, Law of Contracts (Remedies for Breach of Contract) 1971 (1979), 50–51 (in Hebrew).

[65] F.H. 20/82 *Adras v Harlow & Jones* (1988) 42(1) P.D. 221 (*per* Barak J); C.A. 3668/98 *Best Buy Ltd v Fidias* (1999) 53(3) P.D. 380 (*per* Englard J); C.A. 2454/98 *Lindauer v Ringel* (2001) 56(1) P.D. 225. For an approach justifying Israeli law from the point of view of efficiency considerations, see *Daphna Lewinsohn-Zamir*, The Impact of Economic Theory on the Israeli Case Law on Property, (2006) 39 Israel Law Review 5, 27–30.

[66] *Yves Marie Laithier*, Comparative Reflections on the French Law of Remedies for Breach of

The conclusion that the purchaser of non-specific goods will be protected by the property rule is also compatible with the logic in *Adras*. In that case the injured party – a buyer of non-specific goods – became entitled to the gains the party in breach had received from selling his goods to a third party[67]. The injured party's entitlement to the profits was predicated both on his substantive right and the remedial right to enforcement[68]. Unfortunately this important question has not been clarified in the Draft Civil Code.

V. Continuity

The Draft purports not only to harmonise and to clarify the law but also to integrate significant case law that has become part and parcel of the Israeli common law in order to present a full picture of the legal system. A nice example is that of the doctrine of *cy-près*, embodied in s. 449 of the draft. The problem will be illustrated by two examples.

First, under a contract between contractor and buyer the latter is entitled to an apartment A in an apartment-building under construction. It transpires that the apartment was sold to a *bona fide* purchaser, and now our buyer is interested in apartment B; it is located in the same building and has not yet been sold. The original contract cannot be performed any more. Enforcement is therefore impossible[69]. Is the buyer able to claim apartment B?

One might say that nowadays an apartment in an apartment-building is not a unique piece of property, and a similar apartment in the same building may well serve as a substitute for the original one. But even if an apartment is regarded as specific property, a similar apartment may be considered sufficiently close to the original performance so as still to reflect the original intention of the parties.

Israeli case-law dealt with the problem where a contractor, who in breach of his contract sold apartment A to a *bona fide* purchaser, orally promised to deliver apartment B to the buyer. That had posed an easier problem. The Court approved the buyer's right to the other apartment on the basis of either the doctrine of *cy-près*, which was absorbed from trust doctrine obtaining in common law and expanded to specific performance,[70] or the principle of good faith[71]. The question whether the *cy-près* doctrine could apply where no promise had been made

---

Contract, in: Nili Cohen/Ewan McKendrick (eds.), Comparative Remedies for Breach of Contract (2005), 103, 108–116.

[67] See *infra*, n. 28.

[68] This is also the approach advocated in American law by Melvin Eisenberg: *Melvin Eisenberg*, Actual and Virtual Specific Performance, The Theory of Efficient Breach, and the Indifference Principle in Contract Law, (2005) 93 California Law Review 975, 1009–1010; *Melvin Eisenberg*, The Disgorgement Interest in Contract Law, (2006) 105 Michigan Law Review 559, 578–597.

[69] The Contracts (Remedies for Breach of Contract) Law, 1970, s. 3(1); s. 448(a)(1) of the Draft Civil Code.

[70] C.A. 79/49 *Frant v Yehuday* (1950) 4 P.D. 375.

[71] C.A. 289/78 *Eshed v Lober* (1978) 33(1) P.D. 13.

is more difficult. The Anglo-American doctrine of *cy-près*, which came from equity, is unlikely to apply in such a situation[72].

The other example concerns the following case: a buyer was entitled to a specific apartment in a building under construction. In a series of events the seller transferred ownership to the builder, and the builder took upon himself the undertaking towards the buyer. The building was eventually built with one change: the apartments were larger. When the buyer claimed enforcement of his contract, the builder required adjustment of the price. Following a thorough analysis, the Court upheld the claim using the *cy-près* doctrine. Its legal basis was either predicated on the doctrine of good faith or on s. 4 of the Remedies Law which empowers the Court to make enforcement subject to "other conditions necessarily resulting from the contract in the circumstances of the case"[73]. The problem with the last normative source is that the *cy-près* performance does not necessarily result from the contract. Had it been so, it would have been a direct, not a *cy-près* enforcement.

Another problem raised by the doctrine of *cy-près* is whether it is only the injured party who can rely on it or also the party in breach? For example: is the contractor in the last case entitled to impose *cy-près* enforcement on the buyer? In principle the answer is in the negative. The right to *cy-près* performance is available to the innocent party only. If she does not wish to take advantage of it, she is regarded as if she had rescinded the contract. But if the innocent party does not wish to rescind, and the original performance is impossible, she could get only *cy-près* enforcement. In that case the party in breach, who is required to perform, might suggest that the contract be enforced *cy-près*[74].

Cy-près performance may be conceived of as a mirror of the right of the breaching party to limit the power of the injured party to rescind the contract: when the breach is not fundamental, the injured party may not rescind the contract, if the party in breach objects to it and rescission would be unjust[75]. This reflects the two facets of the idea of *pacta sunt servanda* at the remedial level: the party in breach cannot frustrate the aggrieved party's right to enforcement when there is a minor change that prevents exact performance of the original promise. In a similar vein, the aggrieved party cannot frustrate the expectation of the

---

[72] *Austin Wakeman Scott/William f. Fratcher*, The Law of Trusts (4th ed., 1988), vol. III, 271–272, section 208.4. Some courts have considered imposing on a trustee the duty to purchase a similar property for the trust, but it seems too far-reaching to be applied to land.

[73] C. A. 2686/99 *Eismann v Kidmat Eden* (2001) 55(5) P. D. 365, 378 (*per* Englard J).

[74] C. A. 165/78 *Shalit v Societe Anonyme Belge* (1979) 33(2) P. D. 477: original enforcement was coupled with the demolition of a high rise building. That was needed in order to build a cellar which was not, however, built. The result was that the building could not be registered as a condominium. Only this registration enabled transfer of ownership from the seller to the buyer. The *cy-près* enforcement suggested by the seller was to register a lease in the name of the buyer for 99,000 years. The Court found that reasonable and imposed it on the buyer seeking enforcement.

[75] The Contracts (Remedies for Breach of Contract) Law, 1970, s. 7(b). In the Draft Civil Code: s. 453(b).

party in breach that the contract be performed because of a relatively minor breach.

The doctrine of *cy-près* exposes the blurred borderlines dividing right from remedy. If *cy-près* performance is based on the substantive right of the injured party, why should it only be found at the remedial level? On the other hand, since *cy-près* performance substitutes for the original one, it presupposes that enforcement is impossible, and therefore its proper location may appear to be within the remedial sphere. In any case, the question of location seems of little moment. The rule itself is important. Section 449 indeed emphasises that *cy-près* enforcement is an option available to the injured party; that *cy-près* enforcement can be requested only when the deviation from the original performance is not grave; and that a *cy-près* enforcement is deemed to be a regular enforcement, which means that the exceptions to that remedy – in particular the "justice" exception – also apply to it.

The issue of *cy-près* enforcement has been effectively integrated into the code. But the Draft could also have integrated case law which dealt with various issues regarding the "justice" exception in enforcement, for example the impact of change of circumstances[76], laches[77], the blameworthiness of the parties[78], the relative hardship of the parties[79] and public policy[80].

Another problem that could have been addressed with assistance from the case law but was left open is the following: is enforcement likely to be denied if it causes hardship to third parties? In one case the Court held that difficulties faced by third parties should not be considered a ground for denying enforcement[81]. Only hardship of the party in breach may be considered. But in another case it was held that insisting on enforcement while a third party suffers hardship is incompatible with the principle of good faith[82]. Yet the distinction between lack of good faith and injustice is difficult to draw. In sum, more guidance could have been provided regarding the employment of the vast discretionary powers with which the courts are invested in the remedial sphere.

---

[76] C.A. 158/77 *Rabinai v Man-Shaked* (1979) 33(2) P.D. 281 (grave inflation as ground for adjustment of the price).

[77] C.A. 48/81 *Pomeranz v K. D. S.* (1984) 38(2) P.D. 813, 818–820 (minority opinion of Shamgar C.J.).

[78] *Wertheimer v Harari, supra*, n. 13.

[79] C.A. 4796/95 *Alubara v Alubara* (1997) 51(2) P.D. 669 (non-enforceablity if the hardship to the party in breach exceeds the benefit to the injured party).

[80] C.A. 3833/93 *Levin v Levin* (1994) 48(2) P.D. 866 (non-enforceablity of a contract which bars access to court).

[81] *Wertheimer v Harari, supra*, n. 13.

[82] *Ganz v British Colonial, supra*, n. 13.

VI. Change

Two revolutionary matters are included in the draft. The first is the introduction of a deterring order (*astreinte* as it is called in French law) in s. 499. Under that section the court, when ordering enforcement, may impose on the party in breach, from the time the order is given or later, the payment of a sum of money for each day the order has been not complied with. The second novelty is the availability of exemplary or punitive damages. Section 462 provides that if the breach has been maliciously committed the court may impose the payment of damages not related to the loss[83].

When an order of enforcement is not being performed, the injured party may apply to the court to seek the imposition of a sanction based on a contempt of court[84]. This additional proceeding has a penal character but is not used frequently. Failure to obey judicial acts is detrimental to the rule of law and to the validity of the substantive right. The Draft has therefore now added another measure further to deter non-compliance by imposing a monetary sanction on the party who does not comply with enforcement. This deterring order applies to any order of enforcement, whether in tort law (e.g., an order to remove a neighbouring fence), or contract (e.g., an order to deliver certain property). But what is its function? Is the deterring order indeed designed to motivate the party in breach to perform, or is it designed mainly to compensate the injured party for the loss caused by the non-performance? In France – the homeland of this order – there are two types of *astreinte*: provisional and fixed[85]. The provisional order is determined according to the financial position of the party in breach. Its aim is not to compensate but rather to coerce the party in breach into complying with the decree of enforcement. The injured party is not entitled as a matter of right to claim the amount specified. In order to gain it, that party has to apply again to the court in which case the court might reduce the sum to the real loss suffered by the injured party. The fixed order is not subject to reduction, is not conditional on the real loss, and is considered to be more effective.

The draft does not specify the amount that can be imposed or to whom is it payable; this is within the discretion of the court that presumably may hold that the sum is to be paid to the injured party.

---

[83] For clarification on the effect of this order, see *Guenter H. Treitel*, A Comparative Account of Remedies for Breach of Contract (1988), 59–62; Unidroit (ed.), Unidroit Principles of International Commercial Contracts 2004 (2004), Art. 7.2.4 providing for a judicial penalty for non-performance of an order of enforcement.

[84] Contempt of Court Ordinance, s. 6.

[85] *Treitel*, Remedies (n. 83), 60–61.

The deterring factor has been subject to criticism in France[86]: one argument is based on its penal character. As such it cannot be contracted out of[87], and it does not reflect the basic concept of freedom of contract. On the other hand, as a punitive sanction it should benefit the state rather than the injured party. Yet, despite this criticism, it is regarded as a settled mechanism that brings about efficient results.

The introduction of this order into our system raises fundamental questions regarding its compatibility with basic principles of Israeli Law. Thus, one may argue that it creates an undue infringement in property rights incompatible with the principle of the Basic Law: Human Dignity and Freedom[88]. Another difficulty relates to the practical aspect of its application. Has anybody made a survey as to its efficiency? Are there any comparative data indicating the degree of obedience to judicial orders in France and in Israel? What is the basis of the prediction that the transplant of this order might increase the efficiency of enforcement in Israel?

The introduction of a general rule of exemplary damages also raises the question of its compatibility with the principles of the Israeli system of law. The provision in the draft, s. 462, states that such damages may be awarded if the breach is malicious[89].

The word "malice" has the negative connotation of an intentional act done under aggravated circumstances or out of improper motives[90]. The section is not restricted in its application, and thus it applies also to a breach of contract, a problematic point to which I shall shortly refer.

The expression "exemplary damages" is identical to "punitive damages" but different from "aggravated damages". In both situations, damages are over-compensatory. Exemplary or punitive damages focus on public policy considerations and general factors of deterrence[91], whereas in aggravated damages the conduct of the wrongdoer and its impact on the injured party are the focal points[92].

---

[86] *Treitel*, Remedies (n. 83), 62.

[87] Its personal character does not permit taking a surety for it: *Muriel Fabre-Magnan*, Les Obligations (2004), 561.

[88] See s. 3, which provides that "a person's property shall not be infringed".

[89] The torts that require malice are injurious lie (s. 58) and malicious prosecution (s. 60) (they were abolished in the Draft, presumably due to the vast range of application of the tort of negligence).

[90] Does the term refer to motive (internal intention), or purpose (external intention), or both? For analysis, see *John Finnis*, Intention in Tort Law, in: David G. Owen (ed.), Philosophical Foundations of Tort Law (1995), 229, 239, 247. Fleming puts the focus on improper purpose: *John G. Fleming*, The Law of Torts (9th ed., 1998), 685; while to the editors of Clerk & Lindsell the focus is on improper motive: *Clerk & Lindsell*, On Torts (19th ed., 2006), 991, following *Gibbs v Rea* [1998] AC 786, 797.

[91] *Muir v. Alberta* (1996) 132 D. L. R. (4th) 695, 714, referred to in C. A. 140/00 *Etinger v Hachevra Leshikum Uphituach* (2004) 58(4) P.D.486, 562–563.

[92] C. A. 140/00 Etinger v Hachevra Leshikum Uphituach, *supra*, n. 91.

The application of punitive damages in Israeli tort law has been occasionally approved by the courts[93]. But its position in contract law is different. The Remedies Law does not mention it. The argument that s. 13 of the Law, which empowers the court to impose damages for non-monetary loss, may be used also to impose punitive damages, was rejected[94]. An element of punitive damages is provided in s. 28A of the Contract of Insurance Law. That section imposes a specific high interest rate on an insurer who, contrary to good faith, did not pay non-contestable insurance proceeds[95]. It essentially follows some American cases that have occasionally, in these circumstances, regarded the insurer's breach as a tort. The term "punitive damages" not being alien to tort law[96], the classification of the insurer's act as a tort brought about the imposition of punitive damages in this contractual context[97]. Our Draft Civil Code has extended this particular case to a general principle which takes into consideration the fault of the wrongdoer and which aims to deter against malicious breaches. But the possibility of drawing a general conclusion from the specific case is dubious. The insurance context does not reflect contract policies at large. It concerns a regulated area, governed by standard agreements. In this area, policy considerations warrant the imposition of a sanction on the party in breach for the benefit of the injured party: deterrence of the specific party in breach and of future parties; and denunciation reflecting the sense of the community[98]. These considerations may well

[93] For *dicta* in which punitive damages will be awarded in extreme cases, see C.A. 9656/03 *Martziano v Singer* [2005] § 34 (not published yet); C.A. 140/0 *Etinger v Hachevra Leshikum Uphituach*, *supra*, n. 91. Over fifty years ago the imposition of punitive damages was approved in a case of intentional battery: C.A. 216/54 *Sneider v Gluck* [1955] 9 P.D. 1331, 1335.

[94] C.A. 348/79 *Goldman v Michaeli* (1981) 35(4) P.D. 31, 41.

[95] See ss. 317, 318 of the Draft Civil Code. In the context of labour law, see the Salary Protection Law, 1958, s. 17 in which the special damages are imposed for delay in payments of salaries. The Labour Tribunals widely apply the provision which empowers the court to reduce these damages, see *Steve Adler*, Compensation for Delay in Payments of Salaries – Statute and Case Law, (1995) 6 Labor Law Annual 5, 28- 34 (in Hebrew).

[96] Restatement (Second) of Torts § 908(1) (1965) which states that "Punitive damages are damages, other than compensatory or nominal damages, awarded against a person to punish him for his outrageous conduct and to deter him and others like him from similar conduct in the future."

[97] For the development of American case law, see *E. Allan Farnsworth*, Contracts (4th ed., 2004), 760–764 (§ 12.8). The attempt to apply this rule in the employment context has not been successful, but in the insurance context it does apply: *Freeman & Mills Inc v Belcher Oil Co*, (1995) 900 P. 2d 669, 670–80 (California).

[98] All these considerations were reflected in the Canadian case of *Whiten v Pilot Insurance* (2002) 209 D.L.R. (4th) 257 (SCC) in which punitive damages were imposed on an insurer who, during two years, refused to pay the insurance proceeds arguing that the insured person was responsible for the arson. For a critical approach (according to which punitive damages are incompatible with basic notions of contract law, their imposition might lead to uncertainty, and the desired result can be reached by using other contract principles, such as compensation for non-monetary loss), see *Jarvis Swan*, Punitive Damages for Breach of Contract: A Remedy in Search of a Justification, (2004) 29 Queen's Law Journal 596. For a more moderate criticism which praises the court's guidelines in the matter, see *John D. MacCamus*, Prometheus Bound or Loose Cannon? Punitive Damages for Pure Breach of Contract in Canada, (2004) 41 San Diego Law Review 1491.

apply in other public-law-regulated areas governed by standard contracts[99]. But it is not clear whether the principle of punitive damages would serve the whole field of contract law equally well in view of the fact that that field is dominated by the idea of private autonomy.

The rules regarding the deterring order and punitive damages reflect a clear policy of protecting contractual rights and deterring from a breach of contract. In that respect, they echo the *Adras* case, which awarded the injured party the gains derived from the breach of contract[100]. But in contrast to *Adras*, punitive measures deviate from the basic concepts of contract law, and their comprehensive application seems unwarranted.

VII. Epilogue – Prospects and Doubts

In this paper I have not been able to look at the whole of the Draft. This should obviously be done in order properly to evaluate the full scope of the project. Even a quick glance at the Draft in its entirety – both concerning its remedial and substantive aspects – discloses conflicting approaches. On the one hand, an effort was made to create a more detailed regime compared to the existing law. This is evident in the provisions regarding gift[101] and unjust enrichment[102]. On the other hand, ample space for judicial discretion has been left, as is evident in the opening sections concerning the principles of justice, reasonableness and good faith[103]. This is also conspicuous in the area of tort law where specific torts have been omitted. The assumption is that they have become redundant as having been swallowed by the torts of negligence and breach of statutory duty, the anchors of liability in tort law[104].

---

99 For an example, see the Consumer Protection Law, 1981, that includes penal sanctions alongside the civil ones.

100 See Ernest Weinrib who claims that punitive damages and disgorgement of benefits are incompatible with basic principles of contractual corrective justice ("[C]ompensatory damages ... fit within corrective justice. In contrast, disgorgement and punitive damages, which aim at objectives beyond the plaintiff's entitlement, are questionable ..."), at p. 57. Disgorgement is justified regarding proprietary and not contractual rights ("The plaintiff is entitled to the disgorged gains only if the gains came from the alienation of the plaintiff's property; the alienation of property, however, is not a concept applicable to the promisor's failure to perform a contractually obligatory act ..."), at p. 102: *Ernest J Weinrib*, Punishment and Disgorgement as Contract Remedies, (2003) 78 Chicago-Kent Law Review 55; see also *Dagan*, (2000) 1 Theoretical Inquiries in Law 115. But the argument ignores the proprietary features in contract (in particular when the right is enforced *in specie*): public law considers it as property when taking is concerned. Also it does not mention its (proprietary) effect on third parties.

101 See ss. 177–188 Draft Civil Code.

102 See ss. 411–420 Draft Civil Code.

103 See ss. 1–2 Draft Civil Code.

104 Fraud and malicious prosecution were omitted as having been swallowed by negligence. Also all property torts (except for trespass) were omitted, as having been subsumed in the provisions on property protection: *supra*, n. 58.

The process of codification raised the possibility of regulating some of the more complex contracts such as political agreements[105], a promise to marry[106], or contacts of fertilisation[107], but this was not done. These contracts are controversial and charged with conflicting values. Presumably a lack of consensus has left them unregulated.

The remedies section is based on more coherent lines: the major remedies are panoramically drafted; though the rules are detailed, they leave some room for discretion; an attempt has been made to create harmony with regard to substance and terminology. The new regime follows the basic tenet of the Remedies Law to fortify the position of enforcement. A unified approach regarding the formulation of the remedy of enforcement has not, however, been adopted. In some points an attempt has been made to consolidate or clarify the existing case law (e.g., *cy-près* performance and enforcement of debt). But usually a lot of room has been left for judicial discretion, and no attempt has been made to integrate more case law, which might be able to serve as a clearer guideline for limiting the discretion regarding enforcement or damages. Hence the questions concerning the enforcement of the delivery of a non-specific good, the impact of a change of circumstances on enforcement, and the blameworthiness of the parties, the relative hardship with regard to the parties, hardship to third parties, or the impact of public policy on enforcement – they have all been left unanswered. Furthermore, the novelties of the deterring order and punitive damages seem far-reaching and incompatible with existing policies.

The codification project is not disconnected from the law formerly in place. It aims to create a continuity coupled with a certain amount of change. Continuity perpetuates the main problem with which the Israeli legal system is grappling, i.e., the encroachment of broad standards on the range of application of specific rules[108].

There is a common belief that the idea of codification symbolises a preference for rules over standards. Rules are associated with order, stability, certainty, and

---

105 H.C.J. 1635/90 *Zherzhevsky v Prime Minister* (1991) 45(1) P.D. 749, where two contrary opinions were given: one, limiting the enforceability of such an agreement (Elon J); the other, broadening the scope of its enforceability (Barak J).

106 C.A. 5258/98 *Plonit v Almoni* (2004) 58(6) P.D. 209 where a broad enforceability approach was applied, in contrast to previous cases.

107 F.H. 2401/95 *Nachmani v Nachmani* (1996) 50(4) P.D. 661, where, in a majority opinion and following a bitter public and judicial controversy, the Court regarded such an agreement as enforceable.

108 C.A. 4628/93 *State of Israel v Aprofim* (1995) 49(2) P.D. 265; f.H. 2045/05 *Irgun Megadlei Hyerakot v State of Israel* (2006) (not published yet; in both cases the language of the contract was replaced by the reasonable meaning attributed to it by the Court); H.C.J. 1683/93 *Yavin Plast v National Labour Tribunal* (1993) 47(4) P.D. 702 (the contract was supplemented by a restraint of trade provision). On the tension between good faith as an open-ended principle and specific provisions (involving the conflicts between arm's length bargaining and contractual altruism, between judicial arbitrariness and equitable flexibility, and between judicial law making and judicial restraint), see *Marietta Auer*, The Structure of Good Faith: A Comparative Study of Good Faith Arguments (November 17, 2006). Available at SSRN: http://ssrn.com/abstract=945594.

so is a code system. This belief lacks sufficient foundation. The English legal system – the antithesis of a code system – is a striking example in which a proper balance is struck between stability and development, between rules and standards.

The conflict: code or case law, is another example which demonstrates that substance matters more than form. The choice as such cannot transform a legal system, just as the adoption of a constitution does not render a state immediately democratic. The balance between certainty of law and fairness is conditioned by culture and tradition. Culture and tradition are proxies for paying respect to the past which nourishes self-constraint but social responsibility, which is directed to the future, has to guide the decision-maker when to follow the past and when to implement the change.

The draft codification is the product of work spanning twenty years. Within this period thousands of hours were invested in an attempt coherently and harmoniously to draft and arrange hundreds of rules. Such a project naturally reflects sympathy for predetermined rules. Yet, the project leaves wide space for discretion.

The success of the project, which actually means the success of our legal system, will be tested in practice. The big question is whether the Israeli courts will be able to maintain the proper division of labour between them and the creators of the rules, i.e., the legislature and the contracting parties. Will the courts resist the temptation to disregard the rule drafted by the parties? And will the courts be able to preserve the dignity of the statutory rules, a dignity reflecting the values of stability and certainty, which the drafters of the Code sought to preserve?

Remedies for Breach of Contract: Remarks on the Israeli Draft Civil Code from the German and European Perspective

By Hans Christoph Grigoleit

Summary of Contents

I. Introduction

The German law of obligations in general, and the remedies for breach of contract in particular, underwent a fundamental reform in 2002. That reform of the BGB was triggered by certain EC directives, most notably by the directive on consumer sales[1]. While the scope of the modifications required by the directives was rather limited, the German government and legislator used the open door of these reforms to implement much further reaching changes. The other key aims of the reform were: (i) to harmonise the BGB with the judge-made case law since 1900; (ii) to reintroduce certain areas of the law of obligations into the BGB which had hitherto been regulated in a number of individual pieces of legislation; (iii) to adapt the law of obligation to the needs of modern business transactions and (iv) to improve the coherence of the law while disposing of unnecessary distinctions and complications.

The last aspect is of particular interest for the subject of our conference: coherence is equivalent to a default position in favour of generalisation, i.e., allowing distinctions only for valid reasons. The reform of the German law of obligations was aimed at generalising the remedial system for breach of contract and reducing the number of specific rules governing certain types of contracts – sales contracts and contracts for works in particular. Generalisation in the remedial system is apparently also an elementary objective of the draft for a new Israeli Civil Code. With regard to this goal, the Israeli plan is even more radical and courageous in its venture widely to harmonise the remedies of the law of contracts and the law of torts[2]. In comparison, the BGB only deals to some extent jointly with the remedies of both contract law and tort law (e.g. the set of rules governing the extent of damages in §§ 249–255 BGB), while there are specific rules dealing with the breach of contractual (and contract-related) obligations ("Pflichtverletzung"), stating the elements of a claim for damages (§§ 275 ff. BGB) and the conditions of the right to terminate the contract (§§ 323 ff. BGB).

My presentation will focus on these contractual remedies, and it aims to evaluate the basic remedies for breach of contract as provided for under the Draft Civil Code, their requirements and exceptions by comparison to the corresponding concepts and rationales of the BGB. To a large extent, I shall include the solutions of the Principles of European Contract Law (PECL)[3] in my evaluation, taking into account the growing tendency for harmonisation in European private law. I will begin my short survey with the enforcement of obligations, i.e. the issue of specific performance and the defences to specific performance (II.), then turn to the conditions for termination of the contract (III.), deal with the requirements for a claim for damages (IV.), address reduction of the contract price as an independent remedy (V.) and I will close with a brief reference to special rules governing the remedies resulting from specific types of contracts (VI.).

---

[1] Directive 1999/44/EC of the European Parliament and of the Council of 25 May 1999 on certain aspects of the sale of consumer goods and associated guarantees. On the historical background of the reform, see *Reinhard Zimmermann*, The New German Law of Obligations (2005), 5 ff., 30 ff.

[2] Cf. *Nili Cohen*, The Four C's: Coherence, Clarification, Continuity, Change – Remedies for Breach of Contract in Israeli Codification, in this volume, *sub* I.

[3] Cf. *Ole Lando/Hugh Beale* (eds.), Principles of European Contract Law, Parts I and II (2000).

II. Enforcement of Obligations – Specific Performance and Defences

One of the most elementary problems to be solved by a remedial system is whether specific performance is granted as a general rule or whether a claim for damages (in money) is the primary remedy. To the drafters of the BGB specific performance was so essential that it can be found in the first paragraph of the German law of obligations (§ 241 I BGB). This has apparently – at least since 1970 – also been the position of Israeli law[4] and the specific performance approach is also embraced by the Draft Civil Code (s. 524(a) = s. 448(a) new Draft). In the PECL, specific performance is also recognised as the primary remedy for the breach of non-monetary obligations (Art. 9:102 PECL).

The main advantage of granting specific performance as a general rule is the close connection of this remedy with the content of the contract and with the principles of party autonomy and contractual freedom: Specific performance defines the remedy exactly the way the contract defines the obligation. Therefore, specific performance transforms the contractual stipulation and the will of the parties with perfect precision into a remedy. In tort cases, quite similarly, requiring the tortfeasor to restore the damage done in kind, at least as a starting point, can be described as the perfect transformation of the victim's right protected by tort law into a remedy. While, of course, in many cases monetary compensation will be an entirely adequate remedy, restoration in kind is indispensable if only the tortfeasor is in a position completely to restore the victim's rights (e.g. theft of a work of art; false statements damaging the victim's reputation). The parallel in rationales for specific performance or, to put it differently, the character of specific performance as a general principle to protect rights by restoration in kind makes the effort to introduce one rule for both contract and tort law a meaningful move towards coherence. While much more could be said about the specific performance approach in contrast to the common law's focus on damages[5], the correspondence of German and Israeli law in this issue makes it more interesting to focus on the exceptions, i.e. on the conditions under which the debtor is excused from specific performance.

The central defence the debtor has against specific performance (but not against a claim for damages) under German law (§ 275 I BGB) as well as under the Draft Civil Code (s. 524 (a)(1) = new s. 448 (a)(1)) is the defence of impossibility. The "hard" scope of this category covers cases in which performance is physically (e.g. the painting to be delivered has been destroyed) or legally (e.g. delivery is prohibited by an export ban) impossible. For a long time it has been under dispute in Germany and in many other jurisdictions, whether this clearly

---

[4] Cf. *Cohen* (n. 1), *sub* I.

[5] Cf. *Konrad Zweigert/Hein Kötz*, Einführung in die Rechtsvergleichung (3rd ed., 1996), 482ff.; *Guenter Treitel*, Remedies for Breach of Contract (1988), 70ff.; *James Gordley* (ed.), The Enforceability of Promises in European Contract Law (2001). See also *Cohen* (n. 1), *sub* IV., explaining the consistent specific performance approach in the Draft Civil Code.

defined category should be extended to cases of "soft" or economic impossibility, i.e. whether the consequences of impossibility should also apply when performance is not impossible but unreasonably burdensome or unfair to the debtor. In the PECL this idea is expressed by Art. 9:102(2), where an exception from specific performance is made if "performance would cause the debtor unreasonable effort or expense". The Draft Civil Code also embraces the concept of economic impossibility in s. 524(a)(4) (= new s. 448 (a)(4)) according to which a defence is available if "enforcement would be unjust under the circumstances".

In the recent German reform of the law of obligations, however, the concept of economic impossibility was ultimately rejected after thorough deliberation[6]. The crucial factor had been a concern for the principle of *pacta sunt servanda* if exceptions were based on vague concepts like unreasonableness or unfairness. This reservation proceeded from the assumption that the courts may be all too easily inclined to relieve a party only because it has concluded a burdensome contract. The unfairness or unreasonableness test seems like an invitation to achieve whatever is perceived to be social justice on the basis of the judge's discretion ("deep-pocket-mentality").

Yet, there are three other mechanisms in the BGB which may justify exceptions for the debtor in cases of excessive burdens. All these rules were codified during the BGB reform. In comparison to a general unfairness or unreasonableness test, these provisions are designed to *accentuate the exceptional character of any defence to specific performance* and to secure sufficient protection of the creditor's interest.

First, there is a special form of relief for debtors of personal services or work under § 275 III BGB. With regard to such contracts the debtor is excused if performance cannot reasonably be required considering the burden to the debtor as balanced against the interest of the creditor in receiving performance. In addition, under German procedural law the mechanisms of execution cannot be applied to enforce specific performance of personal services (§ 888 III ZPO). The privilege of the personal services debtor is recognised also by s. 524(a)(2) (= new s. 448(a)(2)) Draft Civil Code and by Art. 9:102(2)(c) PECL. It should be noted that these rules provide for an unconditional and general exception from specific performance under substantive law. The German approach, on the other hand, grants an excuse to the debtor of personal services only via the mechanisms of enforcement (§ 888 III ZPO), because enforcement of personal services is impractical and in conflict with basic personal rights. By giving consideration to the relative weight of the *personality interest* compared to the interest of the creditor, as required for the substantive law defence of § 275 III BGB, a balancing

[6] Cf. the original proposal ("Diskussionsentwurf") in: *Claus-Wilhelm Canaris* (ed.), Schuldrechtsmodernisierung 2002 (2002), 3 ff.; Zimmermann (n. 1), 45 ff. Against the concept of "economic impossibility" see *Claus-Wilhelm Canaris*, Die Reform des Rechts der Leistungsstörungen, [2001] Juristen-Zeitung 499, 501 f.

approach is established which is probably more relevant for the damages claim than for specific performance.

The second defence against specific performance protects the debtor against *excessive monetary burdens*, employing a disproportionality standard to this end. According to § 275 II BGB the debtor is relieved from specific performance only if "the burden of performance to the debtor is disproportionate to the creditor's benefit". This rule replaces the unfairness or unreasonableness test with a comparative evaluation of the parties' costs and benefits[7]. Relief from performance is only granted if the creditor's benefit is outweighed by the debtor's costs, i.e. if performance is economically senseless. The cases of defence under § 275 II BGB are therefore quite rare because the creditor usually benefits proportionally when the debtor incurs additional costs of performance. Typically, additional costs of performance will be reflected by an increased market price which the creditor would have to pay for a substitute transaction. If the market price of certain goods goes up, the creditor's interest in the goods increases by the same amount so that performance does not become economically senseless. To give an example: A is under a contractual obligation towards B to produce and deliver a certain amount of goods. Immediately after the contract has been concluded, there is a sharp rise in the price of oil, as a result of which the cost of production of the goods also rises significantly. A, therefore, incurs a loss as a result of the fact that the purchase price agreed upon does not reflect the increase in production costs. B, however, benefits to (about) the same extent because he receives the goods for a significantly lower price than the new, increased, market price. Thus A has no defence under § 275 II BGB. The cases, on the other hand, in which the requirements of § 275 II BGB are met are so rare that the standard textbook example for this exception seems quite foolish: The ring that the debtor is obliged to deliver has sunk to the grounds of a lake and therefore delivery of the ring depends upon the enormous costs of employing divers to search for it or of draining the lake, whereas the creditor's benefit remains the same[8].

The third exception from specific performance under the conditions of the contract is the doctrine of change of circumstance ("Störung der Geschäftsgrundlage", § 313 BGB). That doctrine provides relief if performance is unreasonably burdensome to the debtor, and thereby goes beyond the narrow disproportionality test of § 275 II BGB. However, there are several safeguards in this concept to protect the creditor and the principle of *pacta sunt servanda*. In particular, the doctrine of "Störung der Geschäftsgrundlage" is only operative in the sense of § 313 BGB if a *substantial* change of circumstances (or a mutual *substantial* mistake) has occurred which goes beyond the (regular) contractual and legal distribution of risks. Moreover, the doctrine of "Störung der Geschäfts-

[7] For further details, see *Claus-Wilhlem Canaris*, in: Egon Lorenz (ed.), Karlsruher Forum 2002, 5, 11 ff.

[8] Cf. Bundestags-Drucksache (Printed Papers of the German Parliament) 14/6040, pp. 129 f. The example has been adapted from *Philipp Heck*, Grundriß des Schuldrechts (1929), § 28, 5.

grundlage" leads to an adjustment of the contract, as a general rule, and not to its complete discharge. This legal consequence is supposed to ensure that the debtor is not relieved and the creditor not burdened beyond the absolute demands of good faith and fair dealing. A complete cancellation of the obligation and of the contract can only be achieved on the basis of § 313 BGB if adjustment is inappropriate (§ 313 III BGB).

In the Draft Civil Code, the rules on frustration (ss. 195–201 = new ss. 131–137) are similar to the doctrine of "Störung der Geschäftsgrundlage". In this context, it is worth pointing out that under the Draft Civil Code frustrating events are also relevant only under exceptional circumstances (s. 195 = new s. 131). Furthermore, under the Draft the primary effect of frustration is an adjustment of the contract rather than an exception from specific performance. The PECL also recognise a mechanism for adjustment of the contract in cases of a substantial change of circumstances (Art. 6:111 PECL).

While the BGB's concept of dealing with extraordinary burdens to the debtor is far from being utterly coherent and convincing, it may be instructive on two counts. The first one is that it is probably preferable to choose a restrictive approach in defining the conditions of judicial intervention in the contractual dispositions on the basis of "justness" (s. 524 (a)(4) = new s. 448(a)(4)). Second, considering the interdependence of different concepts of relief, some thought should be given to the demarcation of related doctrines, in particular the exception of "unjust performance" (s. 524 (a)(4) = new s. 448(a)(4)) and the rules on frustration (ss. 195–201 = new ss. 131–137). Otherwise the relief of "unjust performance" might conflict with the restrictive requirements of frustration.

III. Termination of the Contract

Next to specific performance and to damages, termination of the contract – or rescission, as it is called in the translation of the Draft Civil Code – is one of the basic remedies in all legal systems. For the purposes of this evaluation I have decided to focus on three central aspects of termination: the principle of fundamental breach, the issue of a "second chance" for the debtor, i.e. the requirement to fix an additional period for performance after the breach, and finally the specific consequences of termination.

1) The Principle of Fundamental Breach

Many legal systems recognise that not every kind of failure on the part of the debtor but only a "fundamental" breach can lead to termination of the entire contract. This doctrine is expressed in the BGB (§ 323 V BGB), in the PECL (Arts. 9:301(1), 8:103 PECL) and in the Draft Civil Code (ss. 520, 528 = new ss. 444, 452). Despite this conformity in principle some variations in detail are worth mentioning.

The first difference results from the specific conditions of a fundamental breach. Compared with the situation under German law, it will be more onerous for the creditor to show that he is entitled to terminate the contract under the Draft Civil Code or under the PECL. This observation is supported by the wording used to describe the specific character of the breach required for termination. The definition in s. 520 (= new s. 444) of the Draft Civil Code qualifies – in the absence of any specific agreement – a breach as fundamental if the "injured party [is] being *substantially denied* that which he would have been entitled to expect under the contract"[9]. This is in accordance with the definition of fundamental non-performance in Art. 8:103(b) PECL. In contrast, § 323 V 2 BGB merely states that the creditor *cannot terminate* the contract if the breach of duty is insignificant. The criteria "fundamental" and "substantially denied" are more restrictive than the BGB's phrase "not insignificant". In addition, under German law *the debtor* must prove that his breach is insignificant because the case of an "insignificant breach" is treated by § 323 V 2 BGB as an exception ("the debtor cannot terminate, if...") whereas under s. 528 (= new s. 452) of the Draft Civil Code and under Art. 9:301 PECL "fundamental breach" is treated as a condition for termination. This implies that the creditor bears the onus of proof and argumentation. Only with regard to severable performances (e.g., a sales contract relating to several shipments of machines) the conditions for termination in the BGB are formulated in a similarly strict way as in the Draft Civil Code and in the PECL: the creditor can terminate the entire contract for a breach relating to a (severable) part of the contract under § 323 V 1 BGB only if he has no interest in partial performance. This is in accordance with s. 530 (= new s. 454) of the Draft and with Art. 9:302 PECL.

The difference between the conditions for a relevant breach reflects upon different aspects of the principle of *pacta sunt servanda*. While the restrictive approach to termination in the Draft Civil Code and the PECL serves the purpose of saving the contractual exchange and of avoiding the costs of restitution, the more liberal concept of the BGB places greater emphasis on the creditor's interest to realise his expectations as protected under the terms of the contract. The aspect of restitution costs is given more weight under the German concept only with regard to severable contracts, because in these cases the *interest* of the creditor may be *severable* just like the subject matter of the contract. If performance in part fully satisfies the creditor's respective interest, termination of the entire contract is not justified[10].

---

[9] This approach is very much in line with English law in the case of so-called innominate terms, cf. *Guenter Treitel*, The Law of Contract (11th ed., 2003), 795.

[10] For more detail with regard to the rationales of § 323 V BGB, see *Christoph Grigoleit/Thomas Riehm*, Grenzen der Gleichstellung von Zuwenig-Lieferung und Sachmangel, [2002] Zeitschrift für das gesamte Schuldrecht 115 ff.

2) Breach of Collateral Duties Resulting in Termination (§ 324 BGB)

Unlike the Draft Civil Code and the PECL, the BGB provides for a special rule on termination for breach of collateral duties in § 324. Such duties are supposed to secure the protection of the creditor's extra-contractual rights and interests (§ 241 II BGB). As an example, a painter is under a duty not to damage his customer's furniture by drops of paint, the seller of a dangerous machine may be under a duty to inform the buyer about dangers resulting from the use of that machine, and a business consultant may be under a duty to protect the business secrets of his clients appropriately[11].

The central statement of § 324 BGB is that a breach of a collateral duty does not, as a general rule, give rise to a right to terminate the contract, because the contractual obligations are generally not affected by the damage done to extra-contractual interests. Therefore the regular conditions for termination of the contract are modified: The breach of a collateral duty only gives rise to termination if continuation of the contract is unacceptable for the creditor ("unzumutbar"). Normally this presupposes that the breach has destroyed any reasonable reliance in the debtor's ability or willingness to perform. To put it another way, § 324 BGB expresses a special standard of fundamental breach in cases in which the breach does not directly relate to the programme of contractual performance. This special standard can, of course, also be read into the general conditions for fundamental breach, as they are stated in the Draft Civil Code or in the PECL. Thus, § 324 BGB only serves the purpose of clarifying the requirements for termination in certain cases.

3) A "Second Chance" for the Debtor

According to § 323 I BGB the creditor may only terminate the contract after he has given notice to the debtor and fixed a reasonable period for effecting performance or for remedying a defective performance. This requirement, which gives the debtor a "second chance" for performance, applies even in cases of fundamental breach. Exceptions are made only if the debtor has seriously and definitively refused to perform (§ 323 II no. 1 BGB), if time is of the essence under the contract (§ 323 II no. 2 BGB), if exceptional circumstances render the fixing of an additional period unreasonable (§ 323 II no. 3 BGB) and if performance is impossible (§ 326 V BGB). Furthermore, the creditor is relieved from his duty to fix an additional period if the breach of a collateral duty renders performance or the acceptance of the performance unacceptable (§ 324 BGB).

---

[11] From the English tradition, another famous example is the *Moorcock* case. Here, the defendant was contractually obliged to unload the plaintiff's ship at his jetty. With the tide receding the ship stranded and was damaged; cf. (1889) 14 P. D. 64.

Under the Draft Civil Code, the issues of notice, fixing an additional period and remedying a defective performance are dealt with quite differently. The debtor must only be given an extension of the time to perform before termination in cases where non-performance is not fundamental (ss. 528, 529 = new ss. 452, 453). Granting an extra period is thus an exception to the principle of fundamental breach and enables the creditor to terminate even in cases of non-fundamental breach. An additional right to remedying a defective performance is recognised for certain types of contracts with regard to the remedy of reduction (s. 574 = new s. 498). Under the PECL the debtor is treated even more strictly: according to Arts. 8:106(3), 9:301(2) PECL the debtor is given a "second chance" only in cases of non-fundamental *delay*. In cases of fundamental delay and fundamental defects of performance, there is no requirement of notice and of an additional period for performance (Art. 9:301(1) PECL)[12].

The general recognition of a debtor's right to a "second chance" was one of the central elements of the 2002 reform of the German law of obligations. There is a strong economic basis for such right. Firstly, the debtor is given an opportunity to validate an investment, which he has already directed to the contract and which may be wasted in case of termination (e.g. preparatory work, employment of personnel etc.). Secondly, if performance is carried out successfully, the mutual transaction costs of restitution and of assessing damages can be saved. On the other hand, the burden resulting from the time extension to the creditor is not unjust if he is awarded compensation of the damages resulting from the delay – they will in most cases be relatively minor. These rationales apply, as a general rule, even to cases of fundamental breach.

These observations show that the concept of fundamental breach can and should be separated from the issue of granting a "second chance" to the debtor. The issue of the "second chance" can be paraphrased as follows: is it fair – taking into account the creditor's reasonable expectations and the debtor's potential costs resulting from immediately being exposed to the creditor's remedy – to impose a delay on the creditor and to expect him to continue to rely on the debtor's ability and willingness to perform? This question arises equally with regard to the remedies of termination, damages (as far as the damages do not go beyond the value of the performance)[13] and price reduction, and it precedes the issue of whether non-performance is grave enough to justify *termination*. Indeed, the issue of seriousness only comes up if "curing" the performance is impossible, unreasonable or has eventually failed. Here, the test should be whether – after the debtor's final act of performance – the creditor is substantially deprived of what he could expect under the contract, or whether, in the light of the costs of termination, he can reasonably be held to the contract even though his expectations have not been completely fulfilled. *This evaluation is specific to the remedy of termination*. It does not affect the remedies of damages and price reduction be-

[12] See also the explicit comment in *Lando/Beale* (n. 3), 374f.

[13] Cf. *infra* IV. 2) b).

cause these remedies do not give rise to the same transaction costs as termination.

In some situations a breach may be so severe that requiring the creditor to give the debtor a "second chance" would be unjust. This may be the case if the breach was intentional (cf. Art 8:103(c) PECL), or if the character of the breach indicates incompetence on the side of the debtor, with the result that there can no longer be reasonable reliance on the debtor's ability to perform (e.g. the mechanic evidently lacks the requisite qualification or fails to repair a hazardous machine). Such cases are actually quite rare. Apart from them, the significance of the breach does not render the granting of a "second chance" to the debtor unreasonable; for it does not necessarily destroy reasonable reliance in his ability and willingness to perform and thus does not justify throwing away the comparative cost-advantage associated with the opportunity of "curing" performance.

Despite the fact that the PECL have, unfortunately, not consistently taken account of these considerations, an example taken from the PECL[14] may be useful as an illustration: under a contract to install a temperature control system for a wine cellar a defective installation renders the system ineffective. This breach is evidently fundamental, since the temperature control system is of no use to the creditor if it does not work. The creditor's reasonable expectations cannot be met by the means of reduction or an isolated damages claim. However, this is no sufficient reason to deny the debtor an opportunity to remove the defect efficiently by using his specific resources, i.e. his special knowledge about the machine, particular tools, his experience and his specially trained employees. The creditor is sufficiently protected if he can claim damages for the time in which the control system failed to operate.

The same applies in cases of delay: even if there has been no act of performance yet and even if a significant period of time has elapsed, requiring the creditor to notify the debtor and to fix an additional period for performance seems reasonable as a general rule. The debtor may already have incurred considerable costs under the contract while, on the other hand, the costs of notification on the part of the creditor are low and the typically small loss resulting from the delay can be covered by damages.

4) Restitution as a Result of Termination

Concerning the consequences of termination, the BGB provides a specific set of rules covering restitution in kind and in value, compensation for use, risk of destruction and deterioration (§§ 346–349 BGB, "Rücktrittsrecht"), while restitution in cases of void or voidable contracts is governed by the general rules of unjustified enrichment (§§ 812ff. BGB). In the Draft Civil Code, the conse-

[14] Cf. *Lando/Beale* (n. 3), 365.

quences of termination are regulated by reference to the general rules on unjustified enrichment (s. 571 = new s. 495). That is consistent with the Draft Civil Code's aim of generalisation and coherence[15].

The attempt to develop general rules on restitution covering both terminated and void contracts deserves to be supported. Under German law, the coexistence of two sets of rules for restitution is a source of unnecessary complications, permanent dispute and sometimes even unfair results[16]. However, some distinctions may be necessary. Particularly with regard to which party has to bear the risk of loss and deterioration, the cause of restitution and the parties' responsibility for this cause have to be taken into account. Thus, to give an example, under the restitution provisions of the BGB each party bears, as a general rule, the risk for the goods and services received. This is because if restitution cannot be carried out in kind the receiving party must pay compensation for the value of the goods or services received (§ 346 II BGB). However, if one party is responsible for termination, i.e., for the breach of the contract, the other party must pay compensation for losses with respect to the goods received only if he caused them grossly negligently (§ 346 III 1 no. 3 BGB). A similar concept has been adopted by German courts in some cases of unjust enrichment, particularly in cases of incapacity or fraud. Persons subject to an incapacity and defrauded parties are relieved from bearing the risk with regard to the goods received (§ 818 III BGB), while the courts, as a general rule, also attribute the risk of the goods to the debtor in restitution based on a void contract[17].

These distinctions are far from being self-evident and have given rise to serious criticism in Germany. On the other hand, they may indicate that in harmonising the rules of restitution a "one rule for all cases" approach might take generalisation too far[18].

IV. Damages

Under the German law of obligations any damages claim for breach of contract is dependant on certain general requirements dealt with in the general

[15] Cf. *Cohen* (n. 1), *sub* III.

[16] See, e.g., *Timo Fest*, Der Einfluss rücktrittsrechtlicher Wertungen auf die bereicherungsrechtliche Rückabwicklung nichtiger Verträge (2006), 19ff.; *Phillip Hellwege*, Die Rückabwicklung gegenseitiger Verträge als einheitliches Problem (2004), 521ff.; *Phillip Hellwege*, Regelungsmodell für die Rückabwicklung gegenseitiger Verträge, [2005] Juristen-Zeitung 337, 340ff.

[17] These solutions are not explicitly put down in the BGB but the have been developed by the German courts under the famous and heavily disputed *Saldotheorie*. Cf., e.g., BGH of 20 March 2004, [2001] Neue Juristische Wochenschrift 1863; *Hartwig Sprau*, in: Otto Palandt (ed.), Bürgerliches Gesetzbuch (66th ed., 2007), § 818, n. 48. For a thorough critique of the *Saldotheorie* cf. *Karl Larenz/Claus-Wilhelm Canaris*, Schuldrecht II/2 (13th ed., 1994), 334ff.

[18] A meaningful distinction between restitution in case of a breach of contract, and other cases of unjust enrichment, can be found in s. 570 (= new s. 494) Israeli Draft Civil Code; cf. *Cohen* (n. 1) *sub* III.

provision of § 280 I BGB (see below under part one). This provision is complemented by the specific rules of §§ 281 ff. BGB setting up further conditions for special categories of damages (see below under 2).

1) General Conditions of Damages

a) Culpa liability v. strict liability

According to § 280 I BGB every claim for damages requires that the debtor is in breach of a duty, which is equivalent to non-performance of the contractual obligation. Furthermore, the debtor must have been responsible for the breach (§ 280 I 2 BGB). Such responsibility can result from *culpa*, under the definition of § 276 BGB (i.e. negligence or intention), or from the breach of a contractual guarantee. However, there are strict requirements before the courts will find a party liable under a contractual guarantee. In particular, explicit wording is usually required and the courts very rarely derive guarantees and thus strict liability (i.e. liability irrespective of the debtor's *culpa*) from implication.

At first sight, a quite different approach has been adopted by the Draft Civil Code. Under ss. 531 and 533 (= new ss. 455 and 457) the claim for damages is only dependant upon breach by the debtor without an additional requirement of fault. Yet, the claim is limited to the damage that could have been anticipated (s. 457). Under the Draft Code a contract therefore amounts to a guarantee to overcome impediments within the scope of potential anticipation. Here, again, the Draft to a certain extent resembles the rules laid down in the PECL which also establish a damages claim for breach of contract without *culpa* or other fault requirement on the part of the debtor. The PECL also recognise a defence for the debtor similar to the Draft Civil Code in cases in which the impediment is beyond the debtor's control and could not reasonably have been taken into account (Art. 8:108 PECL). The main difference to the Draft is the concept of "sphere of control" under the PECL in addition to the aspect of reasonable anticipation. Under the PECL, the debtor is under a definite guarantee for factors within his control irrespective of whether he could have anticipated them.

However, the difference between the responsibility-based concept of the BGB and the strict liability concept of the Draft Civil Code and the PECL is, in its practical consequences, not as fundamental as it might seem. On the one hand, the strict liability concept operates with defences on the basis of a sphere-of-control or foreseeability test and thus comes very close to a standard of negligent non-performance. On the other hand, upon detailed analysis, the *culpa* requirement under German law comes close to strict liability for two reasons: first, there is a presumption that the debtor is responsible for the breach of duty according to § 280 I 2 BGB, and, second, the standard of due care is formulated objectively, with the result that the debtor is not relieved from his duty by individual shortcomings[19]. Therefore, in cases in which the debtor cannot excuse himself by pointing to the limits of anticipation (Draft Civil Code) or to the limits of his sphere of control and of anticipation (PECL) he is usually also (presumed to be) responsible under § 280 BGB. A significant difference between the two approaches may arise under the PECL standard which burdens the debtor with a definitive guarantee for his sphere of control notwithstanding (a potential lack of) reasonable anticipation. That can, for example, lead to liability in cases of an unforeseeable failure of the debtor's machines, while under German law, and possibly also under the Draft Civil Code, the debtor may relieve himself from liability by proving that he was not at fault with regard to the technical disruption or that he could not have anticipated it.

Taking into account the convergence between the *culpa* and the strict liability approaches in the law of contractual damages it may be worth mentioning that the German *culpa* approach is very much in accordance with the fundamental objective of the Israeli reform effort: the *culpa* principle as a general requirement for liability under both tort and contract law is retained, while the specific responsibility of the debtor in the case of contractual obligations is accounted for by a presumption and the objective standard of negligence.

b) Remote Damage

An aspect which needs to be distinguished from responsibility as to the breach is, whether a responsibility criterion should also apply regarding the causal link between the breach and the resulting damage. That question may arise, for example, if the buyer dies, because the seller was late in delivering the car that he had sold and therefore the buyer cannot get treatment fast enough after the sudden outbreak of a disease. Under German law the element of fault just mentioned only applies to the breach. The debtor who is responsible for the breach in terms of §§ 280 ff. BGB is, as a general rule, liable for all the damage resulting from the breach. There is no further requirement of fault, foreseeability, anticipation etc., with regard to the causal link between the breach and the resulting damage. Only in very exceptional cases, if causation has been brought about under extremely unlikely circumstances, the debtor may be relieved from liability (concept of adequate causation, "Adäquanztheorie")[20].

Under s. 533 (= new s. 457) of the Draft Civil Code (in the translation at hand) the requirement of potential anticipation refers to "damages". Unfortunately, there is no (clear) distinction between responsibility for the breach and remoteness of damages under the Draft Civil Code. The wording of s. 533 (= new s. 457) suggests that the debtor must have been able to anticipate both the breach

---

[19] *Helmut Heinrichs*, in: Palandt (n. 17), § 276, n. 15.

[20] Cf. BGH of 23 October 1951, (1951) Neue Juristische Wochenschrift 711; BGH of 11 January 2005, [2005] Neue Juristische Wochenschrift 1420; *Heinrichs*, in: Palandt (n. 17), Vor § 249, Rn. 57 ff.

and its consequences. Since potential anticipation is formulated as a requirement of the damages claim, it follows that s. 533 (= new s. 457) Draft Civil Code in comparison with German law facilitates the relief of the debtor from liability for remote damages even in cases, in which he has negligently or intentionally breached the contract.

Like German law, the PECL distinguish the issue of responsibility with regard to the breach clearly from the aspect of remote causation and provide a separate rule for the latter aspect in Art. 9:503 PECL. This provision limits liability to losses that could have been reasonably foreseen as likely results of the breach. The PECL approach to the issue of remote causation is similar to the Draft Civil Code solution inasmuch as it does not articulate the exceptional character of a defence of remoteness. However, the scope of the remoteness defence is rather limited under the PECL, because Art. 9:503 PECL does not apply to cases in which non-performance was intentional or grossly negligent. With this exception the PECL strike a balance between the German reservation towards the remoteness defence and a general foreseeability test.

2) The Distinction Between Different Categories of Damages with Specific Requirements

While the general conditions of § 280 BGB are applicable to all claims for damages, four different categories of damages may be distinguished in the provisions of §§ 280 ff. BGB: damages for delay of performance, damages in lieu of performance, reliance damages and general damages. These categories differ with regard to certain additional requirements complementing the general requirements of § 280 BGB in establishing the damages claim.

a) Damages for delay of performance: Notice requirement (§ 280 II, 286 I BGB) and exceptions (§ 286 II BGB)

A claim for damages compensating the specific loss resulting from delay of performance is, in principle, only granted by the BGB under the condition that the creditor has notified the debtor of his delay (§ 286 I BGB). This concept has not been adopted by the Draft Civil Code, where no specific requirements have been set up concerning damages for delay and hence compensation is recoverable under the general conditions of damages for breach of contract (s. 533 = new s. 457). Here, again, the Draft Civil Code is in accordance with the PECL (cf. Art. 9:501 PECL)[21].

The main reason behind the notice requirement of the BGB is to create certainty for the debtor that performance is due and to warn him of the consequences resulting from delay. A notice requirement furthermore promotes cer-

[21] The omission of a notice requirement is explicitly mentioned in *Lando/Beale* (n. 3), 435.

tainty for both parties as to the time for which damages for delay can be claimed, and it therefore saves transaction costs, including possible litigation costs. Usually, the notice requirement imposes a comparatively small burden on the creditor because notification can be carried out easily and the damage that the creditor may incur for the period before notification is limited to delay-related losses[22].

Despite these considerations the practical impact of this condition should not be overestimated. The significance of the notice requirement is, above all, limited by several exceptions according to § 286 II BGB. In particular, the creditor can avoid the notice requirement by fixing a certain date for performance in the contract (§ 286 II no. 1 BGB). This means that the notice requirement makes a difference only for obligations with regard to which the time of performance has not been fixed explicitly and precisely in the contract but is derived from the contract by implication or from a rule of law.

b) Damages in lieu of performance (i.e. for non-performance and defective performance; §§ 280 III, 281 ff. BGB)

Just as, under German law, termination of the contract by the creditor is dependant upon notice and upon the fixing of an additional period for performance or for remedying the defective performance (cf. III. 2)), so is the claim of damages for non-performance and for defective performance under §§ 280 III, 281 BGB. This category is called damages in lieu of performance because the compensation replaces performance by the debtor, inasmuch as it covers the expenditure the creditor has to make in order to fulfil his expectations under the contract by other means than performance through the debtor. Typical examples of damages in lieu of performance are the costs for substitute transactions or for removing defects, the diminution in value resulting from a defect or lost gains of resale. The definition of this category of damages is closely connected with the elementary requirement to fix an additional period for performance or remedying the defective performance, for under this category only such losses are recoverable that could have been avoided by the debtor, if he had performed during the additional period of time[23]. While the claim for damages in lieu of performance is generally dependent upon the requirement of fixing an additional period, in principle the same exceptions apply as with regard to termination according to §§ 281 II, 282f. BGB. The requirement to fix an additional period can be justified in the same way as in the case of termination, in particular by the cost-

[22] For a detailed analysis of the notification requirement, see *Ulrich Huber*, Leistungsstörungen (vol. I, 1999), 412ff.; *Ulrich Huber*, in: Bundesministerium der Justiz (ed.) Gutachten und Vorschläge zur Überarbeitung des Schuldrechts (vol. 1, 1981), 647ff.; *Christoph Grigoleit/Thomas Riehm*, Die Kategorien des Schadensersatzes im Leistungsstörungsrecht, (2003) 203 Archiv für die civilistische Praxis 727, 744ff.

[23] Cf., in greater detail, *Grigoleit/Riehm* (n. 22), 733ff.

efficiency of giving the debtor a "second chance" to perform (or to remove defects) in order to avoid or reduce damages[24].

The interdependence of termination and the claim of damages for non-performance is evident. Without termination, the debtor's obligation and his right to perform is still in force. Therefore, a claim for damages that will put the creditor in the same position as termination (e.g., by claiming the entire costs of a substitute transaction) would be in conflict with the requirements for termination. It is therefore necessary to harmonise the conditions for termination and damages to the extent that termination and damages relate to an economically identical interest. Otherwise the creditor would be able to circumvent the requirements for termination (in particular the requirement that the breach be fundamental) by a damages claim.

Under the Draft Civil Code, it is not specifically stated that damages for non-performance may be connected to termination. However, it would be advisable to introduce such a rule. At least the courts probably will and definitely should harmonise the conditions for termination and damages for non-performance. Apart from the BGB, a further indication for the necessity to harmonise the rules for termination and damages for non-performance can be found in the PECL. Here, the interdependence of termination and certain types of damages is expressed in Art. 9:506 PECL (damages for substitute transactions) and in Art. 9:507 PECL (damages calculated on the basis of the current price). The way in which the claim for damages has to be adapted to the conditions for termination, of course, depends on the specific conditions for termination. Therefore, the distinctions discussed earlier (III. 1) and 3)) will equally influence the claim for damages.

As to the relationship between termination and damages, it may finally be mentioned that under the BGB the creditor is allowed, but not forced, to declare termination if he demands damages in lieu of performance (§ 325 BGB). *Not* to declare termination of the contract may make sense in the (rare) cases where the creditor has a particular interest to fulfil his own obligation. That can happen with regard to contracts of exchange. A and B, two art-dealers, have agreed to swap two oil paintings. Even before the exchange actually takes place, it turns out that the painting to be given to A is a fake. A is, therefore, entitled to terminate the contract, to keep the painting that he has promised to B, and to claim damages for whatever profit he has lost. That profit is then calculated according to the difference in value between the two paintings; with regard to the painting promised to A, of course, the hypothetical value to be taken into account would have to be the value the painting would have had, had it not been a fake. But A might also have an interest in delivering his own painting to B. His damages (in lieu of performance) claim would then extend to the entire hypothetical value of

[24] The recoverability of delay damages and general damages does not depend on the conditions of § 281 BGB. Concerning the interdependence of termination and damages in lien of performance under the PECL, see Zimmermann (n. 1), 53f.

the painting that had been promised to him. By desisting from terminating the contract, A gets rid of the painting that he had promised to B and can avoid any dispute as to the value of that painting which would have to be subtracted from his damages claim in the case of termination.

c) Reliance damages (§ 284 BGB)

The provision of § 284 BGB on reliance damages does, strictly speaking, not introduce an independent category of damages but rather complements the rules on damages in lieu of performance in certain cases. A claim for reliance damages according to § 284 BGB is therefore dependent upon the same prerequisites as any claim for damages in lieu of performance (cf. above). The specific function of § 284 BGB is to secure compensation for the creditor's expenditures even in cases in which he pursues non-profit goals with the contract in question. The general rules on damages do not support a damages claim in these cases, because the creditor would also have "lost" his investment in the contract if the debtor had performed appropriately. Hence, the debtor's non-performance is not a *condicio sine qua non* for the loss[25]. The mere frustration of the creditor's non-profit purpose is not recoverable under the general German rules on damages because it constitutes an immaterial loss which, according to § 253 BGB, is only recoverable in cases of personal injury. A famous example demonstrating the function of reliance damages according to § 284 BGB is the notorious "NPD-City Hall" case[26]. Here, a neo-nationalist political party was denied damages for the expenditures made in preparation of a party convention that had to be cancelled because the owner of the hall in which the convention was to take place failed to perform. While the ruling in this case may have reflected reservations against the neo-nationalist party, it was widely recognised that, as a general rule, the denial of compensation for expenditures with regard to non-profit purposes is unfair.

This consideration led to the introduction of § 284 BGB into the code on the occasion of the 2002 reform. The provision of § 284 BGB allows the creditor to request compensation for the expenditure which he has incurred in reliance on the receipt of performance, even if he pursues non-profit goals. This complication of the German remedies for breach of contract is closely connected to the restrictive approach of the BGB towards damages for immaterial loss expressed in the general rules on damages (§ 253 BGB). As the Draft Civil Code or the PECL do not limit compensation for immaterial loss as strictly as German law, these codes can probably do without a rule such as § 284 BGB[27].

---

[25] If the creditor acts in pursuit of economic profits it is presumed that these expenditures would have paid off ("Rentabilitätsvermutung", BGH of 21 April 1978, BGHZ 71, 234).

[26] BGH of 10 December 1986, BGHZ 99, 182.

[27] Cf. Art. 9:501(2)(a) PECL explicitly recognising damages for non-pecuniary loss.

d) General damages

The final category of damages under the German law of obligations can be called general or simple damages. This category covers all the damages claims that do not result from delay and are not considered to be damages in lieu of performance. Consequently, the specific requirements for damages for delay and for damages in lieu of performance do not apply, and only the general requirements of § 280 BGB have to be fulfilled, i.e., there must have been a breach of contractual duty, and the debtor must have been responsible (*culpa* or breach of a contractual guarantee, cf. above *sub* IV 1 a).

The "negative definition" of general damages, as opposed to damages for delay and damages in lieu of performance, makes this category applicable to losses which do not directly follow from the delay or failure of performance. The losses in question relate to rights which the creditor holds irrespective of the contract. It is therefore characteristic for general damages that the losses covered cannot be limited or removed by (late) performance or remedying a defective performance[28]. Examples for general damages are bodily injury resulting from an accident caused by a defective car, or damage done by the wall painter to the furniture of his customer. Since there are no specific requirements for general damages under German law, this category is in full conformity with both the Draft Civil Code and the PECL, apart from, of course, the issue of responsibility (see above IV. 1)).

V. Reduction

Under German law, a reduction of the price for the contractual performance can be the result of several remedies. The creditor may partly terminate the contract and thereby reduce the price. Yet, this option is only available if the subject matter of the contract is severable (cf. § 323 V 1 BGB). A claim for damages (in lieu of performance) may also lead to reduction of the price but this claim presupposes that the debtor has been responsible for the breach of duty. In order to grant the creditor a right of reduction no matter whether or not the debtor was responsible for the breach of duty, the BGB recognises a specific remedy of price reduction. That remedy is only available for certain types of contracts (i.e. sale, lease, contracts for works, travel contracts; cf. §§ 441, 536, 638, 651d BGB). In the course of the reform of the German law of obligations, it was discussed whether reduction might be formulated as a general remedy for all contracts. The generalisation of reduction was eventually not adopted because that remedy was deemed to be inappropriate with regard to service and labour contracts[29] – a rather unpersuasive rationale.

[28] Cf., in greater detail, *Grigoleit/Riehm* (n. 22), 751 ff.

[29] Bundestags-Drucksache 14/6040 (n. 8), p. 81.

In order to protect the debtor's right to a "second chance", the remedy of reduction, just like termination, requires the fixing of an additional period for performance or remedying the defective performance. The amount of the claim under the remedy of reduction is not necessarily, but can be, smaller than the amount of a damages claim. While the claim of damages covers the whole value of the performance as it was to be expected, and in addition relates to consequential damages, the remedy of reduction diminishes the price by taking into account the actual value of the defective performance in relation to the hypothetical value of the proper performance, while consequential damages cannot be recovered[30].

The Draft Civil Code also provides for an independent remedy of reduction under s. 574 (= new s. 498). According to the translation at hand, this provision is applicable only with regard to obligations "to make property or a piece of work suitable". The requirements for reduction are a breach, and that the debtor is given a "second chance". Assuming that the claim for damages is generally available without being dependent on fault or the fixing of an additional period for performance or cure, the specific function of s. 547 (= new s. 498) is not entirely clear. The provision may possibly cover cases in which the effect of reduction cannot be reached by a damages claim because the breach and/or the damage could not have been anticipated. Furthermore, one may wonder why the remedy of reduction, as stated in s. 574 (= new s. 498) and in contrast to the rules on termination (see *supra* III. 3)), depends on the debtor being granted a "second chance". Finally, it has to be noted that the remedy of reduction is limited to obligations "to make property or a piece of work suitable" and therefore even much more restricted than under German law.

It may be worth noting, that the PECL provide a remedy of reduction as a general rule for all types of contracts (Art. 9:401 PECL). The function of reduction, in contrast to damages, is explained by the authors of the PECL in the official comment: first, reduction applies in cases in which damages are unavailable because the debtor is excused (cf. *supra* IV. 1)) and, second, the measure of reduction is different from the quantum of damages because it is relative to the contract price rather than being based upon the hypothetical value of proper performance[31]. Since these rationales are independent of any specific type of contract, the general approach of the PECL is convincing and might serve as a model for both German and Israeli law. However, it should be noted that the remedy of reduction in the PECL does not offer a clear and convincing solution with regard to the issue of the "second chance" to perform.

---

[30] With regard to the method of calculation, see *Walter Weidenkaff*, in: Palandt (n. 18), § 441 n. 12.

[31] *Lando/Beale* (n. 3), 430f.

VI. Special Rules on Breach concerning Specific Types of Contracts (in particular: Defects of Performance)

The German rules that have been discussed so far are, for the most part, stated in the general part of the law of obligations, and therefore they apply to all contracts[32]. In addition, there are special rules on breach of contract with respect to different types of contract (e.g. sales contracts: §§ 433 ff. BGB; lease contracts: §§ 535 ff. BGB; contracts for works: §§ 631 ff. BGB; travel contracts: §§ 651a ff. BGB). These rules mainly refer to defects of performance typical for that specific type of contract (i.e. defects of the goods sold, works promised, object leased, travel contracted for). Some of them restrict the rights of the creditor (e.g., short periods of prescription and requirements notification) while others extend his rights (see, for example, the non-fault based liability of the lessor according to § 536a BGB; information requirements; relief from the burden of proof).

One of the main objectives of the 2002 reform was to reduce the differences between the general rules of contract law and the special remedial regimes for different types of contracts. In the case of sales and contracts for work, the special rules have been adapted to the new general system of breach of contract and to the remedies implemented by the reform. The rules on lease and travel contracts, however, have not been adapted to the new system. Therefore, it has to be admitted that the German law of breach of contract is far from being perfectly coherent, and much work has yet to be done, both with regard to the general and special rules of contract law.

Unfortunately, the question of the coherence of general contract law and the law relating to certain types of contracts goes far beyond the reasonable scope of this article. It may only be mentioned that the Draft Civil Code also, apparently, cannot do without special rules for certain types of contracts, e.g. on sales contracts (ss. 207–228 = new ss. 155–175), lease contracts (ss. 284–305 = new ss. 231–252) and contracts for work (ss. 241–264 = new ss. 189–212).

VII. Concluding Remarks

The Draft of a new Israeli Civil Code must be praised for its determined move towards clarification, coherence, and generalisation. In fact, these principles are elementary for any code of private law that is committed to achieve rationality and objectivity, and thereby wishes to pursue the idea of justice. With regard to the problem of remedies for breach of contract, the comparative analysis based on the BGB and the PECL has shown, that the Draft Civil Code in many ways meets the high demands of these principles. In some instances, clarity and coherence may be taken even further – e.g., concerning the defences that could be

[32] The rules on reduction provide an exception.

raised against specific performance, and the demarcation of these defences from frustration, concerning the issue of a "second chance" to perform to be granted to the debtor, concerning the definition of the debtor's responsibility for damages in cases of remote causation and concerning the remedy of price reduction. In other respects it can be argued that generalisation should not be an end in itself. While harmonising the remedies for torts and breach of contract is generally feasible and may even be desirable, this effort should not distort the perspective on the specific needs of contract law. Even though the German approach may admittedly take the tendency for subtle distinctions a bit too far, it may turn out to be unavoidable to introduce some additional rules on the remedies for breach of contract into the Draft Civil Code. Examples for the need of further distinctions in the Draft Civil Code are, once again, the defences against specific performance and the requirements for different types of damages claims. It is to be expected that many of these distinctions will be introduced as judge-made law by the courts if they are omitted on the level of the code. Even though, of course, it is not generally objectionable to leave room for judicial development of the law, it should be emphasised at the unique juncture of implementing a new code that it is much more difficult for the courts and their case by case analysis to achieve clarification and coherence than for the drafters of a code.

The Israeli Law of Restitution and the Draft Civil Code

By DANIEL FRIEDMANN

Summary of Contents

I. A Brief Historical Note

The Israeli law of restitution was originally based on English law. Israel was conquered by the British army in 1917, towards the end of the First World War. On 24 July 1922, the League of Nations bestowed upon Britain the Mandate over Palestine and less than a month thereafter, on 10 August 1922, the British enacted the Palestine Order-in-Council which was designed to serve as the "Constitution" of Mandatory Palestine. Art. 46 of the Order-in-Council dealt with the law to be applied by the civil courts in Palestine. It provided in essence that "[t]he jurisdiction of the Civil Courts shall be exercised in conformity with the Ottoman Law in force in Palestine on November 1st, 1914". The Courts were also required to apply subsequent Ottoman legislation that was specifically declared to be in force and, of course, local British Mandatory legislation that would be enacted. In addition it was stated in Art. 46 that as far as these sources of the law "shall not extend or apply" the Courts shall exercise their jurisdiction

> "in conformity with the substance of the common law, and the doctrines of equity in force in England ... Provided always that the said common law and doctrines of equity shall be in force in Palestine so far only as the circumstances of Palestine and its inhabitants and the limits of His Majesty's jurisdiction permit and subject to such qualification as local circumstances render necessary."

This is the famous provision regarding the application of English common law and equity in order to fill lacunae in local law. It proved to be of decisive influence on Mandatory law and subsequently also on Israeli law. Indeed, Art. 46 was used as a pipeline through which a substantial part of English law was imported into Israel including the whole field of unjust enrichment, which at that time was termed "quasi contract"[1].

British Mandate over Palestine ended on 15 May 1948. On this very day the State of Israel was established. A few days thereafter, on 19 May 1948, the Law and Administration Ordinance was enacted. Section 11 of this Ordinance provided that the law which existed in Palestine on 14 May 1948, namely on the eve of the establishment of the State of Israel[2], will remain in force, insofar as it is not changed by Israeli legislation and subject to such modification as resulting from the establishment of the State of Israel and its authorities. The law which existed at the end of the British Mandate was thus absorbed into the law of Israel, and with it Art. 46 of the Palestine Order-in-Council, which served as a conduit for English law as well as for the whole field of "quasi contracts". However Israeli courts developed this branch of the law in a way that led to considerable deviation from the then prevailing approach in England.

The first significant development occurred on the theoretical level. The Israeli courts discarded the English theory of "implied contract" upon which at that time the whole field of "quasi contract" was based. Instead they preferred the approach reflected in Lord Mansfield's decision in the famous case of *Moses v. Macferlan*[3] and held that liability is imposed in order to prevent unjust enrichment[4]. The adoption of the general principle of unjust enrichment was accompanied by the introduction of a new term to this field which is hardly translatable. S. Z. Chechin J. considered that a verse from Jeremiah under which "he that getteth riches, and not by right, shall leave them in the midst of his days"[5] provides the best way to express the underlying idea. This translation does not really provide a good equivalent to the terminology used by Jeremiah and it seems that the only possible way to express a similar idea is by the term "unjust enrichment".

II. The Development of Israeli Case Law

Although the general principle of unjust enrichment was adopted by the Supreme Court of Israel rather early, its application was initially cautious and the

---

[1] *Daniel Friedmann*, The Effect of Foreign Law on the Law of Israel (1975), 61.

[2] *Friedmann* (n. 1), 7. It is interesting to note that while Israel absorbed the pre-existing law as it was on the eve of its establishment, the British who conquered Palestine in 1917 absorbed the Ottoman law which was in force some three years earlier, namely on November 1st, 1914.

[3] 97 E. R. 676 (1760).

[4] *Bar On v. Topol* (1954) 8 P. D. 1065, 1079; *City of Tel-Aviv v. Armon-Aharonowitz* (1956) 10 P. D. 1035. English law adopted the general principle only many years later: *Lipkin Gorman v. Karpnale Ltd* [1991] 2 A. C. 548.

[5] Jeremiah 17:11 (King James' translation).

result in concrete cases followed the English precedents. Consequently, recovery was usually allowed only within the recognised categories known to English law. A major change occurred some twenty years after the establishment of the State of Israel with the decision in *Yafet v. Eastwod*[6]. In that case the District Court dismissed an action for the recovery of money paid under mistake on the ground that the mistake was a mistake of law. That reflected the position of English law at the time[7]. The Supreme Court, by a bench of five Justices, reversed and held that the sharp distinction between mistake of law and mistake of fact should be abandoned and that in the case of a fundamental mistake negating the voluntariness of the payment restitution should be allowed, even if the mistake is one of law and not of fact. English law reached a similar result some thirty years later by virtue of the decision of the House of Lords in *Kleinwort Benson Ltd. v. Lincoln City Council*[8].

The approach reflected in *Yafet* was subsequently adopted by the legislator. The Contracts (General Part) Law, 1973, deals in ss. 14 and 15 with rescission of contract on the grounds of mistake and misrepresentation. For the purpose of these sections "mistake" is defined as being "either of fact or of law, with the exception of mistake as to the profitability of the transaction."

The case of *Yafet* was followed by a number of landmark decisions that have turned Israel into a jurisdiction in which the law of restitution acquired a central role in private law and in which this branch of the law has reached a high state of development, though in some instances the result was not altogether satisfactory.

The adoption of the general principle on unjust enrichment was followed by the recognition of a general defence available against restitutionary claims. In the leading case of *Israel v. Bank Hapoalim*[9] the Supreme Court held that just as the defendant can be liable *ex aequo et bono* to make restitution, so too he may be absolved from liability if the circumstances are such that *ex aequo et bono* he should be free from liability[10]. Thus, the defence of change of position has become available in Israeli law. Again, it may be noted that at that time English law, while recognising the defence of estoppel, did not recognise the defence of change of position[11].

Palimport v. Ciba Geigi[12] is another landmark decision handed down by the Supreme Court of Israel. The defendant in that action obtained in the District Court in a previous action a final injunction restraining the plaintiff from selling

---

[6] (1969) 23(1) P.D. 604.

[7] The source of the rule is *Bilbie v. Lumley* 102 E.R. 448 (1802). The rule was subject to a number of exceptions which need not be discussed in the present context.

[8] [1992] 2 A.C. 349. See Robert Goff/Gareth Jones, The Law of Restitution (6th ed., 2002) 217–228.

[9] (1978) 32(1) P.D. 153.

[10] At 15, per Sussman C.J. referring also to s. 142(1) of the Restatement, Restitution (1937).

[11] This defence was recognised in England only in Lipkin Gorman, *supra*, n. 4.

[12] (1975) 29(1) P.D. 592.

its product, on the ground that that product infringed the defendant's patent. There was no stay of injunction but it was set aside when an appeal was allowed. The plaintiff in the present action claimed that during the period that the injunction was in force it suffered a loss, as it could not sell its product while the defendant made additional profits, since the plaintiff's customers had to turn to the defendant to purchase the competing product. The Supreme Court held that the plaintiff had no cause of action for the loss it had suffered during the period that the injunction was in force. But though the plaintiff was not entitled to damages his claim in restitution was allowed. Sussman J. pointed out that if a person recovers money by virtue of a judgment that is subsequently reversed, the ground that entitled him to keep the money is voided and, if he does not refund the amount received, he is unjustly enriched[13]. In this case the defendant did receive payments from the plaintiff. His enrichment derived from contracts made with third parties, namely the plaintiff's former customers. But the Supreme Court held that the law of unjust enrichment is broad enough to apply to this situation as well. Kahan J. stated that restitution was not limited to the infringement of a property right and stated:

> "With respect to reasons of judicial policy, I do not see any reason why we should restrict the laws of restitution to infringement of a property right ... there are weighty reasons existing against such a narrowing. The principle that we do not order compensation for loss caused as a result of a reversed judgment [deserves] all due respect and should not be tampered with ... However, there is no justification that one who was enriched at the expense of the opposing party following a reversed judgment should retain the profits realised in such a manner, profits which, but for such judgment, would not be his, but rather the opposing party's. In my opinion, the rationale that there was no infringement here of a property right of the plaintiff is meaningless. Is the right of a person to sell his merchandise to his customers and to derive profits not worthy of protection to the same degree as his right to hold movable or real property?"[14]

The Supreme Court reached the correct result, but on this particular point it stands alone. There is no support for this result in any common law jurisdiction and in a recent decision the Court of Appeal in England declined to follow it[15].

Another major decision of the Israeli Supreme Court which had worldwide repercussions is *Adras Ltd. v. Harlow & Jones*[16]. In that case the defendant, a Ger-

---

[13] At 602.

[14] At 607. This part of Kahan J.'s judgment was quoted by Jacob L.J. in *Smithkline Beecham plc v. Apotex Europe Ltd* [2006] EWCA Civ 658, [2006] All E.R. (D) 317.

[15] *Smithkline Beecham plc, supra*, n. 14. The Court also referred to my support of the Israeli decision but was unconvinced. In fact it was *obiter* since the English case concerned a situation in which the injunction was obtained by a third party. In such a case it seems obvious that there is no room for restitution. See *Daniel Friedmann*, Valid, Voidable, Qualified and Non-existing Obligations: An Alternative Perspective on the Law of Restitution in: A. Burrows (ed.), Essays on Restitution (1991), 247, 266, note 75.

[16] (1988) 42(1) P.D. 221. For an English translation, see [1994] Restitution Law Review 23.

man corporation, agreed to sell to the plaintiff 7,000 tons iron c.i.f. Haifa. The price was 570 German marks per ton. Some 5,025 tons were shipped to the plaintiff between January and April 1974, despite the difficulties caused by the "Yom Kippur" war. However, in April 1974 the seller notified the purchaser that because of high storage costs it had to sell the remaining quantity of iron. This sale to third parties in Hamburg was made at a price of 804.70 German marks per ton f.o.b.

The Israeli Supreme Court held by a majority[17] that under the general principle of unjust enrichment profits gained through breach of contract are recoverable. Such recovery may be had not only in the case of a contract for the sale of specific goods but also in the case of a sale of non-specific goods, provided of course that there is a causal connection between the breach of the contract and the gain obtained by the defendant. In the present case, the iron stored in Hamburg and sold to the third parties was destined for the plaintiff. That suffices to establish the causal connection between the breach of the contract and the profit made by the sale to the third parties.

The result reached in *Adras Ltd* was diametrically opposed to the traditional approach of Anglo-American law that in the case of breach of contract recovery is measured by the loss to the plaintiff rather than by the profits gained by the defendant[18]. The traditional approach has been supported by a number of proponents of economic analysis of law. In their view, if the promisor's profits from the breach exceed the loss to the promisee, the promisor should be free or even encouraged to break his contract. Such an "efficient" breach, they argue, leads to a more efficient use of resources and should not, therefore, be deterred by depriving the promisor of his profits[19]. The subject has attracted great attention and become the focus of a voluminous literature[20]. In England the traditional ap-

---

[17] A. Barak J., S. Levin J., and G. Bach J.; M. Ben-Porat J. and D. Levin J. dissenting.

[18] *Sir Guenter Treitel*, The Law of Contract (11th ed., 2003), 927.

[19] *Richard A. Posner*, Economic Analysis of Law (4th ed., 1992), 117–120. For criticism, see *Daniel Friedmann*, The Efficient Breach Fallacy, (1989) 18 Journal of Legal Studies 1; *Melvin A. Eisenberg*, Actual and Virtual Specific Performance, The Theory of Efficient Breach, and the Indifference Principle in Contract Law, (2005) 93 California Law Review 975.

[20] *John Philip Dawson*, Restitution or Damages, (1959) 20 Ohio State Law Journal 175; *Daniel Friedmann*, Restitution of Benefits Obtained through the Appropriation of Property or the Commission of a Wrong, (1980) 80 Columbia Law Review 504; *E. Allan Farnsworth*, Your Loss or My Gain? The Dilemma of the Disgorgement Principle in Breach of Contract, (1985) 94 Yale Law Journal 1339; *Gareth Jones*, The Recovery of Benefits Gained from a Breach of Contract, (1983) 99 Law Quarterly Review 443; *Lionel Smith*, Disgorgement of the Profits of Breach of Contract: Property, Contract and Efficient Breach, (1994) 23 Canadian Business Law Journal 121; *Richard O'Dair*, Damages for Breach of Contract: A Wrong Turn, [1993] Restitution Law Review 31; *Richard Nolan*, Remedies for Breach of Contract: Specific Enforcement and Restitution, in: Francis Rose (ed.), Failure of Contracts (1997), 35; *Andrew Kull*, Disgorgement for Breach, the 'Restitution Interest' and the Restatement of Contracts, [2001] Texas Law Review 2021; *Hanoch Dagan*, Restitutionary Damages for Breach of Contract: An Exercise in Private Law Theory, (2000) 1 Theoretical Inquiries in Law 115; *John D. McCamus*, Disgorgement for Breach of Contract: A Comparative Perspective, (2003) 36 Loyola Law Review 943; *Ernest J. Weinrib*, Punishment and Disgorgement

proach has until recently been maintained[21] but the winds of change had their effect and in a recent decision the House of Lords recognised the possibility of awarding restitution of gains made by breach of contract[22]. A number of American courts have also allowed restitution of profits made by breach of contract[23]. The topic is, however, complex since there are many types of contracts and a breach may occur in a variety of circumstances; for some of them the recovery of profits may not be appropriate. A detailed discussion is not within the ambit of this paper[24].

The case of *Adras Ltd* has another broad aspect. In Israel the topic of remedies for breach of contract is regulated by statute, i.e. the Contracts (Remedies for Breach of Contract) Law, 1970. That Law deals with the well known remedies for breach, namely enforcement (specific performance), rescission, and damages but says nothing about recovering the profits that the party in breach derived from his wrong. The absence of a provision on this issue is presumably because the possibility simply did not occur to the drafters of that Law. Nevertheless the Court in *Adras Ltd* held that restitution is available. This approach demonstrates that the principle of unjust enrichment can be superimposed on various branches of private law even if they are ordered by a statute that is silent on the matter. Obviously this cannot be done where the statute clearly negates this possibility or where it is not in line with its underlying policies. But *Adras Ltd* shows the extent to which unjust enrichment can influence other branches of the law. A similar approach has been adopted with regard to the general defence against restitutionary claims. It was held that this defence is available against statutory provisions in various branches of private law in instances in which the content of the provision indicates that it is founded upon the doctrine of unjust enrichment. An important example is the application of that defence to the provisions in the

---

as Contract Remedies, (2003) 78 Chicago-Kent Law Review 55. See also § 39 of the Preliminary Draft No. 6 (September 2004) of the Third Restatement of the Law of Restitution and Unjust Enrichment (Andrew Kull Reporter), that deals with "Restitution in Cases of Profitable Breach"; *Melvin A. Eisenberg*, The Disgorgement Interest in Contract Damages, (2006) 105 Michigan Law Review 559; *Jack Beatson*, The Use and Abuse of Restitution (1991), 15–17; Robert Goff/Gareth Jones, The Law of Restitution (6th ed., 2002), 515–527; *Andrew Burrows*, The Law of Restitution (2nd ed., 2002), 480–493.

[21] *Surrey County Council v. Bredero Homes Ltd* [1993] 1 W.L.R. 68 (C.A.).

[22] *A-G v. Blake* [2001] 1 A.C. 268 (H.L.). See also *Experience Hendrix v. PPX Enterprises Ltd* [2003] 1 All E.R. (Comm.) 830 (C.A.), discussed in *Peter Jaffey*, Disgorgement and Licence Fee Damages in Contract, (2004) 20 Journal of Contract Law 57. See also *Esso Petroleum Co. v. Niad Ltd* [2001] All E.R. (D) 324.

[23] *Unita Oil Ref. v. Ledford* (1952) 244 P. 2d. 881; *Automatic Laundry Serv. v. Demas* (1958) 141 A. 2d. 497; *Restaurant Supply Co. v. Dib* (1979) 413 N.Y.S. 2d. 835; *Earthinfo Corp. v. Hydrosphere Resource* (1995) 900 P. 2d 113.

[24] *Friedmann* (n. 20), 519–526; *Eisenberg* (n. 20). See also *Daniel Friedmann*, The Creation of Entitlements via the Law of Restitution, in: Charles Rickett (ed.), Essays in Honour of Peter Birks (forthcoming).

contract statutes dealing with restitution upon rescission of a contract[25]. The application of the defence in contractual contexts should be subject to severe limitations but at least in some situations it may conceivably apply[26].

III. Unjust Enrichment and the Creation of New Entitlements

The law of unjust enrichment is essentially a remedial branch of the law[27]. It is predicated on concepts of corrective justice and serves to vindicate and protect entitlements[28] which ordinarily derive from some other branch of the law, such as the law of property, the law of contract or the law of personality[29]. The law of unjust enrichment is called in to intervene where an initial entitlement that belongs to one party has been appropriated, transferred, or inured to the benefit of another in a manner that is not sanctioned by the law. In the absence of such an initial entitlement there is no unjust enrichment. Thus, in *Leibovitz v. Eliahu Ltd*[30], the plaintiff had been the sole importer of Parker pens in Israel and according to his contract with the manufacturer he had the exclusive rights to import these pens. Nevertheless the defendant succeeded in obtaining such pens from a different source abroad and made what has been termed "parallel import". The plaintiff applied for an injunction arguing, *inter alia*, that it invested considerable amounts in advertising and in enlarging the market for these pens and that the parallel importer was thus enriched at its expense. The claim was dismissed on the ground that the plaintiff has no right to a monopoly over the market. Hence, the defendant did not take, exploit, or infringe an entitlement belonging to the plaintiff and was therefore not unjustly enriched at the plaintiff's expense.

The imposition of liability in restitution is therefore generally predicated on a pre-existing right to which the plaintiff was entitled and which became the source of the defendant's enrichment. Yet, the law of restitution is not merely ancillary to the branches of the law that deal with the creation of legal entitle-

---

[25] *Ginsberg v. Ben Yosef* (1993) 47(1) P.D. 540. Cf. *Cheese v. Thomas* [1994] 1 W.L.R. 129 (C.A.).

[26] I have discussed this issue in some detail in *Daniel Friedmann*, The Law of Unjust Enrichment (2nd ed, 1998) (in Hebrew), 776ff. and briefly in *Daniel Friedmann*, Reversible Transfers – The Two Categories, [2003] Restitution Law Review 5.

[27] *Daniel Friedmann*, The Protection of Entitlements via the Law of Restitution – Expectancies and Privacy, (2005) 121 Law Quarterly Review 400.

[28] *Ernest J. Weinrib*, The Idea of Private Law (1995), 114–144. For a discussion of Weinrib's theory in the context of restitution, see *Lionel Smith*, Restitution: The Heart of Corrective Justice, (2001) 79 Texas Law Review 2115. See also *Mark P. Gergen*, What Renders Restitution Unjust?, (2001) 79 Texas Law Review 1927, 1930.

[29] It has also been argued that the law of restitution should protect what has been termed "competition rules", namely the right to participate in a fair competition for resources; see *Ofer Grosskopf*, The Protection of Competition Rules via the Law of Restitution, (2001) 79 Texas Law Review 1981.

[30] (1990) 44(2) P.D. 309.

ments. Both the law of restitution and the law of torts serve an important function in the expansion of existing legal rights and in the developments of new entitlements. The historical role of the law of torts in the development of legal entitlements in English law is well known[31]. The law of restitution fulfils a similar function although on a more modest scale. The decision of the U.S. Supreme Court *International News Service v. Associated Press*[32] provides a classical example. In that case the defendant, a news agency, copied reports published by the plaintiff and sold it to its customers. The time difference between the East and the West coasts enabled the defendant to transmit the news by telegraph and sell them while they were still fresh. The Supreme Court by majority allowed the claim, having concluded that the defendant was "endeavouring to reap where it has not sown" and "appropriating to itself the harvest of those who have sown"[33]. The concept of unjust enrichment was thus utilised in order to recognise, and to grant legal protection to, the interest in "hot news" collected by a news agency against its appropriation by a competitor[34]. There have been numerous other decisions in which the law of restitution was utilised in order to create new legally recognised entitlements, notably in connection with the development of the right of publicity[35]. A similar development occurred in Israeli law. A recent example is provided by a decision of the Supreme Court of Israel in *Aloniel Ltd. v. McDonald.*[36] In this case Ariel McDonald, a well known basketball player, brought an action against Aloniel Ltd, the company running McDonald's chain in Israel, claiming that an Aloniel's advertisement, in which his name was used without his consent, breached his right of privacy, damaged his reputation, and led to Aloniel's unjust enrichment. There is no need to discuss the quite hilarious facts of the case[37]. For our purposes it suffices to point out that the Court discussed at great length the question whether the right of publicity ought to be recognised; and it concluded that the answer should be in the affirmative subject to some limitations deriving from the freedom of expression. The protection to be granted to the economic interest of a person in his name and reputation has

[31] *Friedmann* (n. 27), 400–402.

[32] 248 U.S. 215 (1918).

[33] 248 U.S. 215 (1918), 239–240.

[34] The approach to this decision has for a considerable time been rather cautious. See *George Palmer*, The Law of Restitution (1978), vol. 1, 112–120. Interest in this case was however recently revived with the strengthening of the notions of unfair competition; see *Richard A. Epstein*, International News Service v. Associated Press as Sources of Property Rights in News, (1992) 78 Virginia Law Review 85; *Douglas Baird*, Common Law Intellectual Property and the Legacy of International News Service v. Associated Press, (1983) 50 University of Chicago Law Review 411; *Leo J. Raskind*, The Misappropriation Doctrine as a Competitive Norm of Intellectual Property Law, (1991) 75 Minnesota Law Review 875; *Wendy J. Gordon*, On Owning Information: Intellectual Property and the Restitutionary Impulse, (1992) 78 Virginia Law Review 149. See also Restatement (3rd) Unfair Competition, § 38 and comments, 409–413, 416–422.

[35] For example *Zacchini v. Scripps-Howard Broadcasting Co.* 433 U.S. 562 (1977), 569, 575–576 (with regard to the right to performance as a "human cannonball").

[36] (2004) 58(4) PD 314.

[37] For a summary of the case, see [2006] Restitution Law Review 176.

thus been rooted in the law of restitution. The Court also held that in order to allow recovery there was no need to decide whether the right of publicity is a property right. It suffices to base liability on the fact that such use of another's reputation is unfair and improper. The resulting enrichment is therefore unjust. It should, however, be pointed out that the use of the name and reputation of another's person for commercial purposes constitutes unjust enrichment only if that person has exclusive rights to such use. If he has no such right then the use of his name by others does not constitute unjust enrichment, at least not in the legal sense. Hence, the conclusion that the unauthorised use of another person's name and reputation for commercial purposes constitutes unjust enrichment embodies the recognition of a new legal right, namely the right of publicity.

It is interesting to note that s. 2(6) of the Israeli Privacy Law, 1981, provides that the use of a name, likeness, photo, or voice of a person for the purpose of profit constitutes breach of privacy. The Court considered however that the purpose of the law of privacy and of s. 2(6) is the protection of privacy, namely the right of the person to be left alone and to prevent the disclosure of undesired private information. Section 2(6) is not intended to protect the right of publicity, i.e. the economic interest of a person to exclusive exploitation of his fame and reputation. It would, however, apply in the case in which the name of a celebrity is used for purposes with which he disagrees, or in a way that injures his reputation, as for example in the case of *Onasis v. Christian Dior – NY Inc*[38]. It is thus evident that the Court preferred to attribute the creation of the right of publicity to its power to develop the law of unjust enrichment in order to create a new entitlement, rather than base its decision upon the specific provision embodied in s. 2(6) of the Privacy Law.

However, the Court then moved on to defences, specifically s. 2 of the Unjust Enrichment Law. That defence permits the Court to exempt a party from the duty to make restitution if it considers that the receipt of the benefit did not involve a loss to the plaintiff or if there are "other circumstances [that] render restitution unjust". In this case it was held that since liability is based on unjust enrichment the defence applies and, under the circumstances of the case, it was decided to absolve Aloniel from liability[39].

Another decision of major importance relating to the use of the law of unjust enrichment to create new entitlements is *A.Sh.I.R. Import, Production & Distribution v. Forum Avisarim and Consumption Products Ltd*[40]. The decision was concerned with three cases in which District Courts in Israel granted an injunction enjoining the imitation of industrial products. In none of these cases could the plaintiff base his claim upon specific legislation dealing with intellectual property. There

[38] 472 N.Y.S. 2d 254 (1984).

[39] For a discussion of these circumstances, see the reference above, n. 37.

[40] (1998) 52(4) PD 289. A summary of the decision was published in [2000] Restitution Law Review 412.

was no breach of patent, copyright, or a right of design. Nor did the defendant in any of these cases commit the tort of passing off.

The issue has been dealt with in a number of other district court decisions, which reached conflicting results. Some courts held that product imitation may give rise to a claim based on unjust enrichment while others held that there was no right of action if the product imitation constituted neither passing off nor breach of intellectual property rights as established by the relevant legislation.

An extended panel of seven Justices gave the decision of the Supreme Court. The Court decided to allow the appeal in two cases, with regard to which it was held that there was no room for an injunction. It did, however, decide by a 4 to 3 majority to dismiss the appeal in one case in which an injunction was granted against the imitation of a block relief system. The decision is lengthy and complex, and a detailed discussion is not within the scope of this paper. It suffices to point out that some of the judges considered that there may be circumstances which would justify the application of the unjust enrichment principle to protect ideas, even if they are not within the ambit of the intellectual property legislation, and even though their author has voluntarily consented to their disclosure to the public[41]. However, the exact nature of these circumstances remains rather vague.

Barak C.J.'s decision is in line with that of the majority; however, his reasoning emphasises the approach under which copying a competitor's idea may constitute an act of unfair competition. According to this view, the plaintiff's right is not founded upon a monopoly in his idea, but upon the improper conduct of his competitor. Therefore, the availability of the remedy and its extent depend not only upon the nature of the idea but also upon the conduct of the defendant as well as the other circumstances of the case. In this way, President Barak is trying to alleviate the difficulty arising from the creation of novel intellectual property rights via court decisions. Nevertheless, the conclusion that such a right, perhaps narrow and fragile, has been created, seems unavoidable.

Two dissenting justices (Chechin and Englard JJ.) considered that the law of unjust enrichment should not be utilised to protect ideas that do not enjoy protection under the intellectual property legislation and that became publicly known.

The case demonstrates the expansive application of the principle of unjust enrichment in Israeli law. The main difficulty concerns the vagueness of the guidelines laid down by the Court, and it is submitted that the majority in this case went too far[42]. Yet it is clear that the case created an entitlement, beyond the scope of the intellectual property legislation, to ideas embodied in products,

---

[41] Contrast the view expressed by Brandeis J. in a dissenting opinion, according to which "the noblest of human production – knowledge, truths ascertained and ideas – become, after voluntary communication to others, free as the air to common use": *International News Service v. Associated Press*, *supra*, n. 32.

[42] In addition, there arises the question as to how long the defendant will be enjoined from copying the plaintiff's idea.

though the precise nature of ideas that are the subject of the entitlement and the scope of the entitlement remain vague.

IV. The Israeli Legislation in the Field of Unjust Enrichment and the Draft Code

There are numerous provisions in various Israeli Laws that can be classified as belonging to the law of unjust enrichment such as, for example, the provisions in the Contracts (General Part) Law that deal with contribution among debtors who are jointly and severally liable. These provisions cannot be discussed within the framework of this paper. Rather I shall concentrate on the provisions of the Israeli Unjust Enrichment Law, 1979. The title of the Law speaks of Unjust Enrichment. But only a few of its provisions deal with specific grounds of recovery. Instead, s. 1 adopts the general principle of restitution and imposes liability on a person who receives a benefit "without legal cause". This phrase seems to have been adopted from French law, but it had hardly any influence in Israeli law, and the Israeli courts continue to speak of unjust enrichment. No French influence can be discerned in this branch of the law. The Law adopted in broad terms the general defence to restitution including "circumstances [that] render restitution unjust" (s. 2 of the Law, mentioned above). Some changes introduced by the Unjust Enrichment Law are particularly significant: section 4 that deals with payment of another's debt and s. 5 that deals with an action to protect another's interest. These provisions rejected the strict English position regarding the volunteer and adopted a more liberal approach towards a person who intervenes to protect another's interest. Section 4 provides in essence that a person who pays another person's debt "is not entitled to restitution unless the other person has no reasonable cause to object to the payment ..." The wording of this sentence is somewhat perplexing. It consists of two negative phrases, starting with the proposition that the payor "is not entitled to restitution", but it soon emerges that this proposition is subject to the second part of the sentence ("unless the other person has no reasonable cause to object to the payment") which actually negates the first part that seems to deny restitution. In reality the section means that the payor of another's debt is entitled to restitution unless the debtor has reasonable cause to object to the payment[43]. The puzzling wording of s. 4 reflects the influence of English law that traditionally was highly suspicious of intervention in another's affairs, even though the section itself evidences a break with this tradition.

Section 5 provides another indication of the Israeli approach which in this respect is closer to that prevailing in Continental law. The section grants a right to recovery of expenses by a person who acted in good faith, and reasonably, to

[43] The wording of the section may, however, affect the burden of proof so that it will be incumbent upon the payor to show that the debtor had no reasonable cause to object to the payment.

protect the life, physical integrity, health, honour, or property of another. The section further provides that if the intervener (who is termed the "benefactor") suffers damage as a result of his act, the court may at its discretion order the other party (termed the "beneficiary") to pay the benefactor compensation for property damage, though not for death or bodily injury, if the court "considers it just to do so in the circumstances of the case". The limiting of this possibility to property damage seems paradoxical and indeed it is. The reason presumably lies in the fear of imposing too heavy a liability on the beneficiary. It has also been explained that a rescuer who suffers personal injury while acting to rescue another is entitled to compensation in accordance with the provisions of the National Insurance Law. The position adopted in ss. 4 and 5 of the Unjust Enrichment Law thus reflects an approach that is closer to that obtaining in Continental law but it falls short of completely embracing the legal institution of *negotiorum gestio*. I shall not discuss the differences in any detail. For our purposes it suffices to point out that *negotiorum gestio* in Continental law is, strictly speaking, not part of the law of unjust enrichment but constitutes a separate legal institution[44]. However, the Israeli legislator included the topic in the Law on Unjust Enrichment.

The liberal approach to the intervener and the rescuer reflected in ss. 4 and 5 of the Unjust Enrichment Law presumably results from the Israeli attitude towards the requirement of assisting those in need. It is based on long established Jewish values which led to another piece of legislation entitled "Thou shall not stand against the blood of your neighbour", enacted in 1998. This rather obscure title has been derived from the Bible[45]. It has been traditionally interpreted as imposing a duty to rescue, and the Israeli statute makes it obligatory to come to the rescue of a person whose life or health is in sudden danger, if it is possible to do so without jeopardising oneself or others. Breach of this obligation is a misdemeanour the penalty for which is a fine. A detailed discussion of the issues relating to the duty to rescue is not within the ambit of this article[46].

The Israeli Unjust Enrichment Law is extremely brief. It is in fact the shortest among the statutes on which the new Israeli codification is to be based. It contains none of the "classical" causes of action known to this branch of the law, such as recovery of payment made under mistake. All the pertinent causes of ac-

[44] Thus, in the German BGB the topic is dealt with in §§ 677–687, while the topic of unjustified enrichment is regulated in §§ 812–822 BGB. But the International Encyclopedia of Comparative Law combined the two topics in volume X which is entitled Restitution – Unjust Enrichment and Negotiorum Gestio (*P. Schlechtriem* general editor).

[45] Leviticus 19:16.

[46] There is ample material on the subject. See, e.g., *Ernest J. Weinrib*, The Case for a Duty to Rescue, (1980) 90 Yale Law Journal 247; *Steven J. Heyman*, Foundations of the Duty to Rescue, (1994) 47 Vanderbilt Law Review 673. On the different approaches of English and Continental law, see *Andrew Ashworth*, Principles of Criminal Law (3rd ed. 1995), 49–50. See also *Andrew Ashworth/ Eva Steiner*, Criminal Omissions and Public Duties: The French Experience, (1990) 10 Legal Studies 153. – On the position of Jewish Law, see *Aaron Kirschenbaum*, 'The Good Samaritan' and Jewish Law, (1976) 7 Diné Israel, An Annual of Jewish Law Past and Present 7.

tion were presumably thought to be included in the general principle embodied in s. 1 of the Law. The only additional specific grounds of recovery are those included in ss. 4 and 5 of the Law, discussed above. The reason for their inclusion is presumably that they were intended to change the pre-existing law and expand the "volunteer's" right of restitution. All other potential claims recognised under the pre-existing law were assumed to be included in the general principle.

V. Unjust Enrichment in the Israeli Draft Civil Code

The Draft Civil Code made no attempt to introduce drastic changes. However, the chapter on unjust enrichment is much more detailed than the original Unjust Enrichment Law and consequently considerably longer. The additional material is based primarily on Israeli case law and literature reflecting the law on the subject as it is presently understood to be. In general terms it can be said that the Draft supports the expansive tendencies expressed in Israeli case law. Section 411 of the proposed code adopts the general principle upon which restitution is based and, like s. 1 of the original Law, avoids the term "unjust enrichment". The main change in the new section is that it speaks of the beneficiary gaining the benefit "without being entitled" to it, while the original s. 1 of the Law speaks of receipt of benefit "without legal cause". I do not think that the drafters intended to take a position on the issue that is now raging in English law concerning the difference between the requirement of an "unjust factor" and the more general one of "absence of a legal ground"[47], the latter actually being the idea reflected in the wording of the original s. 1 of the Israeli Law.

Section 412 of the Draft Civil Code is new. It states that the provisions in the chapter on unjust enrichment will apply also to restitutionary obligations included in other parts of the code. It thus adopts the expansive approach of the Israeli literature and case law on that point. This means also that the equitable defence to restitutionary claims will apply to the various provisions dealing with restitution that can be found in various parts of the code, though its application may sometimes be very much restricted in view of the context in which the issue arises[48].

Section 413 of the Draft Civil Code is also new. It seeks to remedy the absence of specific causes of action in the present Unjust Enrichment Law by providing a list of typical situations in which restitution is to be granted. These include instances in which the gain was derived from an unlawful act; a transfer caused by mistake, misrepresentation, duress, or exploitation; a transfer requested by the

[47] See *Jack Beatson*, Unlawful Statutes and Mistake of Law: Is there a Smile on the Face of Schrödinger's Cat?, in: Andrew Burrows/Alan Rodger (eds.), Mapping the Law: Essays in Honour of Peter Birks (2006), 163. See also *S. Meier*, No Basis: A Comparative View, in: *ibid.*, 343.

[48] See *supra* (n. 25, n. 26) and accompanying text.

beneficiary or agreed by him when he knew or should have known that the other party expected consideration; a transfer by virtue of a void cause or a cause that was rescinded or avoided. This latter category seems to include the case of subsequent failure of the ground on which a transfer was made, as is the case, for instance, the where payment has been made pursuant to a judgment that is subsequently reversed. The list is not exhaustive. Thus, for example, it does not include the case of "permissible taking" in which the defendant is entitled to use the claimant's property (notably in case of an emergency) but is required to pay for it[49]. However, s. 413 expressly provides that it does not derogate from the provisions of s. 411 that deal with the general principle. It is thus possible to resort to this principle to supplement the specific causes of action enumerated in s. 413.

Sections 414 and 415 of the Draft Code replicate the provisions that are now included in ss. 4 and 5 of the Unjust Enrichment Law subject to a number of changes. These include the transformation of the double negative statements in s. 4 of the Law, discussed above, into a positive statement under which a person who pays another's debt is entitled to restitution unless the debtor (the beneficiary) had a reasonable ground to object to the payment. In addition, s. 414(2) provides that subrogation will operate in favour of the payor of another's debt, as regards the securities granted to the original creditor.

Section 416 is new. It provides that restoration shall, in the first instance, be *in specie*, but where restoration *in specie* is impossible or unreasonable restitution is to be made in value. Section 417 deals with the measure of recovery. It provides that in calculating the amount of restitution the following elements, among others, shall be taken into account: (1) the profit derived by the beneficiary and his contribution to that profit; (2) the reasonable price that ought to be paid for the beneficiary's use of what he has received, and (3) the market value of the benefit. The possibility of dividing the profits between the parties is not specifically mentioned[50], but it may presumably be included in the first category. There is no guidance as to the choice among the various possibilities. The American Restatement draws a sharp distinction between a defendant who was a conscious wrongdoer and a defendant who acted in good faith. Under the Restatement, a conscious wrongdoer is liable to account for all his profits[51]. The party who acted in good faith is treated much more leniently and his liability generally does

---

[49] See *Vincent v. Lake Erie Transportation Co.* 109 Minn. 456, 124 N.W. 221 (1910) and *Daniel Friedmann*, Restitution of Benefits Obtained through the Appropriation of Property or the Commission of a Wrong, (1980) 80 Columbia Law Review 504, 540ff.

[50] Cf. *Sheldon v. Metro-Goldwyn Pictures Inc.* (1939) 106 F. 2d 45, affirmed (1940) 309 U.S. 390.

[51] See § 40 of the Restatement (3d) Restitution and Unjust Enrichment, Council Draft No. 6 (November 12, 2004), in particular comment b to that section at 38ff. See also § 51 of this Restatement, Council Draft No. 8 (November 29, 2006) at 55ff. But see *ibid.* illustrations 24 at 78, in which a more moderate result is reached.

not exceed the value of what he has received[52]. No such distinction is mentioned in the Draft Civil Code but since the courts have considerable discretion in this matter it may safely be assumed that the qualification of the defendant's conduct will have a considerable effect on the measure of recovery.

The Draft Civil Code also includes provisions relating to the right to the substitute. Section 418 of the Draft provides that if the enriched party received property or a right (termed "a substitute") in exchange for the property owned by another the owner is entitled to the substitute, and until he receives it, the substitute is held in trust for him. The introduction of the trust idea in this context may have considerable implications. It may grant the plaintiff priority over the defendant's other creditors with regard to property (in this instance the "substitute") that is held in trust. In addition if this property appreciates in value, the plaintiff may be entitled to that amount. The Israeli courts have, in the past, applied English rules of tracing. The Draft Code, if eventually enacted, will grant legislative imprimatur to tracing in the field of restitution and may thus lead to its extended application and broader development.

Finally, the Draft Code puts in place the general defence to restitutionary claims (s. 420) and lists a considerable number of considerations that the court may take into account in applying the defence. These include the following: 1) the claimant suffered no loss[53]; 2) the defendant had a moral right to receive the benefit; 3) the defendant changed his position in good faith in reliance on the benefit received; 4) the benefit received is lost, damaged, or transferred in good faith to a third party; 5) the gain was conferred upon the recipient without his consent and he did not derive a benefit from it; 6) the recipient lacks full legal capacity and the award of restitution would conflict with the policy underlying the limitation of legal capacity; 6) restitution would be against public policy.

Broadly speaking, the Draft Civil Code reflects an expansive approach to the law of restitution and maintains the important role that that branch of the law has acquired in Israeli private law. Though it is much more detailed than the present Unjust Enrichment Law, it leaves broad areas to the discretion of the courts, both with regard to situations in which restitution will be available and with regard to the defences to restitutionary claims.

---

[52] § 51 of the Restatement (3rd) Council Draft No. 8, *supra*, n. 51. See also generally *Daniel Friedmann*, Restitution for Wrongs: The Measure of Recovery (2001) 79 Texas Law Review 1879.

[53] This consideration is already mentioned in s. 2 of the present Unjust Enrichment Law. It derives from Jewish law which adopted the rule under which there is no liability where a person gains while the other suffers no loss. A discussion of the ambit of the Jewish rule is not within the scope of this paper. For our purposes it suffices to point out that in these instances Jewish law completely absolves from liability while under the Israeli legislation absence of a loss is merely a consideration that the court may, but does not have to, take into account. Indeed, instances can be found in which the Israeli courts awarded restitution in spite of the fact that the plaintiff suffered no loss. See, e.g., *S. G. M. Henionim v. The State of Israel* (1983) 37(2) P. D. 633.

No Headaches over Unjust Enrichment: Response to Daniel Friedmann

By Christiane C. Wendehorst

Summary of Contents

Professor Friedmann has provided us with a discerning account and brilliant analysis of the Israeli law of restitution, its history, its present state and its future, at least if the proposal we are currently discussing comes into force. I will begin my brief response by showing, first, why Part Four, Subpart Four, Chapter Two of the Draft[1], despite bearing the title "Unjust Enrichment", is not so much about unjust enrichment at all. I will then pose the provocative question whether we need a chapter on unjust enrichment in a civil code or not, contending that we probably do not. And I will close by arguing why, in the case of Israel, these reflections might not be so important after all.

I. Why There Is Not Much Unjust Enrichment in the Chapter on Unjust Enrichment

Let us first take a look at some characteristic features of the Draft which are apt to catch the eye of the comparative lawyer. The first issue I want to address is the difference between restitution and unjust enrichment, and between restitution and unjust enrichment, and legal phenomena that are neither of the two.

1) Restitution and Unjust Enrichment

We owe a lot to our English and Israeli colleagues who have helped to bring out the distinction between unjust enrichment and restitution much more clearly during the past two decades[2]. Restitution is a remedy, like damages or specific performance, the defining feature of which is that it is based on the defendant's gain. Unjust enrichment, on the other hand, is an event giving rise to an obligation, like tort or contract. Another question is whether the two concepts quadrate[3] or not[4], and if not, which of the claims triggering restitutionary remedies are founded on unjust enrichment. In the end, this question is essentially one of terminology[5], and for the purpose of this paper we should simply agree on the usage reflected in s. 412 (ex s. 488) of the Draft Civil Code, i.e. that restitution is broader in scope than unjust enrichment[6]. To put it in the words of the

---

[1] When hereinafter speaking of the "Draft" or of a specific section of that draft, reference is made to the 2006 official Civil Law Code Proposal, available at http://www.justice.gov.il/MOJHeb/Codex2/ (in Hebrew). However, the numbers of the respective sections in the preliminary draft, which is included in this volume, are added in brackets.

[2] There is abundant literature on the issue, which is far beyond the scope of this paper. For references see, e.g., *Robert Goff/Gareth Jones*, The Law of Restitution (7th ed., 2006), no. 1–012.

[3] That was the position still taken by *Peter Birks*, An Introduction to the Law of Restitution (1985), 17–22, but he later changed his mind: cf. *Peter Birks*, Misnomer, in: William Cornish et al. (eds.), Restitution: Past, Present and Future (1998), 1. The view is arguably still held by *Robert Goff/Gareth Jones* (n. 2), no. 1–012; *Andrew Burrows*, The Law of Restitution (2nd ed., 2002), 5–7.

[4] *Graham Virgo*, The Principles of the Law of Restitution (2nd ed., 2006), 8–9; *Peter Birks*, Unjust Enrichment (2nd ed., 2005), 4–5.

[5] The most convincing explanation has probably been given by *Virgo* (n. 4), 8–9, who differentiates between a descriptive sense of unjust enrichment, which quadrates with restitution but is rather empty, and a substantive sense of unjust enrichment.

[6] *David Johnston/Reinhard Zimmermann*, Unjustified enrichment: surveying the landscape, in:

late Peter Birks: unjust enrichment is a distinct causative event, while restitution is a multi-causal response[7]. Or, to pay homage to Birks' predilection for canine metaphors, one might say that unjust enrichment is to restitution as a terrier's head is to a dog's tail. As to the question of what still counts as terrier, we should again refer to the Draft Civil Code and classify as claims in unjust enrichment all claims potentially falling within the ambit of s. 411 (ex s. 487)[8].

2) A Terrier's Head, a Dog's Tail, and Parts of a Cat

In principle, the structure of the Draft recognises the distinction between restitution and unjust enrichment, for Subpart Six deals with remedies, including a chapter on restitution, whereas Subparts Two to Five obviously deal primarily with how obligations arise, including obligations in unjust enrichment as one of several types of non-voluntary obligations. The same holds true, by the way, for liability in tort, for the chapter on tort law deals with grounds of liability only whereas the remedy of compensation is dealt with under Subpart Six (cf. s. 365 of the Draft Civil Code, ex s. 438). Upon closer scrutiny, however, one realises that the distinction between ground of liability and remedy is kept up very stringently with tort and compensation, whereas, with unjust enrichment, the categories become confused. The chapter on unjust enrichment deals both with grounds of liability *and* with the remedy of restitution, and Subpart Six, which is devoted to remedies in general and which does list restitution as one of the basic remedies available to a claimant, itself refers in s. 495 (ex s. 571) to the chapter on unjust enrichment. Obviously, it is the chapter on unjust enrichment that is regarded as the proper place for provisions on restitution in general. This is underpinned by s. 412 (ex s. 488), which states explicitly that the provisions of the unjust enrichment chapter shall also apply to obligations to make restitution, set forth in other chapters of the law.

a) Provisions on Restitution in General

On a closer look, it becomes apparent that provisions on restitution in general are certainly to be found in s. 416 (ex s. 492) of the Draft Code, stating the general principle that restitution must be in kind unless this would be impossible or unreasonable; in s. 417 (ex s. 493), which is about the calculation of the amount due; and in s. 418 (ex s. 494), dealing with the case that the claimant had a pro-

---

David Johnston/Reinhard Zimmermann (eds.), Unjustified Enrichment: Key Issues in Comparative Perspective (2002), 3, esp. 9–14.

[7] *Birks* (n. 4), 4.

[8] It is to be noted that this concept of unjust enrichment does not correspond to the substantive sense (n. 5) of unjust enrichment as it is understood by English writers, as the latter is much narrower and does not include restitution for wrongs (*Birks* (n. 4), 3–38), and perhaps not even the vindication of property rights (*Virgo* (n. 4), 6–17).

prietary right in the asset representing the benefit and that this right was impaired while, at the same time, the defendant has received a substitute in lieu of the original asset. Also, s. 420 (ex s. 496), which lists no less than seven defences against a restitutionary claim, is not inherently linked with unjust enrichment as the underlying principle and cause of action but is equally relevant, for instance, in cases of rescission for mistake, deceit or duress (ss. 110–118, ex ss. 174–182), or rescission for breach of contract (ss. 452–454, ex ss. 528–530)[9]. Thus, ss. 412, 416 to 418 and 420 (ex ss. 488, 492 to 494 and 496) might be thought to form the general law of restitution within the future Israeli Civil Code, governing all kinds of restitutionary claims, but always subject to more specific provisions in other parts of the law, like the modification of s. 416 (ex s. 492) provided for by s. 494(b) (ex s. 570(b)).

As I have already mentioned, this general law of restitution is not to be found in Chapter Five of Subpart Six, which is on the remedy of restitution, but instead in Chapter Two of Subpart Five, which is on the non-voluntary obligation arising from unjust enrichment. The reason for this might be tradition, as the details of restitution–in Israel as well as in other jurisdictions–have most often and most thoroughly been discussed in an unjust enrichment context. Another reason might be that Subpart Six has been explicitly devoted to remedies for breach of an obligation, and it is even more artificial to speak of an obligation not to become unjustly enriched than to speak of an obligation not to commit a tort (cf. s. 445, ex s. 521). Be that as it may, the structure currently adopted by the Draft is rather misleading, and to include the general law of restitution in the subpart on non-voluntary obligations undoes any gains in clarity that might be derived from having a separate subpart on remedies.

Turning from structure to content, I must say that I find the general provisions on the remedy of restitution quite convincing. What is certainly most conspicuous is the vast measure of discretion vested in the courts at three different stages: at the stage of assessing whether it is unreasonable to make restitution in kind, at the stage of calculating the amount due, and at the stage of deciding whether there should be a defence or not. This is certainly a point one might argue about, but I prefer this approach to an approach that *appears* to provide for strict guidelines but has to be modified again and again in order to avoid unacceptable results[10]. As the Draft Civil Code currently stands, one can hardly imagine a situation with which a judge with some common sense might not cope on the basis of ss. 416 to 418 and 420 (ex ss. 492 to 494 and 496).

---

[9] Also the English literature tends to analyse defences that may be available against restitutionary claims at the remedies' level, cf. *William Swadling*, in: William Swadling (ed.), The Limits of Restitutionary Claims: A Comparative Analysis (1997), p. 79–105; *Virgo* (n. 4), 665–757; *Burrows* (n. 3), 509–596.

[10] A perfect example of such an approach is provided by the Draft Principles of a European Law on Unjustified Enrichment, prepared by the Study Group on a European Civil Code (ERA-Forum 2006, 198–203; available also at http://sgecc.net/media/downloads/articles_27.02.06.doc). For a detailed critique see *Christiane Wendehorst*, ERA-Forum 2006, 244–264, esp. 259.

b) Provisions on Deliberate Intervention in Another's Affairs

When pointing out that five out of ten sections ostensibly dedicated to unjust enrichment are really about restitution I did not mean to say that the remaining five sections are substantively about unjust enrichment. Section 415 (ex s. 491) deals with what is commonly called *negotiorum gestio* in continental legal systems and has been the focus of a great deal of terminological creativity in the common law world[11]. It has nothing to do with unjust enrichment as a cause of action, nor, indeed, with restitution as a remedy. The very simple reason why the benevolent intervention in another's affairs in order to preserve his life, physical integrity, health, dignity or property does not create an unjust enrichment is that the enrichment of the beneficiary is not unjust. It is obviously not unjust for the beneficiary to be alive, healthy, and so on. But it is also not unjust for him to have received the "service" of the rescuer's intervention, either because the rescuer acted voluntarily or because he was encouraged or even obliged to provide help to the beneficiary, as is the case in Israel when someone's life, physical integrity or health is in sudden danger[12]. The only promising way to construct rescue cases as unjust enrichment cases is by defining the psychological pressure under which the rescuer was acting as the unjust factor of moral compulsion[13] or necessity[14], but again, this does not really render the enrichment unjust but rather the losses suffered by the rescuer[15]. Therefore, it is only logical that the remedy available to the necessitous intervener is not restitution, but reimbursement of expenses incurred, compensation for damage suffered and perhaps remuneration for services provided (cf. s. 415(a), ex 491(a))[16]. Mixing *negotiorum gestio* up with unjust enrichment is not only confusing cats and dogs, but also reduces intervention in another's affairs to the question of reimbursement and compensation, thus making a coherent codification of the field of intervention including, in particular, duties of the intervener[17], all but impossible.

Things are less clear with payment of another's debt, which is currently dealt with under s. 414 (ex s. 490) of the Draft. On the one hand, to be relieved of an obligation[18] is a benefit obtained by the original debtor which–unlike the integ-

---

[11] *Hanoch Dagan*, The Law and Ethics of Restitution (2006), 86–122 is a treasure trove (also) in this respect; similarly *Hanoch Dagan*, In Defense of the Good Samaritan, (1999) 97 Michigan Law Review 1152.

[12] See the 1998 Law "Thou shalt not stand against the blood of your neighbour", mentioned by *Daniel Friedmann*, The Israeli Law of Restitution and the Draft Codification, in this volume.

[13] *Birks*, Introduction (n. 3), 193–202.

[14] *Virgo* (n. 4), 283–303; *Burrows* (n. 3), 314–322.

[15] Cf. the conclusion drawn by *Burrows* (n. 3), 322.

[16] *Dagan* (n. 11) 112–122, esp. 117, who even pleads for limiting remuneration to the opportunity cost of the intervention.

[17] See, for an example, Study Group on a European Civil Code (ed.), Principles of European Law: Benevolent Intervention in Another's Affairs (PEL Ben. Int.) (2006): only 3 out of 13 articles are about compensation.

[18] For details, see *Daniel Friedman*, Payment of Another's Debt, (1983) 99 Law Quarterly Review 534; *Daniel Friedmann/Nili Cohen*, Payment of Another's Debt, in: International Encyclopae-

rity of his life, health and property – may be regarded as "unjust" in a certain sense as it would have been for him to make payment and as he is better off in the end than he would have been in the normal course of events[19]. Accordingly, most legal systems deal with discharge of another's debt under the heading of unjust enrichment[20]. On the other hand, cases of mistake and compulsion apart, this benefit is not "unjust" exactly *vis-à-vis* the claimant, as she has paid voluntarily and knowing that she was not under an obligation to do so. Therefore, payment of another's debt may also be analysed as a case of *negotiorum gestio* because the payer intervenes in the debtor's affairs, and quite often there will be a clear overlap with the cases covered by s. 415 (ex s. 491) as paying another's debt may serve to save that person's property. Also, the remedy is not restitution in the classic sense as it would not be in the interest of the payer to have discharge of the debt undone even if this was possible, but a specific form of recourse that is limited by both the payer's loss and the defendant's gain (*règle du double plafond*)[21]. This is underpinned by the detailed provisions on the transfer of security interests and guarantees in s. 414 (ex s. 490), which go far beyond restoring the benefit to the payer.

Turning again from classification to content, one must acknowledge that the Draft is less hostile towards meddling with another's affairs than English law[22]. However, it still takes a rather restrictive approach compared with most continental legal systems, as these appear to agree that even bad faith does not hinder compensation of necessary expenses[23]. It is not only a fairness argument, but above all an economic argument that speaks in favour of such minimum compensation, because there should be incentives to preserve any property and thus

---

dia of Comparative Law (vol. X, 1991), ch. 10; *Simon Whittaker*, Performance of another's obligation: French and English law contrasted, in: David Johnston/Reinhard Zimmermann (eds.), Unjustified Enrichment: Key Issues in Comparative Perspective (2002), 433; *Hector L. MacQueen*, Payment of another's debt, in: David Johnston/Reinhard Zimmermann (eds.), Unjustified Enrichment: Key Issues in Comparative Perspective (2002), 458.

[19] Some authors reject the "benefit" analysis and prefer the concept of "unjust sacrifice", especially in cases of payment of another's debt and cases involving services: cf. *Samuel Stoljar*, Unjust Enrichment and Unjust Sacrifice, (1987) 50 Modern Law Review 603; *Garry Muir*, Unjust Sacrifice and the Officious Intervener, in: Paul Finn (ed.), Essays in Restitution (1990), 297; *Jack Beatson*, The Use and Abuse of Unjust Enrichment (1991), 21–44.

[20] For a comparative overview, see *Peter Schlechtriem*, Restitution und Bereicherungsausgleich (vol. II, 2001), 359–392; *Christiane Wendehorst*, Die Leistungskondiktion und ihre Binnenstruktur in rechtsvergleichender Perspektive, in: Reinhard Zimmermann (ed.), Grundstrukturen eines Europäischen Bereicherungsrechts (2005), 47, esp. 100–107, 111–115.

[21] The same holds true where a clear unjust enrichment analysis prevails, as in German law; cf. *Christiane Wendehorst*, Anspruch und Ausgleich (1999), 295–315; *Christiane Wendehorst*, in: Heinz G. Bamberger/Herbert Roth (eds.), Kommentar zum Bürgerlichen Gesetzbuch (vol. 2, 2nd ed. 2007), § 818, no. 3, 140–159.

[22] That holds true, in particular, as far as discharge of another's liability is concerned, where English law arguably allows for restitution only when payment was made under compulsion, *Burrows* (n. 3), 273–293; *Virgo* (n. 4), 187–190.

[23] For a comparative analysis, see *Schlechtriem* (n. 20), 5–52; *Wendehorst* (n. 20), 121, 122.

avoid a waste of resources[24]. Also, the "reasonable grounds" test in s. 414(a) (ex s. 490(a)) leaves the performing party with a great deal of uncertainty as to whether she will be able to seek redress against the debtor or not.

c) The remaining provisions

Section 419 (s. 495) is about the restitution of benefits the defendant has received as a result of the event that had made performance of a pre-existing obligation impossible. Most legal systems would probably prefer to classify this claim as a secondary claim based on the original obligation, in particular in a contractual context[25]. But I agree that, comparative considerations apart, there are no compelling reasons why this situation should not be analysed differently, and the situation recalls the facts of *Adras Ltd. v. Harlow & Jones*[26], where the Israeli Supreme Court constructed the claim of the buyer to the profit the seller had made by selling the goods to third parties as a claim in unjust enrichment. However, as there is a whole subpart in the Draft Code devoted to remedies for breach of an obligation, I would have expected this provision somewhere around s. 494 (ex s. 570), but not here. That leaves only ss. 411 and 413 (ex ss. 487 and 489) for the core of unjust enrichment.

3) Decisions Made and Decisions Avoided

As no more than three or four draft sections within Chapter Two are really about unjust enrichment as a cause of action and, as among these, only ss. 411 and 413 (ex ss. 487 and 489) are on what most legal systems would identify as the core area of unjust enrichment, it will not come as any surprise that these remaining sections hardly address any of the crucial questions that are being discussed so vividly across the civil law and much of the common law world.

To begin with, I want to mention the ambiguity of the Draft when it comes to the issue of "unjust factor" versus "absence of legal basis"[27]. From the wording

---

[24] *Wendehorst* (n. 10), 254.

[25] See, e.g., § 285 BGB (Germany); § 1447 ABGB (Austria); Art. 1302(4), 1303 *Code civil* (France); Art. 1259 *Codice Civile* (Italy); Art. 1186 *Código civil* (Spain). For a comparative analysis, see *Raimund Bollenberger*, Das stellvertretende Commodum: Die Ersatzherausgabe im österreichischen und deutschen Schuldrecht unter Berücksichtigung weiterer Rechtsordnungen (1999).

[26] *Adras Ltd.* v. *Harlow & Jones*, [1994] Restitution Law Review 235. This case is discussed by *Daniel Friedmann*, Restitution of Benefits Gained by Breach of Contract, in: Herbert Hausmaninger, Helmut Koziol et al. (eds.), Developments in Austrian and Israeli Private Law (1999), 93; *Friedmann* (n. 12), *sub* II.

[27] Concerning this choice in general, see *Thomas Krebs*, Restitution at the Crossroads: A Comparative Study (2001). The case for the civilian approach was forcefully put forward by *Sonja Meier/Reinhard Zimmermann*, Judicial Development of the Law, Error Juris and the Law of Unjustified Enrichment, (1999) 115 Law Quarterly Review 556, esp. 560–565; *Sonja Meier*, in: Peter Birks/Francis Rose (eds.), Lessons of the Swaps Litigation (2000), 168; *Sonja Meier*, Unjust factors and

of s. 413 (ex s. 489), one has to conclude that the Draft provides for a combination of both. On the whole, this may even be a wise decision in various respects[28]. Also, separating out the "mistake" test is quite fortunate, because mistake should not be required where a contract is invalid, avoided or rescinded[29]. However, it ought to be made clear that mistake will not trigger restitution when the defendant had a right to receive the benefit[30].

What is more problematic, though, is that the Draft fails to give any hint as to how one should proceed in those notorious three-party relationships[31] in the contractual context, when performance is made to a third party and we have to decide the issue of "leapfrogging" versus "privity principle"[32]. Imagine, for example, the case that B buys a car from C, takes up a loan with A to finance the purchase price and asks A to pay the money directly to C. If the loan contract proves to be invalid, can A seek restitution from B (because the contract was invalid), from C (because A had been acting under mistake) or from any of the two? As the Draft is silent on that point and, at the same time, provides for a very vague definition of "benefit" in s. 411(a) (ex s. 487(a)), restitution will probably lie against all persons involved, with courts having to rule out defendants who deserve protection via a defence, mainly the defence of change of position. This in turn forces plaintiffs to try all potential defendants in court, although only one of them might in effect be liable, which is obviously a waste of resources.

---

legal grounds, in: David Johnston/Reinhard Zimmermann (eds.), Unjustified Enrichment: Key Issues in Comparative Perspective (2002), 37, 67–75. Peter Birks later changed his mind, *Birks* (n. 4), 101–128.

[28] Based on a comparative analysis: *Wendehorst* (n. 20), 139; *Sonja Meier*, No Basis: A Comparative View, in: Andrew Burrows/Alan Rodger (eds.), Mapping the Law: Essays in Memory of Peter Birks (2006), 343, esp. 361.

[29] This, too, finds support in comparative law, as even where the unwinding of contracts is effectuated via *condictio indebiti*, legal systems tend to neglect the requirement of mistake, or fall back on the *condictio causa data causa non secuta*; for details see *Wendehorst* (n. 20), 74; *Wendehorst* (n. 10), 246. Compare also Article 4:115 PECL and Article 3:17 PICC, which give a claim to full restitution even to a party who is guilty of fraud or duress.

[30] This is also the situation under English law: *Kleinwort Benson Ltd.* v. *Lincoln City Council* [1999] 2 A. C. 349, 407–408 (Lord Hope).

[31] The "most notoriously difficult of all enrichment constellations": *Reinhard Zimmermann*, The Law of Obligations: Roman Foundations of the Civilian Tradition (1996), 874.

[32] For details, see *Birks* (n. 4), 89–98; *Virgo* (n. 4), 105–112; and in particular *Dagan* (n. 11), 289–296. For a comparative overview, see *Sonja Meier*, Mistaken Payments in Three-party Situations: A German View of English Law, (1999) 58 Cambridge Law Journal 567; *Daniel Visser*, Searches for silver bullets: enrichment in three-party situations, in: David Johnston/Reinhard Zimmermann (eds.), Unjustified Enrichment: Key Issues in Comparative Perspective (2002), 526. However, the issue seems to be a concern mainly of jurists from the Germanic tradition, where there is abundant literature on the subject; see, e.g., for Germany: *Claus-Wilhelm Canaris*, Der Bereicherungsausgleich im Dreipersonenverhältnis, Festschrift für Karl Larenz zum 70. Geburtstag (1973), 799; *Wendehorst* (n. 21), § 812 nos. 165–271; for Austria: *Karl Spielbüchler*, Der Dritte im Schuldverhältnis (1973); *Helmut Koziol*, Bankgeschäft und Anweisung, [1977] Juristische Blätter 617; for Switzerland: *Natalie Voser*, Bereicherungsansprüche in Dreiecksverhältnissen (2006).

The most surprising inaccuracy, however, lies in the fact that committing an unlawful act towards the benefactor is mentioned as a ground of restitution in s. 413 (ex s. 489). This formulation leaves open whether restitution will be awarded only for breach of statutory duties or also for breach of contract, and equally whether every kind of tort or unlawful conduct may trigger a restitutionary claim or whether such claims are restricted to the infringement of property rights and similar entitlements. Needless to say, it also leaves open how to deal with three-party relationships, as in the standard textbook case of B misappropriating bricks that belong to A and installing them on C's building site.

4) Conclusion

The solution adopted by the drafters of the current proposal for a new Israeli Civil Code is innovative in many respects, but hardly stands up to close scrutiny as far as the chapter on unjust enrichment is concerned. Half of the sections in this chapter (ss. 412, 416 to 418, 420, corresponding to ex ss. 488, 492 to 494, 496) are about the remedy of restitution in general and thus should be included in the subpart on remedies, containing as this subpart does a separate chapter on restitution which is almost entirely lacking in content. Section 415 (ex s. 491) is neither about unjust enrichment nor about restitution, but about something entirely different which civil law countries like to call *negotiorum gestio*. Section 414 (ex s. 490) oscillates somewhat between *negotiorum gestio* and unjust enrichment, as does s. 419 (ex s. 495) between unjust enrichment and contract law. In the end, only ss. 411 and 413 (ex ss. 487 and 489) are left for the core area of unjust enrichment. They are rather well drafted as such, but address few of the more intricate questions involved.

II. Why We Might Not Need a Chapter on Unjust Enrichment At All

So far, I have argued that there is currently not much unjust enrichment in the chapter on unjust enrichment, firstly because only few sections really deal with unjust enrichment as a cause of action, and secondly because these sections fail to address the most crucial issues which are making restitution lawyers worldwide tick. But I am not going to contend that the answer must be to develop those brief and broad outlines into a full-fledged body of law within the new Civil Code. Quite the contrary, the sparseness of the current draft–like, by the way, the sparseness of almost any civil law codification–when it comes to unjust enrichment may be indicative of a deeper problem, and the unanimity among codifications of civil law on the existence of this category may prevent us from asking the pivotal question: do we need unjust enrichment as a source of obligations and do we need a separate chapter in a code dealing with it? Until recently

I thought we did, and I have said so in various contexts[33]. Today I assert rather that we do not[34]. Instead, I assert that, at least for the purpose of codification, we should prefer a split approach, dealing separately with restitution arising in five different contexts: (1) contracts that have failed (including the *datio ob rem* cases), (2) other cases of performance to an alleged creditor or to a third party, (3) intervention in another's affairs (including improvement of another's property and discharge of another's debt), (4) infringement on the claimant's rights, and (5) breach of contract. Despite having been much of a restitution lawyer during my career, when it comes to drafting a new Civil Code, I am surprised to find my argumentation not dissimilar to that of Steve Hedley, probably the fiercest unjust enrichment sceptic[35].

1) First Doubts: A Very High Level of Abstraction

Already at first sight, the existence of a category of unjustified enrichment appears surprising as there is no equivalent category of unjustified loss or disadvantage. The law of obligations as a whole is about gains and losses that are either unjustified from the outset or become unjustified at a later stage. Creating a category of unjustified loss would mean choosing too high a level of abstraction including as it would, for example, losses sustained through breach of contract or breach of pre-contractual duties as well as personal injury or even expenses that have been incurred. Why then should there be a category of unjust or unjustified enrichment?

2) The Gain in Coherence

For there to be a satisfactory answer to this question, the codificatory category of unjust enrichment must pass at least what I like to call the "gain in coherence" test, that is, by grouping together in one chapter the different categories of cases that I have outlined above, the Israeli legislator must add some (local[36]) coherence to the Civil Code. As the idea of coherence may have been somewhat overworked during the past decades and as there appears to be a lack of sufficiently concrete definitions of what coherence really means, I am going to introduce five criteria for evaluating whether and to what extent creating a particular

---

[33] Cf., in particular, *Wendehorst* (n. 20), 96, 138.

[34] *Wendehorst* (n. 10), 260–263.

[35] See, e.g., *Steve Hedley*, Unjust Enrichment as the Basis of Restitution – An Overworked Concept, (1985) 5 Legal Studies 56; *Steve Hedley*, Unjust Enrichment, [1995] Cambridge Law Journal 578; *Steve Hedley*, Restitution: Its Division and Ordering (2001); *Steve Hedley*, A Critical Introduction to Restitution (2001).

[36] For the concept of local versus global coherence see *Hanoch Dagan*, Codification, Coherence, and Priority Conflicts, in this volume, *sub* II. 2).

category would enhance coherence of the law: common underlying principles, congruence of rules, factual connection, the need for consistency, demarcation problems, and the need for a default regime.

a) Underlying Principles

The first and foremost criterion for judging whether or not a codificatory category makes sense is the existence of a unifying justificatory principle or set of principles. As far as the field which I have sketched out above is concerned, a fierce debate has been raging for over a century on whether and, if so, to what extent the resulting claims may be explained by one, single principle of unjust enrichment or at least one generic meta-principle under which a range of sub-principles may be subsumed[37]. At the end of the day, almost everyone will agree that, by moving to a sufficiently high level of abstraction, a common principle of some kind can be found, be it expressed in the famous words of *neminem cum alterius detrimento et iniuria fieri locupletiorem* formulated by Pomponius[38], or in a different, more concrete set of elements.

b) Congruence of Rules

However, a second and at least equally important criterion is a sufficient degree of congruence at the level of rules, i.e. the factual situations covered and the doctrinal patterns that have been developed to cope with these situations in legal terms must share a sufficient number of features or attributes to allow for a sufficiently high proportion of common rules and concepts within the envisaged codification. It is of prime importance that the common rules and concepts would be specific and concrete enough to provide real guidance to the judge as to how to decide a case, although, as we all know, there cannot be absolute certainty and no codification in the world will ever be without gaps and ambiguities. The more commonalities there are between the elements and the more these elements may be submitted to uniform rules, the more a separate category will enhance clarity and simplicity of the law.

At first sight, unjust enrichment appears to fulfil the criterion of congruence to a considerable degree as there are many codifications and treatises that obviously deal with the subject matter under very few and uniform headings such as "benefit", "at the claimant's expense" and "without legal ground" or "unjust". Upon a closer look, however, we realise that these concepts are much too abstract to be of any real help when it comes to solving cases. Therefore, in all the

---

[37] To look more closely at this debate would be far beyond the ambit of my paper. For details, see to the comprehensive analysis by *Frank L. Schäfer*, Das Bereicherungsrecht in Europa: Einheits- und Trennungslehren im gemeinen, deutschen und englischen Recht (2001).

[38] D. 50, 17, 206, Pomp. 9 *ex variis lectionibus*.

jurisdictions with which I am familiar, the subject breaks up into different lines of cases and corresponding sub-concepts.

In the end, it turns out that the different lines of cases do not have much in common except for the fact that the defendant has received a benefit. But that, with respect, is already a precondition for the claimant seeking a restitutionary remedy. Also, they share a set of common defences, in particular the defence of change of position, or its functional counterparts. But again, that has more to do with the remedy of restitution than with unjust enrichment[39]. Apart from that, there are no commonalities: in cases of unwinding of contracts the only further requirement – English law apart – is that the contract has failed, even when there is no mistake[40], and this seems also to be the Israeli approach. In other cases of performance, there is usually some combination of absence of legal ground and an additional factor such as mistake, fraud or duress, with the different legal systems putting different emphasis on each of the two elements[41]. Where someone has benefited another in ways other than by performance, most legal systems differentiate between cases where the benefactor was herself a debtor, for example where she had improved property she has had to return to the beneficiary, and other cases. Within these two categories, legal systems tend to look at the degree of legitimacy with which the claimant was acting, in particular, at whether she was acting in good faith or with a motivation that may be approved of and/or whether she was taking steps that were necessary or at least reasonable[42], and although there is a certain tradition in the common law to equate the "good faith" test with the "mistake" test[43], this equation seems rather artificial. Where it was the defendant himself who has unilaterally caused the enrichment, legal systems tend to ask whether the defendant has committed an unlawful act towards the claimant and/or infringed upon the claimant's rights, especially property rights[44]. And in cases of breach of contract, the claimant has to establish breach and probably some further requirements[45].

Accordingly, the view that the claims dealt with in Subpart Five, Chapter Two of the current draft of an Israeli Civil Code have many elements in com-

---

[39] See n. 9 above.

[40] See n. 29 above.

[41] For a detailed analysis, see *Wendehorst* (n. 20), 94–95.

[42] *Wendehorst* (n. 20), 116–126. For questions of calculation, see *Dirk A. Verse*, Improvements and Enrichment: A Comparative Analysis, [1998] Restitution Law Review 85; *Andrew Kull*, Mistaken improvements and the restitution calculus, in: David Johnston/Reinhard Zimmermann (eds.), Unjustified Enrichment: Key Issues in Comparative Perspective (2002), 369, esp. 383; *James Wolffe*, Enrichment by improvements in Scots law, in: David Johnston/Reinhard Zimmermann (eds.), Unjustified Enrichment: Key Issues in Comparative Perspective (2002), 384.

[43] *Greenwood* v *Bennett* [1973] Q.B. 195; *Virgo* (n. 4), 158.

[44] For a comparative analysis, see *Thomas Krebs*, Eingriffskondiktion und Restitution for Wrongs im englischen Recht, in: Reinhard Zimmermann (ed.), Grundstrukturen eines europäischen Bereicherungsrechts (2005), 141.

[45] For what those requirements might be see, e.g., *Attorney General* v. *Blake* [2001] 1 A.C. 268, 285 (Lord Nicholls).

mon does not stand up to close scrutiny. What they, or at least most of them, do have in common is that they trigger a restitutionary remedy, i.e. a remedy that is based on the defendant's gain. But this, as I have repeatedly pointed out, is a question of restitution, not of unjust enrichment.

c) Factual Connection

The third criterion for deciding whether or not to have a separate codificatory unit is factual connection, i.e. the probability that, in a given case, two or even more of the elements that might or might not be grouped in one codificatory unit come into play. In order to enhance the comprehensibility of the law and to reduce the risk of mistakes by anyone who wants to apply it, a code should try to unite in one chapter as many as possible of the rules that become relevant in the same typical factual setting[46]. Often, but not necessarily so, this criterion runs against the criterion of congruence, as the latter tends to strive for higher levels of abstraction, whereas factual connection usually serves as an argument for being more concrete.

It is quite obvious that the five different contexts which I have sketched out above correspond to five different typical factual settings and tend to exclude each other rather than be relevant in one and the same case. Therefore, the criterion of factual connection does not serve as an argument for having a chapter on unjust enrichment either.

d) Need for Consistency

A fourth, but certainly no less important criterion is the need for consistency. In fact, this criterion is very closely linked with both congruence and factual connection. But whereas the criterion of congruence is about how many common rules are possible for the sake of simplicity and clarity, the criterion of consistency asks to what extent divergent decisions would be harmful because like cases would not be treated alike. And whereas the criterion of factual connection is about whether the issues in question are apt to arise consecutively in one and the same typical case, the criterion of consistency asks whether a decision concerning one of the issues predetermines in any way the decision to be taken concerning another issue.

---

[46] § 816 I, first sentence, BGB may serve as an example of where this criterion has been disregarded: the provision gives the (previous) owner of an asset a claim for restitution of the purchase price which the defendant, who had transferred title to the asset to a third party without being authorised to do so, has received. The factual setting usually requires application of the rules on *bona-fide* acquisition (§§ 929–935 BGB for movables, and §§ 873, 925, 892 BGB for immovable property) and very often also of the rules on the legal relationship between owner and possessor (§§ 985–1003 BGB), and § 816 I is a missing link in both contexts. Nevertheless, the legislator has preferred to place § 816 within the chapter on unjust enrichment.

However, as there are no significant commonalities between the five lines of cases, as far as the elements of a claim are concerned, and as there is clearly no factual connection between them, it is hard to see why there should be much need for consistency, i.e. for a degree of consistency that exceeds the degree which is generally desirable within a legal system. There is an eminent need for consistency in the field of restitution as a remedy, for sure, but not so much in the field of unjust enrichment as a source of obligations.

e) Demarcation Problems

A standard argument that is put forward in favour of creating a specific legislative category, and thus of grouping certain legal issues together in one chapter instead of dealing with them separately, is the difficulty of drawing a clear demarcation line between the issues. Of course, to unite two or more legal concepts or institutions in one codificatory unit does not really release us from the need to differentiate between them, as long as they are not merged into one concept or institution. But it certainly makes irresolution and misclassifications less conspicuous and less momentous than they would be if the concepts or institutions were dealt with in separate chapters of the law.

The demarcation argument is hardly ever a strong argument because there will be borderline cases and hard cases in whatever categorisation we choose[47]. Also in the context of unjust enrichment, the argument does not carry very far because, even though there is some overlap between the five categories of cases, nothing is to be said against an alternative analysis[48].

f) Need for a Default Regime

Last but not least, I want to mention the flexibility, or "miscellaneous cases", argument, i.e. the argument that, first, several concepts, institutions or principles may be subsumed under one generic concept, institution or principle, and that, secondly, it is impossible to divide them up and deal with them in different chapters of the law because any division would not be exhaustive, and there would always be cases that do not fall into any of the potential subcategories but only under the generic category.

It has become commonplace to assert that the law must be prepared for situations where there is a need for restitution but which no one had ever thought of before they arose, or, similarly, that any list of types of enrichment cannot be exhaustive and that there must always be this rubric of "miscellaneous" or "innominate" cases. That argument is no doubt a strong one. But does a general law of unjust enrichment really provide substantial help in deciding such cases? The answer must be no. The only help it can provide is to offer a catalogue of stand-

---

[47] *Birks* (n. 4), 10.

[48] *Birks*, Introduction (n. 3), 44; *Virgo* (n. 4), 428–429.

ard situations where restitution will follow, enabling one to compare the situation at hand with the standard situation within the catalogue that is most akin to it. But that would also be possible if restitution was dealt with in the context of the factual matrix in which the enrichment arose, and as far as the law provides for sufficient flexibility there, a new situation will not pose insurmountable problems.

3) The Opportunity Loss in Terms of Coherence

In my view, the above analysis has shown that there is some, but not much, gain in coherence to be made through having a separate chapter on unjust enrichment. This alone should not prevent us from talking about a category of unjust enrichment which, after all, finds support in the legislative and doctrinal tradition all over the world. Also there is undoubtedly a common set of remedies and defences and of common justificatory principles, though on a very high level of abstraction. I am thus not opposing unjust enrichment as a loose framework[49]. However, talking and writing treatises about a field of law is one thing, but drafting a civil code is another. When structuring a new codification of civil law, a legislator must not only consider the gains in coherence that may be derived by choosing one particular structure, but has to bear in mind also the opportunity loss in coherence he suffers by not choosing a better alternative[50].

So, the point I want to make is that the need for coherence (1) within the field of contracts in general and their unwinding, (2) within a field of performance and discharge of debt in general and what happens if they fail, (3) within a field of intervention in another's affairs in general and reimbursement for expenses, (4) within a field of infringement of rights and other unlawful acts in general and the remedies that are available, and (5) within a field of remedies for breach of contract, including disgorgement of profits, is much stronger than a need for coherence within unjust enrichment. I will address these areas one by one, though in a slightly different order, as the hardest cases will prove to be (2) and (3).

a) Unwinding of Contracts

As far as the unwinding of contracts is concerned, my argument finds support in a line of comparative research that has been conducted during the past five years[51]. If a contract has failed according to the governing law of contract, in

[49] *Dagan* (n. 11), 26.

[50] Compare *Hedley*, Overworked Concept (n. 35), 224.

[51] *Phillip Hellwege*, Die Rückabwicklung gegenseitiger Verträge als einheitliches Problem (2004); *Wendehorst* (n. 20), 80, 83, 139; *Reinhard Zimmermann*, Restitutio in integrum, in: Privatrecht und Methode: Festschrift für Ernst A. Kramer (2004), 735; *Reinhard Zimmermann*, Restitutio in Integrum: The Unwinding of Failed Contracts under the Principles of European Contract

particular if it is invalid or has been avoided or otherwise terminated by one of the parties,[52] this should usually suffice to trigger restitution of the benefits of any performance that has been made, and it is contract law alone that must decide in the end on when exactly and to what extent this is the case. Thus, the criteria of congruence, of factual connection and of the need for consistency are fulfilled in the most perfect way conceivable.

b) Restitutionary Remedies for Breach of Contract

Concerning restitution as a remedy for breach of contract, like in *Adras Ltd. v. Harlow & Jones*[53] or in the English leading case of *Attorney General* v. *Blake*[54], the elements of the claim obviously have very much in common with the elements, for instance, of a claim for damages or for specific performance: in each of the cases the plaintiff has to establish that there is a contract, that the defendant had a specific duty under the contract and that this duty was breached. Similarly, the factual connection between restitutionary remedies and other remedies is self-evident. Last but not least, there is an eminent need for consistency within the field as the law ought to make sure that the response to a breach is proportionate to the gravity of the breach, in particular to the extent to which the claimant was deprived of his contractual rights and to the degree to which the defendant was at fault[55].

c) Restitution in the Context of Wrongs

The situation is very similar with restitution in the context of wrongs. Of course, the kinds of wrong that trigger a restitutionary remedy need not always coincide with the wrongs that trigger a compensatory remedy[56], in particular as far as the requirement of fault is concerned[57], but the elements that have to be

Law, the UNIDROIT Principles and the Avant-projet d'un Code Européen des Contrats, [2005] Uniform Law Review/Revue de Droit Uniforme 719.

[52] For a detailed comparative analysis, see *Izhak Englard*, Restitution of Benefits Conferred Without Obligation, in: International Encyclopaedia of Comparative Law (vol. X, 1991), ch. 5, nos. 64–199.

[53] See *supra*, n. 26.

[54] *Attorney General* v. *Blake* [2001] 1 A.C. 268.

[55] This is also reflected in the PECL: where non-performance is excused, performance and damages are not available (Art. 8:101(2)); where non-performance is not fundamental, termination is not available (Art. 9:301); otherwise, the full range of remedies is available (Art. 8:101(1)). Under the Principles that are being prepared by the Study Group (n. 10) on the basis of PECL, also disgorgement of profits will probably be available, provided further requirements are met.

[56] This argument has been put forward quite vigorously by *Daniel Friedmann*, Restitution of Benefits Obtained Through the Appropriation of Property or the Commission of a Wrong, (1980) 80 Columbia Law Review 504; *Daniel Friedmann*, Restitution for Wrongs: The Basis of Liability, in: William P. Cornish et al. (eds.), Restitution: Past, Present and Future (1998), 133. Cf. also *Beatson* (n. 19), 206ff.

[57] On the role of fault, see *Graham Virgo*, The Role of Fault in the Law of Restitution, in: An-

met will overlap to a considerable extent. Besides, there is certainly a strong factual connection, and also an imminent need for consistency as the law must again provide for a range of remedies that are proportionate to the gravity of the wrong committed[58].

d) Intervention in Another's Affairs

Things are more difficult with benefits that are conferred upon another without his consent. Paradigm cases are the improvement of another's property and the voluntary discharge of another's debt, but there are also many other relevant constellations. At the end of the day, I believe that much is to be said in favour of having a rather broad category of intervention in another's affairs[59] with general provisions on reimbursement for expenses, which should include a graduated scheme of mainly compensatory relief. The major advantage of such an approach would be that reimbursement might be attuned to the intervener's duties and a possible breach of these duties. However, the general provisions must be accompanied by more specific rules in more specific contexts. In particular, the question of recourse after payment of another's debt should be dealt with in the context of the rules that govern the discharge of debts and the possibility of performance by third parties in general, because of the strong functional nexus and the resulting need for consistency.

e) The Core Case: Mistaken Payments

That leaves all those cases of mistaken payment or other kinds of performance, like paying twice, paying too much, paying to the wrong person or otherwise paying in the mistaken belief that there is an obligation to do so. The rather rare cases of payment made due to duress or extortion fall into the same category. It is what Peter Birks has called the core case of unjust enrichment[60], and until recently, I also believed that we need unjust enrichment for this line of cases, as restitution appears not to follow from any other recognised principle and not to fit into any other legislative context[61].

But I had underestimated the genuine force of the principles underlying the law of performance, which would be Subpart One in the Draft or Chapter 7 of

drew Burrows/Alan Rodger (eds.), Mapping the Law: Essays in Memory of Peter Birks (2006), 83.

[58] For a (certainly not universally accepted) model, see *James Edelman*, Gain-Based Damages (2002).

[59] The concept should be broader than that adopted by the PEL Ben. Int. (n. 17), which only apply where the intervener had "a reasonable ground for acting", where the beneficiary approves of the act, or where intervention is in the public interest (Articles 1:101–102). There is no reason why the provisions on duties of the intervener, on damages, etc. should not apply in cases, where the intervener was acting officiously.

[60] *Birks* (n. 4), 3.

[61] *Wendehorst* (n. 20), 96.

the Principles of European Contract Law. I had always considered this area of the law as being rather technical, dealing with claims and obligations but not giving rise to them. However, what happens in the core cases is that someone renders performance but performance essentially fails, i.e. there is no discharge of an obligation, either for want of an obligation, or for want of the obligor's or the obligee's consent, or for want of the performing party's free will. Is it not only natural that a legal action that essentially failed should be undone? And do we really need a principle against unjust enrichment to tell us precisely that, or does it not follow from exactly the same body of law that previously denied discharge of an obligation? I believe that failure of performance is as much an event apt to trigger a remedy as is failure of a contract: something has gone wrong, and what has gone wrong must be reversed.

Even if we do not accept what I have just contended and insist instead on the requirement of a principle against unjust enrichment, it does not follow that this principle and the corresponding rules should be laid down in a separate chapter of a civil code. Rather, the criteria of factual connection and of the need for consistency militate in favour of placing the rules on reversal of a mistaken performance near the rules on performance and discharge of debt in general because it would be unfortunate to grant restitution of a performance that successfully discharged an existing obligation, and vice versa[62].

4) Conclusion

My conclusion from the aforesaid is the following: We need restitution as a remedy, just as we need the remedies of compensational damages, of specific performance, and so on. And, particularly in the case of the Israeli Draft Civil Code which already has a separate subpart on remedies, we should maintain a separate chapter within this subpart which is devoted to restitution and contains roughly what is so far laid down in ss. 412, 416 to 418 and 420 of the present draft (ss. 488, 492 to 494 and 496 of the previous draft). But we do not need a chapter on unjust enrichment as a source of obligations, because this causes a clear opportunity loss in terms of coherence, and thus does not serve but rather undermines the coherence of a civil code.

III. Why All This Is of Limited Importance

Up to this point, I have criticised the Draft in most respects concerning restitution and unjust enrichment, and I have even gone so far as to question the very

---

[62] This statement finds support in comparative research, as most legal systems seem to link the question of restitution to the question of discharge, although there are some exceptions. For details, see *Wendehorst* (n. 20), 91–92, 95, 102–107.

existence of a chapter on unjust enrichment in the proposed Israeli Civil Code. So do disaster and the imminent demise of the whole subject loom on the horizon, should this proposal enter into force? Am I going to call for a thorough revision of the Draft? Certainly not.

As we have learnt from Professor Friedmann and as we know from our experience with the Israeli legal system, restitution in Israel is full of vitality and has always been way ahead of its English parent, be it with regard to mistake of law, restitution for breach of contract, or the defence of change of position. Israel has an excellent judiciary with remarkable comparative knowledge and a good deal of common sense. The solutions adopted by the Draft may not be the most convincing or most elegant solutions one can possibly think of. But there is a widespread conviction that the Draft is more or less a restatement of the law as it stands today, and today's law of unjust enrichment and restitution is working well. There is the old adage: "never change a winning team", which computer people have turned into "never change a running system"; and if we apply this to the field of private law, my only response can be: go ahead!

The Israeli Draft Civil Code: Changes in Tort Law

By Izhak Englard

Summary of Contents

I. A Historical Note

More than thirty years ago, I published a critical analysis of the law of torts in Israel, seen from a comparative viewpoint as a common law codification in a mixed legal system[1]. The original, mandatory Civil Wrongs Ordinance 1944–1947 – that came into effect a few months before the establishment of the State of Israel in 1948 – was not a codification on the pattern of Continental Europe. It was intended by the British Mandatory Legislature as an embodiment of the English common law of torts in statutory form in order to facilitate its introduction into the law of Palestine. It was conceived to be a kind of restatement which did not venture to do away entirely with the prior sources. The draftsmen of the Ordinance considered the statutory nature of their work to be a convenient vehicle for simplifying the common law and accommodating it to local conditions. But they clearly intended to maintain the connection of the local Ordinance to its fountainhead. As a matter of fact, the courts regularly resorted to English law in interpreting the Ordinance. This was inevitable, since the significance of many provisions could only be elicited by having resort to the English precedents that served the draftsmen of the Ordinance in establishing the statutory wording.

The predominant influence of English law upon the Israeli legal system caused considerable misgivings in a number of legal and political circles. On the initia-

---

[1] *Izhak Englard*, The Law of Torts in Israel: The Problems of Common Law Codification in a Mixed Legal System, (1974) 22 American Journal of Comparative Law 302ff.

tive of the Ministry of Justice, a series of Laws in the area of private law were enacted, with the aim to constitute the basis of an independent Israeli Civil Code. Many of these laws are clearly inspired by continental European sources. The present Draft Civil Code is, indeed, the result of the longstanding endeavor to create an independent, comprehensive, self-sufficient, private law codification in the style of continental European codifications. In comparison to the English common law, this means a more abstract and systematic legal framework aimed at coordinating the substantive provisions. The question remains, of course, to what extent such a codificatory endeavor may be able to change the basic mental approach of lawyers and judges, trained in the typical common law style of pragmatic case-to-case reasoning. I have my doubts in this respect, since historical experience shows that in cases of codifications – both in mixed jurisdictions and in common law systems – jurists continue to adhere to the common law style of adjudication, avoiding the more categorical, axiomatic thinking of codified civil law jurisdictions[2].

In my paper I will concentrate on specific changes in the existing Israeli tort law as suggested by the newly proposed Draft Civil Code. However, it has to be noted that the original Civil Wrongs Ordinance – of which a binding new version in Hebrew was enacted in 1968 – underwent some important, substantive and legislative changes by means of direct amendments as well as by separate laws. Mention must be made of the recent amendment introducing a new regime of personal immunity of public employees[3], a major reform that was actually instituted as a result of a draft proposal elaborated by the Civil Code Commission.

The suggested changes by the Draft Civil Code are of different types. I will disregard the manifold purely verbal, or stylistic changes that do not have a substantive significance. A first category of changes are those that integrate judicially established interpretations of provisions, as well as solutions laid down by judicial lawmaking. A second category is the counterpart of the former: changes made in order to alter rules laid down by judicial precedents. These latter changes are relatively rare. A third category contains changes that eliminate obsolete or redundant provisions.

---

[2] *Daniel Friedmann*, Codification of Civil Law in Israel, (1979) 2 The Jewish Law Annual 88, 104–105: "The effect of a code on the legal system depends both on the nature of the code and upon the conditions obtaining in the country in which it is introduced. In some cases the effect may be profound, in others far more moderate. In the case of Israel it seems unlikely that the introduction of codified legislation will transform the legal system into a civil law system. Neither it is likely to change the status of the courts, nor the position which case law occupies in Israeli law." Cf. generally also *John Fleming*, The Restatements and Codification, (1979) 2 The Jewish Law Annual 108, 118–121; *Izhak Englard, Li v. Yellow Cab Co.* – A Belated and Inglorious Centennial of the California Civil Code, (1977) 65 California Law Review 4ff.

[3] Civil Wrongs Ordinance Amendment Law (Nr. 10).

II. General Rules on Obligations

I will concentrate on the more fundamental changes, and especially those that indicate a shift from the traditional common law structures of tort liability to a more abstract, co-ordinated system of liability that fits a codification. Thus, a variety of liability rules that traditionally were specific to tort law, have been transferred to the chapter on remedies within the framework of obligations, contractual and others. As a matter of fact, the very general notion of "obligation" constitutes a departure from the traditional conceptual framework of the common law. As a result, the provisions relating to damages, joint tortfeasors, and contributory negligence have been transferred to the chapter dealing with the general principles of remedies following the violation of obligations. The unification of these rules under the general heading of "obligation" has abolished some differences between tort and contract liability that were idiosyncratic to the common law tradition[4]. Moreover, the Draft Civil Code introduces a number of innovations into the general law of damages: the possibility of paying the compensation for personal injury by way of rent[5]; a limited right of compensation for bereavement[6] as well as detailed rules for the compensation of proprietary damages[7]. In this connection, mention must be made of two important provisions that have been introduced into the general chapter of remedies. They concern the vexing problem of compensation for the "lost years" of a person wrongfully injured by the defendant. The Supreme of Israel recently changed the judicial rule laid down decades ago in tort law that had denied the victim – whose life expectancy had been shortened by the wrongful behavior – of any compensation for the income he could have earned during the lost years[8]. The new rule created a number of difficult problems of application, including problems of monetary assessment, that required further clarifications by the Supreme Court[9]. In the Draft Civil Code, the drafters propose two alternative rules in

[4] Concerning, for example, the rules on the extent of damages to be compensated. The proposed unification of contractual and tortious rules on damages provoked a scholarly discussion: *H. Dagan*, The Risks of Codification: On Over-Coherence and Multiplicity of Remedies, (2006) 36 Mishpatim 249 (in Hebrew); *Y. Adar*, Why Unify Tort and Contract Remedies? A Reply to Professor Dagan, (2006) 36 Mishpatim 357 (in Hebrew).

[5] Sections 474–480 of the Draft Civil Code. The possibility of assessing damages by way of rent had been previously established in the framework of the Traffic Accident Victim Compensation Law of 1975.

[6] See s. 473 of the Draft Civil Code.

[7] See ss. 486–487 of the Draft Civil Code.

[8] C. A. 140/00, 550/01 *The Estate of Michael Etinger and Others v The Company for Restoration and Development of the Jewish Quarter in the Ancient City of Jerusalem and Others* (2004) 58(4) P. D. 486. This judgment, which overruled the precedent laid down in C. A. 295/81 *Sharon Gavriel v. Gavriel* (1982) 36(4) P. D. 533, was handed down on 15. 3. 2004.

[9] L. C. A. 8925/04 *Solel Bone Building and Infrastructure Ltd and Arieh Insurance Ltd v The Estate of Ahman Abed AlHamid and Others* (not yet published; retrospective application of the new rule); C. A. 8022/00 *Orly Raz and Others v Talia Tzuer and Others*, 8156/00 *Menora Insurance Ltd v Orly Raz and Others* (not yet published; rule applicable to traffic accident victim compensation); C. A. 10990/05

ss. 469 and 470: the first alternative maintains the new judicial rule recognising the victim's basic right to compensation for the income of the lost years; s. 469 merely adds the (assessment) principle that the expenses, which the victim would have incurred in the future, have to be deducted from the compensation. The second alternative changes the new judicial rule by limiting it to the pecuniary interest of the victim's dependants. In case of the victim's death, the estate has no right to compensation relating to the income of the lost years; the only rights are those of the deceased person's dependants[10].

III. Nominate Torts v. General Principle

Another major change concerns the specific common law tradition of nominate torts, as distinguished from a general principle of tort liability. As a matter of fact, the Mandatory legislator expressly stated in an explanatory note to the Ordinance that it does not incorporate a general principle of tortious liability, but a series of defined tortious acts. However, the recognition of a general duty of care in the (nominate) tort of negligence created a wrong that, because of its high level of abstraction, was very close, if not identical, to a general principle of liability[11]. The tendency of the Israeli courts was to give the tort of negligence a broad application, thus transforming it practically into a general principle of liability. In this spirit, the courts decided that the abstract wording of the relevant section in the Ordinance included intentional acts as well as negligent ones. As a result, difficult problems of co-ordination were created in respect of express nominate torts that required a particular, more limited, mental state, such as willfulness or intention or special knowledge, or required some other limiting conditions. A good example is presented by the tort of fraud[12]. It requires that the false representation be made with the intent to mislead. In the case of a false representation to obtain credit, money or goods, the Ordinance requires the further condition of a document signed by the defendant. The problem now is whether, for example, a false representation relating to credit which is made negligently and not in a signed document can nevertheless be actionable under the tort of negligence. This would mean that all the more restricted nominate torts – which, besides fraud, include also injurious falsehood and malicious prosecution – lose their independent existence and functional importance, since all their specific limiting conditions can be circumvented by a reliance on the tort of negligence. The tendency of the courts was to admit, in principle, the broad application of negligence. A similar problem was created in relation to vicarious

---

David Fintz v Harel Insurance Ltd, 11214/05 *Harel Insurance Ltd v David Fintz* (not yet published; method of assessment).

[10] See ss. 470 (1st alternative), 471 of the Draft Civil Code.

[11] See ss. 35, 36 of the Civil Wrongs Ordinance [New Version].

[12] See ss. 56, 57 of the Civil Wrongs Ordinance.

liability. In some torts – assault, false imprisonment, and malicious prosecution – the master or principal is not liable for the act of his servant or agent, unless he authorised or ratified the act[13]. Can the victim avoid this restriction by assimilating the act into negligence, where vicarious liability prevails?

In the Draft Civil Code almost all these questions have been resolved by some substantial changes. First and foremost, the traditional civil wrongs of fraud, injurious falsehood, passing off and malicious prosecution have been completely removed. The assumption is that these wrongs are covered by the general torts, i.e. negligence and breach of statutory duty. Equally, the "authorisation/ratification" restriction in the above form of vicarious liability has been removed. Two of the remaining nominate torts, which under the Draft Civil Code require the specific state of mind of knowledge, i.e. assault and false imprisonment[14], have been retained, subject to particular defenses. Nevertheless, there is no doubt that a negligent violation of bodily integrity or of personal freedom entails liability under the general tort of negligence. The third remaining tort, "knowingly causing breach of obligation", constitutes a special case that will be dealt with later in this paper.

IV. Property Torts

Important changes have been introduced in relation to the so-called proprietary torts. Here, according to the common law tradition, tort liability has a dual task: compensation for wrongful damage and enforcement of the proprietary right itself. The right is a function of, and co-extensive with, the remedy and is defined through its scope of protection: *ubi remedium ibi ius*. In other words, the existence of the proprietary right is to be inferred indirectly from the tortious protection it is given against invasion. A result of this dual function was that tort liability, as protection of the right itself, did not require real damage to have been incurred. It was actionable *per se*. Hence, the owner or possessor of the property was entitled to an injunction, based on the tortious liability of the defendant, even where the violation of the proprietary right did not involve any damage. However, Israel has separate laws that deal with ownership and possession in the Continental European way, namely by express and immediate recognition of these proprietary rights and by a concomitant protection of them by means of real actions (*rei vindicatio* and *actio negatoria*)[15] that are not based on tort liability.

---

13 See ss. 25, 28, 61 of the Civil Wrongs Ordinance.

14 See ss. 389–390, 391–392 of the Draft Civil Code. Under the Civil Wrongs Ordinance, assault consists of "intentionally applying force". False imprisonment, on the other hand, does not require a specific state of mind and thus constitutes a case of strict liability; the Civil Code, therefore, suggests mitigating the liability in tort.

15 Sections 16, 17 of the Land Law, 1970; for possessory actions, see ss. 18, 19 of the Land Law. These provisions are applicable equally to chattels: Chattels Law, 1971, s. 8.

The existence in tandem of the two different systems of protecting property rights created difficult problems of co-ordination[16].

However, the very fact of a dual function of proprietary torts – direct enforcement of the right and compensation for its damaging violation – created a tension within the principles of tortious liability. Since no clear distinction was drawn between the two functions, the result was that in every case where actual damage was caused by the invasion of the proprietary right, the duty to pay compensation depended on the same criterion which determined the availability of a real action. This situation created a serious problem where the invasion of the protected interest did not involve any negligent conduct. Strict liability is justified where the enforcement of the right itself is concerned, since it is most reasonable that the owner of the proprietary right should have the means to put an end to the invasion, whatever the cause. But why burden the wrongdoer with payment of compensation when he is not guilty of negligent conduct? The result of strict liability for compensation would be that the protection of property rights is wider than the protection of a person's bodily integrity[17].

Both problems, that of co-ordinating proprietary torts with proprietary (real) actions and that of strict liability in relation to compensation for damage have been addressed under the Draft Code.

First, a number of the traditional common law proprietary torts have been completely removed, namely those of "unlawful detention", of "conversion", and of "interference with daylight"[18]. The remaining torts are "trespass"[19] and "nuisance"[20]. The new "trespass" combines the former "trespass to immovable property" and "trespass to movable property". The new provisions on nuisance maintain the distinction between "public nuisance" and "private nuisance" and conserve the special tort of "prevention of support from neighboring land"[21].

The problem of co-ordination between the action in tort and that in property has been resolved by way of direct reference. Thus, s. 393 of the Draft Code provides: "Trespass to property is a violation of the right stated in s. 504". Section 504(a) defines the proprietary action: "The owner of property and the person entitled to its possession have the right that another person shall not seize the property and hold it unlawfully, and that he will not unlawfully cause damage to the property". Section 504(b) adds: "The provisions of subsection (a) shall apply, with the necessary changes, to the unlawful possessor of the property".

As a result, the scope of the tortious action is, in principle, co-extensive with the proprietary one. Moreover, there is no longer any need to resort to the his-

---

[16] See *Englard*, (1974) 22 American Journal of Comparative Law 321–324.

[17] On the distinction between accidental and intentional trespass and its influence on the problem of strict liability, see *Englard*, (1974) 22 American Journal of Comparative Law 311–314.

[18] See ss. 48, 49–55 of the Civil Wrongs Ordinance (New Version).

[19] See ss. 393–394, of the Draft Civil Code.

[20] See ss. 395–399 of the Draft Civil Code.

[21] This nominate tort was introduced by the Land Law of 1969, s. 165.

torical, complex English common law rules and distinctions relating to the nominate property torts.

Similarly, private nuisance is defined in s. 397 of the Draft Civil Code by reference to the corresponding proprietary action in s. 505 that provides: "The owner of property, the possessor of property and the user of it, are entitled that another person, who has no right to it, shall not interfere materially with the reasonable use and enjoyment of the property, having regard to the situation and nature thereof". Here again, the possible tensions between the two systems of protection have been avoided by way of direct reference.

Equally, the problem of the scope of strict liability has been resolved by express provisions. Thus the torts of trespass and nuisance are subject to the following rule: "A person will not be liable for damages under these torts except if there was negligence on his part" (ss. 394, 399). In the Draft, an alternative qualification for the torts of nuisance is added in s. 399: "However, if the court found that there are special reasons for imposing damages [upon the claimant] even in the absence of negligence, it may do so".

The Draft Code, by limiting the strict liability to the enforcement of the proprietary right and by subjecting the duty of compensation to the test of negligence, will eliminate an element of incoherence in the general principles of tort liability.

V. Other Important Changes

Another interesting change has been suggested in relation to the traditional tort of knowingly causing a breach of contract[22]. The scope of liability will be extended to causing the breach of any obligation, whatever its origin[23]. Thus, causing a breach of statutory duties will henceforth be equally subject to tortious liability. However, the Draft Code does not resolve the above-mentioned problem of the relationship between this specific tort and the general tort of negligence. In other words, what about negligently causing breach of contractual and statutory duties? The specific tort requires knowledge, which is more restrictive than negligence. The answer probably continues to lie in the policy considerations that have to be weighed in the context of establishing a duty of care[24].

Some important changes are suggested in relation to causation. Under the existing wording of the relevant provision, the starting point and dominant element of causation is the "cause in fact". The major statutory exceptions to the principle of "equivalence of causes" concerned the cases where the contributing factors were an act of God or another person's fault that constituted a decisive

---

[22] Section 62 of the Civil Wrongs Ordinance.

[23] See s. 400 of the Draft Civil Code.

[24] See the comprehensive analysis of the problem, as it currently stands, in *Nili Cohen*, Causing Breach of Contract (1986), 169–204 (in Hebrew).

cause in the damaging occurrence[25]. Notwithstanding the existence of that explicit provision, case law admitted additional policy considerations under the (common law) heading of "cause in law". The Draft Civil Code now ratifies this judicial approach by defining the relevant policy consideration in the framework of the new statutory causal notion of "sphere of risk"[26].

Another important innovation in causation concerns the case where the court cannot determine who among a number of persons guilty of tortious behavior actually caused the damage. Section 367 of the Draft Civil Code provides that in this case all of the wrongdoers are liable for the damage in full or in part, as the court sees fit to apportion it. The Draft Code, therefore, enables the court to solve the cases of indeterminacy of causation by a broad discretion that could include also the doctrine of "market share liability"[27]. It has to be noted that there exists already a tendency in Israeli case law to apply the new doctrine of liability for "evidential damage" that entails procedural and substantive solutions for causal problems[28].

Some changes have been made in relation to defences: the general immunity of children under twelve years has been abolished[29]; on the other hand, a new defence for acts done by persons under automatism has been established[30].

Finally, notwithstanding the comprehensive nature of the Draft Civil Code, some special fields of tort liability have been excluded from it. Thus, the liability for defamation, for infringement of privacy, and for commercial torts have been left in the special statutes dealing with these wrongful acts. The reason is that these statutes also establish rules for criminal liability that would have to be left, in any case, outside the Draft Civil Code. Equally, the important special statutory regime for traffic accident compensation has been left outside the Draft Code. There is some continuity on a higher level though; section 364(b) of the Draft Civil Code provides that the Code's general principles apply also to tortious liability that has been established by other statutes.

---

[25] See s. 64(1) and (2), of the Civil Wrongs Ordinance.

[26] See s. 366(c) of the Draft Civil Code.

[27] See especially *Ariel Porat/Alex Stein*, Tort Liability under Uncertainty (2001), 59–67.

[28] The doctrine has been elaborated by *Porat/Stein* (n. 27), 160–206. See also C. A. 361/00 P. D. 59(4) 310; f.H. 1912/05 (not yet published); C. A. 6732/97 (not yet published).

[29] In the Table comparing the old and new sections, the explanatory note to the omission of s. 9 of the Civil Wrongs Ordinance states that it is done in the light of the tendency to assimilate the legal status of the minor to the general rules of tort liability. For the same reason, the exemption from the principle of *volenti non fit iniuria* of a child under 12 years (s. 5(c) of the Ordinance), has been omitted, as well as the special provision regarding the causal connection in relation to children invitees injured by property (s. 64(3) of the Ordinance).

[30] See s. 374 of the Draft Civil Code.

Changes in Israeli Tort Law: A Continental European Perspective

By Helmut Koziol

Summary of Contents

I. Introduction

First of all I would like to stress that I am grateful for the opportunity to deal with the very interesting draft of a new Israeli Tort Law. Thanks to that I have gained valuable new insights into problems of tort law and have been greatly stimulated by it. But since only a very short time is available, I have decided to concentrate on some main points. Also, I think it more interesting to deal with those provisions which appear problematic to me as a Continental European lawyer rather than with those with which I fully agree. As a result, my paper may paint a negative picture which does not conform to my general impression. I apologise for this in advance, and I do hope that, with this statement, I can avoid misleading you. Furthermore, I have to add that unfortunately only an old version of the draft from 2004 was available to me in English. I am very grateful that Professor Englard told me which of my remarks are no longer of relevance, but I have had no opportunity to study all the new provisions.

As Englard points out, the present Israeli Draft Civil Code is the result of longstanding endeavours to shift from common law structures towards a code in the style of Continental European legal systems. As to the style, I feel that that goal has undoubtedly been reached; but the substance of the code is – and this is in line with Englard's remarks – still influenced to some extent by common law. I will concentrate on such influences.

II. Common Law Thinking Patterns

1) Injunctions, Punitive Damages

Section 439 (new version 366) offers illustrative material. At the beginning of the chapter on tort law it presents a classical general clause:

> "Tort liability is liability for damage caused by wrongful conduct or liability for the conduct itself."

A continental lawyer may have quite some difficulties in understanding the second part of the rule: the first part provides liability for the damage caused, but in contrast the second part imposes liability for the conduct itself. Thus it seems that, under tort law, a defendant may incur liability without having caused any damage at all. That would be astonishing for continental lawyers; and I also wonder whether this complies with s. 438 (now 365) which states that the one who suffered injury as a result of a tort is entitled to remedies. A clear inconsistency would exist if "injury" means damage. But it may be that one can interpret "injury" also as the pure violation of a right which does not require any damage (cf. s. 5, now 6). If the authors of the code have that interpretation in mind, then in s. 439 (second half) common law thinking still comes through, namely the concept of the so-called proprietary torts and the dual function of tort law in this area: A result of this dual function was that tort liability, as protection of the right itself, did not require the occurrence of real damage[1]. However – as Englard points out – the injunction based on the defendant's tortious liability no longer fits into the new system. This observation is supported by the fact that, in the chapter on property, ss. 580 and 581 (now 504 and 505, with some textual changes) accept a demand for the surrender of property and the obligation to refrain from any act that constitutes an interference with the use of the property. It would also not fit into the continental European way of thinking as it is almost generally accepted that the primary aim of tort law is the compensation of loss suffered by the victim[2]. As far as I am aware, the widespread opinion is that injunctions are not a subject of tort law and that they need fewer requirements than claims for compensation[3].

Further evidence of the influence of common law thinking is a provision which touches upon the fundamental question of the aims of tort law. Section 564 of an older version and now 462 (but unfortunately not included in the version printed in this volume) provides for a claim for punitive or exemplary damages:

---

[1] Cf. *Israel Gilead*, Tort Law, in: International Encyclopaedia of Laws, Israel (2003) no. 190.

[2] See *Ulrich Magnus* in: European Group on Tort Law (ed.), Principles of European Tort Law (2005), art. 10:101 no. 5ff.

[3] Cf. *Helmut Koziol*, Gedanken zum privatrechtlichen System des Rechtsgüterschutzes, Festschrift für Claus-Wilhelm Canaris I (2007), 635.

"The court may award to an injured person damages which are not damage-related, provided it finds that the breach was malicious."

In Europe, punitive damages are known to the English[4] and Irish[5] tort law systems, but continental European systems deem such damages to be even contrary to their *ordre public*[6]. The EU legislator appears divided internally on this issue: There are – unfortunately – some pieces of legislation that provide for punitive damages[7], while others explicitly declare this to be in violation of European public policy[8]. There exists also a certain tension in the Israeli Code considering s. 532 (now: 456) which reads:

"The purpose of compensation for a breach is to put the injured party, to the extent possible, in the position he would have been in were it not for the breach."

As a matter of course, damages independent of damage, i.e. also of immaterial damage, do not put the injured party in the same position but in a much better position.

2) Strict Liability

On the other hand, the absence of rules on strict liability also seems to be a consequence of the common law influence. English law dislikes strict liability and therefore – strikingly, from a continental perspective – even the liability of keepers or drivers of motor cars is based on fault[9]. Israeli law does not go as far as that and recognises strict (absolute) liability of owners and drivers of motor vehicles and, of course, of the producer of defective products. But there exists no

---

[4] *W. V. Horton Rogers*, Damages under English Law, in: Ulrich Magnus (ed.), Unification of Tort Law: Damages (2001), no. 3.

[5] For example, ss. 14(4) & 14(5)(b) Competition Act 2002, s. 59 Industrial Designs Act 2001, ss. 128(1) & (3) and 304(3) Copyright and Related Rights Act 2000, s. 5(3) Hepatitis C Compensation Tribunal Act 1997.

[6] German Federal Supreme Court in BGHZ 118, 312; Greek Supreme Court (*Areios Pagos*) (Full Bench) 17/1999, NoB 2000, 461–464.

[7] See, for example, Council Directive 75/117 EEC (equal pay); Council Directive 76/207/EEC (access/working conditions etc.); Council Directive 86/378/EEC (occupational social security schemes); Council Directive 97/80/EC (on burden of proof in sex-discrimination cases); Council Directive 2000/43/EC (equal treatment (race)); Council Directive 2000/78/EC (equal treatment in employment and occupation); and Council Directive 2002/73/EC (amending Directive 76/207 EEC).

[8] Thus, Art. 24 Proposal for a Regulation of the European Parliament and the Council on the Law Applicable to Non-Contractual Obligations ("Rome II") COM (2003) 427 final, 22. 7. 2003, provides: "The application of a provision of the law designated by this Regulation which has the effect of causing non-compensatory damages, such as exemplary or punitive damages, to be awarded shall be contrary to Community public policy."

[9] *W. V. Horton Rogers*, England, in: Bernhard A. Koch/Helmut Koziol (eds.), Unification of Tort Law: Strict Liability (2002), no. 25.

rule at all regarding strict liability in the new Code. This is in contrast to the development of continental European tort law: many of the new codes or draft codes recognise strict liability; this is true not only for the Eastern European countries but also for the Swiss[10], the French[11] and the Austrian[12] drafts. Further, the strict liability of the *gardien*[13] under French law has to be mentioned. However, the new Israeli draft contains a rule on dangerous things providing a somewhat stricter fault based liability by reversing the burden of proof[14]. Section 486(a) (now 410(a)) reads:

> "Where injury was caused by a thing that is dangerous by its nature or due to the escape of a thing likely to cause injury by its escape, and the defendant had control over the dangerous thing, or over the thing that escaped immediately prior to its escape, the defendant has the burden of proof to show that he was not negligent in failing to prevent the injury; for this purpose, it makes no difference if the grounds of the action against the defendant is a tort of negligence or another tort."

This is highly interesting, as many continental codes know only individual rules, e.g. §§ 833, 834 and 836 of the German Civil Code, regarding animals and constructions, but not a general rule which implements the fundamental idea of strict liability. The situation in Austria is similar but the new Austrian draft contains a general provision on strict liability for sources of high danger as well as a general rule on liability for sources of lesser danger which is based on fault but with a reversal of the burden of proof.

3) Dominant Position of the Courts

The influence of common law patterns, especially the dominant position of the courts, may also help explain why the code quite often leaves the solution to the courts without any signposts. For example, ss. 394, 399 in the new version provide for the torts of trespass and nuisance that a person will not be liable for damages except if there was negligence on his part. As Englard points out, in the proposal an alternative qualification for the tort of nuisance is added in s. 399:

---

[10] Art. 50 Swiss Draft (1999): "The operator who runs a particularly dangerous activity is liable for compensation of any damage resulting from the realisation of the characteristic risk inherent in this activity, even if such activity is tolerated by the legal order."

[11] Art. 1362 French Draft Alain Levasseur (2006): "Unless particular legislation is to the contrary, one who undertakes an abnormally dangerous activity, even lawfully, is bound to compensate for any harm that ensues from such activity."

[12] § 1302 Austrian Draft (2005): "The keeper of a source of high danger is liable insofar as this danger results in damage. Who is the keeper depends on who has a special interest in the source of the danger, who bears the costs and who exercises the actual power of disposition."

[13] *Suzanne Galand-Carval*, France, in: Bernhard A. Koch/Helmut Koziol (eds.), Unification of Tort Law: Strict Liability (2002), no. 13.

[14] *Israel Gilead*, Israel, in: Bernhard A. Koch/Helmut Koziol (eds.), Unification of Tort Law: Strict Liability (2002), no. 24.

"However, if the court found that there are special reasons for imposing upon him damages even in the absence of negligence, it may do so".

Further, s. 563 states:

"Where non-monetary damage has been caused, (and such damage is not the result of bodily injury [deleted in the new version]), the court may award damages to him for such damage in an amount that it finds appropriate under the circumstances."

Thus the courts have to decide fundamental questions without any indication from the legislator as to which factors should be relevant. For example, as far as s. 563 is concerned, it is unclear whether persons closely related to a victim who is killed have a claim for compensation of their suffering; whether the immaterial damage in case of sexual abuse, of intentional or serious discrimination because of gender, disability, ethnic origin, religion or comparable reasons or of an invasion of privacy has to be compensated; or whether in case of damage to items of property, sentimental value has to be compensated. I feel that such questions should be answered at least to some extent by the legislator if he wants to codify private law.

It may be that the blame for some of the deficiencies in the area of causation can also be attributed to the common law or, to be more precise, to the dominant position of the courts in that system[15]. Thus, the difficult and vehemently discussed problems of concurrent causes (multiple sufficient causes) and superseding causes are not mentioned at all in the code. As a result, the business of the legislator will have to be done by the courts. As Englard mentions, there is now a provision on alternative causation in the latest version of the code which concerns cases where the court cannot determine who among a number of persons guilty of tortious behaviour actually caused the damage: s. 367 of the Draft Civil Code provides that in this case all of the wrongdoers are liable for the full or partial damage, according to the court's decision. Again, however, the legislator avoids a decision on whether the tortfeasors are fully or only partially liable and he does not even give any indication as to which reasons may be advanced in favour of the one or the other solution. The Principles of European Tort Law[16] and also the Austrian draft[17] provide for partial liability.

III. Key Concepts

I do not think that common law thinking can be blamed for the following difficulties; possibly they are caused by translation problems. I refer to the issues

[15] The definition of "actual cause", incidentally, is not very helpful since it is a circular definition: "Actual cause means the cause without which the damage would not have been caused" s. 439(b)(1) (now 366(b)(1)).

[16] Art. 3:103(1).

[17] § 1294(2).

of wrongfulness, negligence and fault. To start with, I find the inclination to use circular definitions astonishing. Section 461(a) (now 387(a)) reads:

> "Negligence is a negligent act causing damage[18] to a person towards whom the malfeasor owes a duty not to act negligently under the circumstances."

Also remarkable is the definition of "negligently" in s. 461(b) (now 387(b)):

> "Acting negligently is doing an act, including an act done intentionally, that a reasonable person would not have done under the circumstances."

Thus, intent becomes a subcategory of negligence! Further, who knows a really reasonable person and how such a wonderful ideal person would have behaved? (The new version mentions an alternative. Section 387(b) states:

> "Acting negligently is a conduct, including intentional conduct, that a reasonable person would not have adopted under the circumstances because of its foreseeable risks; the reasonableness of the said conduct will be evaluated, among other things, by paying attention to the costs involved in the prevention or reduction of the said risks by means of an alternative conduct, and to the social value of these conducts."

This seems to me a great advance as many relevant factors in establishing negligence are pointed out.)

But my real difficulties relate to the following points. Section 439(a) (now 366(a)) states: "Tort liability is liability for damage caused by wrongful conduct or liability for the conduct itself." But as far as I can see, no definition of what is wrongful exists. Further: paragraph (c) subsection (3) mentions culpability without defining that term; as mentioned, s. 461 (now 387) defines negligence without great success; and, last but not least, s. 479(a) (now 403 (a)) stresses that a manufacturer shall compensate one who has suffered bodily injury as a result of a defect in a product, regardless of whether the manufacturer was at fault. It is not really clear whether there is in substance any difference between these different terms, what that difference may be, and whether negligence and fault have to be measured against an entirely objective yardstick or are, at least to some extent, subjective criteria. That question is of even greater importance here than under most European legal systems[19] – with the exception of the French – as there exists, as far as I am aware, no special provision for liability of minors or mentally ill persons. Thus, liability of such persons depends on whether, in establishing negligence, subjective circumstances have to be taken into account or not. If the latter is true, minors and mentally ill persons would be exposed to a far reaching liability.

One final remark: Englard underlines that in the Draft a variety of liability rules, traditionally forming part of tort law, have been transferred to the chapter of "Remedies in the framework of obligations, contractual and others". That is

---

[18] It has to be mentioned that negligence can also be present if no damage has been caused.

[19] For more details, see the country reports in: *Miquel Martin-Casals* (ed.), Children in Tort Law, Part I: Children as Tortfeasors (2006).

true, for instance, of the provisions relating to damages, joint tortfeasors and contributory negligence. This is to some extent astonishing as, for example, joint tortfeasors cause less problems with regard to remedies than to establishing liability. On the other hand, it seems reasonable to draft common rules on tortious and contractual liability as far as there are no differences. However, I wonder whether this is the case only with regard to remedies. §§ 249 ff. BGB tackle a broader area and the Austrian Code even adopts the opposite course: §§ 1293 ff. ABGB cover the entire law of liability, be it tortious or contractual, and only provide different rules to the extent that they are necessary.

Codification, Coherence, and Priority Conflicts

By Hanoch Dagan*

Summary of Contents

I. Introduction

The recent publication of a proposal for a new Israeli Civil Code could turn out to be an important landmark in the development of Israeli private law, a "constitutional moment" of sorts[1]. A codification process – let alone an ambitious one aimed at the codification of private law in its entirety[2] – is a perfect opportunity for critical reflection on fundamental conceptual, jurisprudential,

* Thanks to Jennifer Shkabatur for her excellent research assistance and to the participants of the Conference on the Israeli Draft Civil Code at the Max Planck Institute for Comparative and International Private Law for their penetrating comments.

[1] The Draft Civil Code is available at http://www.justice.gov.il/MOJHeb/Codex2/. The term "constitutional moment" is borrowed, of course; see *Bruce Ackerman*, We the People (1991), 170.

[2] The text is overstated. The proposed code does not cover the entire field. The two most conspicuous omissions insofar as property is concerned are those of marital property law and the important doctrine governing the purchase of new apartments. See also Ofer Grosskopf's paper on Consumer Contracts in this volume.

and normative questions. There is, to be sure, no doctrinal barrier to such a reflection at other times. But experience demonstrates that the life of the law gives us only a limited number of such "magical moments" of (partial) transcendence from the daily evolution of law[3]. The invocation of such a moment within the Israeli legal community is, in and of itself, a reason for celebrating the proposed civil code.

In this piece, I hope to contribute to such critical reflection in two ways. On the more jurisprudential side, I discuss the risk – or, at least one of the most significant risks – of codification, namely: the temptation towards over-inclusiveness[4]. The risk of over-inclusiveness derives, I argue, from overzealousness for coherence, or more precisely from insufficient attention to the virtues of local coherence and the vices of global coherence. This risk is not merely theoretical. As I will show in Part II, this risk has in fact affected the proposed Israeli code quite crucially and quite detrimentally in at least two important respects.

My discussion of coherence will also be the foundation for the remainder of this article, in which I will discuss one particular area of private law: the law governing priority conflicts, that is: cases of contradictory proprietary claims raised by parties who are not bound by contractual privity. Part III celebrates one of the most significant innovations of the proposed code: the formal entrenchment of this body of law as a legal category. I will argue that this innovation is worthwhile precisely because it nicely captures the important coherence underlying the various categories of priority conflict cases. Part IV is more critical than Part III. This part surveys some important doctrinal refinements Israeli case law has developed regarding priority conflicts. Unfortunately, these refinements are not sufficiently reflected in the proposed code. Thus, even in this area of the law where the codifiers' commitment to coherence was actually helpful, the risk of over-inclusiveness is still manifest and potentially damaging.

II. Risks of Codification

Both the goals of the proposed Israeli Civil Code and the explanatory text produced by the codifiers emphasise coherence (at times using other words like harmony, unification, or co-ordination) as a primary purpose of the current codification effort[5]. To be sure, the proposed code may well be promoting other

---

[3] See, e.g., *Roscoe Pound*, Mechanical Jurisprudence, (1908) 8 Columbia Law Review 605, 606–608, 611–612; *Roscoe Pound*, Liberty of Contract, (1909) 18 Yale Law Journal 454, 462.

[4] As the text implies, there are other risks. The prime example in the proposed code is the indiscriminate multiplication of remedies for breach of private law obligations. See *Hanoch Dagan*, Risks of Codification: On Over-Inclusiveness, Excessive Unification and Multiplicity of Remedies, (2007) 36 Mishpatim (The Hebrew University Law Review) 249, 277–287 (in Hebrew).

[5] See s. 1c to the Draft Civil Code (n. 1); ss. 14 & 24 to the Introduction to the Draft Civil Code, available at: http://www.justice.gov.il/MOJHeb/Codex2/.

normative purposes that justify, or even require, legislative reform. But it is difficult to explain the choice of having a code, as opposed to a series of legislative amendments, without mentioning coherence. At least in this sense coherence is the *raison d'être* of codification.

Coherence sounds like an indisputable legal ideal. But in fact it is not, or rather it is not always, a worthy goal. In this part I argue that overzealousness in pursuing coherence can generate a damaging over-inclusiveness and I further demonstrate the two main manifestations of this difficulty in the proposed Israeli civil code. In order to set the stage for making this claim I begin with some preliminary conceptual work devoted to the distinction between the coherence of rules and normative coherence as well as the distinction between global (normative) coherence and local (normative) coherence.

1) Coherence of Rules

Consider first the coherence of rules. A coherentist argument, in this sense of the term, is an argument in which the fit between a legal rule (existing or proposed) and other such rules is a good reason, perhaps even the only reason, for its adoption. It is not easy, however, to explain why such a rule is indeed preferable to the other candidates, which do not fit as neatly into the doctrinal fabric. Legal prescriptions, after all, affect people's lives. Therefore, humanistic lawyers must base their choices, directly or indirectly[6], on their judgments concerning the human good, broadly defined[7]. When facing a legal question that has better and worse answers from the normative perspective, they should choose the normatively superior answer even if this would entail an inelegant result when judged from the viewpoint of doctrinal aesthetics.

There are, nonetheless, some cases where promoting the coherence of rules is justified. These cases typically deal with the more technical aspects of the law. One such case is already implicit in the prescription to choose the normatively justified rule over the coherent one. This prescription, on its own terms, does not proscribe reliance on the coherence of rules where the competing alternatives are morally equivalent to each other, so that the choice amongst them is purely a matter of co-ordination (think, for example, of many – albeit by no means all – possible rules regarding timing). Quite the contrary: as Joseph Raz

---

[6] As the text implies, there are contexts in which normative considerations justify some local use of formalist legal techniques. But then, by definition, these techniques rely on such normative considerations. Roy Kreitner aptly describes this approach as local instrumental formalism. See *Roy Kreitner*, Fear of Contract, (2004) 2004 Wisconsin Law Review 429, 437–438.

[7] See, e.g., *Ronald Dworkin*, Law's Empire (1986), 76–85; *Guido Calabresi*, An Introduction to Legal Thought: Four Approaches to Law and the Allocation of Body Parts, (2003) 55 Stanford Law Review 2113, 2121.

explains, in these cases it is in fact important to adhere to whichever option we end up choosing, thus facilitating certainty, stability, and efficacy[8].

On its face, there is another type of case in which it is normatively desirable to bolster the coherence of rules: harmonising a doctrine which at the present time includes conflicting rules. Promoting the coherence of the rules in this type of case seems to be quite obviously desirable: making contradictory requirements is surely a clear violation of one of the most fundamental tenets of the rule of law[9]. One example of such a "coherentist" move can show us, however, the limited justificatory role that the sheer reference to the coherence of rules can play: Israeli existing doctrine is quite equivocal in its treatment of the issue of self-help, so that currently the same act can be legitimate insofar as property law is concerned and illegitimate for torts purposes, or vice versa[10]. This predicament definitely cries out for revision. But the existing incoherence is silent as to the direction of the desirable cure. In order to choose between the conflicting rules – or maybe opt for another one altogether – we must openly engage in normative arguments. The reference to coherence cannot assist us there.

2) Normative Coherence: Global v. Local

Another, and much more significant, form of coherence as a legal virtue is normative coherence, namely: the coherence of the values underlying the legal doctrine. In fact, as we have just seen, many legal arguments that are presented in terms of rule coherence are in fact ones of normative coherence. This is the meaning of the prevalent legal argument propounding a rule that would cohere with another rule that applies in a similar case. As such, this argument – as we have just seen – is a *non sequitur* because it does not explain why the same regulation should apply to both cases and why it is desirable to extend the existing rule. But this argument can be read in a better light, as implying that there are in fact good reasons for treating the two cases at hand similarly and that the existing rule whose rationale is claimed to be expanded is (at least) satisfactory. This charitable reading exposes the real nature of the type of argument under consideration as one of normative coherence.

In what follows, I present the two most prominent accounts of normative coherence. My purpose in this brief discussion is to point out a second important distinction for our purposes: that between global coherence and local coherence. This distinction will help us to identify the main risk of codification and the main pitfalls of the proposed Israeli code.

---

[8] See *Joseph Raz*, The Relevance of Coherence, in: Ethics in the Public Domain: Essays in the Morality of Law and Politics (1994), 261, 301.

[9] See *Lon L. Fuller*, The Morality of Law (2d ed., 1969), 65–70.

[10] See s. 26 to the Introduction to the Draft Civil Code (n. 5), referring to s. 18 to the Land Law, 5729–1969 and s. 24(2) to the Torts Ordinance [New Version]. For the treatment of this matter by the proposed Code, see ss. 393, 394, 397, 504, 505 to the Draft Civil Code (n. 1).

One approach to normative coherence is identified with Ronald Dworkin's theory of law. In this view, each judge approaches (or at least should approach) adjudication like a chain novelist, attempting to write the next chapter so that it presents the legal story – the doctrine in its entirety – in the best light possible. This analogy implies that the choice between doctrinal alternatives is guided by the set of values that optimally complies with two criteria: (i) its "fit" (or coherence) with a broad range of existing (legislative or judge-made) rules; and (ii) normative justification. This form of adjudication, insists Dworkin, presents legal practice in its best light because it provides the best justification for law's coercive power; it also facilitates a vision of the state as a special type of community that is endowed with a unique sense of integrity, which therefore deserves the obedience of its citizens[11].

This view, in which coherence is an independent legal virtue, is controversial. Raz discusses the conflict between commitments to coherence and to pluralism and prefers the latter over the former. The reason for this is that our moral system is not reducible to one ultimate value from which all the other values derive; that morality includes a set of intrinsic values that are incommensurable. Raz insists that we not only disagree on many moral questions; rather, we believe that in many – although by no means all – moral issues there is more than one right answer. This is why it is reasonable – even desirable – for the law to adopt more than one set of principles and thus more than one set of coherent doctrines. In a world of incommensurable human values, a monistic legal voice is repressive, whereas the plurality of normative voices may be key to our collective coexistence. For this reason coherence should be rejected as an independent value. But there is still room for more modest forms of coherence in law. In particular, Raz acknowledges the virtue of normative *local* coherence if, but only if, it derives from the normative injunction to found a given area of the law on one certain value (or a given balance among the pertinent values)[12].

Fortunately, for our purposes there is no need to resolve this dispute, because even Dworkin recognises a practice of "local priority". Judgments about fit, in his view, always refer to a series of concentric circles, centered on the issue at stake, so that the weight of the fit with a relatively internal circle is higher than that of the fit with a relatively distant one. Notwithstanding his initial preference for global coherence, Dworkin agrees that we should respect "departments" of law if (and only if) this legal categorisation is premised on a solid normative foundation[13]. Thus, even Dworkin, who does find independent value in legal coherence – indeed he is the ultimate spokesperson of the virtues of legal coher-

[11] See *Dworkin* (n. 7), 164–258. Dworkin believes that citizens' commitment to the law is premised on the role played by the law in constituting modern heterogeneous societies. He argues that in order for the law to perform this task it needs to talk to the people with one normative voice.

[12] See *Raz*, The Relevance of Coherence (n. 8), 281–282, 291–304. Raz also rejects Dworkin's account of the role of law in constituting the community of the modern state as well as his related account of obedience to law.

[13] See *Dworkin* (n. 7), 250–254.

ence – agrees that important normative concerns can, and should, justify substantial deviations from "the coherent predicament."

3) On Over-inclusiveness

Most of the coherentist changes of the Draft Civil Code are not aimed at resolving contradictions of technical rules respecting issues of no particular normative significance. Rather, they seek to promote normative coherence, as is evident from the structure of the current proposal, which includes "a thick layer of uniform rules"[14].

Analysing a codification process from the perspective of normative coherence invites a focus on the risk of over-inclusiveness, namely an exaggerated tilt towards global (as distinct from local) coherence. Over-inclusiveness seems to be a fundamental risk of such an enterprise because there is a fine line between the natural interest of the codifiers in the code's structure and their understandable wish to make it harmonious – "going from the general and common to the particular and separate"[15] – and an inflated emphasis on doctrinal aesthetics. Such an attitude is worrying as it tends to understate (at times even ignore) important normative concerns. As we have just seen, even friends of coherence as an independent legal virtue condemn a doctrinal unification that flattens normatively significant doctrinal distinctions[16].

Over-inclusiveness tends to undermine some important virtues of private law at least insofar as the common law tradition is concerned. Private law, in this tradition, is divided into narrow categories that represent a tentative suggestion for slicing the social universe into economically and socially differentiated segments, recognising that each "transaction of life" has some features that are of sufficient normative importance to justify distinct legal treatment[17]. The different institutions of private law offer a way (which is, to be sure, always tentative and imperfect) for structuring our interpersonal relations in differing social contexts, adjusting the normative fine-tuning of the competing values that the doctrine promotes to the characteristics of the pertinent human relation[18].

---

[14] See *Miguel Deutsch*, On the Codification Vision and the Property Chapter in the Code, (2007) 36 Mishpatim 289, 296 (in Hebrew).

[15] See s. 15 to the Introduction to the Draft Civil Code (n. 5).

[16] As the text implies, Raz and Dworkin may well disagree as to the degree of the normative significance of these distinctions, and thus on the degree of the required caution regarding doctrinal unification. Insofar as the normative significance of these distinctions is marginal, or even small, Dworkin may opt for the coherent solution. But even Dworkin's view recommends caution where this significance is substantial.

[17] See *Herman Oliphant*, A Return to Stare Decisis, (1928) 14 American Bar Association Journal 71; *Karl N. Llewellyn*, A Realistic Jurisprudence: The Next Step, in: Jurisprudence: Realism in Theory and in Practice (1962), 3, 27–28, 32, 34–36; *Karl N. Llewellyn*, Some Realism about Realism, in: *ibid.*, 42, 56–57, 62, 73.

[18] For a more detailed account of this view in the context of property law, see *Hanoch Dagan*,

To be sure, like every aspect of the law, the existing legal categorisation should be critically examined; lawyers should never be complacent about the possibility that legal categories neither follow social categories nor improve on our social structure[19]. But there is a danger in understating the importance of multiplicity. If law is to sustain and facilitate the richness of our social world, which is typified by a broad spectrum of ways in which people interact with one another[20], legal categories (existing or new) should be appropriately narrow. Narrow legal categories are commendable also because they help sustain and inculcate one of the most important advantages of judges as lawmakers: their daily and unmediated access to actual human situations and problems in contemporary life[21].

There is no reason to suspect that legislative interventions in private law – such as the ones that were enacted in Israel during the 1960s and the 1970s – necessarily entail the surrender of these merits. Furthermore, even the mission of incorporating various private law statutes into one comprehensive code is not an inevitable recipe for such an unhappy consequence. But some of the coherentist moves of the current proposal seem to fall into this very trap. This deficiency would be particularly worrisome if courts were to take the codifiers' emphasis on the virtue of legal coherence too seriously.

4) Two Pitfalls in the Israeli Draft Civil Code

Two of the most important, and the most radical, reforms of the proposed code are particularly vulnerable to the problem of over-inclusiveness and thus run the risk of flattening the rich social fabric regulated by private law.

The first problematic proposal is to unify "the remedial principles of contract law and tort law," and prescribe one unified regime for "remedies for the breach of obligations." The codifiers justify this radical reform – which is almost[22] un-

---

The Craft of Property, (2003) 92 California Law Review 1517, 1558–1565. For similar conclusions regarding contract law, see *Todd D. Rakoff*, The Implied Terms of Contracts: Of "Default Rules" and "Situation Sense", in: Jack Beatson/Daniel Friedmann (eds.), Good Faith and Fault in Contract Law (1995), 191; *Alan Schwartz*, The Default Rule Paradigm and the Limits of Contract Law, (1994) 3 Southern California Interdisciplinary Law Journal 389, 415–419; *Kreitner*, (2004) 2004 Wisconsin Law Review (n. 6), 461–478.

[19] See, e.g., *Llewellyn*, A Realistic Jurisprudence (n. 17), 3, 27; *Walter Wheeler Cook*, Scientific Method and the Law, in: William W. Fisher III et al. (eds.), American Legal Realism (1993), 242, 246.

[20] See *Michael Walzer*, Spheres of Justice: A Defense of Pluralism and Equality (1983); *Elizabeth Anderson*, Value in Ethics and Economics (1993), 157.

[21] See *Oliphant*, (1928) 14 American Bar Association Journal (n. 17), 73–74, 159. Joseph Raz's analysis of the phenomenon of distinguishing cases brings home a similar point. See *Joseph Raz*, The Authority of Law (1979), 183–97. For an extended treatment of these virtues of lawyering, see *Anthony T. Kronman*, The Lost Lawyer: Failing Ideals of the Legal Profession (1993), 72–73, 223–225.

[22] There are only a few examples of codes that blur the distinction between remedies for breach of contact and remedies for torts, or – more generally – between contracts and torts. The Dutch

precedented[23] – by claiming that "there is insufficient justification for the "disconnected" development of the rules in these two fields," because "once the plaintiff has a right to a remedy for a breach of an obligation, the legal source of this right has quite limited significance"[24].

The desirability of this proposal is quite dubious. There are important and rather fundamental normative distinctions between contracts and torts. Space does not permit me to explore these differences here in any detail. For our purposes it is enough to mention that at least from the viewpoint of the fundamental value of human dignity and freedom – the ultimate value in Israeli law[25] – the purposes of contracts and torts are distinctly different[26]. Contracts are usually understood as conventional frameworks of voluntary promises that the law enforces in order to allow people to promote their own goals by using other people

---

Code is an example of the former category; the Civil Code of Québec, of the latter one. See respectively *Arthur S. Hartkamp*, Law of Obligations, in: Jeroen M.J. Chorus/Piet-Hein M. Gerver/Ewoud H. Hondius/Alis K. Koekkoek (eds.), Introduction to Dutch Law (1999), 123, 129–135; the Civil Code of Québec: Book Five, Title One, Chapter III "Civil Liability" and Chapter VI "Performance of Obligations".

[23] The classic Continental codes such as the German, the Italian, the French and the Swiss – include, to be sure, rules that are common to the law of obligations in its entirety; yet these codes maintain the distinction between contracts and torts insofar as remedies are concerned. Thus, although both the *Bürgerliches Gesetzbuch* and the *Codice Civile* include unified rules dealing with the operational aspects of remedies for the breach of civil obligations, they have separate – at times quite narrowly tailored – rules respecting the more fundamental issue of the choice of remedies in contracts and in torts. For Germany, see the BGB: §§ 249–254 (dealing with operational aspects); §§ 272–282, 320, 323–325, 440, 459 ff., 537 ff., 633, 645 (dealing with remedies in contracts); § 823 (dealing with remedies in torts); see also *Basil S. Markesinis/Werner Lorenz/Gerhard Dannemann*, The German Law of Obligations – The Law of Contracts and Restitution: A Comparative Introduction (1997), 398–426; *Basil S. Markenis/Hannes Unberath*, The German Law of Torts – A Comparative Treatise (2002), 24–27; *Werner f. Ebke/Matthew W. Finkin*, Introduction to German Law (1996), 224–225; *Nigel Foster*, German Law & Legal System (1993), 231–237. For Italy, see the *Codice Civile*: Art. 1176–1217, 1236–1240, 1241–1252 (dealing with operational aspects); Book Four, Title I (focusing primarily on contracts) and Title IX (dealing with torts); see also *Thomas Glyn Watkin*, The Italian Legal Tradition (1997), 252–256. The distinction between contracts and torts (and unjust enrichment) is even sharper in the French and the Swiss codes. For France, see the *Code Civil*: Book III, Title III, Chapter III "On the Effect of Obligations" (dealing with contracts) and Title IV, Chapter II "On Intentional and Unintentional Wrongs" (dealing with torts); see also *John Bell/Sophie Boyron/Simon Whittaker*, Principles of French Law (1998), 305, 340–357. For Switzerland, see *Obligationenrecht*: Art. 1–40, 97–101 (dealing with contracts); Art. 41 (dealing with torts); see also *P. Tercier/D. Dreyer*, Torts, in: f. Dessemontet/T. Ansay (eds.), Introduction to Swiss Law (2nd ed., 1995), 125–139; *Eugen Bucher*, Law of Contracts, in: *ibid.*, 111.

[24] See s. 27 to the Introduction to the Draft Civil Code (n. 5); *Miguel Deutsch*, Interpretation of the Code (2005), 25, 291 (in Hebrew). See also Nili Cohen's contribution to this volume.

[25] See Basic Law: Human Dignity and Liberty (1992), Sefer Hachukim 150.

[26] Even the economic analysis of the law recognises the difference between contract law and tort law. While the former is aimed, according to this view, at maximising the welfare of contractual parties, the latter is preoccupied with minimising the costs of accidents and the costs of their prevention. See, e.g., *Alan Schwartz/Robert E. Scott*, Contract Theory and the Limits of Contract Law, (2003) 113 Yale Law Journal 541 and *Guido Calabresi*, The Costs of Accidents: A Legal and Economic Analysis (1970).

(or their resources) without immorally instrumentalising these people[27]. By contrast, from the viewpoint of autonomy, tort law is mainly focused on prescribing rules of action and liability that fairly reconcile the competing claims of liberty and security[28].

The distinction between contracts and torts is by no means sharp: they do contain overlapping or mixed doctrines, such as products liability law and the law governing medical malpractice. But this is a common legal phenomenon that cannot serve to disprove the existence of easy or core cases. Furthermore, I do not dispute the normative continuity between contracts and torts[29], notably due to their common pursuit of autonomy. But this similarity is so abstract that its significance is quite limited. After all, most (if not all) legal fields promote the fundamental values of the legal system, including – at least in liberal settings – autonomy. Thus, even though the ultimate values of torts and contracts are similar, or even identical, their differing contexts of application yield differing purposes. This heterogeneity should serve as a warning against a hasty unification of the remedial aspects of torts and contracts.

Rather than assume – as the current proposal does – that the remedies for breach of contract and those for the commission of torts are a priori similar, the different purposes of these legal fields call for a careful analysis of the appropriate remedial consequences of these two types of cases[30]. Though a thorough investigation is beyond the scope of this article I feel confident recommending against the proposed unification[31]. This is a safe statement because it is a mistake to ana-

---

[27] See *Charles Fried*, Contract as Promise: A Theory of Contractual Obligation (1981), 7–17; *Daniel Markovitz*, Contract and Collaboration, (2004) 114 Yale Law Journal 1419.

[28] See *Dan B. Dobbs*, Torts and Compensation: Personal Accountability and Social Responsibility for Injury (2d ed. 1993), 8–9; *Arthur Ripstein*, Equality, Responsibility, and the Law (1999), 6; *Gregory Keating*, Rawlsian Fairness and Regime Choice in the Law of Accidents, (2004) 72 Fordham Law Review 1857, 1862–1870. There are, to be sure, also other accounts of the role of autonomy in torts. Thus, for example, Ernest Weinrib insists that corrective justice is the regulative principle of torts (and more generally of private law). See *Ernest J. Weinrib*, The Idea of Private Law (1995). But Weinrib too sees important distinctions, with significant remedial consequences, between contracts and torts. See *Ernest J. Weinrib*, Punishment and Disgorgement as Contract Remedies, (2003) 78 Chicago-Kent Law Review 55.

[29] This continuity may explain the reciprocal influence of conventional accounts of contracts and torts: the use of the cheapest cost avoiding party analysis for contract law and the reference to a hypothetical contract as a means to justify the rules of torts.

[30] It has been argued that all private law remedies serve one purpose: corrective justice. See *Yehuda Adar*, Why Unite the Remedies in Contracts and Torts: A Response to Professor Dagan, (2007) 36 Mishpatim 357, 376 (in Hebrew). Pointing to corrective justice as the normative common denominator of the law of remedies may well be correct, but is unhelpful, because reference to corrective justice begs the question unless it relies on a distributive foundation that shapes the underlying entitlements and thus also the appropriate response to their infringement. See *Hanoch Dagan*, The Distributive Foundation of Corrective Justice, (1999) 98 Michigan Law Review 138.

[31] In fact, the multiple types of contracts and the multiple types of interests protected from non-consensual interference may even suggest that such an inquiry may end up calling for a move in the opposite direction. See, respectively, *Roy Kreitner*, Multiplicity in Contract Remedies, in: Nili

lyse remedies merely as means to protect rights[32]. Rather, remedies are constitutive features of these rights[33]. Because different remedial responses constitute differing types of rights, which in turn can promote different human values[34], it is implausible to suppose that legal doctrines that promote different purposes would implicate an identical remedial apparatus[35].

The second proposed reform that may end up as a problematic over-unification involves property law, which is also the focus of the remainder of this article. Existing doctrine prescribes that the rules governing land law apply to chattels as well and – "as far as appropriate to the matter and *mutatis mutandis*" – to rights more generally[36]. The Draft Code substitutes this doctrinal structure with a more elegant one. The fourth part of the Draft is titled "Assets", thus conveying a stricter commitment to unification. The internal structure of this part further fortifies this coherentist outlook. It begins with a "trunk of common rules that would govern assets generally" – these rules are mostly imported from the existing land law dealing with topics like co-ownership and the protection of ownership and possession – and it concludes with "special rules for land … and special rules for chattels"[37]. This structure implies that insofar as the "trunk" is concerned, the unification is strict rather than mediated through analogical application *(mutatis mutandis)*. The definition clause of the proposed code is somewhat more careful, defining "assets" as "land and chattels, as well as, insofar as it fits and with the necessary changes, proprietary rights"[38].

This proposed coherentist reform raises two difficulties[39]. The first problem assumes that future interpreters and appliers will take the cautionary note in the definition clause seriously. The question here – which, in fact, also pertains to the existing law – concerns the application of rules that also govern land to chat-

---

Cohen/Ewan McKendrick (eds.), Comparative Remedies for Breach of Contract (2005), 19; *Hanoch Dagan*, Unjust Enrichment: A Study of Private Law and Public Values (1997), chapters 2–4.

32 As the text implies, other features of claims in contracts and in torts which are less fundamental to the definition of the entitlements vindicated by these two distinct fields of law – such as prescription or the assignability of causes of action – may well be justifiably unified.

33 See *Llewellyn*, A Realistic Jurisprudence (n. 17), 8–18, 21–23; *Llewellyn*, Some Realism about Realism (n. 17), 63; *Karl N. Llewellyn*, The Bramble Bush (1930), 93–94, 96–97.

34 For more detailed analyses in the contexts of restitution and contracts, see respectively *Dagan*, Unjust Enrichment (n. 31), ch. 2; *Roy Kreitner*, Frameworks of Cooperation: Competing, Conflicting, and Joined Interests in Contract and Its Surroundings, (2005) 6 Theoretical Inquiries in Law 59, 64, 67–70, 74–80.

35 Furthermore, even if such a result had been demonstrated by happenstance, it still would have been desirable to resist the temptation of unification. A uniform law of remedies is bound to facilitate easy cross-references between contracts and torts, thus blurring the important distinction between wrongs and breaches of contract, and therefore skewing the development of the law. For a critique of the treatment of breach of contract as a species of legal wrongs, see *Hanoch Dagan*, The Law and Ethics of Restitution (2004), 268–272, 278–282.

36 See ss. 8, 9(e) to the Movable Property Law, 5731–1971.

37 See s. 20 to the Introduction to the Draft Civil Code (n. 5).

38 See s. 6 to the Draft Civil Code (n. 1).

39 On a happier note, the limitation of assets to proprietary rights, rather than rights more generally, is a commendable improvement on existing law.

tels with no adjustment mechanism whatsoever. Even those who believe that the co-ownership of land and chattels, as well as the protection of possession and of ownership of land and chattels, should be similarly regulated, acknowledge that the differences between land and chattels may require corresponding doctrinal distinctions; but they insist that these distinctions are at the application level, and that they do not justify, in any event, a "bizarre and cumbersome repetition of the same basic regulation in two different places"[40]. For me, this aesthetic cost is rather marginal, especially compared to the possible material detrimental consequences of excessive unification. Moreover, once we acknowledge the need for some refinements before rules pertaining to land can properly apply to chattels as well, we realise that the more careful – albeit less elegant – *mutatis mutandis* mechanism is preferable to the elegant – but more blunt – mechanism of unification.

The second possible problem with this proposed reform relates to assets besides land and chattels. Even if we ignore the rather awkward way in which the definition clause conveys the message that in these cases analogical application is in place, it may still be questionable whether the combination of (i) the location of this prescriptive norm in the definition clause (494 sections before the beginning of the assets part of the Draft Civil Code); (ii) the creation of a new "super legal category" of assets; and (iii) the codifiers' strong emphasis on coherence, might generate a judicial tilt toward unification. Put differently, whereas the existing doctrine makes the analogical extension of land law to other assets somewhat cumbersome, the proposed structure might render it almost obvious.

This contingency would be quite unfortunate because the traditional property law distinctions between the regulation of different types of resources are neither accidental nor arbitrary. Quite the contrary: the categories of resources that property law constitutes – such as land, chattels, copyrights, patents, etc. – lie on a spectrum. On one end of this continuum are resources that are constitutive of their owners' personhood (land – in particular, a home – is a classic example). The other end of the continuum consists of resources, such as money and other mostly fungible assets (e.g., trade secrets or patents), the possession of which is purely instrumental. Israeli property law, like the property laws of other states, respects the personhood value of property. Therefore, it accords owners of constitutive resources a rather fortified sovereignty, while giving more space to other property values (such as utility, social responsibility, and distributive justice) insofar as the more fungible resources are concerned[41]. These normative distinctions entail, of course, doctrinal consequences; they justify the distinction between the various legal regimes governing different resources[42]. The proposed

---

[40] *Deutsch*, (2007) 36 Mishpatim, 299.

[41] For a more extended treatment see *Hanoch Dagan*, Property at a Crossroads (2005), 38–42, 67–74, 86–96 (in Hebrew).

[42] Thus, for example, there may well be good reasons to distinguish between co-ownership of a copyright – one of the most constitutive categories recognised by law – and other types of co-

reform – in particular, the creation of an all-encompassing legal category of assets – might flatten these distinctions by generating a dynamic of hasty analogies from one category to the other. That detrimental contingency is admittedly not unavoidable. In this context – as indeed in (almost) any other doctrinal context – reflective judges can remedy, at least to an extent, legislative failures. And yet it is surely preferable not to codify a legislative reform that would require such judicial aid, especially where the better regulation is already reflected in the existing law.

III. A New Legal Category: Priority Conflicts

Thus far I have discussed coherence – both as a virtue and as a potential vice of codification efforts – and demonstrated the risks of codification using the main two pitfalls of the proposed Israeli code as my examples. I shift gears now to the second main goal of this article: to discuss at some more length one particular, and particularly difficult, area of property law and examine its codification in the proposed code. So the remainder of this article will deal exclusively with one type of property dispute: cases that involve contradictory claims raised by parties with no contractual privity, such as conflicts between two parties holding contradictory contractual commitments from the same intermediary, conflicts between sellers and transferees of buyers, and triangular conflicts emerging from bailment or theft.

In current Israeli legislation each such case is covered by a separate rule typically appearing in a separate statute[43]. But in recent years courts have increasingly looked at these cases as if they belong to one legal category and have thus adopted interpretive strategies, such as analogy, that make these separate rules more coherent[44]. This approach is significantly fortified in the proposed code, which dedicates a separate chapter to the law of priority conflicts, in which the scattered rules, of which it is currently composed, are assembled and unified[45].

The basic thrust of this proposal is both important and desirable because we are indeed dealing with a group of cases that raise similar problems and frequently invoke similar normative judgments. In what follows I will try to delineate the common normative infrastructure of the law of priority conflicts. (Part of the discussion will expose some possible normative disagreements that run through this area.) In Part IV I will consider some important differences be-

---

ownership. See *Gilad Wekselman*, Co-operation in Copyrights (Tel-Aviv University, Doctoral Dissertation, forthcoming 2007) (in Hebrew).

[43] The first academic complaint against this important deficiency appears in *Daniel Friedmann*, Rights of the Owner against a Third Party in Modern Israeli Legislation, (1975) 4 Tel Aviv University Law Review 245 (in Hebrew).

[44] An important landmark is C. A. 109/87 *Havat Makura Ltd. v. Hassan* (1993) 47(5) P. D. 1.

[45] See ss. 508–512 of the Draft Civil Code (n. 1).

tween the sub-fields of the law of priority conflicts and thus criticise some excesses in the Draft Code's coherentist approach.

1) Priority Conflicts as Legal Accidents

Menachem Mautner has conceptualised priority conflicts cases as "legal accidents". The parties to these legal dramas, typically an original owner and a third party, each interacted with an intermediary for the same right. In the typical case, the intermediary turns out to be judgment-proof, so that achieving priority with respect to this right is the conflicting parties' only or most significant possible remedy. Therefore, resolving the conflict between these parties – prescribing priority rules – can be compared to resolving accident cases. Both accidents and priority conflicts require the allocation of harm resulting from the parties' attempt to use the same resource simultaneously. In a "factual" accident, they both attempt to have recourse to the same physical resource. In priority conflicts, they both attempt to have recourse to the same legal resource: the right in dispute[46].

Following the accident analogy, Mautner astutely suggests that some of the same normative concerns that guide tort law in dealing with factual accidents also guide decisions about priority rules in dealing with legal accidents. Applying the economic analysis of tort accidents, which, in his view, also represents concerns of justice, Mautner sets out three guiding considerations for priority rules[47]. First, *ex ante* efficiency concerns (which he also recasts in terms of retributive justice) recommend imposing liability on the party who put the fewest resources into avoiding the risk of the legal accident to encourage people in this situation to invest sufficient resources to prevent the very occurrence of conflict. Second, *ex post* allocative efficiency (minimising the losses suffered by the litigating parties) and the need criterion of distributive justice entail a preference for the party "likely to suffer the greater loss if the other party prevails"[48]. These two considerations, translated into legal doctrine, typically require the third party who seeks priority to be a good faith purchaser for value. Bad faith clearly indicates opportunism and easy (cheap) avoidance, as well as culpability; and without significant investment ("value") in reliance on the interaction with the in-

---

[46] See *Menachem Mautner*, "The Eternal Triangles of the Law:" Toward a Theory of Priorities in Conflicts Involving Third Parties, (1991) 90 Michigan Law Review 95, 95–96, 102.

[47] *Mautner*, (1991) 90 Michigan Law Review 100–126. For a similar analysis, see, e.g., *Craig Rotherham*, Proprietary Remedies in Context: A Study of Judicial Redistribution of Property Rights (2002), 70–73.

[48] *Mautner*, (1991) 90 Michigan Law Review, 101–106. For an opposite view, in which need-based concerns have no place in private law see, e.g., *Ernest J. Weinrib*, Right and Advantage in Private Law, (1989) 10 Cardozo Law Review 1283. For the intrinsic role of need-based concerns in the justification of property, see *Jeremy Waldron*, Property, Justification, and Need, (1993) 6 Canadian Journal of Law and Jurisprudence 185.

termediary, the third party's potential loss if the right is allotted to the original owner is likely to be relatively small[49]. Third, priority rules minimise litigation and uncertainty costs, which may overwhelm a system in which both the least cost avoiding party and the least vulnerable party are determined on a case-by-case basis[50]. This third consideration, along with other virtues of the rule of law, explains and justifies the law of legal accidents' articulation of precise rules for typical cases, rather than vague standards requiring the evaluation of every case on its own terms.

2) Normative Tensions

A difficult question concerns the weight to be assigned to each of these three considerations. One aspect of this problem, beyond the scope of this article, concerns the balance between the two substantive considerations on the one hand and the third consideration (litigation costs) on the other hand[51]. For our purposes it is enough to stipulate my support of relatively clear rules and proceed to focus on another aspect of this problem – namely, the relationship between *ex ante* efficiency, or the identification of the least cost avoiding party, and *ex post* efficiency, or the identification of the least vulnerable party. Mautner appears to suggest that the *ex ante* considerations are of primary importance, while *ex post* considerations enter the picture only when the parties' relative preventive ability is in doubt[52]. This approach focuses on maximising incentives for least cost avoiding parties. On its face, such a rule of lexical ordering seems justified also because the *ex post* efficient allocation is likely to emerge regardless of the way the law allocates rights between the parties, assuming that the transaction costs between the original owner and the third party are negligible[53]. Even if the law is wrong from the perspective of *ex post* efficiency, this mistake will be corrected quickly, because the loser in the priority litigation, by definition, will then be willing and able to purchase the right from the winner.

In many types of cases, most notably regarding legal accidents in a purely commercial context, this account is sufficient. But other types of cases do not follow the reasons justifying lexical priority for *ex ante* efficiency, or may present other reasons that support a more significant emphasis on *ex post* considerations. Thus, in certain categories of cases, the assumptions underlying this approach, that the law's messages reach their addressees (or are in some way intuitive to most people) and that people will be able to change their behaviour accordingly,

---

[49] *Mautner*, (1991) 90 Michigan Law Review, 110–112.
[50] *Mautner*, (1991) 90 Michigan Law Review, 107–109.
[51] See *Dagan*, Property at a Crossroads (n. 41), 214–215.
[52] *Mautner*, (1991) 90 Michigan Law Review, 100.
[53] See *Ronald H. Coase*, The Problem of Social Cost, in: The Firm, the Market, and the Law (1988), 95.

are likely to be fanciful, or at least questionable[54]. In such cases, even where the comparative avoidance ability test yields a definite answer – let alone where it is somewhat ambiguous – *ex ante* efficiency should not enjoy exclusive emphasis. Likewise, in many cases of legal accidents, conflicting parties face non-negligible transaction costs following the legal accident. Frequently, legal accidents entail an all-or-nothing battle for a unique asset, such as land or art, that constitutes a large part of one or both parties' estates, and on whose ownership both parties have relied. In such cases, the litigating parties frequently are locked into a bilateral monopoly[55], and thus are subject to strategic behaviour that may hinder mutually beneficial transactions[56]. The result of such "legal wars of attrition" might be dictated more by the parties' relative wealth, which determines their resiliency in a long and exhausting legal struggle, than by the balance of harm or utility[57].

The discussion thus far has merely established that economic efficiency does not justify awarding a strong preference to the comparative avoidance ability issue over the comparative vulnerability test. This conclusion is important because economic efficiency is a proxy – albeit at times one that is regressively tilted – of social welfare[58], which is in turn an important property value[59]. But it is not the only pertinent property value. Three other such values – social responsibility, distributive justice, and personhood[60] – should also importantly inform the law of priority conflicts. The first fortifies the weight of the comparative avoidance ability test; the second supports the comparative vulnerability test; and the third highlights an additional important distinction that the law of priority conflicts should follow.

Social responsibility requires that owners (or owners-to-be), who can avoid a legal accident at a relatively low cost, do so in order to prevent the severe harm

---

[54] See *Robert D. Cooter/Edward L. Rubin*, A Theory of Loss Allocation for Consumer Payments, (1987) 66 Texas Law Review 63, 89–90; see also, e.g., *Robert C. Ellickson*, Order Without Law: How Neighbors Settle Disputes (1991), 144–145; *Izhak Englard*, The Philosophy of Tort Law (1993), 43–44. Some versions of the cheapest cost avoidance test incorporate factors of information and rationality into the calculus of comparative avoidance ability. If these considerations have already been taken into account, they should not, of course, be reintroduced again at this stage.

[55] A bilateral monopoly is a situation in which, concerning a specific resource or right, there is only one seller and one buyer, who are locked into dealing with each other. See, e.g., *Richard A. Posner*, Economic Analysis of Law (6th ed., 2003), 60–61.

[56] See *Ward Farnsworth*, Do Parties to Nuisance Cases Bargain After Judgment? A Glimpse Inside the Cathedral, (1999) 66 University of Chicago Law Review 373, 384; *Stewart E. Sterk*, Neighbours in American Land Law, (1987) 87 Columbia Law Review 55, 70–74.

[57] In other words, in many cases the wealthier party will obtain the asset, and the one with more limited resources will lose out or will be forced into an uncomfortable compromise, even if he or she is more in need of the disputed asset or likely to gain more utility from obtaining it.

[58] See *Anthony T. Kronman*, Wealth Maximization as a Normative Principle, (1980) 9 Journal of Legal Studies 227, 240.

[59] I discuss social welfare as a property value in *Dagan*, Property at a Crossroads (n. 41), 46–51.

[60] For a discussion of these three property values, see *Dagan*, Property at a Crossroads (n. 41), 51–55, 55–65, and 38–42, respectively.

another person is likely to incur if the accident takes place. In other words, the moral prescription embedded in the comparative avoidance ability test is not one of retributive justice (a concern that should very rarely, if ever, inform private law). Rather, it is our commitment to the social responsibility of landowners that joins the property value of social welfare in condemning a least cost avoiding party who did not bother to prevent a legal accident.

By contrast, a commitment to distributive justice pushes in the opposite direction. We must give the comparative vulnerability test attention even when it has no impact on ex post efficiency (i.e., even if mutually beneficial transactions are not hindered by bilateral monopolies) because even in these cases the legal allocation of entitlements determines the identity of winners and losers[61]. The ensuing distributive implications make the comparative vulnerability test always relevant, although the reason for its significance varies according to the type of case at hand.

Consider first categories of cases – such as the "combination transactions" discussed in section III. 3) below – in which the socio-economic status of the parties is more or less equal. As Mautner himself noted, in these cases the comparative vulnerability test can serve as a proxy for the more general question of the parties' relative needs, so that distributive sensitivity would suggest imposing the accident's costs on the party who is likely to suffer the lesser loss if the other party prevails[62]. Here bilateral distributive considerations – as opposed to the broader ones I discuss momentarily – help determine the normatively desirable rule.

But even types of cases that deviate from this paradigm – in which the conflicting parties typically belong to different social strata – lead to a similar conclusion. To be sure, in some categories of legal accidents the groups of original owners or third parties can hardly be characterised as discrete subgroups of society, making the distributive question much less significant[63]. When such a characterisation can be made, however, a commitment to distributive justice requires paying attention to the variance among people competing for disputed rights and giving some (not necessarily determinative) preference to rules that favour deprived groups[64].

---

[61] See, e.g., *Kronman*, (1980) 9 Journal of Legal Studies, 240; *Richard Craswell*, Passing on the Costs of Legal Rules: Efficiency and Distribution in Buyer-Seller Relationships, (1991) 43 Stanford Law Review 361, 385–387.

[62] *Mautner*, (1991) 90 Michigan Law Review, 105–106.

[63] In these cases, too, the difficulties of characterising the original owner and the third parties may follow from our being entrenched in existing social categories. This constraint actually may increase the advantage of making the competing parties confront each other as a possible way of exposing "hidden social categories" and other relevant private information.

[64] In many cases this rule would also promote bilateral distributive justice as well as social welfare. The former conclusion follows from the declining marginal utility of money; the latter derives from the observation that stronger parties are more responsive to the law's incentives than weaker ones.

Finally, the personhood value of property can also make a difference. This value requires that the law make a qualitative distinction between the ways it treats constitutive resources (of which people's homes are a prime example) and fungible resources (such as money). The relevant prescription here is that where the type of conflict at hand confronts a party, whose interest in the right at stake is purely fungible, with a party for whom the resource is constitutive, some preference for the latter is in order. (This prescription can be restated as suggesting a qualitative vulnerability test, as opposed to the quantitative vulnerability test discussed above.) Applying this prescription is not easy, though, not only because there are bound to be cases in which the other pertinent considerations push in the other direction. It may also be complicated because cases of constitutive resources are heterogeneous. It is not only that different resources stand in varying places along the constitutive-fungible spectrum, but also that there is a difference between the personhood value of an existing right in a constitutive resource and an expectation to have such a right[65].

IV. Over-inclusiveness in Action

By laying down the normative infrastructure of the law of priority conflicts, Part III justifies the main innovation of the Draft Civil Code in this area: the unified regulation of these cases in one chapter of the code. But even in this context – of a coherentist move that is desirable – the proposal goes too far by generalising down to a rather limited number of sections (six). As we will see in this part, priority conflicts arise in different contexts, and this heterogeneity entails normative, and thus also doctrinal, implications. The Draft Code preserves – and rightly so – the distinction between "regular" cases of priority conflicts and cases in which the defendant has purchased the disputed entitlement under market overt conditions[66]. But it ignores some crucial distinctions which Israeli jurisprudence has developed between important categories of priority conflicts law. In this sense, the proposed code may end up constituting a setback, rather than a step forward, in Israeli property law.

In what follows, I survey the state of the law with respect to the three most prevalent priority conflicts regarding land: conflicts between purchasers and the general creditors of the seller; conflicts between two parties to whom an inter-

---

[65] For the last point, see *Dagan*, The Law and Ethics of Restitution (n. 35), 266–267.

[66] See s. 509 to the Draft Civil Code Proposal (n. 1). The main reason and justification for separating out the market overt doctrine is that the third party involved in these cases, e.g., the government running the land registry or the merchant dealing in the sale of the type of good under dispute, can serve as the insurer of the legal accident. Such a party takes much of the bite out of these types of conflict. I argue elsewhere that focusing on the capacity of that third party as an insurer – in terms of both avoidance capabilities and coverage – is the proper key to understanding and interpreting the specific market overt rules. See *Dagan*, Property at a Crossroads (n. 41), 263–284.

mediary sold the same right; and conflicts that emerge out of the so-called "combination transactions," i.e., those between landowners and purchasers of apartments that were built (or contracted to be built) by a contractor on the land before the contractor breached his obligations to the landowner (or went bankrupt). As we will see, the pertinent case law on all three fronts is rather sophisticated and in most cases corresponds to the theoretical analysis offered above. Unfortunately, the Draft Civil Code deals explicitly only with two of these three categories, and even there prescribes somewhat unsatisfactory rules.

1) Purchasers v. General Creditors

Our first category includes cases in which the seller of a piece of land turns out to be a "suboptimal debtor", thus triggering a priority conflict between the purchaser and the seller's general creditors. The main type of case discussed by Israeli courts came about where a general creditor attempted to impose an attachment on the land and the purchaser, of course, raised an objection[67]. The development of this particular doctrine is somewhat complex and need not be recapitulated here[68]. All that is important for our purposes is the skeleton of this narrative and a somewhat more detailed analysis of the *Aharonov* case[69], which is the contemporary leading case in this context.

There are four important signposts in the history leading to the *Aharonov* case. (1) Prior to the Land Law of 1969, Israeli case law applied an equitable norm, which it borrowed from English law, according to which the purchaser prevails over a creditor who seeks to impose an attachment to the extent of the money the purchaser theretofore had actually paid[70]. (2) In 1969, s. 161 of the Land Law, entitled "no equitable rights," was enacted, prescribing that "from the coming into force of this Law, there shall be no right in immovable property except under Law." (3) Soon thereafter, and based on both s. 161 and the Land Law's efforts to upgrade the land registry system and render registration of land constitutive – rather than merely evidentiary – the Supreme Court overruled the old equitable doctrine. The *Boker* case prescribes that a land transaction does not furnish any priority to the purchaser in the conflict with the seller's general creditors even where – as was the case at hand – the purchaser has actually taken possession. If such a purchaser wants to set aside the creditors' attachments, she

[67] Another context involves the status of such purchasers in the debtor's bankruptcy, namely: the question of whether they enjoy a priority *vis-à-vis* the general creditors, or whether the land is part of the pool of the debtor's assets to be distributed *pro rata* among all the creditors (including these purchasers). See *infra* (n. 74).

[68] See *Dagan*, Property at a Crossroads (n. 41), 216–225.

[69] C. A.189/95 *Bank Otzar Hakhayal Inc. v. Aharonov* (1999) 53(4) P. D. 199.

[70] See C. A. 392/65 *Sigalov v. Etzion Cooperative for Wood Works Ltd.* (1966) 20(1) P. D. 442, 446–447; C. A. 528/66 *Stern v. Helka 36 Gush 6127 Company Ltd.* (1967) 21(2) P. D. 342, 352–353; f.H. 30/67 *Stern v. Stern* (1968) 22(2) P. D. 36, 40–42, 49; the *Aharonov* case (n. 69).

needs to pay off the debtor's debts[71]. (4) Following *Boker* the Land Law was amended to negate the *Boker* rule where the purchaser registers a cautionary note before the imposition of the attachment. The added s. 127(b) – which is incorporated also into the proposed code[72] – prescribes that

> "where after a cautionary note has been entered an attachment is imposed on the land, or the right in land, which is the subject of the note, or a receiving order in bankruptcy or a winding-up order is made against the owner of the land _ then, so long as the note has not been struck out, such attachment, order or appointment shall not affect the rights of the person entitled, arising from the undertaking which is the subject of the note."

After some initial confusion, the case law now recognised that with this section, a cautionary note functions as a security interest on the land[73].

The *Aharonov* case dramatically overruled the 30-year-old *Boker* rule, holding that even without a cautionary note a purchaser of land who parted with full value and took possession prevails over the general creditors of the seller even though her right has not yet been duly registered[74]. Two lines of reasoning were advanced in support of the unanimous decision. The first, propounded by the majority, held that when a seller undertakes to sell the ownership of land, the purchaser receives not merely a contractual right, but an "Israeli-made" equitable right. (Section 161, these justices argued, only put an end to the incorporation of English equity into Israeli law, as opposed to the development of indigenous equitable rights.) This is a quasi-property right, which prevails over the right of a creditor of the seller's who has imposed a later attachment.

The majority founded its judgment of this quasi-property right on an argument from the coherence of rules. Although the Land Law does not directly prescribe the content of the right purchasers of land receive, they argued, s. 9 of the Law, governing conflicting transactions, implies that this right is a quasi-property right. Section 9, which will be discussed in some detail below, prescribes that where a person sells rights in land, and – before the transaction is completed by registration of the purchaser's rights – the seller undertakes to effect a conflicting transaction with another purchaser, the rights of the earlier

---

[71] See R.C.A. 178/70 *Boker v. The Anglo-Israeli Company for Management and Responsibility* (1971) 25(2) P.D. 121. Two judges allowed an exception to this rule in extreme cases, where there was a conspiracy between the debtor and one of his general creditors or where a creditor in fact was aware of the sale and the transfer of possession at the time at which he advanced some credit to the seller. See *Boker* (as above), 132, 134.

[72] See s. 676 to the Draft Civil Code (n. 1).

[73] See C.A. 261/88 *Bank Ha-Mizrachi Ha-Meuchad v. Rozovski* (1994) 48(2) P.D. 102, 118, 123, 125. See also C.A. 2659/96 *Rosen v. Bank Ha-Mizrachi Ha-Meuchad* (2001) 55(2) P.D. 529, 536–538.

[74] At first blush the *Aharonov* rule does not cover cases of a bankrupt seller. But as the Court correctly noted in a later case, its rationale also necessarily applies to these cases. See C.A. 3911/01 *Kaspi v. Nes (*2002) 56(6) P.D. 752, 760–761. For an analysis, as well as a critique of the more limiting approach to *Aharonov*, see *Dagan*, Property at a Crossroads (n. 41), 234–236.

purchaser shall prevail, provided that where the later purchaser has acted in good faith, given value, and the transaction with her was registered while she was still acting in good faith, her right shall prevail. The *Aharonov* majority insisted that the *Boker* Court failed to give sufficient weight to this rule which is, they claimed, a fundamental rule with myriad effects across the legal spectrum. For our purposes, the Court held that because s. 9 prescribes that a later purchaser who failed to register her rights in good faith while giving adequate value must yield to the earlier purchaser's rights, that provision must be interpreted as precluding the ability of a sheer creditor to defeat the earlier purchaser because the entitlement of the former cannot possibly be more robust than that of a later purchaser[75].

Like most other claims of the coherence of rules, the majority's reasoning cannot withstand critical scrutiny. As we have seen[76], absent a normative analysis doctrinal incoherence can never prescribe its own cure. This general lesson is vividly vindicated here, because while the majority's opinion bolsters the significance of s. 9 of the Land Law, it renders s. 127(b) of the Land Law superfluous: even without a cautionary note, the earlier purchaser's right in the land – a quasi-property right – trumps a subsequent attachment[77]. (Likewise, nothing in the doctrinal materials necessitates the majority's intuitive argument that the prescription in s. 9 that a later purchaser fails to prevail over an earlier one should clearly apply respecting a general creditor.) I am not suggesting that this difficulty renders the majority's doctrinal structure indefensible: while the popular rule of construction, according to which expression of one thing excludes another, would limit the jurisdiction of a statutory rule to the specific circumstances mentioned therein, the opposite result can just as easily be established by employing analogical reasoning that expands such jurisdiction[78]. But this (unsurprisingly) means that the doctrine alone cannot settle the case; after all, nothing in the doctrine itself tells us that s. 9 is more fundamental or more germane than s. 127(b) (or vice versa). As usual, normative arguments are needed in order to settle the doctrinal indeterminacy; and to choose which of these conflicting rules should direct the regulation of the case at hand.

Fortunately, Strasberg-Cohen J.'s separate opinion, which placed much less emphasis on s. 9, can fill this gap. The crux of her opinion lies in arguments of

---

[75] See *Aharonov* (n. 69), 239–240, 244, 246–247, 249, 251–254, 261, 264–265, 271, 277, 287.

[76] See *supra*, *sub* II. 1).

[77] Cheshin J. attempted to overcome this difficulty by suggesting that s. 127(b) is still relevant for cases that involve a bankrupt seller: *Aharonov* (n. 69), 278. This suggestion is unconvincing because there is no possible reason to distinguish these two cases. See also *supra*, n. 74.

[78] This is, of course, only one example of the doctrinal indeterminacy of our canons of interpretation – see *Karl N Llewellyn*, Remarks on the Theory of Appellate Decision and the Rules or Canons about How Statutes Are to Be Construed, (1950) 3 Vanderbilt Law Review 395, 405 – which is, in turn, an example of the phenomenon of rule multiplicity, which is the ultimate reason for the indeterminacy of legal doctrine. In any specific setting, of course, most lawyers would converge in prescribing the scope of conflicting rules of interpretation. But – like legal determinacy more generally – the entailed determinacy is conventional, not doctrinal. See *Hanoch Dagan*, The Realist Conception of Law, (2007) 57 University of Toronto Law Journal 607.

normative coherence, analysing the conflict between purchasers and general creditors in terms of the normative infrastructure of the law of priority conflicts. In this context, Strasberg-Cohen suggested three reasons for the *Aharonov* rule: (1) A contractual right to purchase a specific property is weightier than an attachment imposed on the same property by a general creditor because the former is a substantive right in that specific property while the latter is merely a procedural instrument which is used in order to secure the realisation of the creditor's rights against the debtor's estate; (2) prioritising purchasers of land is justified because typically purchasers are likely to suffer much greater harm should a later attachment trump their rights. This is true because while attachments are generally imposed by profit-making institutions such as banks, which can self-insure against the risk of a debtor's failure, purchasers are usually ordinary people who invest their life savings in this one land transaction and who will be devastated should the law allow the imposer of the attachment to prevail; (3) while in some contexts the possibility of registering a cautionary note is a viable – indeed the cheapest – way of avoiding a priority conflict, there are many cases in which such registration is impossible and, even if it were possible, would not have helped prevent the creditor's predicament[79]. (The reason for this is that in many cases the latter has advanced credit before the sale of the debtor's land or, in any event, without possibly relying on the debtor's continuous entitlement in that land[80].)

This reasoning nicely fits the analysis of Part III of this article. It considers both the parties' comparative avoidance ability (which is the point of Strasberg-Cohen's third reason) and their comparative vulnerability (which is what her second reason is all about). It does not accord the former issue a lexical priority over the latter. And it shows how the personhood value of property can be translated into legal rules, proposing in effect that we need to consider the qualitative vulnerability of the competing parties and not only their quantitative vulnerability (that is the crux of Strasberg-Cohen's first reason). Although the *Aharonov* rule is not doctrinally predetermined, it is indeed the correct rule, because it is clearly required by all the pertinent normative considerations[81].

The lessons from this analysis are all relevant to the codification project. The *Aharonov* case vividly demonstrates the inevitable failure of most attempts to reason based on the coherence of rules. More specifically, as the remainder of this section demonstrates, by following the approach of the majority, the pro-

[79] See *Aharonov* (n. 69), 219, 221, 232–233, 235–236.

[80] The reason for this last observation, which Strasberg-Cohen does not mention, is that general creditors cannot in any event preclude the possibility of a subsequent sale of their debtor's land and moreover cannot know how many more creditors will seek recovery from that land.

[81] In her comment to this article, Eva-Maria Kieninger defends the German rule which is solely based on registration. See *Eva-Maria Kieninger*, Codification of Property Law – Comments from a German Perspective, in this volume. The reason for the divergence between the two legal systems on this front may derive from the striking difference between the rather heavy formalities which German law requires in order to make a valid transaction in real estate and the very loose requirements of Israeli law on this very point. Nothing in the text above should be read as supporting the position of Israeli law on this last front; it simply accepts it as a given.

posed codification of the *Aharonov* rule leads to undesirable practical consequences.

Section 513 of the Draft Civil Code prescribes a rather sharp rule that privileges the purchaser ("beneficiary" in the language of the proposal) over a creditor of the seller ("the benefactor") who attempts to impose an attachment over the sold property[82]. This rule provides an answer to one practically important question that remained open in *Aharonov*: whether its rule also applies where the purchaser has not yet parted with full value[83]. According to s. 513 – or, for that matter, the approach of the *Aharonov* majority[84] – the purchaser's priority comes into effect from the moment the seller's obligation to sell came into being. Therefore, such a purchaser prevails over the seller's general creditors even when she has only so far given partial – maybe even nominal – payment in consideration for the property[85]. That outcome is normatively inferior to the pre-*Boker* rule, which limited the purchaser's priority to her actual out-of-pocket payment[86]. As I show below, the need for a different doctrinal treatment of priority conflicts that involve purchasers who in fact did not part with a great deal of money derives from the appreciation of the significance of the context to the normative analysis, vindicating again the superiority of local coherence over global coherence.

Indeed, priority conflicts that involve purchasers who have not yet parted with full value require some modifications in the analysis of the pure *Aharonov* scenario. First, the quantitative comparative vulnerability test is not as determinative as regards a purchaser who paid only a fraction of the value of the land at stake as it is regarding a fully-paid purchaser: for the former type of purchaser it is no longer the case that her potential loss dramatically outweighs the loss of the general creditors such as the seller's suppliers, employees, or tort victims[87]. Second, the qualitative comparative vulnerability test is likewise affected: the earlier the contractual stage of the purchaser-seller transaction, the weaker her claim that the asset at stake is constitutive for her personhood and thus the higher the similarity between purchaser and general creditor. The pre-*Boker* rule captures these important distinctions[88]. Notice that where this rule applies, a

---

[82] The only cases in which this rule does not apply are of revocable obligations to give a gift. See s. 513(b) and s. 183 to the Draft Civil Code (n. 1).

[83] One may hope that s. 513 does not intend to limit the scope of the *Aharonov* rule so that it would not apply in cases of the debtor's bankruptcy; see n. 74.

[84] The reason for this is that the question of how much value the earlier purchaser has already parted with is irrelevant under s. 9 of the Land Law.

[85] See *Aharonov* (n. 69), 247–248, 285–286 (*per* Barak and Englard, JJ.).

[86] Indeed, two Justices – Strasberg-Cohen and Dorner – were reluctant to join Barak and Englard's suggestion on this front. See *Aharonov* (n. 69), 238, 288.

[87] This observation derives from the function of value actually paid by the parties as proxies for their relative vulnerability.

[88] One may be tempted to learn from these observations that each case of a partially paid creditor should be analysed on its own facts. That temptation should be resisted because here – as elsewhere in the law of priority conflicts – vague standards are inferior to clear rules.

purchaser who wishes to complete the transaction needs to buy her priority from the general creditors by paying them the value of that portion of the asset with respect to which they are prioritised. This means that in many cases – where the present value and the contract value of the asset are roughly the same – there is no practical difference between reviving the pre-*Boker* rule and furnishing the partially-paid creditor with full priority, because in both cases such a mutually beneficial deal is likely to follow[89]. The practical effect of the choice between these relates to the allocation of the entitlement to increases of the value of the asset from the time of the transaction to the time of the seller's failure. Applying the *Aharonov* full priority rule allocates this entitlement to the purchaser, while the pre-*Boker* rule allocates it to the general creditors. The pre-*Boker* rule fully protects the purchaser's investment (her reliance interest), while insisting that she cannot also expect to enjoy the full benefits of a transaction (her expectation interest) when the seller's general creditors compete over his meagre estate. This middle of the way solution seems justified given that both quantitative and qualitative comparative vulnerability tests require that the priority of the partially-paid purchaser will be weaker than that of the fully-paid purchaser.

2) Conflicting Transactions

Another type of priority conflict that the proposed code explicitly regulates is that of conflicting transactions. Section 512 of the proposal – which is supposed to replace s. 9 of the Land Law[90] – can be read as the culmination of a long process of common law evolution. As we will see, the main thrust of this process, and thus the core effect of s. 512, is normatively desirable. Furthermore, I also have no quarrel with the width of this category of priority conflicts. As long as s. 512 is not expected to govern other types of conflicts (such as the one discussed under 3)), the Draft Civil Code, like s. 9 of the existing Land Law, cannot be faulted for over-inclusiveness. And yet, even in this happy context a few substantive comments are appropriate.

A brief description of the two most important developments in the history of the modern (Israeli) law of conflicting transactions may help explain both my endorsement of the core point of s. 512 and my specific criticisms. First there was the *Wertheimer* case[91]. This case involved a classic tragedy of conflicting transac-

[89] The pre-*Boker* rule is unlikely to encourage general creditors to hold out on their consent because this is clearly also the best deal for them, given the significant savings in transaction costs associated with following through with this completed transaction, and given the low probability, known to both parties, of finding a third party who would be interested in buying the portion of the asset to which they are entitled. In any event, the unlikely case of such a holdout is likely to be deemed by a court as an illegitimate (*mala fides*) abuse of rights. See s. 14 of the Land Law, 1969.

[90] As well as s. 80 of the Land Law and s. 12 of the Chattels Law, which regulate, respectively, conflicting leases and conflicting chattels sale transactions.

[91] f.H. 21/80 *Wertheimer v. Harari* (1981) 35(3) P.D. 253.

tions: The Hararis sold their apartment twice – first to the Wertheimers and then to the Binyaminis. The former paid only a nominal sum of money, while the latter paid a substantial amount. Neither transaction was registered. The majority of the Court applied s. 9 strictly and thus held that because Binyamini failed to register their rights, Wertheimer must prevail notwithstanding the fact that Binyamini's loss was 70 times higher than the loss of Wertheimer would have been had Binyamini been declared victorious. The majority insisted that it could not circumvent the explicit wording of s. 9, and thus rejected the suggestion of the minority to avoid this uncomfortable outcome by applying s. 3(4) of the Law of Contracts (Remedies for Breach of Contract) Law, 1970, which prescribes that a contract is unenforceable where justice so requires. It further justified its conclusion by arguing that conflicting transactions should be subject to clear rules, rather than vague standards, and by claiming that without more information regarding the conflicting parties' overall predicaments, the sheer gap between the payments cannot determine their comparative vulnerability. In passing, the Court on its own initiative raised, but left open, the question of whether an earlier purchaser's failure to register a cautionary note, where such registration was possible, should affect the outcome.

This last *obiter dictum* brought about a vibrant legal discourse. As Nili Cohen explained, the doctrinal source of the difficulty lies in the mixed message of the Land Law. On the one hand, s. 9 prioritises an earlier purchaser unless a later purchaser registers her rights in good faith while giving adequate value. On the other hand, ss. 126 and 127 established a new regulatory mechanism – the registration of a cautionary note – that facilitates the ability of an earlier purchaser easily and cheaply to notify third parties about his claims, thus preventing the occurrence of legal accidents in the first place. The existence of such a mechanism may imply that one who fails to employ this means should not be allowed to prevail should such an accident eventually take place[92].

For many years the Court was reluctant to settle the matter, and in practice allowed earlier purchasers to prevail notwithstanding their failure to register a cautionary note. But in the *Ganz* case it dramatically changed its course[93]. *Ganz* held that the omission of an earlier purchaser who was able, but failed, to register a cautionary note regarding his rights in the land for a long period of time amounts to an infringement of the overarching duty of good faith. Therefore, in such cases, even later purchasers who have not registered their own right will prevail despite s. 9. The Court did not purport to resolve the doctrinal indeterminacy just mentioned by resorting to purely doctrinal means. Rather, in line with one of the main themes of this article, it invoked normative arguments to substantiate as well as refine the scope of its new holding.

---

[92] See *Nili Cohen*, A Minor's Contract to Acquire an Interest in Land, as Against the Vendor's Creditor, (1993) 41 Ha-Praklit 161 (in Hebrew).

[93] C.A. 2643/97 *Ganz v. British & Colonial et al.* (2003) 57(2) P.D. 385.

The crux of the Court's reasoning lies in the comparative avoidance ability test, which in many such cases yields the definite answer advanced by the Court. In the typical case the registration of a cautionary note is an obvious and rather trivial means to prevent a legal accident. Failure to do so in such circumstances invites such unfortunate contingencies and is thus tantamount to an inexcusable disregard for other people's interests in clear violation of the social responsibility value of property. Depriving an earlier purchaser who failed to register a cautionary note of the priority set by s. 9 is an appropriate *ex post* response as well as a proper incentive for other such parties to do the right thing.

This simple but persuasive rationale explains two exceptions to the *Ganz* rule mentioned by the Court, in which the earlier party is clearly *not* the cheapest cost avoider of the legal accident, namely: cases in which it is impossible to register a cautionary note; and cases in which the earlier purchaser's failure did not cause the legal accident, either because the later purchaser actually knew about the first transaction, or because she made the purchase without examining the registration or the land that was already possessed by the earlier purchaser. Moreover, explaining the *Ganz* rule on this basis also justifies excluding from its coverage cases in which inducing the registration of a cautionary note by the earlier party is undesirable, hence the third exception mentioned in *Ganz* concerning cases in which the first contender in time is married to the formal owner.

Section 512 of the Draft Civil Code adopts the general thrust of the *Ganz* holding, and it is indeed for this reason that it is generally desirable. However, *Ganz* left open at least three questions[94]. Unfortunately, regarding all three, the position adopted by s. 512 is rather disappointing.

The first open question in *Ganz* is how stringent this new rule is. There are two aspects to that question, one of form, the other of substance. The former was implicitly raised in *Ganz* by Matza J., who urged the Court to restate its holding as making the earlier purchaser's priority subject to the good faith duty without prescribing specific rules regarding the registration of cautionary notes, or implying that there are no other ways in which this duty can be deemed violated[95]. In addition, two other justices, who also concurred in the *Ganz* outcome, insisted that the failure to register a cautionary note can upset the priority rule of s. 9 only in exceptional cases, such as the case at hand, in which the delay in registration was outrageous (17 years!) and the later purchaser had already taken title[96]. Even Barak J., who delivered the main opinion in this case, opened the door to the possibility of limiting *Ganz* by suggesting that it may not apply where the earlier purchaser and the formal owner agree to postpone the registra-

---

[94] There is in fact a fourth issue: whether the later purchaser's own failure to register a cautionary note deprives her of the ability to rely on the *Ganz* rule in order to gain priority. In *Ganz* the Court seemed to answer this question in the negative; *Ganz* (n. 93), 408. The Draft Code prefers the opposite answer. See the suffix of s. 512(b). As I explain elsewhere, the Court's rule is preferable. See *Dagan*, Property at a Crossroads (n. 41), 255.

[95] *Ganz* (n. 93), 425–426.

[96] *Ganz* (n. 93), 415–416, 430–432.

tion of a cautionary note until the latter perform certain acts, such as the payment of a certain percentage of the agreed price[97].

At least a literal reading of the proposed s. 512, which reverses the priority of an earlier purchaser (a "first assignee" in the language of the proposal) if her failure to register a cautionary note is negligent suggests, or in any event opens up the possibility of, recasting the earlier purchaser's obligations as open-ended (along the lines of Matza J.'s position) and furthermore may allow an exception based on the terms of his agreement with the formal owner. Both of these directions seem to me misguided. *Ganz*'s rather precise formulation of the circumstances in which a failure to register a cautionary note is preferable to Matza J.'s approach because, as I have already intimated, there is a particular significance in our context to keeping the law clear and predictable. The law of conflicting transactions affects many cases, which typically involve significant amounts of money. The social welfare value of property requires prescribing clear rules in such cases. Such clear rules minimise the parties' litigation costs. Even more importantly, they preserve the clear message of the law that in general only by registering a cautionary note – and thus preventing a potential legal accident – can earlier purchasers be secure against conflicting transactions. Furthermore, in such conflicts over what is typically a constitutive resource to both parties, the parties are likely to be locked into a bilateral monopoly, which is in turn likely to produce regressive outcomes[98]. Therefore, the distributive justice value of property also opposes the use of open-ended standards of liability in our context.

The possibility of allowing the seller and the earlier purchaser to bypass the *Ganz* rule via a consensual arrangement should likewise be firmly rejected. Supporters of this putative exception to *Ganz* found it on the freedom of contract and further explain that it is particularly warranted in cases where the seller's objection to the registration of a cautionary note is temporary and is indeed limited to the first stages of this transaction, until the earlier purchaser parts with a substantial amount of money[99]. This reasoning is a *non sequitur.* There is neither a conceptual nor a normative connection between the proper scope of the liberty of contracting parties consensually to shape the terms of their agreement and the rights of third parties who may be affected by such an agreement[100]. More specifically, an accommodating approach to freedom of contract – which is, by and large, to be supported – should not be interpreted as validating terms that are detrimental to third parties. Even where the contractual parties find such terms appealing, the law has good reasons to intervene and prevent such negative externalities, either by invalidating these terms as being opposed to public policy

---

[97] *Ganz* (n. 93), 400, 404–408.

[98] See *supra*, text accompanying note 57.

[99] *Miguel Deutsch*, The Burden of Registering a Warning Note – The *Ganz* Ruling and Its Effects, (2003) 47 Ha-Praklit 181 (in Hebrew).

[100] See *Dagan*, (2003) 92 California Law Review, 1543–1557.

or by negating their detrimental effect on third parties. This last result seems particularly called for in the case of a temporary delay in placing the cautionary note. The seller's request of such a delay is understandable and an earlier purchaser's concession on this front may well facilitate their transaction. But the risk this term imposes on third parties cannot be redeemed by virtue of this happy union of the two parties' wills. Furthermore, the fact that the earlier purchaser did not yet part with any significant value cannot salvage this unjustified external effect. If anything, such a lack of detrimental reliance seems to point in the other direction, because it implies that this purported consensual exception applies where the comparative vulnerability test suggests that the later purchaser must prevail.

The second question left open in *Ganz* is whether the *Wertheimer* rule is still good law. In *Ganz* Barak J. insisted that it is, explaining that the new rule he prescribed does not sanction the consideration of the parties' comparative vulnerability, but only the consideration of their relative ability to avoid legal accidents[101]. The two other Justices who addressed this question questioned that view, implying that once the law relieves the stringency by which it enforces the priority set by s. 9 of the Land Law, the way is cleared for a reassessment of *Wertheimer* allowing for taking into account a later purchaser's excessive vulnerability, in particular where by the time the conflict was brought to light she had already taken possession[102].

Section 512 does not take any affirmative position on this front, but at least on its face seems to endorse the *Wertheimer* rule, so that in cases where the earlier purchaser was justified in his failure to register a cautionary note, he will prevail even if he parted with much less value than the later purchaser. It would be unfortunate if this moment of reconsideration of Israeli private law were not used for an explicit reversal of the undesirable *Wertheimer* rule. To be sure, I do not claim that *Ganz* logically requires such a reversal. As a formal matter, both rules are indeed doctrinally possible. But *Ganz* does set the stage for the reconsideration of *Wertheimer* by its implicit recognition that nothing in the language of s. 9 of the Land Law necessitates the dominance ascribed to it in *Wertheimer.* More precisely, it implies that just as the registration provisions and the duty of good faith can set limits to the scope of s. 9 in cases of the earlier party's failure to register a cautionary note, so can s. 3(4) of the Law of Contracts (Remedies for Breach of Contract) Law provide a possible doctrinal hook in order to refine its prescriptions. The sheer doctrinal indeterminacy is obviously not a good reason in and of itself to upset *Wertheimer* (although it does mean that, as usual, the *Wertheimer* Court's claim that it is bound by the language of s. 9 was simply fallacious). But there are good, normative reasons to seize the opportunity and reverse *Wertheimer.*

The crux of the matter lies in *Wertheimer*'s disregard for the significance of the comparative vulnerability test. Recall that the *Wertheimer* Court addressed this

---

[101] *Ganz* (n. 93), 398–399, 408–409.

[102] *Ganz* (n. 93), 415, 429, 431.

concern and insisted that in order to take it into account a comprehensive examination of the conflicting parties' overall predicament, rather than a much narrower comparison of the values they parted with, is required. Clearly, this proposition is correct insofar as our goal is to insure that we always make accurate assessments. Thus, if we had known that Wertheimer was in fact extremely poor while Binyamini belonged to society's uppermost echelon, we would have admitted that even a rather minor objective harm to the former would be more severe than a much larger (70 times larger) objective harm to the latter. (This conclusion derives, of course, from the diminishing marginal utility of money.) But the Court's conclusion in *Wertheimer* does not follow from this observation. The Court presents the strategy of a comprehensive assessment of the parties' overall predicament and the option of ignoring altogether the comparative vulnerability test as if they had exhausted all alternative courses of action, and opts for the latter due to the obvious problems (in terms of commercial stability as well as the rule of law) of the former. But this binarism is simply wrong: alongside these two alternatives, there is a third possible course of action, which is in fact more desirable than either of the other two: using the comparison of the payments made by both parties as a proxy for their comparative vulnerability. As a proxy, it is admittedly imperfect, as the hypothetical of a poor Wertheimer and a wealthy Binyamini demonstrates. But this is indeed a rather exaggerated hypothetical. In many, perhaps most cases, purchasers of a given piece of real estate belong to roughly the same socio-economic stratum[103]. And in these cases the technical and innocuous comparison of the payments they parted with – in other words, their respective losses should they each lose in the priority conflict and find themselves with an almost worthless claim against the intermediary – *is* a good indication of their comparative vulnerability.

Finally, the *Ganz* case left open the question of its relationship with the *Aharonov* rule, and the Draft Code does not help in resolving this difficulty. On its face, these two cases run in opposite directions: while *Aharonov* curbs the role of the land registry and fortifies s. 9, *Ganz* strengthens the reliance on registration and limits the scope of s. 9. But a proper appreciation of the important qualitative distinctions between these two types of priority conflicts, and thus of the normative underpinnings of these two seminal cases, demonstrates that both of these rules can, and indeed should, be easily accommodated together. Recall that the *Aharonov* rule regulates conflicts between a purchaser and the seller's general creditors in which both the quantitative and the qualitative vulnerability tests privilege the former and the comparative advance test does not lean, at least not heavily, in favour of the latter. By contrast, the *Ganz* rule deals with conflicting transactions in which in many cases the parties' vulnerability is less determinative, while their comparative avoidance ability is rather sharp. Therefore,

---

[103] The most conspicuous exception to this may be cases in which one party purchases one apartment for its own use and the other party purchses it in order to rent it out.

Ganz should not be read as reversing *Aharonov*[104], at least not insofar as the purchaser is an individual, as opposed to a commercial entity, who buys real estate for his or her own use[105].

3) Combination Transactions

I turn now to the third and final type of priority conflict to be considered in this article: the important and rather prevalent case of "combination transactions", which end up in conflicts between landowners and third parties who purchase apartments built on the owners' land from an intermediary: the contractor. The Draft Civil Code, like the current Land Law, is silent on this matter. This silence is puzzling given the rich jurisprudence that has been developed over the years. As the paragraphs below demonstrate, Israeli common law nicely adjusts the general normative underpinnings of the law of priority conflicts laid down in Part III above to the particular setting under consideration. The codification process should and can supply a fine opportunity for codifying, and maybe also refining, this emerging body of law.

A combination transaction is a transaction according to which a contractor builds an apartment building on someone else's real estate. The completed building is then registered as a condominium and the landowner transfers a defined set of its apartments to the contractor or to those who in the meantime purchased from the contractor the right to receive such apartments, while the landowner nevertheless remains the owner of the other apartments. An important benefit of such an arrangement to the parties involved is that most or all of the needed financing is supplied from the sales of the apartments that are yet to be built.

Difficulties arise, however, where the contractor materially breaches his obligations to the other parties, which typically occurs where he becomes insolvent or is on his way to insolvency. The landowner can obviously cancel her contract with the contractor. The important question is, however, whether she can also strike out the cautionary note registered by the purchasers based on the claim that such cancellation amounts to the elimination of the cause underlying that cautionary note[106]. An affirmative answer to this question places the costs of the legal accident at hand on the apartment purchasers; a negative answer places it on the landowner.

The rule adopted by the Court opts for the latter alternative, prescribing that in cases of combination transactions the registration of cautionary notes on a landowner's real estate creates an independent legal relation between her and the

---

[104] This point was recognised in C.A. 790/97 *Bank Ha-Mizrachi Ha-Meuchad v. Gadi* (2004) 59(3) P.D. 697.

[105] P.M. (Jerusalem) 2247/03 *Reshef – as a General Receiver v. Yosseph* (2004) (not yet published).

[106] See s. 132(a)(2) to the Land Law, 1969.

apartment purchasers (or their financing banks). This rule implies that a landowner's consent to the registration of cautionary notes creates a direct obligation towards the purchasers (or their financiers) that protects them in the interim period in which she still owns the land[107]. Thus, cancelling the landowner's contract with the contractor does not affect, in and of itself, the validity of the cautionary notes and cannot justify their eradication[108].

The direct obligation doctrine is normatively desirable because it mimics the rule that most rational parties are likely to adopt, thus facilitating the maximisation of the contractual surplus that combination transactions offer[109]. The reason for this is intimately related to the normative infrastructure of the law of priority conflicts: this rule assigns the burden of legal accidents that may occur following such transactions to the cheapest cost avoider of such accidents. As Uriel Reichman noted, because the landowner is the most effective risk avoiding party, landowners who allow apartment purchasers to register cautionary notes on their land and fail to protect themselves by taking any kind of security from the contractor, should bear the cost of any ensuing legal accident[110]. This proposition, in turn, seems valid for two reasons: (1) in most cases there are many apartment purchasers and only one (or a few) landowner(s), so that it is more efficient to concentrate the avoidance efforts on the party that is least likely to face collective action difficulties performing it; (2) the landowner typically enjoys (probably due to economies of scale) superior legal advice and better ability to affect and supervise the triangular arrangement. Given this conclusion of the comparative avoidance test – and the fact that typically there is no reason to believe that landowners are more (or less) vulnerable than apartment purchasers – the direct obligation doctrine is indeed warranted.

This conclusion does not mean, to be sure, that the doctrine should be immutable. Quite the contrary: unlike the other types of priority conflicts discussed above, conflicts that result from combination transactions occur in a contractual setting. Thus, the fact that there are good reasons for prescribing the direct obligation rule as the default rule, should not affect the parties' freedom of contract should they decide to assign the risk of the failure of their triangular

---

[107] The landowner's obligations are assignable to the purchaser's transferees, see C.A. 886/97 *Burstein v. Hudad* (1998) 52(4) P.D. 68.

[108] C.A. 813/85 *Nachshon v. Shay* (1988) 42(1) P.D. 340; C.A. 250/89 *Bank Ha-Atzmaut for Mortgages and Development Ltd. v. Shpouch* (1993) 47(1) P.D. 593, 602–607; C.A. 3380/92 Farge v. David (1995) 49(2) P.D. 61, 72–75; C.A. 540/88 *G.E.G. Investments (in liquidation) v. Land Registrar in Petah-Tikwa* (1995) 49(2) P.D. 735; *Burstein* (n. 107), 74; C.A. 5549/94 *K.I.M.A. for Investments and Building Ltd. v. Grinfeld* (1997) *not published*; C.A. 6439/99 *"Tfachot" Bank for Mortgages in Israel Ltd. v. Perach* (2003) 58(2) P.D. 106, 119.

[109] The justification the Court itself provided for this rule is dubious. See *Dagan*, Property at a Crossroads (n. 41), 258–259.

[110] *Uriel Reichman*, Cautions – Nature, Recordation and Protection against Conflicting Transactions, (1984) 10 Tel Aviv University Law Review 297, 352 (in Hebrew). For further discussion on this and other issues in combination transactions, see Ofer Grosskopf's contribution to this volume, *sub* IV. 3).

arrangement in a different way. The law should allow the parties to opt out of this rule in cases where it doesn't fit their preferences as long as the apartment purchasers are fully aware of the consequences of such an opt out so that they can properly price the added risk that is thus shifted to them. This indeed is the rule of the Israeli common law in our context. The Court is rather strict with landowners who want to opt out, requiring that they use explicit and unequivocal language[111]. But once such language is employed, it is given full effect even where this means assigning the risk of a contractor's insolvency to apartment owners who are thus treated as any other creditor, and notwithstanding the fact that they may already possess an apartment in the building[112]. This result is difficult but nonetheless justified because the existence of an explicit and unequivocal proviso to the landowner's obligation in the contract of the apartment purchaser with the contractor renders such purchaser the better avoider of any legal accident that derives from her reliance on a more robust obligation.

In addition to the benefit of putting these desirable rules into statutory language, a section in the Draft Civil Code that dealt with combination transactions would facilitate the resolution of at least one important question that is still open[113], i.e., whether the direct obligation rule applies also in cases where the contractor has in fact not yet started the construction of the building and the apartment purchasers accordingly have only parted with relatively nominal sums of money[114]. If the law were to focus exclusively on the comparative avoidance test, this fact would be deemed irrelevant. But if, as I have argued above, the comparative vulnerability test should also be considered, these cases should prompt an exception to the direct obligation rule, so that following the contractor's breach the landowner will be able to erase the cautionary notes she allowed to be registered.

V. Conclusion

The codification of private law is a heroic enterprise. A codification process can facilitate the re-examination and the refinement of our existing rules and furthermore contribute to their coherent coexistence. We should, however, take codifiers' attempts to improve the coherence of private law with a pinch of salt remembering that in most cases the only defensible coherentist moves are normative (rather than doctrinal) and local (rather than global). This important lesson requires rethinking two unfortunate suggestions included in the proposed

---

[111] C.A. 570/87 *Burstein v. Zeev-Lev-Har, Company for Building and Investments Ltd.* (1990) 44(2) P.D. 793.

[112] See *G.E.G.* (n. 108), 746–747.

[113] Another open question deals with the precise content of the landowner's (default) obligation. Here the better answer seems to be that the cautionary note serves as a security interest. See *Reichman*, (1984) 10 Tel Aviv University Law Review 346–352.

[114] This issue was debated between Shamgar and Goldberg JJ. in *Nachshon* (n. 108), 350–352.

Israeli Civil Code: unifying the remedial principles of contract law and tort law and creating a super-category of property covering all types of assets.

By contrast, the proposed consolidation in one chapter of the law of priority conflicts is a laudable suggestion. The rules regulating this amalgam of cases need to face similar normative questions and thus justify unified treatment. Yet, even in this context important factual differences between the different types of conflicts entail significant contextual refinements that an overly broad treatment obscures. An improved version of the Israeli Draft Civil Code should clearly address these subtleties, which the existing common law already reflects.

Codification of Property Law: Comments from a German Perspective

By Eva-Maria Kieninger

Summary of Contents

I. Codification and Coherence

Hanoch Dagan's contribution starts with a discussion of the merits and dangers of codification in general. He criticises the Draft Israeli Civil Code for being, at least in part, overzealous in its attempt to reach coherence of rules. He distinguishes between coherence of rules and normative coherence. Technical coherence may be desirable but cannot guide us when it comes to normative questions. Here, a coherence of values is asked for (normative coherence). But even the attempt to reach normative coherence can be dangerous if it is applied on a global rather than on a local scale. Codification carries the risk of too much global coherence, or – in other words – the risk that overarching principles are given too much weight, that they get out of control. This is perhaps one of the reasons why there is such a strong opposition in common law jurisdictions to codification. There is a fear that solutions to individual problems might get determined by dogmatic considerations rather than by good common sense and the interests of the parties.

Property law is often said to be more strongly determined by general principles than other areas, because of the absolute character of real rights. Every textbook on German property law invariably starts with a discussion of the general principles, such as the absolute character of proprietary rights, the *numerus clausus*, the specificity and publicity principles, as well as the famous principles of separation and abstraction[1]. Nevertheless, German law has, at least in my view, largely escaped the dangers of over-inclusiveness and global coherence by not taking its own principles too seriously. They function as tools of analysis and as means of structuring a solution, rather than as determinants of a certain outcome of an individual case. It is perhaps significant that none of the principles that are commonly named as being most fundamental for German property law are actually spelled out in the Code. Also, compared to the Draft Israeli Civil Code, German property law does not attempt to reach the same level of coherence and abstraction. There is no general notion of "asset" in property law that would include movable and immovable tangibles as well as intangibles. The notion of "patrimony" (*Vermögen*) is used in the law of obligations, but not in property law. In contrast to the Israeli Draft Civil Code, the BGB does not contain any general rules on priority conflicts. Also, despite the BGB's love for general parts, there exists neither a general part of property law (apart from §§ 90–103 BGB, which in any case form part of the first, not the third, book), nor are the rules that apply to movables and immovables alike very numerous (cf. §§ 854–872, 903 ff., 985–1011 BGB).

As far as the fundamental principles of property law are concerned, it is a well-known fact that to some of them court practice only pays lip-service. Perhaps the most prominent example is secured transactions law. Traditionally, German property law is said to adhere to the principle of publicity[2]. The means of publicity are possession in the case of movables and registration in the case of immovables. The principle is not expressed directly but rather through its different functions. The person who has possession of a movable asset, or is duly registered as the owner of a piece of land, is deemed to be the owner (§§ 1006 I first sentence, 891 I BGB). Transfer of possession and registration in the case of an immovable are prerequisites for the acquisition of ownership (§§ 929, 873 BGB). Likewise, possession and registration are the basis of *bona fide* acquisition from a non-owner (§§ 932 ff., 892 BGB).

Nevertheless, with respect to movables, possession as an indication of ownership has almost completely lost its meaning through the recognition of non-possessory security interests such as the fiduciary transfer of ownership and the prolonged and extended forms of retention of title[3]. This development began even before codification. The first cases on security transfer of ownership had already been decided by the Imperial Supreme Court (*Reichsgericht*) before the BGB entered into force in 1900[4]. With the exception of the possessory pledge

---

[1] Cf., for example, *Karl Heinz Schwab/Hanns Prütting*, Sachenrecht (32th ed., 2006), 9.

[2] *Schwab/Prütting* (n. 1), 14.

[3] Cf. BGH of 18 June 1980, BGHZ 77, 274.

[4] Cf. RG of 2 June 1890, RGZ 26, 180, where the *Reichsgericht* already spoke of security transfer of ownership as being an established institution according to dominant opinion and long-standing jurisdiction.

the whole body of securities in movables stayed out of the codification process and was deliberately left to case law[5]. The courts, in turn, did not apply the principles underlying the possessory pledge, namely the requirement of publicity through dispossession (§ 1205 BGB) and the prohibition of the *pactum commissorium* (§ 1229 BGB), but instead built a secured transactions law on ownership in circumvention of the principles underlying property law. It is interesting to note that in traditional common-law jurisdictions such as the United States, Canada or New Zealand, we find coherent statutes on securities in movables, whereas German law in this area consists almost exclusively of judge-made law, which is – at least partly – in direct contradiction to the principles and provisions of the Civil Code.

Another example for this contradiction is the way in which the courts uphold retention of title clauses in manufacturing situations. § 950 BGB states that the manufacturer acquires ownership unless the value of the manufacturing process is considerably lower than that of the material. As a matter of principle, property law is not subject to party autonomy. Nevertheless, the BGH constantly holds that the question who is a manufacturer within the meaning of § 950 BGB is to be decided by taking into account the contract between the seller under retention of title and the buyer-manufacturer[6]. Thus, the parties are effectively allowed to circumvent § 950 BGB by stipulating that the buyer produces the new goods for the seller.

By reminding the reader of these developments in the context of codification and coherence, it is not the intent of the author to recommend the same path to other jurisdictions. But the German experience might be a useful example to show that codification and a wish for coherence can live side by side with a recognition of commercially sound practices and good common sense. In the absence of a well-functioning statutory body of secured transactions law, the German courts were compelled to develop a judge-made system, in which they largely had to disregard the property law principles of the Code. So, my overall comment on the first part would be that overarching principles can be a useful tool of analysis but do not necessarily hamper the development of reasonable judge-made law if the principles are not applied too rigorously.

II. Priority Conflicts

Te second part of Hanoch Dagan's contribution deals with priority conflicts. There is a great variety of possible priority conflicts, see e.g. the list of priority

[5] Cf. *Hans Friedhelm Gaul*, Lex commissoria und Sicherungsübereignung, (1968) 168 Archiv für die civilistische Praxis 351, 357 ff., with further references.

[6] BGH of 3 March 1956, BGHZ 20, 159 (163); BGH of 28 June 1954, BGHZ 14, 114 (117); BGH of 15 October 1966, BGHZ 46, 117 (118).

rules in the Uncitral Legislative Guide on Secured Transactions[7]. But, following Hanoch Dagan, I will only cover the three most basic situations. They are (1) the conflict between an owner and a *bona fide* purchaser, (2) the conflict between a transferee of a real right and the general creditors of the transferor, and (3) the conflict between two transferees of real rights in the same assets.

German law treats all three situations separately and does not attempt to put them together under one heading. In fact, the term "priority conflict" in the wide sense of covering all possible conflicts between persons who claim to have a right in the same asset or entity of assets, is hitherto hardly known to German legal terminology.[8]

Nevertheless, it is certainly possible to analyse German property law rules according to their solution of priority conflicts. The first category (owner versus *bona fide* purchaser) is covered by the rules on *bona fide* acquisition, the second group (transferee of a real right versus general creditors of the transferor) by the rules on transfer of real rights in general, and the third category (two transferees of real rights in the same assets) either, if the real right in question is ownership, again by the general rules on transfer of ownership, or, if the right in question is a limited real right – such as a mortgage or a hypothec – by the rules on ranking. In addition, the conflict between a holder of a (limited) real right and the general creditors of the transferor is also covered by the rules on execution and insolvency. The following paragraphs explain the basic German rules and compare them to the Israeli Draft Civil Code.

1) Bona Fide Acquisition from a non-Owner

The rules that are contained in ss. 508–511 (= ex ss. 584–587) of the Israeli Draft Civil Code would, in German law, be considered as rules on *bona fide* acquisition. Nevertheless their substance, compared with German law, is quite different, as a brief comparison of the main provisions on movables, immovables and rights demonstrates.

a) Movables

Israeli law stands in the tradition of English law. Both – as a matter of principle – adhere to the *nemo dat* rule[9]. Acquisition of good title from a non-owner is not

---

[7] A/CN.9/637 of 28 September 2007, recommendations nn. 73ff. (cf. http://www.uncitral.org).

[8] An exception is the use of the term *"Rang"* by *Jan Wilhelm*, Sachenrecht (3rd ed., 2007) para. 2460, as including the relationship between a former owner of an asset and a subsequent purchaser. Usually however, "Rang" only covers the relationship between two or more parties having security rights in the same immovable, cf. *Jürgen F. Baur/Rolf Stürner*, Sachenrecht (17th ed., 1999) § 17 para. 1.

[9] Cf., for English law, *Michael Bridge*, in Eva-Maria Kieninger (ed.), Security Rights in Movable

based on the doctrine that possession is tantamount to title, but rather on practical exceptions to the *nemo dat* principle, such as the so-called "market overt" rule. In addition to good faith and consideration, this rule requires that the seller has to deal with property of the same kind as the assets in question and that the sale was in the ordinary course of business. In German law, no such additional requirements exist. Whether the sale was in the ordinary course of business will, however, influence the decision on the issue of good faith. Consideration is also not required for *bona fide* acquisition under German law. But if the transaction is gratuitous, the acquirer has to re-transfer the asset on account of a claim in unjustified enrichment (§ 816 I second sentence BGB). Last, but not least, *bona fide* acquisition of movables is not possible under German law, if the owner or the person in whose hands he has left the asset has involuntarily lost possession. Under the provisions of the Israeli Draft Civil Code, these cases are probably captured by the ordinary course of business rule, so that my guess would be that, with respect to the practical outcome, there will not be such a great difference as it seems on a theoretical level.

b) Immovables

For immovables, the Draft Israeli Civil Code – probably in conformity with the traditional rules – requires good faith, consideration and reliance on registration. In German law, only positive knowledge of the incorrect registration will prevent acquisition from a non-owner. With immovables, grossly negligent ignorance of the fact that the seller is not entitled to transfer ownership (or another real right, as the case may be) is irrelevant. Active reliance on the registration in the land register is also no condition of *bona fide* acquisition under § 892 BGB. It is fully sufficient that the transferor is entered in the register as the owner or the holder of the right in question. Whether the acquirer had any knowledge of the content of the register and whether he in any way relied on it, is of no importance. Yet again, it may well be that the practical implications of this difference are marginal because, even under German law, every acquirer or at least his legal counsel will check the land register before entering into a transaction.

c) Assignment of Rights

The most distinct difference between German law and the Israeli Draft Civil Code with respect to *bona fide* acquisition concerns assignments. Section 509(3) Israeli Draft Civil Code (= ex s. 585[3]) provides for a *bona fide* acquisition of rights, which also includes claims. By way of contrast, in German law, acquisition of a claim from a non-owner is only possible if the claim is secured by a

Property in European Private Law (2004), 326; for Israeli law, see s. 508 Draft Civil Code (= ex s. 584).

mortgage (§ 1138 BGB)[10] and in the case of § 405 BGB. Apart from this exception, there is no *bona fide* acquisition of claims.

d) Right of Redemption

Last but not least, the Israeli Draft Civil Code also includes a right of redemption (s. 511 [= ex s. 587]). A similar rule is known to Swiss law (Art. 934(2) *Zivilgesetzbuch*, so-called "Lösungsrecht"), but not to German property law. Under the BGB *bona fide* acquisition is a case of "all or nothing". The only remedy that is left to the deprived party is a claim in unjustified enrichment for the purchase price which the non-owner has received from the *bona fide* purchaser (§ 816 I first sentence BGB).

2) Conflict between Transferee and General Creditors of the Transferor

The general question that is posed in this priority conflict is the following: which steps does a transferee have to complete in order to safeguard his rights against the general creditors of the transferor? For German law, this question is quite easily answered. As far as full ownership is concerned, we do not think in the category of priority conflicts. We simply ask whether the transferee has acquired ownership or a real right that is deemed to be as good as ownership, i.e., a so-called expectancy ("Anwartschaftsrecht"). As a matter of principle, German law does not distinguish between the proprietary relationship *inter partes* and *erga omnes*. Therefore, if the transferee has acquired ownership vis-à-vis the transferor, he is also owner with respect to the world at large, and vice versa.

The commonalities and differences with current and future Israeli law can be demonstrated by using the *Aharonov* case[11] cited by *Hanoch Dagan*: the case concerns the conflict between a purchaser of a piece of land and a general creditor of the seller who attempts to execute against the land. According to *Aharonov*, the purchaser, whose ownership has not yet been registered in the land register, nevertheless prevails over the executing general creditor, if the purchaser has already given full value and taken possession of the land. Contrary to the previous *Boker*-rule[12], it is no longer necessary that the purchaser has registered a cautionary note before the attachment on behalf of the general creditor took place. *Hanoch Dagan* concurs with this solution and criticises the Draft Civil Code for parting with the requirement that the purchaser must have given full

---

[10] *Schwab/Prütting* (n. 1), 279; contra: *Dieter Eickmann*, in Münchener Kommentar BGB (vol. 6, 4th ed., 2004), § 1153, n. 13.

[11] C.A. 189/95 *Bank Otzar Hakhayal Inc. v. Aharonov* (1999) 53(4) P.D. 199.

[12] R.C.A. 178/70 *Boker v. The Anglo-Israeli Company for Management and Responsibility* (1971) 25(2) P.D. 121.

consideration. By also privileging purchasers who have only parted with a small or even nominal sum, the future law loses its normative foundations.

What would the solution under German law be, and does German law live up to the "cheapest cost avoider test" and the "smaller loss test", which should govern the resolution of priority conflicts?

In German law, due to the separation principle, the conclusion of a contract of sale does not give the purchaser any real right, not even if he has parted with full value and/or taken possession of the land. Even the conclusion of the real agreement, which with respect to the purchase of land is called *Auflassung* (§ 925 BGB), with or without consideration and possession offers no security. There are only two ways in which the purchaser can protect himself. First, he could send an application to the land register for registration of his ownership, accompanied by documents that show his entitlement to demand registration as owner ("Auflassung", "Eintragungsbewilligung"). The time of application decides on the time of entry in the register which in turn decides the priority question.

The second possibility is used when, for whatever reason, some time will elapse between the conclusion of the sales contract and its actual fulfilment. In order to secure the purchaser against subsequent dealings, a so-called *Vormerkung*, in this case an *Auflassungsvormerkung*, can be entered in the land register (§ 883 BGB). Its function seems to be comparable to that of the cautionary note under Israeli law. Technically, the *Vormerkung* renders all real transactions, that have been entered into after registration of the *Vormerkung*, invalid against the party whose right is secured by the *Vormerkung* (§ 883 II BGB). This also applies to transactions in execution or insolvency proceedings.

Again, the decisive element in law is the registration, not the question whether the purchaser has given full, partial or even no value or whether he has taken possession. In practice however, a seller of land will only give his consent to the registration of a *Vormerkung* if he has received at least partial value, because although formally the *Vormerkung* does not block the owner's ability to deal with the immovable, in practice it does.

The German system is clearly quite different from the present and future Israeli system in not paying attention to the payment of consideration or the taking of possession, but solely looking at registration. The reasons for this difference are to be found in the general rules on the transfer of ownership and other real rights in immovables, especially the system of land registration ("Grundbuch"), the role of the notaries and the strict formalities that have to be observed when dealing with immovables. Nevertheless, one might ask, whether the German rules are in conformity with the twofold test put forward by economic analysis: Is the loss suffered by the party who is typically the cheapest cost-avoider? Usually, as has been said, a purchaser will not part with his money unless he is either secured by a *Vormerkung* or the application for registration has been handed in at the land register, so that another party can no longer interfere with his future proprietary right. The loss will therefore be suffered by the general creditor, but usually only from the moment in which the land register would give him the possibility to learn about the competing right. The general creditor will loose the priority conflict without having the relevant information at hand only during the time between the application for registration and the actual registration. But usually, with the introduction of electronic land registers, this period is relatively short. It is therefore probably safe to conclude that the general creditor who has to inform himself about the creditworthiness of his debtor is not unduly disadvantaged if he suffers a loss because he did not check the land register. As to the second question, who is likely to suffer the smaller loss, I would concur with Hanoch Dagan, that ownership of land very often is decisive for a person's or a family's patrimony and life, so that considerations of social responsibility and personhood should also have to play a role. From this point of view, the strong protection which German law offers to a transferee, who observes the usual steps when purchasing land, seems to be justified.

This happy state of affairs, however, is restricted to immovables. In the first part, it has already been pointed out that German secured transactions law is judge-made. It is laudable in its effort to provide security rights that do not rest on dispossession and can thus be used in practice. However, priority questions cannot satisfactorily be solved by a system that does not provide for some element of publicity, ideally registration. Of course, judges cannot invent a registration system. Therefore, the basic priority conflict rule in German law is: first in time, first in right, and this also applies to security transactions concerning movables and rights. But because the time of the creation of the first right cannot be found out by third parties other than by questioning the parties privy to that first transaction, it is often difficult, if not impossible, for the third party to avoid the conflict and to secure its interests. Notice-filing as it exists, for example, in the United States[13], Canada and New Zealand and has been introduced in some of the Eastern European reform countries, would provide market participants with a priority rule whose relevant point in time would be easily accessible. In this area, I would therefore suggest that German law does not efficiently solve priority conflicts and should be reformed[14].

3) Conflict between Two Transferees of Real Rights in the Same Assets

On the last category of priority conflicts, that between two or more transferees of the same asset, my comments can be very brief, because the rules in German law are largely the same as those for general creditors. The decisive question, again, is: who has first completed the necessary prerequisites for acquiring the real right in question? The basic answers are the same, whether the compet-

---

[13] Cf. *Harry Sigman*, Security in movables in the United States – Uniform Commercial Code Art. 9: a basis for comparison, in: Kieninger (n. 9) 54.

[14] See, more generally, *Eva-Maria Kieninger*, Nationale, europäische und weltweite Reformen des Mobiliarsicherungsrechts, [2005] Wertpapier-Mitteilungen 2305.

ing parties are unsecured creditors seeking an attachment, or second transferees.

4) Conclusion

What lessons can be drawn from the German experience with priority conflicts? Above all, the considerations for solving priority conflicts with regard to movables and immovables are quite different. Registration of the real right or a cautionary note in the land register should be decisive in solving priority conflicts concerning land. With movables, even if one adopts a registration system for security rights, such a register would have to take quite a different form. It would have to be debtor-based rather than asset-based and its function would be to raise a "warning flag" and determine the relevant time for priority questions rather than to give detailed information on the security right, the collateral or the secured debt in question. So, a very general comment on the way in which the current Israeli Draft Civil Code deals with priority conflicts could be that the drafters should be very careful in treating movables and immovables alike.

Limitation of Civil Actions

By Israel Gilead

Summary of Contents

I. Introduction

In an endeavour to reform a 50-year-old law that regulates the limitation of civil actions[1], one has to reconsider the basic questions that underlie this complex field of law[2]. First, what are the present goals that justify the imposition of time limits on the ability of people to vindicate their alleged rights? Are the traditional justifications to the defence still valid in our rapidly changing society? Second, given these goals and justifications, what should the correct method be for achieving them today: Should we adhere to the approach that converts these goals into predetermined statutory rules and then applies these rules to particular cases, or should we now try to achieve these goals directly by deciding in each particular case whether time limits are required (as does the law of laches)? Or is it, perhaps, preferable to adopt an intermediate approach that allows for considerable judicial discretion within the general framework of predetermined statutory rules? Third, what changes, if any, should be made in each of the four components of the law of limitations: rules of accrual; limitation periods; rules that suspend the limitation period, postpone its expiry or renew it; and upper time limits ("long-stop"). Fourth, should we continue to adhere to the perception that limitation is a procedural defence that bars the legal action which seeks to enforce a substantive claim through judicial remedies? The alternative would be to embrace the concept of a substantive defence that not only bars the legal action but also either extinguishes the underlying substantive claim or affects it otherwise.

These four questions are discussed in the following sections, as are other topics that may raise interesting aspects of comparative law. These topics include succeeding defendants and claimants, collateral rights such as mortgage and pledge, set-offs and counterclaims, and declaratory judgments. Further topics, such as: which claims are not subject to limitation, claims of contribution and subrogation, the procedural stage at which the defence should be raised, and the limitation of claims regarding rights in land, need await another opportunity for discussion. Similarly, the delicate questions regarding the limitation of claims which stem from sexual offences against minors[3] will not be addressed here as they are now being reconsidered by the Ministry of Justice.

Before proceeding it may be helpful to clarify the meaning attached to major terms that may otherwise be interpreted in divergent ways. A "claim" is the as-

[1] The Limitation of Actions Law, 1958.

[2] The following discussion of the proposed reform refers to Part Six of the 2004 version of the Draft Civil Code. That Part (sections 807–840) is entitled "Limitation of Actions". It should be noted that this Part is undergoing a separate legislative process. It has been incorporated into the "Limitation of Actions Bill, 2004", a Bill which has passed a preliminary vote in the Knesset and which is now being discussed by a parliamentary committee as part of the advanced stages of its enactment.

[3] Section 832a Draft Civil Code.

sertion, the allegation, that one person is entitled to a legal remedy against another person, namely, that one person has a "right" against another person[4]. Such a claim may be founded or unfounded, true or false. The person who has, or who makes, this substantive claim is the "claimant". The legal procedure through which "claims" are verified and enforced by courts is termed "action". A claimant who files an action on a claim[5] becomes a "plaintiff". The term "claimant" therefore refers both to actual plaintiffs and to potential plaintiffs. A "defendant" in our vocabulary is a person against whom a claim exists. Here also a distinction is drawn between "actual defendants", who have to cope with filed actions based on substantive claims, and "potential defendants", who are exposed to the "threat" of future actions.

II. Goals and Justifications

Regarding the goals of limitation and its justifications, the Draft Civil Code is founded on traditional ground. The explanatory comments reiterate the major conventional justifications for imposing time limits on the ability to vindicate alleged rights: the need to protect defendants, actual and potential, against the evidential and the financial burden and the other evils of stale claims; the reduced commitment of society to the resolution of disputes which the passage of time has rendered less relevant, more burdensome, and more susceptible to mistaken judgments; and the need to encourage claimants to file their claims in a timely manner, and to reduce neglect and unfair strategic behaviour in this regard.

True, in this digital age, where documents can be scanned and stored in virtual space, the argument that time limits are required to protect defendants from the deterioration of documented evidence and the costs of its preservation may lose some of its force. But then again, the reliability of virtual evidence is disputable. In any case, computer technology does not solve the problem of fading memories and the weakening ability to ascertain past events in their relevant context. Nor does it solve the problem of financial resources diverted from better uses to serve as reserves for covering risks of stale claims. Moreover, as society becomes more and more litigious, resulting in an added burden on courts in particular and on society's limited resources in general, the screening role of limitation law may become even more important. The conclusion, then, is that the traditional rationales of limitation law have not lost their relevance. Limitation law still serves important goals.

---

[4] Section 808 Draft Civil Code provides: "A claim for the enforcement of a right that any person has vis á vis another person (in this Part – a claim) is subject to limitation of claims."

[5] See s. 809 Draft Civil Code which provides: "The court should not entertain an action on a claim that has been limited."

III. Judicial Discretion?

Can the goals of the limitation law be better served, not by the traditional method of predetermined statutory rules, which convert its rationales into a body of rules applied to specific cases, but rather by a direct application of these rationales themselves on a particular case? At first glance, such a "direct" approach may seem attractive. Obviously, answers to issues such as whether the passage of time negatively affected a defendant; whether the claimant neglected his rights or acted in bad faith; whether the public interest would be harmed by the resolution of the dispute; and whether the public interest would be harmed by burdensome litigation prone to mistakes depend to a large extent on the circumstances of each case. If this is true, perhaps the court should decide whether or not to apply the defence in each case, as it does under the law of laches?[6] Interestingly, such a tendency can be discerned in some recent Supreme Court decisions which seem to inject judicial discretion into the present, traditional regime of predetermined statutory rules. This tendency has taken two forms: First, the Court held that the statutory rules should be interpreted in each case in a way that corresponds to the relevance of the particular rationale of limitation most relevant to the specific case[7]. This is obviously a very problematic approach that may lead to inconsistency: the same statutory rule or rules that bar a claim might be interpreted broadly in one case, when the rationale seems to be more relevant, and interpreted narrowly when they seem less relevant. The result would be amorphous rules that change from one case to another. Second, some justices apparently support the idea, already embraced by lower courts, that the defence of limitation can be denied on the ground that it was not pleaded in good-faith[8]. In Israeli legal culture subordinating the statutory defence to the objective standard of good-faith may become a discretionary controlling-device, depolyed or ignored by the courts depending on the perceived merits of the case.

The Draft Civil Code, although allowing for more judicial discretion than the present law, remains within the traditional concept of statutory rules, and limits judicial discretion to narrowly defined contexts. The option of broader discretionary arrangements, such as the discretion given to the English courts in cases of death and bodily injury[9], was considered but rejected. The reason was the concern that broad judicial discretion may create uncertainty regarding the risk

---

[6] A colleague of mine, Ehud Guttel, has suggested transforming the limitation defence from an "all or nothing" to a "proportional liability" defence. According to his suggestion, in every case in which the defence is raised the court will examine the extent to which the ability of the defendant to defend has been reduced due to the delay in the filing of the action, and then reduce the defendant's liability accordingly. See Ehud Guttel/Michael T. Novick, A New Approach to Old Cases: Reconsidering Statutes of Limitation, (2004) 54 University of Toronto Law Journal 129ff.

[7] *Yechezkeli v Gluska* (2002) 57(1) P.D. 289, 306–7.

[8] See, e.g., *Nagal v. Ganey Tikva Local Authority* (31. 1. 2005) (unpublished decision).

[9] Section 33 of the Limitation Law 1980 ("Discretionary exclusion of time limit for actions in respect of personal injuries or death").

of future claims and thereby undermine one of the major goals of limitation law which is to reduce uncertainty and its costs. Limitation law, let us recall, is meant to protect not just actual defendants but all potential defendants from costs associated with preserving evidence and the need to divert financial resources for long periods. The aim of statutory rules of limitation is therefore to notify potential defendants in advance when the risk of potential claims substantially subsides. Such early notice reduces the costs of uncertainty for potential defendants and for other parties also negatively affected by it. Judicial discretion may frustrate this goal because it leaves potential defendants susceptible to the risk of future claims. As the court's discretion remains an unknown factor, a regime of "uncertain limitation" can hardly reduce those costs. True, such a regime may do justice in a particular case, and this is arguably what the courts have in mind. It is often maintained that justice should take precedence over certainty. Yet, justice and certainty are not opposites. Uncertainty may be a kind of injustice to those who incur its costs. Moreover, and most importantly, there is a fundamental difference in scale between those who benefit from the certainty that a non-discretionary regime produces and those who benefit from the flexibility of a discretionary regime. As almost all members of society are potential defendants, almost all of us benefit from the certainty that a non-discretionary regime produces. In contrast, a discretionary regime benefits only those relatively few who have failed to meet the time limits. A discretionary regime aimed to help those of these few who have "deserving" claims, might, due to the unavoidable increased uncertainty that it produces, cause injustice to the "silent and invisible majority" who are forced to incur the costs of this increased uncertainty.

IV. The Four Components of Limitation – An Overview

The defence of limitation consists of four components. The first component is the date of accrual – the date on which the cause of action is born for limitation purposes. The second component is the limitation period – the time to be measured on the "limitation clock" as regards the relevant claim before the defence can be raised. The third component is composed of rules that suspend the limitation period, postpone its expiry, or trigger the start of a new running of the period. The effect of these rules is to extend the effective time span between the accrual of the cause of action and its limitation. The fourth component is a "long-stop", an upper time limit that bars a claim after a prescribed maximum period even though the limitation period has not yet expired due to rules of suspension, postponement of expiry, or renewal.

The role of the first component is to identify the starting point that triggers time counting. The role of the second component is to determine the period during which people are expected to file their actions in the normal course of events. This is a period after which the filing of an action is considered delayed. The role of the third component is to determine which delays in the filing of actions are "acceptable and recognised" causes of delay that justify the extension of the limitation period by its suspension, postponement of expiry, or renewal. The fourth component counterbalances the third by creating an additional upper time limit after which a claim is subjected to limitations, despite the operation of the different rules of extension.

It appears that the basic dilemma of the modern law of limitation is to devise the boundaries of the third component – the scope of the "acceptable and recognised" delays. These boundaries represent the balance that a society strikes between "fairness to claimants" and their basic right to enforce their claim, and "fairness to defendants" and the interests of society. This is the balance between "innocent" claimants who can introduce an acceptable excuse for the delay in the filing of an action and "innocent" actual and potential defendants who will have to incur the costs of such delays without contributing to them. As the fourth component, which counterbalances the third, also affects the boundaries of "recognised delays" through the upper time limit, it should be conceived as another factor in this basic dilemma.

Obviously, the first and the second components too can be used as balancing tools between the interests of claimants and those of defendants. A later date of accrual and a longer period of limitation benefit the former to the detriment of the latter and vice versa. Nevertheless, it is preferable not to perceive these components as policy-based balancing devices but rather as "neutral" components which determine when a cause of action is born and the period during which claimants should file their claims in the absence of acceptable delays. The discussion below of the four components begins with these two allegedly "neutral" components.

V. The First Component – Rules of Accrual

1) Actions v. Causes of Action – The Problem of Roots and Branches

Common sense tells us that the cause of action should accrue for the purposes of limitation law when a claim becomes actionable, namely, when conditions for a *prima facie* successful claim are met and the claimant is entitled to remedies against the defendant. From that date onwards, the limitation period clock should begin to tick; subject, however, to recognised delays that suspend, postpone the expiry, or renew this period under the third component.

Behind this apparently simple answer hides an array of difficult questions. A major difficulty has to do with the distinction between a particular claim and the action based on it, on the one hand, and the cause of this action, on the other hand. A given claim (and the action based on it) is a combination of specific factual events including type of damage, specific legal bases of liability, and specific remedies. Change any of these and you get a different particular claim and ensuing action. A cause of action, in contrast, is a wider concept. It is the core, the common denominator, of a group of particular claims and ensuing actions. It contains the material elements that lie at the core of each particular claim: the material facts, material legal bases of liability, and the material types of remedies. All the particular claims with the same material elements belong to the same cause of action. Therefore, when one of these particular claims is limited, it means that the cause of action has also been limited, and as a result all of the other particular claims which belong to the same cause of action are limited, including those which have not yet come into being. The explanatory comments to the Draft Civil Code use the concept of roots and branches as a metaphor. The material elements are the roots that sprout branches over time. These branches are the particular claims. When one branch (a particular claim) looses its vitality due to the passage of time (so that an action based on this claim is barred), the roots (the cause of action) also lose their vitality, and with them all the other branches that sprout from these roots (all actions based on these claims are barred)[10]. On the other hand, when particular claims differ in material elements (facts, legal bases, or remedies), i.e., when their roots differ, the limitation of one claim does not necessarily lead to the limitation of other claims.

This may sound simple, but it is not. The question of materiality is a difficult one. What makes one fact material and another fact immaterial? What makes a legal base or a type of remedy material or immaterial? The present Limitation of Actions Law is silent on this point[11]. The Draft Civil Code, in contrast, tries to cope with this complex question.

2) Cause of Action – Claims that are "Essentially Identical"

The Draft Civil Code's answer to the question of how to determine which facts, bases of liability, and remedies of a particular claim are material, and which are not, is the following. To determine whether the cause of action of a given particular claim has been limited, one has to compare its particular combination of facts, legal bases, and remedies with the equivalent combination of another particular claim that has already been limited and which originates in the same general interaction between the parties. This is a purpose-orientated, functional comparison. It asks whether there are differences in facts, legal bases, or remedies between the two claims which justify a conclusion that the actual claim should not be limited together with the other claim that has already been limited. Such a justification should be based on the aims and rationale of limitation. When

[10] In the words of s. 813 Draft Civil Code: "A claim shall be limited on the day on which the period of limitation that was set forth for it pursuant to the provisions of this law or other legislation ends; however, claims arising from the same cause of action shall be limited together, on the earliest date on which the period of limitation that was set forth for one of the claims has run."

[11] See s. 6 of the Limitation of Actions Law, 1958, which refers laconically to the accrual date of the cause of action as the starting point of the limitation period without any attempt to explain or define this term.

such justification is detected, it renders the differences in facts, legal bases, and remedies material, and accordingly leads to the finding that the two claims do not belong to the same cause of action. In the Draft Civil Code's words, different particular claims are barred together only when they are "essentially identical" for limitation purposes[12].

Under this approach, it should be noted, the notion of accrual-of-cause-of-action is casuistic and situation-related. Whether a given element of a claim (facts, legal bases, and remedies) is material or immaterial depends on the particularities of the claims being compared and the interaction between the parties that gives rise to these claims. Assume, for example, that a breach of contract entitles a claimant to specific performance at the date of breach and to compensation at the (later) date when damage has materialised. Assume further that the action for compensation is filed when the claim for specific performance has already been limited. Should the action for compensation be barred on the ground that it originates in the same cause of action as the claim for specific performance? This depends on whether one would expect a claim for specific performance after the breach, and that depends on the circumstances.

This general criterion for defining the cause of action, which determines the materiality of facts, bases of liability, and type of remedies, by the "essentially identical claims" test, is accompanied by provisions, discussed below, that regulate a specific aspect of that materiality: the materiality of later losses.

3) Cause of Action – The Materiality of Later Damage

Quite often particular claims differ from each other only with regard to the particular damage that is the subject matter of the claims. A given breach of contract may often result in a sequence of losses which materialise over a long period, or an accident may cause a sequence of bodily injuries that are spread over a long time span. When such claims are compared and it is found that they are based on the same material facts, material bases of liability, and material kinds of remedies, the question remains whether the difference only in the particular damage can be perceived as a material difference.

The Draft Civil Code states that, as a rule, differences in the particular damage are considered immaterial. That means that claims which differ only in this regard belong to the same cause of action[13]. That rule is actually self-evident. If

[12] Section 814 Draft Civil Code provides: "(a) Claims that are different from one another with respect to their facts, the rights whose enforcement is claimed, the law that establishes such rights or the relief requested – shall be considered, for the purposes of section 813, as claims arising from the same cause of action, if they are essentially identical so as to justify their limitation together at the time set forth in that section".

[13] Section 814 Draft Civil Code provides: "(a) … (b) Claims for compensation, that are different from one another only with regard to the damage for which the compensation is claimed, shall be considered claims arising from the same cause of action, as set forth in subsection (a)."

each and every new form of damage could be considered a material fact which establishes a new cause of action there would be no limitation. In the above examples of the breached contract and the accident, potential defendants would be exposed to the risk of claims for the later losses and injuries regardless of how much time has already elapsed since the breach and the accident, and since the limitation of earlier losses and injuries.

The Draft, however, establishes an exception to this rule. There are cases in which a relatively small damage, although an actionable one, is followed by a damage of a much greater magnitude. In such cases it might be unjust to limit the claim for the much greater damage only because the claim for the significantly smaller damage has been limited. A special provision of the Draft provides for the conditions under which a claim for a later damage will not be limited together with a claim for earlier damage[14].

4) Can the Distinction between Actions and Causes of Action be Avoided?

In his comparative assessment of the Draft Civil Code Professor Reinhard Zimmerman argues that the complexity involved in drawing this subtle distinction between actions and causes of action can be avoided[15]. In his view the need for such a distinction arises only under a procedural concept of limitation of actions, while under the "weak" substantive concept of prescription the simple rule is that "each claim has to be looked at in isolation"[16]. But can the distinction be avoided? Arguably, the problem of whether different claims belong to the same cause of action is an unavoidable one. It has to be coped with under all concepts of time limits, including the substantive one, whether "weak" or "strong". Assume, following Professor Zimmerman's examples, that a contract is breached causing damage A. Years later the same breach causes damage B which is of the same type and magnitude as damage A. Now assume further that the claim for damage A was prescribed under the "weak" substantive concept. Has the claim for damage B also been prescribed? If, as suggested by Professor Zimmermann, "each claim has to be looked at in isolation", the answer would be

[14] See s. 814 Draft Civil Code provides: "(a) ... (b) ... (c) Notwithstanding the provisions of section 813, where the limitation has run on a claim for compensation for specific damage (in this subsection – earlier damage), the claim for compensation for later damage (in this subsection – later damage) arising pursuant to the provisions of subsection (a) from the same cause of action shall not run on the same day as the claim for the earlier damage, if all of the following are fulfilled: (1) the plaintiff refrained, on reasonable grounds, from filing an action for compensation for the earlier damage; (2) the later damage is substantially greater than the earlier damage; (3) the plaintiff did not delay in filing an action for the later damage. (d) For the purposes of this section, increase in the monetary value of specific damage shall not be considered to be other damage."

[15] See his chapter in the present volume, *Reinhard Zimmermann*, Limitation of Actions under the Proposed Civil Code for Israel, *sub* VI.

[16] For the distinction between "weak" and "strong" approaches to prescription see below, *sub* X.

negative, which means that no matter how old the breach is the defendant will always remain liable for fresh damage. This may thwart the basic aims of prescription law. Such an undesirable outcome can be avoided once it is recognised, in accordance with the above analysis, that the claim for damage A and the claim for damage B belong to the same cause of action, and therefore that the claim for the later damage prescribes with the claim for the former. The same applies also to claims that differ in other factual aspects or in their legal bases. These differences too may be either material (different causes of action) or immaterial (same cause of action).

5) Continuous Causes of Actions?

The question of what constitutes a cause of action for the purposes of limitation has another challenging aspect – the concept of "continuous" causes of action. Where the relations between the parties are such that they give rise to similar and consecutive claims over a period of time, courts are occasionally inclined to cumulate these "daily" claims and to form, through their aggregation, a "continuous cause of action" that stretches from the time the first daily claim became actionable to the moment when the last daily claim became actionable. The particular claims, it is perceived, are welded together to form a "consolidated cause of action." Prominent examples of such continuous claims are claims for continuous trespass and nuisance, and for failure to perform a periodical obligation.

Whenever such "a continuous cause of action" is recognised, courts must determine its date of accrual. That date may be the date of last claim, the date of first claim, or any intermediate date of a claim that lies in between.

Notably, the present law applies the "continuous cause of action" approach to torts actionable *per se*. It provides that if an act or omission which constitutes such a tort is of a continuing nature, the cause of action accrues on the day on which that act or omission ceases.[17]

The Draft Civil Code rejects the concept of "continuous cause of action"[18]. The major reason is that when a cause of action accrues, the mere existence of similar and consecutive causes of action that emerge from the same interaction between the parties provides no justification for postponing or predating its date of accrual. For instance, if a service is not provided on a given day and this amounts to a breach of contract, it is unclear why the recurrence of other such breaches should affect the day of accrual of this particular claim. Another reason for rejecting the continuous cause of action concept is that not every new claim

[17] See s. 89(1) of the Civil Wrongs Ordinance [New Version].

[18] See s. 814a Draft Civil Code which provides: "Where a number of causes of action arise consecutively from an on-going event, the limitation shall run as to each cause of action in its turn."

constitutes a new cause of action. We have just seen that recurring injuries or losses which a given accident or breach of contract generate constitute new particular claims but not necessarily new causes of action.

There are continuous relationships, though, such as marriage or guardian-wardship, where the nature of the relationship may justify an extension of the limitation period. Yet, this has to be done not through rules of accrual (first component) but rather through rules of suspension or postponement of expiry (the third component)[19].

6) Notices and Demands

Sometimes an action based on a claim cannot be brought by a claimant unless he/she makes a prior demand or gives notice in advance. In such cases the preliminary question for the courts is whether such a notice or demand is an element of the substantial claim or just a procedural prerequisite. In the latter case the failure to make a demand or a notice does not affect the time of accrual. If, however, the demand or the notice is an element of the substantive claim and a material fact, the claim will not accrue until such demand or notice is made. But such a rule may create a problem. It provides a potential claimant with control over the commencement of the limitation period. That control may be misused by a claimant who either neglects his/her claim or who intentionally delays the filing of the claim in order to gain an unfair advantage over the defendant. To protect defendants against claimants who have failed to make such a demand or give such a notice within a reasonable time due to inexcusable neglect, and to prevent strategic behaviour, the Draft provides that when accrual is contingent on demand or notice, it will nevertheless take effect on the date when a reasonable claimant would have made such a demand or given such a notice[20].

VI. The Second Component – The Limitation Period

Under the present law, the general limitation period for claims other than claims relating to land is seven years[21]. A shorter period of three years applies to strict product liability for bodily injury[22] and to insurers' liability under insur-

---

[19] See below, *sub* VII. 4).

[20] Section 816 Draft Civil Code.

[21] Section 5(1) of the Limitation of Actions Law, 1958. It has been decided, for various reasons, that the present law regarding the limitation of claims related to land should remain basically unchanged: section 838a Draft Civil Code. The limitation period for such claims is 15 years or 25 years: section 5(2) of the 1958 Law.

[22] See s. 6(a) of the Defective Products (Liability) Law, 1980.

ance policies[23]. A period of two years applies to actions for breach of privacy[24], to some actions to recover money under statutory provisions, and to actions regarding carriage by air or sea.

The Draft Civil Code preserves the policy of one general limitation period. The alternative, a variety of limitation periods tailored to the various bases of liability, was never a real option. The reason is simple: Israeli law allows for different bases of liability to concur. For example, a given occurrence may give rise to concurrent claims in tort, contract, and unjust enrichment. Given this concurrence, claimants could easily circumvent the shorter period tailored for one basis of liability by resorting to a longer period under another applicable basis of liability. Obviously, a general period reduces uncertainty and avoids the complex classifications of causes of actions required under the "supermarket approach."

What should the length of the general limitation period be? The role of this component, let us recall, is to determine the period during which people are expected to file actions based on their claims in the absence of recognised causes of delay. Coping with these delays is the role of the third component which extends the limitation period. The question, then, is in the regular course of events, what is the length of the period during which actions are expected to be filed, and after which filing can therefore be perceived as delayed. The Draft provides for a period of four years. This is obviously a sufficient period to prepare and file an action as well as to exhaust the alternatives of negotiation and settlement. Professor Zimmermann comments, in this regard, that it would be more appropriate to embrace the standard which is increasingly accepted internationally, a general limitation period of three years[25]. Well, a three-year period may well be preferable and it was indeed considered. Yet, it has always been apparent that such a drastic cut of the existing limitation period is politically unattainable. Actually, given the protective approach in Israel to the rights of plaintiffs and given the widespread dislike of the defence of limitations, which is perceived to be a procedural restriction of substantive rights, even the cut from seven to four years has triggered a loud outcry and fierce opposition; and indeed it is uncertain whether it will be approved by the legislator.

There are exceptions to the general four-year period. One exception is a seven-year period for claims to execute a final court judgment[26]. As the worthiness of this claim cannot be disputed, and the only question is whether the debtor has complied with the judicial order, such a claim "deserves" a longer active life[27].

---

[23] See s. 31 of the Contract of Insurance Law, 1981.

[24] See s. 26 of the Protection of Privacy Law, 1981.

[25] *Zimmermann*, Limitation of Actions (n. 15), *sub* III. 1).

[26] See s. 834 Draft Civil Code.

[27] The 25 year period under the present law is obviously an exaggeration. Professor Zimmermann suggests embracing the 10 year period chosen in many legal systems. That suggestion seems adequate and should definitely be considered. The running of the limitation period on an enforceable judgment, it should be noted, ends once the creditor applies to the Execution Chamber for a judicial execution order (this probably provides the answer to Professor Zimmermann's query re-

Another exception is a seven-year period for claims of a mixed nature: arising out of contract but relating to rights in immovable property[28]. This period would usually apply to claims based on an obligation to transfer a right in immovable property. Other exceptions – the seven-year period for claims of minors and for the expiry of rights in chattels, and the special periods regarding the limitation of mortgage and pledge – are discussed below. As to the present three-year limitation period which applies to strict product liability for bodily injury and to insurers' liability under insurance policies, and the two-year period for the infringement of privacy, these periods are supposed to be extended to four years to match the general period, as is indeed recommended by Professor Zimmermann[29].

Finally, the Draft Civil Code, like the present law, allows parties to a potential future dispute to adjust the limitation period to their special needs by agreeing either to shorten or to extend the period[30]. However, for paternalistic and protective reasons, the Draft does not allow an agreed period shorter than one-year (six months under the present law), and it also requires that the agreement be written as an independent document. The extension of the minimum period from six months to a year may prove to be overprotective and inefficient, and Professor Zimmerman rightly comments that it curtails the parties' autonomy too severely[31].

VII. The Third Component – Acceptable and Recognised Delays and the Extension of the Limitation Period

1) Which Delays Should be Recognised – The Search for the Right Balance

The role of the third component, as mentioned, is to determine which delays in the filing of actions are acceptable and recognised causes of delay, and whether each recognised delay suspends, postpones the expiry, or renews the limitation period. By setting the boundaries of this component the law strikes a balance between "innocent claimants" who introduce an acceptable cause of delay and "innocent defendants" who may have to incur the costs of such delays. It is the balance between the basic right to bring a claim and "fairness to claimants", on the one hand, and "fairness to defendants" and the interests of society on the other hand.

It therefore follows that not all the acceptable delays, i.e., those which can be characterised as normal, understandable, or reasonable in the circumstances, are

---

garding the lack of provision which deals with "attempted execution" – *Zimmermann*, Limitation of Actions, *sub* IV. 3).

[28] See s. 838a(c)(1) Draft Civil Code.

[29] *Zimmermann*, Limitation of Actions (n. 15), *sub* III. 2).

[30] See s. 838 Draft Civil Code.

[31] *Zimmermann*, Limitation of Actions (n. 15), *sub* V.

to be recognised as causes for suspension, postponement of expiry, or renewal of the limitation period. If all acceptable delays were recognised, innocent claimants would benefit, but at the expense of innocent defendants. Moreover, such an all-encompassing recognition would increase the costs of uncertainty to all potential defendants. These costs, as pointed out above, are multiplied by the great numbers of potential defendants (actually all of us) who bear the burden of uncertainty. In contrast, the benefits in terms of fairness to claimants are much more limited in scope. The conclusion, then, is that recognition should usually be granted to acceptable delays when the overall positive outcomes on claimants exceed the overall negative outcomes on actual and potential defendants.

This type of "cost/benefit analysis" of outcomes may have a theoretical appeal but is practically very difficult to implement because these outcomes can hardly be measured and compared. Nevertheless, decisions have to be reached, even when based on common sense and intuition. So what are the major differences between the present balancing regarding "recognised delays" and the balance proposed by the Draft Civil Code?

2) The Late Discovery Rule

The major recognised cause of delay under the present law is the rule of late discovery. The running of the limitation period is suspended until the actual or the reasonable possibility of discovery by the claimant of the facts that constitute the relevant cause of action. The Draft Civil Code basically preserves the existing rule[32]. It also specifies, in accordance with the case law, which facts constitute the cause of action for the purpose of the discovery rule: the identity of the defendant, the act or omission of the defendant that is the subject of the claim, the injury to the defendant that is the subject of the claim, and the existence of a causal relationship between the said act or omission and the said injury. Notably, these facts do not include the "legal fact" that the claimant is vested with a legal right. This means that when a potential claimant knows all the facts that constitute his or her cause of action, but does not know, for acceptable reasons, that these facts constitute a cause of action, this kind of non-discovery does not trigger the discovery rule. Time will continue to run on this claim despite the reasonableness of the non-discovery. The exclusion of this "legal fact" from the scope of the discovery rule can be justified on the grounds that the risk of a legal mistake, even a reasonable one, should lie with claimants and not with defendants. After all, when the mistake can be attributed to negligent legal advice, the claimant may have an alternative remedy – suing the negligent advisor. Moreover, the inclusion of this "legal fact" in the discovery rule may be problematic

[32] See s. 818(1) Draft Civil Code. However, the Draft Civil Code abolishes an older and problematic rule of late discovery which now presently limits the scope of the general rule of suspension with regard to major tort claims: s. 89(2) of the Civil Wrongs Ordinance [New Version].

when courts change the law retrospectively and recognise causes of action that were not recognised before. Claimants with such retrospectively recognised causes of action may argue that they became discoverable only when the court changes the law retrospectively. Still, despite these considerations, it has been argued that the discovery of this "legal fact" should not be excluded from the scope of the discovery rule as it is not materially different from the discovery of the other facts to which the rule does apply.

3) Legal Incapacity

Under the present law the mental disability of an adult which results in inability to take care of his or her affairs suspends the running of the limitation period; this is prior to the appointment of a guardian. The Draft Civil Code preserves this rule of suspension[33]. In contrast, it proposes to change the law with regard to minors. Presently time does not run on claims of minors (under the age of 18 years): the limitation period is suspended regardless of whether the minor has a guardian or not. The Draft takes a different view and states that as a rule time will run on claims of a minor who has a guardian[34]. This significant change of approach is based on the view that if society entrusts the bodily and mental integrity of minors, their education, and many other aspects of their well-being to the hands of their parents who bear the responsibility for their deeds and misdeeds in this regard, the same should apply to the conduct of the minor's legal affairs. After all, there is no necessary built-in conflict of interest between parents and their descendants in this regard. On the contrary, their interests often correspond. A fair risk allocation therefore requires that as a rule the costs of delayed claims should remain within the family rather than be externalised to third parties who are innocent in this regard. This is especially so given the long period of suspension, which may extend to up to 18 years.

On the other hand, the drafters were aware of the conflicting considerations. As parents might neglect their children's interests, is society not obliged to protect these children by a rule that suspends the limitation period during minority? Moreover, is it just that the beneficiaries of such parental neglect would be third parties who escape their liability to the minors? An earlier version of the Draft therefore "balanced" the abolition of the suspension rule with a longer period of limitation that applies to minors, seven years rather than four, and by providing that a limitation defence against minors would not take effect before the age of ten years[35]. Yet, this proposed new balance was still criticised for being too harsh

[33] See s. 818(2) Draft Civil Code.

[34] Section 812 Draft Civil Code.

[35] Section 812 Draft Civil Code. The rationale behind the "10 years old" rule is to provide sufficient time for filing claims in medical negligence cases where it can take years before the injury caused at birth, or in its aftermath, becomes definable.

on minors. As a result this earlier version was amended and the Draft Civil Code now also includes an exception to the rule of non-suspension. It provides that in cases of bodily injury, time may be suspended when the claimant is a minor, special circumstances have prevented the guardian from filing the claim, and the severity of the prejudice to the minor, when compared to the alternative prejudice to the defendant, justifies the suspension[36]. It is yet to be seen whether this further "softening" of the non-suspension rule will persuade the legislators to accept the proposed changes, or whether the vociferous opposition will succeed in its effort to reinstate the suspension rule into the Civil Code.

Professor Zimmermann notes in this regard that "[t]hese complex rules appear to be overprotective. There is no reason to treat minors differently from other persons subject to an incapacity, as is evidenced by the great majority of regulations internationally."[37] Yet, as he later acknowledges, "... established comparative wisdom, whether it is to be found in legal literature or international restatements, may ... not suit a particular legal culture."[38] Obviously, the great sensitivity to the protection of minors' rights, which led to this complexity, is a matter of legal culture.

4) Special Relationships

Relationships based on guardian-ward or marriage affinities are a cause for suspension under the present law and remain so under the Draft Civil Code[39]. Professor Zimmermann notes, regarding the cause of marriage that "it is difficult to see why the rule should not be generalised so as to cover other closely related persons living in a common household."[40] Indeed, this kind of extension has already been made by the Draft with regard to the proposed definition of "dependants". This definition now includes "any other person who is a member of [the person's] household."[41] The question which kinds of interpersonal relations should be encouraged and protected by law, and to what extent, is a delicate one and requires further consideration.

A suggestion that physician-patient relationships and employer-employee relationships should also be recognised as causes for suspension has been considered but was rejected. One of the reasons for the rejection was the excessive uncertainty such a rule could generate. Another reason was that a new rule of suspension, discussed below[42], partially tackles this problem.

---

[36] Section 818(4) Draft Civil Code.
[37] *Zimmermann*, Limitation of Actions (n. 15), *sub* IV. 2).
[38] *Zimmermann*, Limitation of Actions (n. 15), *sub* VII.
[39] See s. 818(5) and (6) Draft Civil Code.
[40] *Zimmermann*, Limitation of Actions (n. 15), *sub* IV. 3).
[41] See s. 520 Draft Civil Code.
[42] *See* VI. 4).

5) Delays Caused by the Defendant – Admission and Partial Performance

It is unfair and against public policy that a defendant who knowingly and improperly prevents the claimant from filing an action should benefit from the running of the time. Yet, the present law fails to recognise such a delay as a cause of suspension or postponement of expiry. This omission is rectified by the Draft Civil Code. It establishes a new rule of suspension that suspends the limitation period whenever the delay is caused because the defendant knowingly misleads the claimant, improperly exercises power or authority over him, threatens him, or exploits his distress[43]. "Misleading" includes concealment of the facts to which the late discovery rule applies, and also an admission and partial performance which induce the claimant not to file the action on time. The limitation period is suspended until any of the above delaying factors cease to exist. This new rule of suspension, as noted, provides at least partial protection to employees and patients who, because of the nature of their continuous relationship with their employers or physicians, delay the filing of their claims. Whenever such a delay can be attributed to an explicit or implicit threat or pressure from the defendant, the running of time would be suspended.

Prof. Zimmermann, however, suggests that in coping with delays caused by the defendant's misconduct it may have been preferable to rely on the fundamental principle of "good faith" rather than to form a detailed, but still incomplete, list of misconducts[44]. Yet, as mentioned, an unconstrained subjection of the limitation defence to the general plea of "lack of good faith" may, under Israeli legal culture, undermine the defence and jeopardise the attainment of its goals[45]. The combination of an objective, demanding, and open-ended principle of good faith with the prevalent hostility to the "procedural" defence of limitation may increase the degree of uncertainty surrounding the defence to such an extent that it might become devoid of any real value. Even the mere raising of this procedural defence by a "strong" defendant against the substantive claim of a "weak" plaintiff may be considered by Israeli courts as an act of "bad faith". The channelling of the plaintiff's general "bad faith" plea against the defendant into a specified list of misconducts reduces this risk. Actually, Professor Zimmermann also thinks that a specific manifestation of the principle of good faith deserves a special provision – a provision that postpones the expiry of the limitation where the parties have negotiated a settlement[46]. The Draft Civil Code, however, did not embrace such a provision because negotiations *per se* were thought not to justify postponement of expiry or suspension. They justify it only where they mislead the claimant into believing that the preparation of the legal action or its filing may be delayed. Moreover, answering questions such as what constitutes

---

[43] See s. 818(8) Draft Civil Code.

[44] *Zimmermann*, Limitation of Actions (n. 15), *sub* IV. 3).

[45] See above, *sub* III.

[46] *Zimmermann*, Limitation of Actions (n. 15), *sub* IV. 3).

negotiations, when have they started and when have they ended, may involve many practical difficulties.

Notably, under this new rule of suspension the defendant's admission of the claimant's right or the partial implementation of this right by him or her would suspend the running of the limitation period only where such conduct improperly induces the claimant to delay filing. Otherwise it does not affect the limitation period. Under the present law, in contrast, such admission or partial implementation, regardless of whether it causes a delay in filing, triggers a new period of limitation, unless the claim is already barred[47]. This rule of renewal, which "deletes" the period that has already begun, was rejected by the Draft Civil Code for the following reasons. Firstly, the rule is based on the assumption that admission and partial implementation establish a new and independent obligation which supersedes the claimant's original claim. In reality, however, a debtor who admits the claimant's alleged right or partially implements it often had no intention to form a new obligation and there may be no justifiable grounds to attribute to him or her such an intention. Secondly, it is a complex rule that generates uncertainties and raises difficult questions. For example, are inadvertent, indirect, or partial admissions sufficient to trigger this rule? And what are the effects of these admissions on individuals other than those who made them and their recipients in cases of joint liabilities and joint entitlements? Moreover, in the case of several debts, to which debt should partial implementation be attributed?

Prof. Zimmermann remarks that as a misleading acknowledgement is a momentary event "it is difficult to see how long prescription can be seen to be suspended as a result of it."[48] The solution, as explained, is that the limitation period should be suspended as long as the claimant is misled by the acknowledgement, or by a partial performance, and consequently delays the filing of the legal action.

6) Absence from Israel

The present law suspends the running of time for the period during which any party stays in another country and the claimant is unable to conduct the litigation in Israel due to the nature of the relationship existing between Israel and the other country, or because of conditions existing in that foreign country. The Draft Civil Code draws a distinction in this regard between absentee defendants and absentee claimants. It suspends the running of time as long as the claimant is unable to pursue the legal proceedings due to the defendant's absence[49]. In contrast, when the claimant is absent, the running of time usually continues, be-

---

[47] See s. 9 of the Limitation of Actions Law, 1958.

[48] *Zimmermann*, Limitation of Actions (n. 15), *sub* IV. 3).

[49] Section 818(7) Draft Civil Code.

cause such an absence is generally voluntary. However, the court is authorised to postpone the expiry of the limitation period in instances where it finds that the conditions and circumstances which prevent the absent claimant from pursuing his claim in Israel justify such an extension of the period. This extension, when granted, allows the claimant to file an action within one year from the day on which he or she returns to Israel or from the day on which such conditions and circumstances cease to exist[50].

7) Previous Legal Proceedings

Should the running of the limitation period on a particular claim be suspended, or its expiry be postponed, because of "related" previous legal proceedings between the parties? Such an extension of the limitation period can be justified where the previous proceedings indicate that the claimant does not sit idle and that he or she may file actions not just for the initial claims made in these previous proceedings but also for all other "related" claims. This signal should put the defendant on alert about the possibility of such future actions based on the "related" claims. Previous proceedings in this regard may either be past proceedings that have ended in a manner that allows for the future filing of "related" claims (past proceedings),[51] or an ongoing action which is amended by adding a new claim (amendment).

The present law takes the previous proceedings into account when the initial claim made in the previous proceedings and the claim made in the later proceedings belong to the "same cause of action". When this condition is met, different techniques are used with regard to past proceedings and with regard to amendment. With regard to past proceedings, the running of the limitation period for the later claim is suspended for the time during which the initial claim was adjudicated in the past proceedings[52]. With regard to amendment, the later claim is "related back" to the time at which the initial claim was made in the ongoing proceedings. These different techniques may well "save" the later claim from limitation. Present law, however, provides no guidance as to when the initial claim and the later claim belong to the "same cause of action."

The Draft Civil Code makes two major changes in this regard[53]. First, it lays down a different criterion for determining whether the initial claim and the

---

[50] Section 822(a) Draft Civil Code.

[51] In accordance with the rules of *res judicata*.

[52] See s. 15 of the Limitation of Actions Law, 1958.

[53] This relatively complex arrangement is embodied in s. 823 Draft Civil Code that provides: "(a) Where an action was filed on a claim (in this section – original action and original claim), and the proceedings in the action have ended in such a manner that the plaintiff is not barred from filing another action on the original claim or on a related claim, the period of limitations of the original claim or of the related claim, as is the case, shall not end until one year has passed from the day that the judgment in the original action became final; (b) Where an application to amend the original

later claim are "related." Instead of the multi-faceted concept of "the same cause of action" it establishes a criterion of "relation" tailored to this specific context. The two claims are related when the action on the initial claim signals to the defendant that actions on claims such as the later claim may also be filed by the claimant. Claims A and B are related when the initial action on claim A "prepares" the defendant for the later action on claim B by putting him on notice. Second, with regard to past proceedings, the Draft replaces the rule of suspension with a rule of postponement of expiry. As past proceedings may continue over years, a rule of suspension may extend the limitation period for a too long period. The Draft Civil Code therefore does not suspend the time but rather allows the claimant to initiate the new proceedings for the later claim within a year after the ending of the past proceedings.

8) Other Causes for Postponement of Expiry

The Draft Civil Code, as we have just seen, substitutes rules of postponement of expiry for rules of suspension in two respects: plaintiff's absence from Israel and previous legal proceedings. As Prof. Zimmermann observes, postponement of expiry is a "milder form of interference with prescription than suspension" and "it has increasingly gained ground internationally."[54] The other causes of postponement of expiry recognised by the Draft are also recognised by the present law. "Where the plaintiff could not file an action on a claim, due to an unexpected break in the course of the work of the court of jurisdiction", expiry is postponed "until 60 days from the day on which the work of the court of jurisdiction was resumed."[55] Expiry is also postponed, in favour of a deceased claimant's estate, for six months from the date of the issuing of the inheritance order or the appointment of an executor[56]. Yet another provision "blends" suspension with postponement by stating that where the running of the period of limitation was suspended, "the period of limitation shall not end prior to the expiration of six months from the day on which the grounds for the suspension ceased to exist."[57]

---

action was filed in order to include in it an additional claim, and on the day the application was filed the period of limitation regarding the additional claim had already expired, the court shall not accede to the application, unless the additional claim was a related claim; (c) In this section "related claim" is to be a claim with respect to which all of the following are fulfilled: (1) it originates in the same event that gave rise to the original claim; (2) the defendant is the defendant in the original claim or his successor; (3) the period of limitation with respect to it had not yet expired on the day the original action was filed; (4) the defendant knew or should have known, due to the filing of the original action, of the possibility that an action would be filed against him on the related claim, in addition to or in place of the original action."

[54] *Zimmermann*, Limitation of Actions (n. 15), *sub* IV. 1).

[55] See s. 824 Draft Civil Code.

[56] See s. 825.Draft Civil Code

[57] See s. 821 Draft Civil Code.

In addition, the Draft Civil Code launches a novel and "experimental" rule of postponement of expiry which is discussed below.

9) A Novel Procedure – Judicial Postponement of Expiry within the Limitation Period

We have seen that some acceptable causes of delay are not recognised as causes of suspension or postponement of expiry in the balancing which takes place under the third component. These include unexpected and uncontrollable events (such as *force majeure*, accidents, or illness), lack of sufficient evidence to support a claim, temporary legal inability to sue, and other causes. The reason for their exclusion is that in the overall balance struck between fairness to the relatively few innocent claimants on the one hand, and fairness to the huge group of innocent actual and potential defendants, and the costs of uncertainty, on the other hand, the scales tip in favour of the latter. Moreover, the risk that a claim may be lost due to *force majeure* may encourage claimants to predate the filing of their actions rather than wait until the last day. In any case, the negative effect that the non-recognition of these causes of delay has on claimants can be reduced or even avoided by a novel procedure embraced by the Draft Civil Code[58]. Under this procedure a potential claimant may ask the authorised court, within the limitation period, to postpone the expiry of the limitation period for a given claim, and the court, if it finds the request justified, may grant such an extension of the period for the necessary, nominal period of time. If the request is denied, the claimant would nevertheless have at least 60 days to file an action after denial. The major idea behind this novel approach is that an extension that takes place within the limitation period, with the full knowledge of potential defendants, does not raise problems of uncertainty and of unexpectedly delayed actions. The benefits to claimants may therefore exceed the costs to defendants, and thus the courts should be allowed to extend the period in such cases. To discourage misuse of this procedure, claimants must bear the costs of these special proceedings.

VIII. The Fourth Component – The Upper Limit (Long-Stop Period)

The role of the fourth component, as mentioned, is to counterbalance the third component by creating an additional time limit with the effect that, upon its expiry, a claim is barred even though the normal limitation period has not yet expired as a result of the fact that it has been extended by the operation of rules of suspension and postponement of expiry. This additional limit, the long-stop, is supposed to restore some degree of certainty to potential defendants.

[58] See s. 826 Draft Civil Code.

The present law establishes an upper time limit in two restricted tort contexts. First, a ten-year period limits tort claims in cases where the limitation period has not yet expired because the damage was not reasonably discoverable[59]. The countdown begins once the damage occurs. Second, another ten-year period limits strict product liability claims when they are made under the Defective Product (Liability) Law, 1980. This ten-year period begins to run once a product leaves the control of the manufacturer[60].

The Draft Civil Code brings about significant changes in this regard[61]. To start with, as the major role of the upper limit is to counterbalance rules of suspension and postponement of expiry which apply to all private law actions and not just in isolated tort contexts, the Draft extends the application of the upper limit to all civil actions governed by it. The second major change is that the under the Draft the upper limit, the long-stop period, begins to run not from the day of accrual, as does the limitation period, but from the day of the defendant's relevant act or omission, even when this conduct predates the accrual of the cause of action. This early trigger provides potential defendants with a greater sense of certainty. While they often have no idea when "external" events establishling causes of actions against them occur (such as late damage to the claimant), potential defendants are usually knowledgeable about their own acts or omissions which may trigger future liability. This renders the starting point of the long-stop period more ascertainable than the starting point of the limitation period and thereby restores some degree of certainty. The third change is the extension of the long-stop period from 10 to 25 years. This extension is justified on two grounds: the early trigger of this period which may precede the accrual of the cause of action, and the long period that may elapse before latent diseases and latent defects materialise into discernible damage. Arguably, it would be preferable to shorten the long-stop period to 15 years and apply the 25-year period only to these exceptional cases of latency[62]. Finally, the Draft Civil Code provides that the rules of a suspension and postponement of expiry applying to the limitation period do not apply to the long-stop period[63]. After all, the whole idea behind the upper limit is to counterbalance the uncertainty caused by suspension and postponement of expiry. The only exception, dictated by public policy, is the rule which suspends the limitation period where the delay in filing

---

[59] See s. 89(2) of the Civil Wrongs Ordinance [New Version].

[60] Section 6(b) of the Defective Products (Liability) Law, 1980.

[61] Section 827–829 Draft Civil Code.

[62] An indication of such a desirable change is an amendment to the original provision of s. 827 Draft Civil Code made in s. 21(b) of the Limitation of Actions Bill, 2004. The new provision shortens the long-stop period to 18 years in cases of medical malpractice (22 years if a minor is involved). Support for the shortening of the 25-year period is provided also by Professor Zimmermann who notes that good arguments can be advanced for a uniform upper limit of 15 years: *Zimmermann*, Limitation of Actions (n. 15), *sub* III. 3).

[63] See s. 828 Draft Civil Code.

the action is caused by the defendant's misconduct: this rule applies also to the long-stop period.

Professor Zimmermann agrees that with regard to claims for damages the count of the upper limit, the maximum period, should begin not from the day on which the damage occurred, but rather from the day of the defendant's relevant act or omission that later caused the damage. He rightly observes that under the Draft Civil Code, because of this early trigger, "the upper limit has become another period of prescription which runs alongside the general period."[64] Yet, in his view it is preferable, for the sake of clarity and uniformity, that there should be only one "point of departure for the general period of prescription and the maximum period."[65] This uniformity in the point of departure can be attained, according to Prof. Zimmermann, by "a general rule to the effect that prescription begins to run ... in the case of claims for damages, from the date of the act which gives rise to the claim." In other words, he suggests that the early trigger would apply not just to the maximum, long-stop period, but also to the general period. The problem with this suggestion is that it can hardly be reconciled with the basic rule of commencement, namely, that the count begins only "on the day on which a claim becomes actionable, i.e. when the creditor has the possibility of enforcing his claim in court"[66]. Where a claim becomes actionable only when damage occurs, as is often the case under existing tort law, the count simply cannot begin on the earlier date of the act or omission that later caused the damage, because on that early date there was no actionable claim to enforce[67].

IX. Other Topics

1) Succeeding Defendants and Claimants

The present law is not sufficiently clear with regard to the effect that the devolution of rights and liabilities from one person to another has on the running of the limitation period. The Draft Civil Code is more detailed in this re-

---

[64] *Zimmermann*, Limitation of Actions (n. 15), *sub* III. 4).

[65] *Zimmermann*, Limitation of Actions (n. 15), *sub* III. 4).

[66] *Zimmermann*, Limitation of Actions (n. 15), *sub* III. 4).

[67] In Professor Zimmerman's view the time gap between the early trigger (the creation of a risk of damage) and the later actionability (the occurrence of the damage) can be bridged by the rule of late discovery which suspends the counting of the limitation period until the damage becomes discoverable (simultaneously with its occurrence or later). But the late discovery rule, being a rule of suspension, seems to apply only to actionable claims where the facts that constitute their actionability have already occurred but have not yet been discovered. Where the damage, as a constitutive element of the claim, has not yet occurred, there is no actionable claim and therefore no object of discovery. Indeed, Professor Zimmermann acknowledges that the BGB (§ 199) and the Principles on International Commercial Contracts (Art. 10.2(2)) also embrace the "two different triggers" approach: *Zimmermann*, Limitation of Actions (n. 15), *sub* III. 4).

gard. It clarifies that the devolution of rights or liabilities from one person to another does not create a new cause of action and therefore does not trigger a new limitation period[68]. This rule of continuation also applies to subsequent conversions of chattels[69] and, by analogy, to successive squatters on land. The more complex question, however, is the effect that the devolution of rights or liabilities has on the operation of rules of suspension. In this regard the Draft Civil Code differentiates between devolution of rights and devolution of liabilities. When liabilities are devolved, all rules of suspension apply to the successor in the same manner as they apply to the predecessor[70]. They do not cease to operate in favour of the claimant who should not be worse off because of the devolution of liabilities. When, however, it is rights which are devolved, a distinction is drawn between voluntary transfers on the one hand and transmission by the operation of inheritance law on the other hand. When rights are transferred voluntarily, the only rules of suspension that operate in favour of the successor are suspension due to the absence of the defendant, suspension due to delays caused by the defendant's misconduct, and suspension due to non-discovery of the cause of action by the successor and his predecessor[71]. The idea behind not allowing the successor to rely on the other causes of suspension is to avoid manipulation. The concern is that a person who has no cause of suspension that operates in his favour may transfer the right to another person to whom a cause of suspension is applicable and thereby gain control over the running of the limitation period. No such concern exists when rights are transmitted by the operation of inheritance law, and therefore all causes of suspension operate in favour of the heir with only one exception: when the predecessor has discovered or should have discovered the material facts of the cause of action – the late discovery rule is then unavailable to the heir[72].

2) Collateral Rights – Mortgage and Pledge

How should the limitations of a claim affect another claim which is collateral or ancillary to it? Should the latter be barred with the former or be barred independently according to its "intrinsic" time table?

With regard to the ancillary liability of a surety, the present law provides that it is barred simultaneously with the claim for the debt covered by the surety unless it has been barred before[73]. In contrast, it provides that charges that secure a debt, a mortgage or a pledge, are not barred with the secured principal claim.

---

[68] See s. 819(a) Draft Civil Code (devolution of entitlements) and s. 820(a) (devolution of liabilities).

[69] See s. 830(b) Draft Civil Code.

[70] See s. 820(b) Draft Civil Code.

[71] Section 819(b)(1)(2) Draft Civil Code.

[72] Section 819(b)(3) Draft Civil Code.

[73] Section 7(b) of the Guarantee Law, 1967.

Moreover, it appears that under present law charges are not subject to limitation at all[74].

The Draft Civil Code is more consistent in this regard. It embraces the principle that a claim which is ancillary to another claim is barred along with the latter unless it has been barred before[75]. As to mortgage and pledge the Draft takes an intermediate stance[76]: On the one hand, and at variance with the present law, mortgage and pledge are subject to limitation. Moreover, the court, upon a request from an interested party, may order their removal from the relevant registration once they are barred[77]. On the other hand the Draft Civil Code provides for special and longer limitation periods for these charges. The limitation period for a mortgage is ten years after the limitation of the secured debt and for pledges three years after the limitation of the secured debt[78]. Why are the limitation periods longer for charges than they are for the debts secured by these charges? The answer lies in their special status. Charges are property rights, as opposed to the secured debt which is often only an obligatory right, and as such they protect the creditors against the debtor's insolvency. This protection provides creditors with a degree of comfort and makes them less anxious to enforce these rights promptly. Moreover, as the enforcement of charges, mortgages in particular, is costly and painful to both parties, the creditor may prefer to negotiate a settlement or to look for less painful and costly solutions. Longer limitation periods for charges encourage these alternatives while shorter periods may press creditors to enforce their securities before they exhaust their preferable options.

3) Set-offs and Counterclaims

When potential adversaries to potential litigation have claims agaist each other which are co-extensive, none of the parties has a real incentive to file a claim because each claim will offset the other. This balance of mutual deterrence serves the interest of society in preventing pointless and costly litigation. Limitation law, however, may disrupt this balance when A's claim is barred before B's claim. In such a case, B can wait until A's claim is barred and then sue A. To avoid this legal risk, A has an incentive to file an action on his claim before it gets barred. This "strategic" behaviour can lead either to unfair results, where A is stripped of the defence of set-off, or to redundant costly litigation, where A files a "defensive" claim to be offset by B's claim.

---

74 Section 20 of the Limitation of Actions Law, 1958.

75 Section 833 Draft Civil Code.

76 Section 832 Draft Civil Code.

77 Section 832(c) Draft Civil Code.

78 Section 832(a)(b) Draft Civil Code.

To counteract the incentives for such strategic behaviour, the Draft Civil Code, basically following the present law[79], denies the defence of limitation when it is raised against a claim with regard to which set-off is possible[80]. Such denial undermines the incentives of both parties to litigate. The defence is allowed only with regard to a claim that has been barred before the defence of set-off became available.

4) Declaratory Judgments

Arguably, judicial declarations regarding the actual state of affairs, whether factual or legal, should not be subject to limitation. Such a declaration only describes and verifies factual or legal realities. Yet, following case law, the Draft Civil Code provides that when a court is asked by one party to litigation to give a declaratory judgment against another party, the latter can raise the defence of limitation to prevent such a judicial declaration[81]. The idea is that when declaratory judgments negatively affect the interests of a party to the litigation, for example, when they allow the other party to enforce a limited claim through non-judicial proceedings, the rationales of limitation law apply. Therefore, this kind of indirect remedy should be limited in the same way that direct remedies are.

On the other hand the Draft, unlike the present law, empowers the courts to grant a declaratory judgment which affirms that a given claim between the parties has been limited[82]. Such a declaration has the advantage of clarifying the liabilities and the entitlements of the parties, thereby reducing uncertainty concerning their legal and financial situation. This would benefit not only the parties, who would know where they stand, but also third parties such as creditors and investors.

X. A Note on the Procedural/Substantive Distinction

It is a common view in Israel that there are two kinds of limitation of actions: substantive and procedural. According to this view, substantive limitation (prescription), extinguishes the substantive claim. Therefore, with the expiry of the limitation period, any attempt to enforce the extinguished claim, either through the courts (by way of legal action) or otherwise, would fail if the defence is raised. In contrast, procedural limitation, according to this view, does not extinguish the claim. It only limits it in the sense that the claimant is prevented from

[79] See s. 4 of the Limitation of Actions Law, 1958.

[80] See s. 837 Draft Civil Code.

[81] See s. 835 Draft Civil Code.

[82] See s. 836 Draft Civil Code.

enforcing the claim through the courts. Once the defence is raised the legal action based on the claim is procedurally barred.

Obviously, the present law is dominated by the procedural concept of limitation. The Limitation of Actions Law of 1958 explicitly states that limitation *per se* does not extinguish the right itself[83]. The Draft Civil Code seems to follow that course. It states that, unless it is otherwise provided in the legislation, limitation does not extinguish the right[84]. Non-extinction is the "default rule".

Against this background, Professor Zimmermann clarifies that substantive prescription has more than one meaning. There is a concept of "strong" substantive prescription and a concept of "weak" substantive prescription. Under the "strong" approach, a limited claim is indeed extinguished. Under the "weak" approach, however, a limited claim is not extinguished but is only "weakened": the debtor is granted the right to refuse to perform[85]. Professor Zimmermann finds the "weak" approach, which is gaining ground internationally, superior to the "strong" approach, and intimates that it may also be superior to the procedural approach of Israeli law[86].

Is the "weak" substantive approach in fact superior? Arguably the question is misphrased: a legal system should not attribute superiority to any of these three approaches, or to any other approach concerning the nature of the defence. Why not? Because what should matter is not the notional characterisation of the defence and its conceptual classification, but rather its consequences. Where the law has to decide between different possible consequences of the limitation/prescription defence, and this has to be done in a wide variety of contexts, the right approach would appear to be to choose those consequences which best promote the goals of this important legal institution. Such a functional, purposive, choice should be made regardless of whether the desired consequence fits into the procedural concept, or rather into the "weak" or the "strong" substantive concepts. These concepts should not become obstacles on the road to the best possible solutions. They should serve as instruments, not as constraints.

The choice that the law of limitation/prescription has to make between different consequences in different contexts is exemplified by the following questions. Should self enforcement of a right (self help) be allowed after the limitation period has expired? Is a debtor who mistakenly paid a barred debt entitled to restitution? Do amendments to the law apply retrospectively or prospectively? The law of which jurisdiction should apply when a right is established under one jurisdiction and adjudicated in another? Can property rights be acquired, in land or in goods, through adverse possession during the limitation period? Does a mortgage or pledge that secure a debt expire with the limitation of the debt? As suggested, the right answer to each of these questions should be derived not from

[83] See s. 2 of the Limitation of Actions Law, 1958.

[84] See s. 810(a) Draft Civil Code.

[85] *Zimmermann*, Limitation of Actions (n. 15), *sub* VI.

[86] *Zimmermann*, Limitation of Actions (n. 15), *sub* VI.

the alleged superiority of a concept, whether it is procedural or substantive ("weak" or "strong"), but rather from the desirability of the consequences. In some contexts the "procedural consequence" may be more desirable than any of "substantive consequences" and vice versa. A rigid rule which dictates an answer just because it fits into a preferred concept is prone to lead to undesirable and unjust consequences.

Having that in mind, a closer look at the Draft Civil Code reveals that it is less rigid and less committed to any superior concept than may appear at a first glance. Although it states that, as a rule, limitation does not extinguish the right, and thereby excludes the "strong" substantive concept as a rule, the Draft explicitly allows statutory exceptions to this "non-extinction" rule. Moreover, it embraces consequences that fit into the "strong" substantive approach. Unlike the present law, it provides that property rights in goods are extinguished after a special period of seven years on the claim to recover possession has run its course and it sanctions the acquisition of title in such a property by its possessor[87]. Dissimilar to the present law, as we have seen, it states that after the end of the special period of limitation, mortgage and pledge expire and can be removed from the register[88]. In these contexts, limitation is not only a procedural shield but also a "strong" substantive sword. It is also provided that amendments to present law which extend the period of limitation do not apply to claims which have already been barred[89]. Arguably, under a "pure" procedural approach such amendments only remove procedural bars and therefore may be applied to "save" claims that were barred under the old law. Furthermore, "procedural consequences" are not taken for granted as one would expect from a "pure" procedural approach. The Draft Civil Code, unlike present law, explicitly allows self enforcement of a barred claim[90] and explicitly denies restitution from a person who mistakenly fulfilled a barred obligation[91]. Moreover, as Prof. Zimmerman observes, the latter "no-restitution" consequence can also be considered as a manifestation of the "weak" substantive approach[92].

Finally, it is worth reiterating that on the conceptual level, at least under Israeli law, the subject matter of procedural limitation is not only the "action" (in the sense of the legal procedure through which substantive claims to remedies are verified and enforced), but also the substantive claim itself. It is the limitation of the substantive claim that leads to the procedural barring of the action based on the claim.[93] It therefore appears that the major difference in consequence between the procedural approach and the "weak" substantive approach is the

---

[87] See s. 830 Draft Civil Code

[88] See s. 832 Draft Civil Code.

[89] See s. 44 of the Limitation of Actions Bill, 2004, based on the Draft Civil Code.

[90] See s. 810(b) Draft Civil Code.

[91] See s. 837a Draft Civil Code.

[92] *Zimmermann*, Limitation of Actions (n. 15), *sub* VI.

[93] See ss. 808 and 809 Draft Civil Code and the clarification of terms in the last paragraph of the Introduction.

following: under the former, rights to remedies are denied only where enforcement is sought through the courts, while under the latter they are also denied where enforcement is sought through recognised means of "self help". So which of these two alternative consequences is more desirable? As mentioned, the Draft Civil Code explicitly allows self help. But it is questionable whether this choice of consequence is indeed appropriate. After all, its main beneficiaries are governmental authorities who are equipped with very effective means of self help, and it has consequently been argued that this choice unfairly favours these authorities. Indeed, "[t]here is no reason why it should only be possible to plead prescription in Court."[94]

XI. A Short Conclusion and a Comparative Note

The major challenge facing the new law of limitation is to improve the existing balance between the need to protect actual and potential defendants against the costs and injustices of delayed suits and to reduce these costs to society, on the one hand, and the basic right to pursue and exercise one's alleged legal rights, on the other hand. This balance is relatively easy to strike when the delays are unjustified. It becomes more complex when the balance is between "innocent claimants" and "innocent defendants," actual and potential. In its search for a better balance, the Draft Civil Code changes the present law in both directions – in some respects favouring claimants and in other respects favouring defendants. Hopefully, the new balance, if enacted, will produce fairer results, greater success for meritorious claims, less success to undeserving claims, reduced uncertainty, and lower costs to parties and society.

Viewing the Draft from a broad comparative perspective, Prof. Zimmermann, who should be thanked for the array of most useful and inspiring comments, observes that the Draft "confirms the general impression that the law of prescription is converging internationally" and that "in a number of important respects, the proposed provisions reflect the general international development."[95] This is encouraging. Moreover, given that most of the Draft's provisions date back to as early as 1995, when its first version matured, it appears that in some respects it has even predated international developments. Yet, Prof. Zimmermann also notes that the Draft's provisions do not fully reflect these developments and that "in other respects, they continue to deviate from solutions that have come to be recognised as a result of comparative research and international cooperation"[96]. Well, whether the above discussion provides sufficient reasoning for the provisions which Prof. Zimmermann finds "deviating" is left for the reader to judge. Arguably, the following "particularities" appear justified and should not be re-

---

[94] *Zimmermann*, Limitation of Actions (n. 15), *sub* VI.

[95] *Zimmermann*, Limitation of Actions (n. 15), *sub* VII.

[96] *Zimmermann*, Limitation of Actions (n. 15), *sub* VII.

considered: the four year basic period; the "protective" approach to minors; the concretisation of the "bad faith" plea; the exclusion of "*force majeure*", acknowledgement *per se* and negotiation *per se* from the list of causes of recognised delays; the different triggers for the long-stop period and the limitation period; and the emphasis on consequences of limitation rather than on its underlying superior concepts. Some other provisions, however, should be reconsidered in the light of Prof. Zimmermann's comments[97].

Finally, regarding the novel, "experimental", provisions of the Draft Civil Code (mainly the *ex ante* time extension by courts and the distinction between actions and causes of action), it may be interesting from a comparative perspective to see whether these provisions, if enacted, will indeed contribute to the attainment of the goals of limitation/prescription law, goals which lie at the heart of our discussion.

---

[97] As the principal point of reference for Professor Zimmermann's comparative assessment is not the prescription section of the BGB (§§ 194 to 218), but rather the Principles of European Contract Law (Art. 14:101 to 14:601), one could have raised a concern that these Principles naturally focus on the contractual aspects of prescription, while the Civil Code has also to accommodate the "special needs" of all the other fields of private law. Yet, Professor Zimmermann assures us that the Principles relate to obligations in general: *Zimmermann*, Limitation of Actions (n. 15), *sub* I.

Limitation of Actions under the Draft Civil Code for Israel

By Reinhard Zimmermann

Summary of Contents

I. Introduction

It is my task to attempt a first comparative assessment of the law on limitation of actions in the Draft of a new Civil Code for Israel. As far as the object of this assessment is concerned, I have two sources of information at my disposal: an English translation of the Draft Civil Code that has been prepared at the request of the former Chief Justice, Aharon Barak[1], and the paper written by Israel Gilead for this symposium[2]. I am very grateful to Aharon Barak and to Israel Gilead for making the translation and the paper available to me. For linguistic reasons I have not, unfortunately, been able to consult whatever *travaux préparatoires* there

[1] The translation received in August 2006 relates to a Draft Civil Code of 2004. That Draft contained a special part devoted to limitation of actions (on the terminology, see *infra*, VI.): Part Six, beginning with s. 807 and ending with s. 840.

[2] *Israel Gilead*, Limitation of Civil Actions; a revised and extended version of that paper appears in the present volume.

may be. My principal point of reference for the comparative assessment will be the Principles of European Contract Law. Part III of these Principles, published in 2003[3], contains a chapter on prescription which, notwithstanding the title under which the Principles have been published, relates not only to contractual obligations but to obligations in general. The draftsmen of the Principles have made every effort not to base their work on any individual national legal system. They have attempted, as far as possible, to identify the common core of private law of all the EU member states and to create a workable system on that basis[4]. Prescription, however, is one of the areas of the law where none of the codifications based on traditional civilian doctrine, nor documents such as the English Limitation Law, contain a satisfactory set of rules. Here the draftsmen of the Principles had to look at more recent developments which, in spite of a far-reaching nationalisation of private law and private law scholarship, still display a common pattern. Comparative analysis of these patterns of development provided the basis for devising a modern uniform regime, as now proposed in Chapter 14 of the Principles.

The Principles have been designed for a number of purposes[5]. Thus, for instance, they can be used by arbitrators who have to decide a case according to "internationally accepted principles of law"; and they provide a conceptual and systematic infrastructure for community legislation concerning contract law. Equally significant, however, is the fact that they may serve as a source of inspiration for national legislatures, courts of law and legal doctrine[6]; and, indeed, Chapter 14 of the Principles has already had a significant impact on the new German law of prescription[7] and on the *Avant-projet de la réforme du droit des obligations et du droit de la prescription* in France[8]. It is in this spirit that I want to use the Principles as a background document for the comparative assessment of the proposed new rules in Israel. This appears to be appropriate in view of the close historical links between Israeli law and the European legal systems (particularly

[3] *Ole Lando/Eric Clive/André Prüm/Reinhard Zimmermann* (eds.), Principles of European Contract Law, Part III (2003). The text of the black letter rules is also easily available in *Oliver Radley-Gardner/Hugh Beale/Reinhard Zimmermann/Reiner Schulze* (eds.), Fundamental Texts on European Private Law (2003).

[4] In a way, therefore, the Principles were inspired by the idea of a Restatement of European Contact Law; see *Ole Lando/Hugh Beale* (eds.), Principles of European Contract Law, Parts I and II (2000), xxvi.

[5] *Lando/Beale* (n. 4), xxiii ff.

[6] *Reinhard Zimmermann*, The Principles of European Contract Law: Contemporary Manifestation of the Old, and Possible Foundation for a New, European Scholarship of Private Law, in: Florian Faust/Gregor Thüsing (eds.), Beyond Borders: Perspectives on International and Comparative Law, Symposium in Honour of Hein Kötz (2006), 141 ff.

[7] On which see *Reinhard Zimmermann*, The New German Law of Obligations: Historical and Comparative Perspectives (2005), 122 ff.

[8] On which see *Reinhard Zimmermann*, "Extinctive" Prescription under the *Avant-projet de reforme du droit des obligations*, (2007) 15 European Review of Private Law 805 ff.

those of England, Germany and Italy)[9]. In addition, it may be kept in mind that there is now a second set of model rules which is comparable, in many respects, to the Principles of European Contract Law even if it pursues the aim of global rather than European harmonisation of contract law: the Principles of International Commercial Contracts of Unidroit[10]. They also contain a chapter on "limitation periods". Though displaying a number of differences in detail, Chapters 14 of the European Principles and 10 of the Unidroit Principles are characterised by a far-reaching correspondence in matters of principle which enhances their persuasive authority[11].

II. The General Framework

As has just been said, a number of dominant trends are evident in the international development of the law of prescription, and they have fundamentally shaped both the European and the Unidroit Principles[12]. In the first place, there is a clear tendency favouring a general period of prescription applying as widely as possible. Secondly, that general period should be relatively short. Thirdly, and closely related to the latter point, the idea has been gaining ground that the general period of prescription should not run unless the creditor knew (or ought reasonably to have known) about his claim. A fourth characteristic of a modern prescription regime follows from the latter point: a maximum period after which a claim can be defeated, regardless of the creditor's knowledge, appears to be necessary as a counterbalance to the discoverability principle. Today, this scheme is very widely thought to provide a reasonable balance between a number of conflicting interests. The introduction of prescription periods can be justified on the basis of the following considerations[13]: (i) as the years pass by, it becomes more and more difficult for the debtor to defend himself against the creditor's claim; (ii) the lapse of time engenders the reasonable expectation that an incident which might have given rise to a claim may be treated as closed, and that potential debtors may adjust their behaviour accordingly; and (iii) that it is in the public interest that legal disputes are resolved swiftly so as not to create a source of uncertainty, unfairness and increased cost of litigation. Considerations (i) and (ii) focus on the protection of the debtor, consideration (iii) on the public inter-

---

[9] See, e.g., *Stephen Goldstein*, Israel, in: Vernon V. Palmer (ed.), Mixed Jurisdictions Worldwide: The Third Legal Family (2001), 448ff.

[10] Unidroit (ed.), Principles of International Commercial Contracts 2004 (2004).

[11] For a comparative assessment, see *Reinhard Zimmermann*, The Unidroit Principles of International Commercial Contracts 2004 in Comparative Perspective, (2006) 21 Tulane European and Civil Law Forum 8ff.

[12] For details of what follows, see *Reinhard Zimmermann*, Comparative Foundations of a European Law of Set-Off and Prescription (2002), 85ff.

[13] For details, and further references to the pertinent literature, see Comparative Foundations (n. 12), 63ff., 76ff.

est. They can be advanced in favour of having a prescription regime and of making it bite as hard as reasonably possible. In determining what is reasonably possible, however, the creditor's interests also have to be taken into account. A creditor, in a way, is acting against the precepts of good faith and fair dealing if he sits on his rights without exercising them and pounces upon the debtor at some later stage. But the creditor's behaviour can be held against him only if he has had a fair chance to pursue his claim. It would be manifestly unjust to hold a creditor accountable for not bringing an action against his debtor if he either was unable, or could not reasonably be expected, to do so. He must, in other words, have had a fair chance of pursuing his claim. This explains, in particular, the discoverability criterion and a number of grounds for suspension of prescription. It is a consideration that is neatly embodied in the old maxim of the *ius commune*: *agere non valenti non currit praescriptio*[14].

III. Key Features of the Draft Civil Code

From Israel Gilead's paper I gather that these policy considerations essentially also underlie the proposed new law on limitation in Israel. Also, the latter remains within the tradition of converting these considerations into a body of discrete statutory rules and operating with fixed periods of prescription rather than leaving everything to the discretion of the court. How about the general structure of the proposed new regime then? It does indeed reflect the tendencies set out above. There is a general prescription period of four years[15]. The running of this period is suspended as long as the creditor did not know, and did not need to know, essential facts concerning his claim, particularly its existence[16]. And there is a maximum period which has been fixed, in principle, at 25 years[17]. Four points deserve to be commented upon.

1) Length of the General Period

The first is the length of the general period. Anything, I think, between two and four, possibly even five years, appears to be defensible. There can be no rational ground to choose two rather than three, or three rather than four years; the choice is largely arbitrary. In view of this it appears to be unfortunate that the draftsmen of the proposed new code have fixed the period at four rather than

[14] On which, see *Karl Spiro*, Zur neueren Geschichte des Satzes "Agere non valenti non currit praescriptio", in: Festschrift für Hans Lewald (1953), 585ff.; Comparative Foundations (n. 12), 132f.; *Mauro Tescaro*, Decorrenza della prescrizione e autoresponsabilità: La rilevanza civilistica del principio contra non valentem agere non currit praescriptio (2006).

[15] Section 811 Draft Civil Code.

[16] Section 818(1) Draft Civil Code.

[17] Section 827 Draft Civil Code.

three years. It will quite unnecessarily bring Israeli law out of step with a standard that is increasingly accepted internationally, for we find a general period of three years not only in places such as South Africa[18], Russia[19] or Québec[20], but also in Germany[21], in the *Avant-projet* for the reform of the French law of obligations and prescription[22] and in the Report of the English Law Commission on Limitation of Actions[23], and we find it in both of the international model codes mentioned above[24]. A period of three years also appears to be emerging as a uniform limitation period in European Union legislation[25]. Thus, it is the period laid down in the Product Liability Directive[26] and also, significantly, in s. 483 of the Draft Civil Code for Israel concerning liability for defective products.

2) Range of Application

This brings me to the second point. The general period laid down in s. 811 of the Draft Civil Code does not apply as widely as it might. There is the three-year period, just mentioned, for product liability, there is a three-year period for the payment of insurance benefits[27], and there are seven-year periods for claims of minors (s. 812) and for claims established by legal proceedings (s. 834)[28]. Just about every special period has the potential to undermine the great advantages associated with having a general period of prescription and therefore has to be scrutinised particularly carefully. The only one, I think, that passes such scrutiny is the relatively long period laid down in s. 834. For, on the one hand, here we have a clearly distinguishable type of claim that does not interfere with any others. On the other hand, a claim established by judgement is as firmly and securely established as is possible and, therefore, is much less affected by the "obfuscating power of time"[29] than other claims[30]. Seven years, however, is shorter

---

[18] South African Prescription Act 68 of 1969, s. 11(d).

[19] Art. 196 Russian Civil Code.

[20] Art. 2925 *Code civil du Québec.*

[21] § 195 BGB.

[22] *Avant-projet de réforme du droit des obligations* (Articles 1101 à 1386 du Code civil) *et du droit de la prescription* (Articles 2234 à 2281 du Code civil); Rapport à Monsieur Pascal Clément Garde des Sceaux, Ministre de la Justice, 22 Septembre 2005, Art. 2274.

[23] The Law Commission, Limitation of Actions, Law Com No. 270, 2001, s. 1(1).

[24] Art. 14:201 PECL; Art. 10.2(1) PICC.

[25] *Christian von Bar,* The Common European Law of Torts, vol. I (1998), n. 395.

[26] Art. 10(1) Council Directive 85/374/EEC of 25 July 1985 on the approximation of the laws, regulations and administrative provisions of the Member States concerning liability for defective products.

[27] Section 377 Draft Civil Code.

[28] Israel Gilead also mentions a two year period applicable to actions for breach of privacy; it does not appear to be contained in the Draft Code.

[29] *Bernhard Windscheid/Theodor Kipp,* Lehrbuch des Pandektenrechts (9th ed., 1906), § 105 (at 544).

[30] Comparative Foundations (n. 12), 112ff.

than the periods chosen in most other legal systems for claims established by judgement[31]. Art. 14:202 PECL, for example, has a period of ten years.

3) The Upper Limit

Thirdly, the upper limit of 25 years laid down in s. 827. Here, as in prescription matters generally, we have the choice between differentiation and uniformity. Differentiation would have to be along the lines of personal injuries claims versus other claims. Most situations that have been specified as being particularly problematic (sexual abuse of children, asbestosis, medical malpractice) fall into the category of personal injuries claims. The reasons for treating them differently are that there is often a long latency period and that life, health, and the bodily integrity in general are particularly valuable objects of legal protection: personal injuries are usually considered to be more serious than property damages or economic harm. For the latter a long-stop of ten years is widely regarded as sufficient. For personal injuries, most prescription regimes have a period of thirty years. We find this dichotomy, e.g., in Art. 14:307 PECL, § 199 II-IV BGB and Art. 2278 Avant-projet. There are also, however, good arguments in favour of a uniform upper limit: a compromise solution which accommodates both personal injuries and other claims while not providing a perfect solution for either of them[32]. Yet, for such compromise solution, 15 years would appear to be more appropriate than 25.

4) Commencement of Prescription

The fourth point concerns the commencement of prescription. Here, some of those who subscribe to the subjective system[33] imagine that the discoverability criterion has to determine when prescription starts to run. The new German law of prescription as well as Art. 10.2 PICC are based on that idea. According to Art. 14:301 PECL, on the other hand, the fact that the creditor does not know, and could not reasonably know, of the identity of his debtor, or the facts giving rise to his claim, constitutes a ground for suspending the running of the period of prescription. Elsewhere I have argued that the latter approach is preferable because, *inter alia*, it leads to an equitable distribution of the onus of proof[34]. It is very much to be welcomed that the draftsmen of the Israeli Civil Code project

[31] See the references in Comparative Foundations (n. 12), 112; *Lando/Clive/Prüm/Zimmermann* (n. 3), 167.

[32] Comparative Foundations (n. 12), 102ff. On Art. 10.2(2) PICC see, in this context, (2006) 21 Tulane European and Civil Law Forum 14f.

[33] For the terminology, see New German Law of Obligations (n. 7), 129ff.

[34] Comparative Foundations (n. 12), 106ff.; *Lando/Clive/Prüm/Zimmermann* (n. 3), 177f.; (2006) 21 Tulane European and Civil Law Forum 13f.

appear to have taken the same view. At the same time, they have, to some extent at least, given away the systematic advantages that could have been reaped from that approach. According to s. 815 of the Draft Civil Code, prescription begins to run "on the day on which the cause of action was created". It is not quite clear what this means; but presumably it refers to the day on which a claim becomes actionable, i.e. when the creditor has the possibility of enforcing his claim in court. In terms of substantive law, one would refer to the time when the debtor has to effect performance (due date)[35]. For the upper limit, however, a different commencement date is envisaged in s. 827(b), for the 25 years count "from the date of the act of the defendant that is the subject of the claim". The thinking behind this provision appears to be the following.

The due date for performance is clearly inappropriate as a period of reference for any maximum period of prescription concerning claims for damages. For it is specifically the "latent damages" problem that can lead to a long delay of prescription. A right to payment of damages for harm caused by another is generally due as soon as it comes into being. But it comes into being only when all requirements of the rule imposing liability have been met. One of them will often be the occurrence of damages; and damages will sometimes only occur many years after the act giving rise to liability has been committed. If a legal system accommodates the reasonable interests of the creditor by suspending prescription as long as the damage is not discoverable, it cannot sensibly operate with a maximum period running from the moment when the damage occurs. That would be a long-stop that does not bite. A maximum period counting from the act giving rise to liability is therefore clearly desirable. It counterbalances both the emphasis on the creditor's interests and the uncertainty inherent in the discoverability criterion. But, if that maximum period counts from the act giving rise to liability rather than due date, the general period of prescription can quite safely be made to run from the same moment. For the suspension rule of Art. 14:301 PECL, s. 818(1) Draft Civil Code, focusing on the moment of discoverability, ensures that prescription does not run before the damage has occurred. Thus, there should be a general rule to the effect that prescription begins to run from the time when the debtor has to effect performance or, in the case of claims for damages, from the date of the act which gives rise to the claim[36]. Such rule would have the structural advantage of providing one and the same point of departure for the general period of prescription and the maximum period. That maximum period would then really be an upper limit for extending the general period of prescription. This is a scheme that would promote clarity and uniformity in prescription matters and that we find in the Principles of Eu-

---

[35] See Art. 14:203 PECL and *Lando/Clive/Prüm/Zimmermann* (n. 3), 168 ff.; Comparative Foundations (n. 12), 105 f.

[36] Art. 14:203 PECL.

ropean Contract Law[37]; considering their choice of terminology[38], the draftsmen of the Draft Civil Code for Israel project appear to have aimed for something similar. In fact, however, the upper limit has become another period of prescription which runs alongside the general period.

IV. Suspension of Prescription

1) Suspension, Postponement of Expiry, Renewal

The enactment of a relatively short general period of prescription enhances the importance of determining under which circumstances it may be extended or "interrupted". If the period is interrupted, the time which has elapsed before the interrupting event is not taken into account: the period of prescription begins to run afresh. Today, the traditional civilian term "interruption" (based on the *interruptio temporis* of the Roman sources) is increasingly replaced by the more descriptive term "renewal"[39]. It is the most radical interference with the running of a period of prescription. Less radical is the mere extension of a given period either by way of suspension (i.e. the period during which prescription is suspended is not counted in calculating the period of prescription; when the cause of suspension ends, it is therefore the old prescription period that continues to run its course) or by way of postponement of its expiry (i.e. the period of prescription runs its course but is only completed after the expiry of a certain extra period). While suspension of prescription is a device well known in European civil codes, postponement of expiry is of more recent vintage but has increasingly gained ground internationally as an even milder form of interference with prescription than suspension[40]. While the Draft Civil Code does not accept the notion of interruption (or renewal), it does recognize the devices of suspension (subject to an interesting modification)[41] and postponement of expiry[42].

---

[37] Art. 14:307 PECL. But see Art. 10.2(2) PICC and the criticism in (2006) 21 Tulane European and Civil Law Forum 14; New German Law of Obligations (n. 7), 138ff. – Professor *Gilead* remains unconvinced by the scheme proposed both here and in the Principles of European Contract Law. He argues (*sub* VIII. *in fine*) that the count cannot begin before the occurrence of damages in view of the fact that such occurrence is a constitutive element of a damages claim. This, I would venture to suggest, is a very conceptualist view. A legal system is perfectly able to state that a period of prescription shall begin to run, in the case of a right to damages, from the time of the act which gives rise to the claim (see Art. 14:203 (1) PECL), and to suspend prescription as long as the creditor does not know, and could not reasonably know, of the facts giving rise to the claim (see Art. 14:301 PECL). That suspension rule, then, does not only apply to cases where the damage has occurred but has not yet been discovered, but also to cases where it has not yet occurred.

[38] Chapter 6 of Part Six of the Draft Civil Code is entitled "Upper Limit on Limitations".

[39] Art. 14:401 PECL; § 212 BGB; Comparative Foundations (n. 12), 124f.

[40] Comparative Foundations (n. 12), 138f.; *Lando/Clive/Prüm/Zimmermann* (n. 3), 178.

[41] See ss. 818–820 Draft Civil Code. The modification is that where the running of the period of prescription was suspended, "the period of prescription shall not end prior to the expiration of six months" from the day on which the ground of suspension has ceased to exist (s. 821 Draft Civil

2) Persons subject to an Incapacity

The most important ground for suspending prescription has been mentioned already: the creditor does not know, and cannot reasonably be expected to know, essential facts concerning his claim[43]. But ignorance is not the only problem that may prompt a legal system to extend a period of prescription. Another such problem is mental disability which results in a person not being able to take care of his or her affairs. But a general rule according to which prescription does not run against a person subject to a mental disability would, arguably, overshoot the mark. Special protection is only required in two situations: where the person subject to a mental disability is without a guardian who can act on his or her behalf, and as far as claims between the person subject to a mental disability and his or her guardian are concerned. This is recognised by modern prescription regimes such as the one contained in the Principles of European Contract Law as much as by the Draft Civil Code for Israel[44]. Yet, while the Draft makes use, for these two situations, of the device of suspension, postponement of expiry along the lines of Art. 14:305 PECL would appear to be quite sufficient. Minors, according to the law presently in force in Israel, enjoy an all-round protection: prescription does not run against them, regardless of whether they have a representative adult capable of proceeding on their behalf or not[45]. The Draft now proposes to change that and to confine the law's protection to the two situations just mentioned for persons subject to a mental disability[46]. However, a complete transition to the new model appears to have been regarded as too radical. That is why it is proposed to (i) subject claims of a minor to a special prescription period of seven years (though no more than four years from the time when he or she reaches the age of majority)[47], (ii) determine that the defence of prescription cannot be raised against a minor before he or she reaches the age of ten[48], and (iii) provide a special suspension regime concerning claims for bodily injury[49]. These complex rules appear to be overprotective. There is no reason to treat minors

---

Code). See also Art. 10.8 PICC where, however, we find a one-year period. But we are still dealing with the device of suspension, not of postponement of expiry.

[42] See ss. 822–826 Draft Civil Code (concerning, i.e., absence from Israel, and previous legal proceedings).

[43] *Supra, sub* III. 4) first para. Section 818(1)(b) Draft Civil Code specifically states that ignorance of the law does not suspend prescription. This is in line with the old adage *error iuris nocet, error facti non nocet* and conforms to the approach underlying § 199 BGB (see *Helmut Heinrichs*, in: Palandt, Bürgerliches Gesetzbuch [66th ed., 2007], § 199, n. 26), Art. 14:301 PECL and Art. 10.2(1) PICC (see Unidroit Principles 2004 [n. 10] 316).

[44] Art. 14:305 PECL; s. 818(2) and (5) Draft Civil Code; cf. also §§ 207, 210 BGB; and see Comparative Foundations (n. 12), 134 ff.; *Lando/Clive/Prüm/Zimmermann* (n. 3), 188 ff. On Art. 10.8(2) PICC, see (2006) 21 Tulane European and Civil Law Forum 19 f.

[45] See the paper by *Israel Gilead, sub* VII. 3).

[46] Section 818(3) and (5) Draft Civil Code.

[47] Section 812 Draft Civil Code.

[48] Section 812 Draft Civil Code.

[49] Section 818(4) Draft Civil Code.

differently from other persons subject to an incapacity, as is evidenced by the great majority of regulations internationally[50].

3) Other Grounds of Suspension

In a number of codes, claims between spouses have been subjected to the same regime as claims between persons subject to an incapacity and their representatives: prescription is suspended as long as the marriage persists[51]. The Draft Civil Code for Israel also contains a provision along these lines[52]. It has been argued elsewhere that the underlying policy may be questionable today. Marriage should not have the effect of removing protection against stale claims[53]. Moreover, even if the rationale underlying suspension concerning claims between spouses were to be regarded as sound, it is difficult to see why the rule should not be generalised so as to cover other closely related persons living in a common household[54].

Prescription is also suspended in cases where the plaintiff refrained from filing an action because he was misled by the defendant, because the defendant employed force against him, threatened him, or exploited his distress[55]. This is a generalised version of a *fraus omnia corrumpit* provision that we find in a number of legal systems[56], and it appears to cover cases which, under the Principles of European Contract Law, would be subsumed under Art. 14:304 (postponement of expiry in case of negotiations)[57], Art. 14:401 (renewal by acknowledgment)[58], or under the general good faith provision of Art. 1:201 PECL[59]. It is not obvious to me why the problem of a creditor relying on the debtor's acknowledgement and thus refraining from instituting an action should be dealt with by suspending rather than (as is generally accepted internationally) renewing prescription. After all, an acknowledgment is a momentary event and it is difficult to see how long prescription can be seen to be suspended as a result of it. That negotiations

---

[50] See Art. 14:305 PECL; Art. 10.8(2) PICC; § 210 BGB; Comparative Foundations (n. 12), 134 ff.; and see the references in *Lando/Clive/Prüm/Zimmermann* (n. 3), 191 f.

[51] § 207 I 1 BGB; for other national legal systems, see Comparative Foundations (n. 12), 139; *Lando/Clive/Prüm/Zimmermann* (n. 3), 192.

[52] Section 818(6) Draft Civil Code.

[53] Comparative Foundations (n. 12), 139 ff.; *Lando/Clive/Prüm/Zimmermann* (n. 3), 190.

[54] Generally, see *Karl Spiro*, Verjährung und Hausgemeinschaft, in: Festschrift für Friedrich Wilhelm Bosch (1976), 975 ff.

[55] Section 818(8) Draft Civil Code.

[56] Comparative Foundations (n. 12), 145 ff.; *Lando/Clive/Prüm/Zimmermann* (n. 3), 195 f.

[57] Art. 14:304 PECL; § 203 BGB. But see, concerning commercial contracts, Unidroit Principles 2004 (n. 10), 328.

[58] Art. 14:401(1) PECL; Art. 10.4(1) PICC; § 212 I no. 1 BGB; Comparative Foundations (n. 12), 126 ff.

[59] Art. 1:201 PECL; Art. 1.7 PICC; § 242 BGB.

should not constitute a trap for the creditor is also very widely recognised[60]. The concern is sufficiently important to be taken care of by a special provision[61] even if, of course, that provision has to be regarded as a special manifestation of the principle of good faith. That principle is also regarded as fundamental in the Draft Civil Code for Israel[62], and any hard cases apart from those where the creditor is prevented by an acknowledgment, or by negotiations, from instituting an action may safely be left to it rather than to a special provision with specific requirements that may be difficult to apply in practice and, moreover, still do not cover all imaginable situations. Surprising, from a comparative perspective, is the lack of provisions suspending prescription in cases where the creditor is prevented by *force majeure* from pursuing his claim[63] and as long as judicial or arbitration proceedings on the claim are pending[64]. The former situation appears to be taken care of by the possibility, granted to a creditor, to apply within the period of prescription to the competent court to be granted an extension[65]. But what about situations where *force majeure* not only prevents the creditor from pursuing his claim but also from lodging an application to be granted extension? The proposed rule does not appear to cover that situation. Equally surprising is the lack of a provision on renewal of prescription by attempted execution[66].

V. Agreements concerning Prescription

The statutory determination of a relatively short period of prescription can also be balanced by the possibility being granted to the parties to agree upon a longer period. The Draft Civil Code for Israel is even more liberal in that respect than the Principles of European Contract Law and the new German law, for it does not recognise any ceiling[67]; according to the European Principles and Ger-

---

[60] See the country reports and the comparative evaluation in Reinhard Zimmermann/Simon Whittaker (eds.), Good Faith in European Contract Law (2000), 493ff. and 530f.

[61] Comparative Foundations (n. 12), 142ff.

[62] Section 2 Draft Civil Code.

[63] See Art. 14:303 PECL; Art. 10.8(1) PICC; § 206 BGB; Comparative Foundations (n. 12), 129ff.; *Lando/Clive/Prüm/Zimmermann* (n. 3), 184ff. The Draft Civil Code does have a rule concerning "an unexpected break in the course of the work of the court of jurisdiction" (s. 824). The idea underlying this provision is that, under the circumstances, it is impossible for the creditor to file an action (*agere non valenti non currit praescriptio*). The same consideration, however, also applies to other situations of *force majeure*. Cf. also § 206 BGB new version as opposed to § 203 BGB old version (where closure of the courts was also specifically singled out, though as a specific instance of *vis major*).

[64] See Art. 14:302 PECL; Art. 10.5–10.7 PICC; § 204 BGB; Comparative Foundations (n. 12), 117ff.; *Lando/Clive/Prüm/Zimmermann* (n. 3), 179ff.

[65] Section 826 Draft Civil Code.

[66] See Art. 14:401 PECL; § 212 I no. 2 BGB; Comparative Foundations (n. 12), 125f.; *Lando/Clive/Prüm/Zimmermann* (n. 3), 200f.

[67] Section 838(a) Draft Civil Code.

man law the parties cannot agree upon a period that is longer than thirty years[68]. Effectively, therefore, the parties in Israel will be free to exclude a claim from prescription. It is doubtful whether such regime would pay sufficient attention to the public-interest dimension of prescription[69]. The Draft Civil Code also allows the parties to shorten the statutory period of prescription, though not to less than one year[70]. The latter qualification should be abandoned. Agreements facilitating prescription are much more widely recognised internationally than those rendering prescription more difficult. Moreover, they do not conflict with the public policy based concerns underlying the law of prescription (nor, of course, with the policy considerations turning around the protection of the debtor). The autonomy of the parties would be curtailed much too severely, and without any good reason, if they were not allowed, by way of individually negotiated agreement, to fix a prescription period of six months, or less[71].

VI. Prescription/Limitation: Substantive or Procedural in Nature?

There is one centrally important point that has not been mentioned, so far: the effect of prescription[72]. Closely related to it is the question of whether prescrip-

---

[68] Art. 14:601 PECL; § 202 II BGB; cf. also Art. 10.3(2)(c) PICC, imposing a ceiling of fifteen years; and see Comparative Foundations (n. 12), 166; *Lando/Clive/Prüm/Zimmermann* (n. 3), 208.

[69] *Supra* text after n. 13.

[70] Section 838(a) Draft Civil Code.

[71] § 202 BGB and New German Law of Obligations (n. 7), 154f. But see Art. 14:601(2) PECL; Art. 10.3(2)(a) PICC.

[72] There are also some other points that have not been covered. They include s. 816 Draft Civil Code: in cases where a claim is contingent upon delivery of notice or demand on the part of the plaintiff prescription starts to run on the day the notice or demand is delivered, or on the day when a reasonable plaintiff would have delivered the notice or demand. The first part of this rule states something that appears to be self-evident considering that the claim, under these circumstances, is actionable only once the notice or demand has been given. The second part of the rule appears to be based on the fear that, by protracting the notice or demand, the creditor may be able to manipulate the date of commencement of prescription. That fear, however, is based on very theoretical considerations. Creditors are not normally guided in their behaviour by the desire to secure for themselves the benefit of a long prescription period. German law used to have a rule very similar to s. 816 Draft Civil Code (§ 199 BGB old version) which has been of very little practical significance. It has therefore been abandoned in the reform legislation of 2002, following the recommendations of *Frank Peters/Reinhard Zimmermann*, Verjährungsfristen: Der Einfluß von Fristen auf Schuldverhältnisse; Möglichkeiten der Vereinheitlichung von Verjährungsfristen, in: Bundesminister der Justiz (ed.), Gutachten und Vorschläge zur Überarbeitung des Schuldrechts, vol. I (1981), 245f. Presumably for the same reason, neither the PECL nor the PICC contain a provision on this point; see Comparative Foundations (n. 12), 153f. – The Draft Civil Code also tackles the question of what effect a transfer of a claim has on the running of the period of prescription for that claim: s. 820. It is, I think, unnecessary: a change in the person of the creditor cannot affect the running of the period of prescription as long as it is recognised that the claim remains the same. Of course, in determining whether prescription is suspended (i.e. discoverability) the position of the new creditor is now relevant. Since all of this follows from general principle, neither German law nor the international restatements provide a regulation on this point. In German law, a problem is

tion is conceived as an institution of substantive law, or whether it is procedural in nature. The Draft Civil Code for Israel, following English law in that respect, subscribes to the procedural view: it refers to limitation of actions rather than prescription[73], it requires limitation to be pleaded in court[74], and it sees the creditor exclusively in the role of claimant. Apart from that, the Draft Civil Code determines that limitation does not extinguish the right of the creditor[75]; and it specifies that whatever has been performed in order to discharge an obligation may not be reclaimed merely because the period of prescription had expired[76]. The latter two rules are in accordance with what is very widely recognised today in the national legal systems and what is also, therefore, reflected in both sets of international model rules[77]. But it does not follow, as those responsible for the Draft Civil Code appear to have assumed, that prescription must be procedural in nature. Even if a legal system regards prescription as matter of substantive law, it may take what is often dubbed a "weak" or a "strong" approach[78]. Once the period of prescription has run out, the claim may be held to have ceased to exist (strong effect); or the debtor may merely be granted a right to refuse performance (i.e. prescription constitutes a defence on the level of substantive law; weak effect). It is this latter approach that has been gaining ground internationally[79]. It

only seen to exist with regard to claims based on a right *in rem* because transfer of the object concerned extinguishes those claims. That is why § 198 BGB preserves, whatever portion of the period of prescription has elapsed, for the benefit of the successor in title; for Israel, s. 819 Draft Civil Code pursues the same policy. The PECL and PICC do not have a rule on this point because they do not cover prescription of rights *in rem*. – Section 833 Draft Civil Code (effect of prescription on ancillary claims) essentially corresponds to § 217 BGB and Art. 14:502 PECL (the PICC do not have a rule on this point: see [2006] 21 Tulane European and Civil Law Forum 16); s. 832(a) Draft Civil Code (sexual abuse of minors) is motivated by the same concerns as § 208 BGB (on which see New German Law of Obligations (n. 7), 150 ff.) but goes even further by eliminating the defence of prescription altogether; and s. 825 Draft Civil Code, just as § 211 BGB, Art. 14:306 PECL and Art. 10.8(2) PICC, provides for an extension of prescription in certain situations where the creditor (though not where the debtor!) has died; cf. also Comparative Foundations (n. 12), 141; *Lando/Clive/Prüm/Zimmermann* (n. 3), 192. – On the effect of prescription on set-off, see § 215 BGB, Art. 14:503 PECL, Art. 10.10 PICC; Comparative Foundations (n. 12), 160 f.; New German Law of Obligations (n. 7), 153 f.; (2006) 21 Tulane European and Civil Law Forum 20. Section 837 Draft Civil Code deals with this question but it is difficult for me to comment on the proposed rule because it appears to be uncertain whether set-off has a retrospective or merely a prospective effect under Israeli law; information kindly supplied by Talia Einhorn, Tel Aviv.

[73] That, at least, is the term used by *Israel Gilead* in his paper.

[74] Section 809 Draft Civil Code.

[75] Section 810(a) Draft Civil Code.

[76] Section 837a Draft Civil Code.

[77] See Art. 14:501(2) PECL; Art. 10.9(1) and Art. 10.11 PICC; § 214 II BGB; Comparative Foundations (n. 12), 154 f.

[78] Comparative Foundations (n. 12), 72 ff.; *Lando/Clive/Prüm/Zimmermann* (n. 3), 202 f.

[79] Art. 14:501(1) PECL; Art. 10.9(1) – (2) PICC; § 214 I BGB. – The main point of these remarks in my original paper was to draw attention to the fact that one does not have to resort to a procedural concept of prescription if one rejects all, or some, of the consequences of a "strong" substantive approach. In the new version of his paper (*sub* X.), Professor *Gilead* has taken up this point. Of course, I entirely agree with him that one should first look at the legal consequences for

is superior to the former for a number of reasons[80]. Thus, for example, it is quite unnecessary for a legal system to foist its protection upon a debtor who is willing to pay and who can thus be taken to acknowledge the obligation to do so. But it is also superior to the procedural approach. For there is no reason why it should only be possible to plead prescription in Court. Such an approach would appear to engender rather than reduce litigation, and that is hardly in the public interest. Arguably, recognition of the substantive nature of prescription would also avoid the necessity to draw subtle distinctions between actions and causes of action[81]. A cause of action, according to Professor Gilead, contains the material elements that lie at the core of a group of actions; but Professor Gilead acknowledges that the question of materiality is a difficult one and that the decision will often depend on the circumstances of each case[82]. Civilian legal systems which subscribe to the substantive view of prescription in the weak variety and which tie prescription to the notion of "claims"[83] do not have these kinds of problems. A contract may, presumably, be regarded as a cause of action. It can give rise to a variety of claims. Each claim has to be looked at in isolation. If the purchaser demands specific performance, the seller can raise the defence of prescription if and when three years have elapsed after his claim has become due (i.e., normally, three years after conclusion of the contract). If he demands damages for non-performance, he can raise the defence of prescription three years after *that* claim has become due (i.e., normally, if and when the seller has failed to perform and has, as a result of such failure, incurred damages). If the seller has delivered a defective object, the purchaser is entitled to terminate the contract. Once again, subsequent to termination, the claims to restore what has been delivered are subject to the normal rules of prescription, i.e. they prescribe three years after the contract has been terminated. Concurrence of claims can also not throw up specific prescription problems, as long as a legal system provides for a uniform prescription regime. Difficulties, as has been mentioned before, can arise with regard to claims for damages in view of the "latent damages" problem. The Principles of European Contract Law and the Draft Civil Code for Israel take account of these difficulties in ways which are very different in form but similar in substance[84]. Concerning ongoing obligations, Art. 14:203(2) PECL and s. 814a of the Draft Civil Code also essentially pursue the same policy.

---

all the relevant problems and not be led by conceptual blinkers. Still, however, it appears to be legitimate to inquire how these consequences can best be conceptualized; and here, I am happy to see, that Professor *Gilead* also appears to incline towards the "weak" substantive approach, particularly as far as the question of self-help is concerned; see his criticism of s. 810(b) *sub* X. *in fine*, with which I completely agree.

[80] Comparative Foundations (n. 12), 73 f.; *Lando/Clive/Prüm/Zimmermann* (n. 3), 202.

[81] See *Gilead sub* V. 1).

[82] *Gilead, sub* V. 1), 2).

[83] *Lando/Clive/Prüm/Zimmermann* (n. 3), 157 f.

[84] *Supra* III. 4). – In the revised version of his paper, Professor *Gilead* argues (*sub* V. 4)) that the distinction between actions and causes of action is necessary in order to be able to cope with the situation where a breach of contract first causes damage A and, many years later, damage B "which

VII. Conclusion

All in all, I think, it can fairly be said that Part 6 of the Draft Civil Code for Israel on limitations of actions confirms the general impression that the law of prescription is converging internationally. In a number of important respects, the proposed provisions reflect the general international development, even if they do not do so fully. In other respects, they continue to deviate from solutions that have come to be recognised as a result of comparative research and international cooperation. To be sure: established comparative wisdom, whether it is to be found in legal literature or international restatements, may be based on mistaken assumptions; it may be favouring an inappropriate solution; it may not suit a particular legal culture; or it may be questionable for other reasons[85]. But if a legal system decides to follow its own path, such decisions should be based, in each and every instance, on a reasoned motivation, and a critical reflection of other views. Only then Israeli law may, in turn, be able to influence the international legal development.

---

is of the same type and magnitude as damage A". Here it would clearly thwart the aims of prescription if the injured party were still able to claim for damage B in spite of the fact that the period of prescription for his damages claim has elapsed. Professor *Gilead* and I are in complete agreement in that respect. But it is not necessary to resort to the complex notion of a cause of action in order to reach this result; see Art. 14:301 PECL (running of the period of prescription is suspended as long as the creditor does not know, and could not reasonably know of "... the facts giving rise to the claim including, in the case of a right to damages, the type of damage"; and see the explanation in *Lando/Clive/Prüm/Zimmermann* (n. 3), 176.

[85] See, concerning the Principles of European Contract Law, Symposium Kötz (n. 6), 144: "In the first place, ... it is the task of legal scholarship to take note of the Principles, to provide critical comment and discussion, and intellectually relate them to the various national legal systems. This does not have to be, and indeed should not be, a one-way process. For as much as national legal developments have to be evaluated against the yardstick provided by the Principles, the Principles may not pass muster when they are evaluated against the background of national legal experiences which have been gathered over a long period and by sophisticated courts and legal writers".

The Draft Civil Code for Israel: Closing Remarks

By Kurt Siehr

Summary of Contents

I. Types of Codifications

There are two basic types of codifications. There is, first of all, the unifying type as, e.g., the French *Code civil* of 1804 or the German BGB of 1896 which unified the territorially different legal systems in France and in Germany. This unification was necessary in order to abolish concurring and conflicting regional laws within the same country and to grant equal treatment to all citizens[1]. The other type of codification is more of a reforming nature; it is one which, like the *Nieuwe Burgerlijk Wetboek* of the Netherlands in 1992, revises and modernises an outdated older code. The forthcoming Israeli Civil Code will have both features in common. It will be unifying and modernising private law in Israel. It will integrate and revise many of the already existing statutes on civil law matters and, at the same time, will include additional matters and thereby unify Israeli private law, a legal system with different layers or "Schichtenrecht" so called by Wladimir Zeltner (1909–1977)[2] who established the close contact between

---

[1] Jean-Etienne-Marie Portalis (1745–1807), conseiller d'Etat, said in his speech of 4 ventose an XI [23 February 1803] on the forthcoming Code civil to the legislators: "La loi, partout opposée à elle-même, divisait les citoyens au lieu de les unit. Cet ordre de choses ne saurait exister plus longtemps. Des hommes qui, à la voix puissante de la patrie, et par un élan sublime et généreux, ont subitement renoncé à leurs privilèges et à leurs habitudes, pour reconnaître un intérêt commun, ont conquis le droit inappréciables de vivre sous une commune loi", in: *Portalis*, Discours préliminaire du premier projet de Code civil (1999), 62.

[2] *Wladimir Zeltner*, Einführung in das israelische Privatrecht, in: Gesellschaft zur Förderung der wissenschaftlichen Zusammenarbeit mit der Universität Tel Aviv e.V. (Hrsg.), Beiträge zum deut-

the University of Tel Aviv Faculty of Law and the Max Planck Institute in Hamburg under the directorship of his friend Konrad Zweigert (1911–1996).

II. Qualities of Codifications

From our own experience in Germany and from other European codifications of private law we know that such a codification must have at least three basic qualities[3]: (i) it must be clear, systematically organised, and try to avoid burying basic principles under the details of minor problems. That means that a codification has to be relatively short and resist the temptation to provide specific rules for each and every situation. (ii) The codification has to be intellectually consistent and has to avoid contradictions and superfluous repetitions. In short: It must be enforceable[4]. (iii) It must be comprehensive with respect to the matters covered by the code and not only a restatement of existing case law with all its lacunae. It must be guided by, and meet the needs of, modern society.

III. Value of Codifications

After having carefully and comprehensively revised and finished your work on the draft for the Israeli Draft Civil Code you will be rewarded in three important aspects. You will get: (i) certainty and security with regard to private law transactions and legal problems. People will know about their legal situation and will not take every case to court. (ii) You will have a single source of law for private law matters and will abandon the scattered individual acts on specific problems of private law. (iii) Scientific progress and the status of Israeli legal research will be reflected in the Israeli Civil Code[5] and encourage academic research to correct any deficiencies.

---

schen und israelischen Privatrecht. Deutsch-israelisches Juristensymposion Köln 1975 (1977), 9–29.

[3] Cf. also *Aharon Barak*, Towards Codification of the Civil Law, (1975) 1 Tel Aviv University Studies in law 9, 11 (the opening address to the 1973 Symposium on Codification of the Civil Law of Israel).

[4] Cf. *Eugen Huber*, Recht und Rechtsverwirklichung. Probleme der Gesetzgebung und der Rechtsphilosophie (1921), 242ff.

[5] Wladimir Zeltner at the end of his lecture, more than thirty years ago, stated: "Ihre Schaffung [eine Theorie des israelischen Rechts] scheint die dringlichste Aufgabe des israelischen Juristen zu sein". Cf. *Zeltner* (n. 2), 27. This task seems to have been achieved and will encourage further progress.

IV. Destiny of Codifications

Even if not all wishes and aspirations may become true, you deserve some words of consolation and encouragement from historical examples.

As the first modern codification of private law, the *Allgemeine Landrecht für die Preussischen Staaten* (ALR) was promulgated in 1794. King Frederick II (1740–1786), who was afraid of judicial activism, had already ordered that any gaps had to be filled not by the judges but by a legislative commission, called the *Gesetz-Commission*[6]. Yet, the Prussian ALR has given rise to multi-volume commentaries[7] and multi-volume treatises[8]. They have been written mainly by law professors, but also by judges and practising lawyers. Legal scholarship and judicial development of the law cannot be stopped by governmental fiat.

Ten years later the French *Code civil* of 1804, later called *Code Napoléon* (1807–1816, 1852–1870), was enacted; it was to be imitated and copied in many European and Latin American countries. Napoléon is reported to have said on St. Helena: "Ma gloire n'est pas d'avoir gagné quarante batailles et d'avoir fait la loi aux rois … Waterloo effacera le souvenir de tant de victoires … Mais ce que rien n'effacera et que vivra éternellement, c'est mon Code civil."[9] Three years ago the 200th anniversary of the Code civil was celebrated and it was pointed out how much has been changed in the Code civil due to modern needs and new perspectives[10]. This is a good example for the common experience that no codification is ever perfect. Sooner or later it must be adjusted to changed circumstances and to new demands.

Next came the Austrian *Allgemeines bürgerliches Gesetzbuch für die gesammten deutschen Erbländer der Oesterreichischen Monarchie* (ABGB); it was promulgated by Emperor Francis I and entered into force on January 1, 1812. It seems to have been the first civil code which openly admitted that it cannot be perfect and stated that gaps have to be filled according to principles of natural justice[11].

---

[6] Cf. *Grundsatz* 27 of the *Cabinetts-Ordre* of 27 July 1780 in: *Hans Hattenhauer* (ed.), Allgemeines Landrecht für die Preußischen Staaten von 1794 (3rd ed., 1996), 42 and 47.

[7] Cf., e.g., *Friedrich Christian Koch*, Allgemeines Landrecht für die Preussischen Staaten, 8 vols. (1852–1883).

[8] Cf., e.g., *Heinrich Dernburg*, Lehrbuch des Preussischen Privatrechts, 5 vols. (1875–1894); *Franz Förster/Max Ernst Eccius*, Theorie und Praxis des heutigen gemeinen preussischen Privatrechts auf der Grundlage des gemeinen deutschen Rechts (Preussisches Privatrecht), 7 vols., Berlin (1865–1896); *Eduard Gans*, Beiträge zur Revision der Preussischen Gesetzgebung, (1830–1832).

[9] *Charles-Tristan de Montholon*, Récits de la captivité de l'empereur Napoléon à Ste Hélène, vol. I, (1847), 401.

[10] *Le Code civil 1804–2004. Livre du Bicentenaire* (2004); *1804–2004. Le Code civil. Un passé, un présent, un avenir* (2004).

[11] § 7 ABGB reads: "Läßt sich ein Rechtsfall weder aus den Worten, noch aus dem natürlichen Sinne eines Gesetzes entscheiden, so muß auf ähnliche, in den Gesetzen bestimmt entschiedene Fälle, und auf die Gründe anderer damit verwandten Gesetze Rücksicht genommen werden. Bleibt der Rechtsfall noch zweifelhaft; so muß solcher im Hinblick auf die sorgfältig gesammelten und reiflich erwogenen Umstände nach den natürlichen Rechtsgrundsätzen entschieden werden."

Other civil codes followed that example,[12] and the Swiss Civil Code even copied Aristotle[13] by providing in Article 1(2) and (3): "Where no provision is applicable, the judge [now: the court] shall decide according to the existing Customary Law and, in default thereof, according to the rules which he [it] would lay down if he [it] had himself [itself] to act as legislator. Herein he [it] must be guided by approved doctrine and case-law."[14]

The German *Bürgerliches Gesetzbuch* (BGB) of 1896 has been characterised as "the child of the deep, exact and abstract learning of the German Pandectist School with all the advantages and disadvantages which that entails"[15]. It has been decried as patriarchal, insensitive to social issues, not readily comprehensible, and too heavily Romanist in spirit and substance[16]. Yet, the BGB has survived and for more than a hundred years the German judiciary, supported by legal scholars, have created a fair balance between stability and adjustment to modern needs[17].

One hundred years ago the Swiss *Zivilgesetzbuch* (ZGB) was enacted and entered into force on 1 January 1912. Eugen Huber (1849–1923), who mainly drafted the bill, wanted to create a popular codification. "The statute must reflect the ideas of the nation. The common man, who reads it and has considered the needs of our time, must have the impression that the statute is voicing his innermost thoughts"[18]. The ZGB was written for the lay public, not for lawyers. Every household received a free copy of the code so as to familiarise it with its

[12] Article 3(2) of the Italian Civil Code of 1865 referred to "i principii generali di diritto"; Article 1(4) of the Spanish Código civil of 1889 still refers to "los principios generales del derecho".

[13] *Aristotle*, The Nicomachean Ethics (translation by H. Rackham, 1990), 315 (book V, 10, 5): "When therefore the law lays down a general rule, and thereafter a case arises which is an exception to the rule, it is then right, where the lawgiver's pronouncement because of its absoluteness is defective and erroneous, to rectify the defect by deciding as the lawgiver would himself decide if he were present on the occasion, and would have enacted if he had been cognizant of the case in question."

[14] Article 1(2) and (3) of the Swiss Civil Code read: "Kann dem Gesetze keine Vorschrift entnommen werden, so soll der Richter [das Gericht] nach Gewohnheitsrecht und, wo auch ein solches fehlt, nach der Regel entscheiden, die er [es] als Gesetzgeber aufstellen würde. Er [es] folgt dabei bewährter Lehre und Überlieferung." The brackets refer to the new gender neutral version in force since 1 January 2000.

[15] *Konrad Zweigert/Hein Kötz*, Introduction to Comparative Law (translation by Tony Weir, 3rd ed., 1998), 144.

[16] *Otto von Gierke*, Der Entwurf eines bürgerlichen Gesetzbuchs und das deutsche Recht, (1889); *Otto von Gierke*, Das Bürgerliche Gesetzbuch und der Deutsche Reichstag (1896), 39ff.; *Anton Menger*, Das bürgerliche Recht und die besitzlosen Volksklassen (3rd ed., 1903), 14ff.

[17] Cf., e.g., *Basil S. Markesinis/Hannes Unberath*, The German Law of Torts (4th ed., 2002), 592ff., 687ff.

[18] "Das Gesetz muß aus den Gedanken des Volkes heraus gesprochen sein. Der verständige Mann, der es liest, der über die Zeit und ihre Bedürfnisse nachgedacht hat, muß die Empfindung haben, das Gesetz sei ihm aus dem Herzen gesprochen." These excerpts of the explanations of the ZGB are cited by *Theo Guhl*, Eugen Huber, in: Hans Schultheß (ed.), Schweizer Juristen der letzten hundert Jahre (1945), 348.

civil rights and obligations. The character of the Swiss Civil Code has been aptly described by the professor and federal judge Virgile Rossel in his obituary of Eugen Huber in 1923: "En particulier si l'on a pu dire du Code Napoléon qu' îl était la 'raison écrite', nous avons cru travailler dans le sens de l'esprit national en moralisant notre droit autant que faire se pouvait, et nous serions heureux si l'on disait un jour du code civil suisse qu'il est un peu la conscience écrite."[19] In spite of this, the Swiss codification was not able to solve all ills, and lawyers are needed in Switzerland, as everywhere, to interpret and apply the code.

One of the latest modern civil codes is the *Dutch Burgerlijk Wetboek* (BW). It is interesting also insofar as it has entered into force since 1992 in instalments. The work on that project started in 1947 und will eventually comprise all matters of general private law and commercial law[20]. Although deviating from the old model of the French *Code civil* the new BW will remain an open and flexible codification[21].

From all these experiences of the past three conclusions may be drawn. First that all codifications, except for the Prussian ALR that was abolished by the BGB, have survived. They managed to adjust to changed circumstances. Each code in its own way was revised innumerable times and was corrected in many respects. Yet, they all preserved many of their original features. The *Code civil* is still "the constitution civile de la France" which celebrated its 200th anniversary in 2004[22] and in the future may be subject to a "re-codification"[23]. The Austrian ABGB is still a liberal code awaiting its 200th anniversary in the near future, and the German BGB preserves its character as a scholarly codification for jurists rather than for laymen[24]. Also the Swiss ZGB has been modernised several times and will continue to keep up with contemporary needs. In all countries there is a certain danger of "de-codification" consisting of the creation of private law statutes outside the civil code[25]. This, however, can be avoided. The BGB has not only revised its law of contractual obligations but has also inserted a range of

---

[19] Cited in *Guhl* (n. 18), 342.

[20] *Ewoud Hondius*, Das neue Niederländische Zivilgesetzbuch, (1991) 191 Archiv für die civilistische Praxis 378.

[21] *Arthur Hartkamp*, Das neue niederländische Bürgerliche Gesetzbuch aus europäischer Sicht, (1994) 57 Rabels Zeitschrift 664, 679.

[22] *Yves Gaudemet*, Le Code civil, "constitution civile de la France", in: *1804–2004. Le Code civil* (n. 10), 297 ff.

[23] *Jean-Luc Aubert*, La recodification et l'éclatement du droit civil hors le Code civil, in: *Le Code civil* (n. 10), 123 ff.

[24] *Rudolph Sohm*, Ueber den Entwurf eines bürgerlichen Gesetzbuchs für das Deutsche Reich in zweiter Lesung (1895), 5 ff.; *Ernst Zitelmann*, Die Rechtsgeschäfte im Entwurf eines Bürgerlichen Gesetzbuches für das Deutsche Reich, in: E.J. Bekker/O. Fischer (eds.), Beiträge zur Erläuterung und Beurteilung des Entwurfes eines Bürgerlichen Gesetzbuches für das Deutsche Reich (7 and 8, 1889), 3 ff.

[25] For Switzerland, cf. *Susanne Genner*, Dekodifikation. Zur Auflösung der kodifikatorischen Einheit im schweizerischen Zivilrecht (2006).

consumer law statutes into the codification[26]. There is no separate *Code social* as in France. A codification of private law is a living body of legal provisions and provides the framework for revisions and additions.

Second, the judiciary is an important part of the legal culture in all codified legal systems[27]. Even if there are no formally binding precedents, the judgments of the courts of last resort provide important guidelines for lower courts, practising lawyers and the public. There are, however, two very significant features of case law in codified legal systems. Courts do not stick to the literal meaning of statutory words and phrases. They try to determine the purpose and teleological meaning of a provision in order to implement this aim and to apply it also for the solution of open problems. In cases of lacunae courts often attempt to behave like a legislator by filling those gaps *modo legislatoris*. The other significant feature is that the case law still keeps in touch with the statutory provisions. The Civil Code is considered to provide the intellectual framewok within which any case law development takes place. Therefore, case law is always related to certain provisions of the Civil Code and discussed under the relevant heading.

Finally, a note of prophecy. When the German BGB was about to enter into force, Ernst Zitelmann, a famous law professor of Roman law and private international law, raised the question whether the new codification could endanger legal scholarship[28]. He argued that legal scholarship might lose some of its attraction as a result of being fettered by the code. Obviously, Zitelmann's fears did not come true. Legal scholars continued their dialogue with the judiciary and the legislature. They wrote commentaries on the BGB, published treatises and wrote streams of law review articles on the new code. They never declined to act as critical, but co-operative, partners in the constant endeavour for clarification and improvement of the Civil Code and German legal culture in general. Almost all judicial developments have been preceded by scholarly studies, often based on comparative law. At the same time German law professors taught the new BGB to young students according to the universally known proverb: "You can't teach an old dog new tricks."

V. Israeli Civil Code

Very soon Israel will join the family of countries with a codified private law. The Hamburg Max-Planck-Institute has observed this development with great interest. More than 30 years ago Wladimir Zeltner, Professor of the Tel Aviv

---

[26] *Per Zumbansen*, The Law of Contracts, in: Mathias Reimann/Joachim Zekoll (eds.), Introduction to German Law (2nd ed. 2005), 190ff.

[27] Cf. for Germany *Reinhard Zimmermann*, Characteristic Aspects of German Legal Culture, in: Reimann/Zekoll (n. 26), 19–22 (Case Law in a Codified System). For French law, cf. the annotations to Article 1382ff., *Code civil* (French tort law) in the edition of the *Code civil* by Dalloz.

[28] *Ernst Zitelmann*, Die Gefahren des bürgerlichen Gesetzbuches für die Rechtswissenschaft (1896).

University Faculty of Law and President of the Tel Aviv District Court, told us about the plans to codify Israeli private law and to fuse the individual statutes on private law matters into a comprehensive Civil Code[29]. Since then the connection between the Tel Aviv University Faculty of Law and the Hamburg Max Planck Institute has become a very close and friendly one. Students of the Tel Aviv University take part in the biannual workshops on European and German private law in Hamburg and on European and German public law in Heidelberg, common conferences have been held in Israel and in Germany (at *Schloss Ringberg*), and the Institute has been delighted to host many Israeli colleagues from Tel Aviv and Jerusalem. Yesterday and today we have enjoyed listening to extremely interesting papers on the draft of the Israeli Civil Code. We all hope that ultimately an Israeli Civil Code will be passed and become a successful codification of Israeli private law.

---

[29] As to the history of the Israeli codification cf. *Alfredo Mordechai Rabello*, L'influence du Code civil sur la nouvelle législation israélienne en marche vers la codification, in: *Le Code civil* (n. 10), 549, 558ff.

Professor Amos Shapira: on the Occasion of His 70th Birthday

By Gunther Kühne

Dear Amos, members of the Shapira family, distinguished guests,

tonight we have gathered here in this elegant ambiance to honour a man who is deeply connected to many of us personally and to the city of Hamburg, in particular its most renowned institutions of legal research (the Max Planck Institute) and learning (Bucerius Law School). Thanks go to Professors Zimmermann and Siehr for having made possible the inclusion of this evening in the program of the conference.

But Amos Shapira's contacts with Germany go far beyond his connections with Hamburg and other institutions of legal research. I shall – for a few minutes – concentrate on a deeper layer of Amos Shapira's relations with Germany and German culture. Their origins can be traced back to medieval Germany, as evidenced by his name: The root of the word "Shapira" is nothing else but the German city of Speyer. The Shapiras, Shapiros or Spiros are supposed to originate from Speyer which is not as surprising as it may seem at first glance. Together with Worms and Mainz, Speyer were the area of the most famous Talmudic scholars of the time and had great influence far beyond their geographical boundaries, for instance with the outstanding figure of Salomo ben Isaac, called Rashi. The communities of Speyer, Worms and Mainz, throughout the Jewish world, at that time gained a high reputation as centres of Jewish learning and deeply influenced Jewish law through their religious ordinances, called "Takkanot SHWM" (S(peyer), W(orms), M(ainz)), commonly known as "Shum"*. As we all are sadly aware, this heyday of Judaism in Germany was destroyed in the 12th and 13th centuries by the crusades and their aftermath. Most Jews in Germany including our Shapiras had to seek refuge in Eastern Europe. The majority of them settled in Poland and in the Baltic States, especially Lithuania. And here again, during the 17th, 18th and 19th centuries, we see the Shapiras embedded in an atmosphere and culture illuminated by an exceptional level of Talmudic learning geographically concentrated on the cities of Wilna (Vilnius), called the

* "Shum", in Hebrew, means "garlic". That is why the three communities carried a bulb of garlic as their pictorial symbol.

"Jerusalem of the East", and Kowno (Kaunas) (Amos Shapira's parents' residence of origin), with most important religious schools ("Jeshivot") and outstanding Talmudic authorities, the most famous of them being the Gaon of Wilna and Israel Lipkin of Kaunas, the founder of the moralistic Mussar Movement.

The Shapira family – Amos' father was a Hebrew teacher in Kaunas -presumably has been all along in contact with and, therefore, influenced by the religious and intellectual life in the Lithuanian Jewish or, as it came to be called, the Litvak community. In this respect it is noteworthy that, within the cosmos of East European Jewish religious factions, Lithuania was a stronghold of rationalistic, moralistic and even austere religious attitudes vigorously opposing mysticism, irrationalism and Chassidism. From religious rationalism to *Aufklärung*, or "enlightenment", is not too far a step. The Enlightenment or Haskala Movement, in the 18th and 19th centuries, had gained ground within East European Jewish communities and was stimulated by the striking success the *Aufklärung* had achieved among German Jews under the inspiration of Moses Mendelssohn. The *Aufklärung* integrated German classical literature and philosophy into the Jewish cultural horizon also in Eastern Europe, a development that was facilitated by the linguistic Germanic basis of Yiddish. And that is why the works of Goethe, Schiller and Lessing were to be found also in the Shapira family's bookcase as in those of many other educated Jewish families in the East.

The turbulences and excesses of the history of the 20th century in Europe were bound to uproot the living conditions also of Lithuanian Jews and with it of the Shapira family. Lithuania was a bone of contention between Poland, Russia and Germany, and rampant Lithuanian nationalism left many Jews with no option but to leave: either to the world at large, which many did – South Africa is an example – or to choose emigration to Erez Israel (Palestine) or "aliyah". For the Shapira family, deeply impregnated with Zionist convictions and personally involved in the aspirations to reestablish Hebrew as the language of the Jewish nation, the latter choice was clear. And in practicing "aliyah" in 1935, Amos Shapira's family was blessed with foresight in the light of the horrors that – only a few years later – were to be inflicted on Lithuanian Jews in general and on those in Kaunas in particular.

With this family heritage bestowed on Amos Shapira at his birth in 1937, he has had, by now, a life span of 70 years as a most successful and respected Israeli law professor and a visible part of Israel's intellectual upper-class. While being what Israelis call a "sabre", he, nonetheless, already early developed a universalist life perspective by going both to Columbia for the LL.M., and to Yale for the J.S.D. And it was his Yale thesis on "Interest Analysis in Choice of Law" which was to become the igniting spark of the relationship between Amos Shapira and myself.

I had used that book while being in residence at Columbia in 1970/71. When, six years later, I accompanied my then boss, the German Parliamentary State Secretary in the Federal Ministry of Justice, Dr. de With, as his personal assistant on a lecture tour to Israel and, during the introduction ceremony, heard the name "Professor Amos Shapira" I immediately asked him: "Are you the author of that yellow book?" and within a fraction of a second an explosion of mutual sympathy filled the room. Ever since that moment, our friendship has deepened and extended first to our wives and then to other members of the family as well as to quite a few friends of ours in Israel and in Germany respectively. Together we have experienced a wide range of emotional reunions in quite a few places of the world – happy reunions as, e.g., the Passover Seders in Ramat Aviv, which strengthened my own inherited bonds with Jewish tradition, or the many highlights of meetings – both professional and private – in Europe and in America, but also pensive or even sad reunions. And with regard to future reunions, we very much hope there are a lot more to come.

So, tonight, we are delighted to have among us a man with a multi-faceted personality and a rare blend of ingredients – loyalty, a sense of tradition, intellectualism, rationalism, universalism and pragmatism – some of which I have tried to explain out of Amos Shapira's background. And all this is wrapped in personal charm and a most lovable nature.

In Germany, it is customary on occasions such as this to express the wish "ad multos annos". In this respect, Jewish tradition is more precise and demanding: here, the wish runs up to 120 years and therefore I would like to ask the audience to join in the traditional "Ad mea ve'essrim shanah" together with a most cordial "Mazal tov" to our most esteemed friend Amos Shapira.

Draft Civil Code for Israel

Part One: Principles of the Civil Code[1]

Chapter One: Fundamental Principles

1. *Objectives of the Law* – The objectives enumerated herein are among the objectives of this law:

(a) Ensuring justice, fairness and reasonableness;
(b) Promoting security, certainty and efficiency in the legal process;
(c) Coordinating the various civil procedural laws;
(d) Preserving established rights;
(e) Protecting the appropriate expectations and reliance of the parties.

2. *Good Faith* – In making use of a right, in carrying out a legal transaction and in fulfilling an obligation, one must act in good faith.

3. *One who violates the law is not rewarded* – The court may deny or limit the right of a person, when to do so is justified because the right arose due to behavior of the one holding the right that violates the law or public enactments.

4. *Trivialities* – A complaint shall not be filed for a deed of little importance, about which a reasonable person would not complain.

4A. *Legal Competence re rights and obligations* – Legal competence regarding rights and obligations is accorded to a person from the time his birth is completed until the day of his death, and with respect to a company – in accordance with the provisions of the law.

Chapter Two: Definitions

5. *General Definitions* – In this act –

"Adult" – a person who has reached the age of 18 years;

"Spouse" – including a common law spouse;

"Breach" – an act in violation of an obligation;

"Land Law" – The Land Law [Registration], 5729–1969[2];

"Adjudication of Interest Law" – Adjudication of Interest Law, 5721–1961[3];

"The Planning and Construction Law" – The Planning and Construction Law, 5725–1965[4];

"Ward" – one for whom a court has appointed a guardian, or one regarding whom a court is authorized to appoint a guardian, even if it has not yet been determined if the conditions for such an appointment have been fulfilled, as is the case;

---

[1] *Footnotes to the legislative version:* In this proposal there are three kinds of footnotes. The first, the normal footnote, is a citation of various laws. The second, cites parts, chapters, or sections of the proposed law in order to make finding provisions in the law easier. The third, is found in places in which in the current version there are a number of possibilities, and it interprets the rationale of the different versions.

Regarding the name of the law, other names were considered such as "The Civil Code", "The Civil Book of Laws", "The Civil Law", "The Collected Civil Laws". The public is invited to suggest other names.

[2] SH 5729, p. 259; the law will be amended and provisions regarding registration will remain – cf, sec. 848.

[3] SH 5721, p. 192.

[4] SH 5725, p. 307.

"A person of limited competence" – a person whom a court has declared to be of limited competence pursuant to section 9;

"Moveable property" – tangible property, excluding real property;

"Act" – including acts of omission;

"A person's place of residence" – the place where his life is centered; regarding a minor, a person of limited competence or a protected person, there is a presumption that his place of residence is the place of residence of his guardian, as long as it has not been proven that his life is centered elsewhere;

"immoveable property" – land, anything built or planted on it and any other thing permanently connected to it;

"physical injury" – death, illness, injury or physical, emotional or mental impairment;

"property" – real property and moveable property, and to the extent appropriate, and with the necessary changes, rights in property;

"injured party" – one towards whom an obligation was breached;

"minor" – A person who has not yet attained eighteen years of age;

"relative" – spouse, father, mother, son, daughter, brother, sister grandfather, grandmother, grandson, granddaughter.

★★ Sec 6–74 were dropped from the final version of the code

Part Three: Legal Acts

Chapter One: General Provisions

Article One: Legal Act

75. *Kinds of Legal Acts* – A legal act can be unilateral or multilateral, in accordance with the legislation or the contract pursuant to which it is carried out.

76. *Method of Carrying out a Legal Act* – A legal act may be carried out orally, in writing or by means of behavior.

77. *Irrevocability of Legal Transaction* – A legal act is irrevocable effective from the date on which it was completed.

Article Two: Unilateral Legal Act

78. *Reception of Unilateral Legal Act* – A unilateral legal transaction must be received by the person whose rights are affected by the act (in this Part – addressee of the transaction).

79. *Completion of Unilateral Legal Act* – A unilateral legal act is completed upon its receipt by the addressee of the act, or on the date that notice of the act reaches his residence.

80. *Notice of Unilateral Legal Act* – (a) Notice of a unilateral legal act is to be transmitted as is customary under the circumstances.

(b) Where the unilateral legal act is known to the addressee of the act, this is regarded as if notice was transmitted to him in the manner set forth in subsection (a).

81. *Addressee of Act who was not Located* – Where it is not possible to locate the addressee of the transaction through reasonable means, the unilateral legal act will be completed when the one who undertook the act has taken reasonable steps to transmit the notice as set forth in section 80.

82. *Legal act that Exercises an Option* – Where the legal act was the exercise of the right of a choice that was created due to the breach of an obligation by the addressee of the act

or due to a defect in the will of the one carrying out the act as set forth in sections 87, 177(a) and 178 through 180, the act will be completed within a reasonable time from the sending of a notice for collection, even if the notice arrived late to the addressee of the act or if it did not arrive at all, on the condition that the one carrying out the act sent the notice as is customary and under the circumstances it was reasonable to expect that the notice would reach the addressee of the act on time.

83. *The Time for Carrying out an Act* – The time for carrying out a unilateral legal act is within a reasonable time from the time when the person knew of his right to carry out the act.

Chapter Two: Competence to Carry Out a Legal Act

84. *Legal Competence* – Every person is capable of carrying out legal acts, unless he has been deprived of this capacity or it has been restricted by law or by the judgment of a court of law.

85. *Legal Act of one whose Competence has been Restricted* – (a) The provisions of this chapter regarding a minor will apply, *mutatis mutandis*, to a legal act carried out by one whose capacity has been limited.

(b) Where, at the time a legal act was carried out, it was possible to declare a person to be of restricted legal competence pursuant to section 9 and the addressee of the act knew or should have known this, such person will be considered as one who was declared to be of restricted capacity for the purposes of the provisions of this Chapter.

86. *Guardian's Consent to the Legal Acts of a Minor* – Legal acts of a minor require the consent of his guardian; the guardian's consent may be granted in advance or subsequently, for a particular act or for a kind of act, and he may withdraw his consent as long as the act has not been performed.

87. *Invalidation of Legal Act of a Minor* – (a) A legal act of a minor performed without the consent of his guardian may be invalidated by the guardian, and if the minor does not have a guardian – by the Attorney General or his legal representative, within a reasonable time from the day that he knew of the act.

(b) If the guardian or the Attorney General is requested by the addressee of the act to notify him of his position regarding the act, he will notify him within 30 days from the day on which he received the request; if he does not so notify him, the act will be regarded as having been consented to.

(c) If the minor has reached the age of majority before the guardian or the Attorney General, whichever one is applicable, becomes aware of the act, or before the reasonable time period for invalidating the act has passed, the minor who has reached the age of majority is entitled to invalidate the act, within a reasonable time from the day on which he reached the age of majority; the provisions of subsection (b) will apply, *mutatis mutandis*, to the right to invalidate pursuant to this subsection as well.

88. *Legal Acts of Minors that cannot be Invalidated* – A legal act of a minor, of a kind commonly performed by minors of his age, or a legal act between a minor and a person who neither knew nor should have known that the person performing it was a minor cannot be invalidated unless substantial harm is caused to the minor.

89. *Void Acts by a Minor* – A legal act involving receipt of credit by a minor, that is not among the kinds of acts that it is common for minors to perform, will be void unless the guardian's consent to the act is received within a reasonable period of time.

90. *Restitution for a Void or Invalid Act* – Where a legal act is void or voided as set forth,

each party will be entitled to restitution of what he gave to the other party; the Chapter Unjust Enrichment[5] will apply to the right of restitution.

91. *Court Approval of a Minor's Legal Transaction* – (a) A legal act of a minor, that is one of the acts listed below, requires court approval, regardless of whether it is performed by the minor or by his guardian on his behalf:

(1) An act whose validity is contingent upon registration in a registry that is kept pursuant to legislation;
(2) assignment of a right to receive a right in property, where the right is contingent upon registration in a registry kept pursuant to legislation;
(3) transfer, encumbrance or partition of rights in an apartment or in an economic unit in an agricultural, industrial, craft or commercial enterprise;
(4) the making of a gift, other than gifts and contributions customarily made in similar circumstances;
(5) providing a guarantee;
(6) a legal act between the minor and his guardian or relatives of his guardian, other than the receipt of gifts given to the minor;
(7) a legal act between two minors who each have the same guardian;
(8) a lease to which the Tenants' Protection Law applies;

(9) A commitment to perform any of the acts set forth in paragraphs (1) through (8); if approval of a commitment has been given pursuant to this subsection, no additional approval will be required regarding the performance of the act that is the subject of the commitment.

(b) A legal act as described in subsections (a)(6) and (a)(7) require prior approval by the court; if the minor was a ward, such prior approval may also be given by a guardian who was appointed for the purpose of giving such approval.

92. *Court Approval of a Ward's Legal Act* – Section 92 will also apply, *mutatis mutandis*, to acts performed by a guardian on behalf of the ward.

93. *Who may Submit a Petition for Court Approval* – An application to receive court approval of a legal act may be submitted by the guardian of the minor or the ward, by the ward, or by the other party to the legal act.

94. *Act of Guardian in Absence of Court Approval* – The act of a guardian that is subject to court approval pursuant to this Chapter, or to consent pursuant to section 41(2), will be valid even without such approval or consent, if it was performed with respect to a person who did not know, and was not required to know, that it was subject to such approval or consent.

95. *Action of Guardian whose Appointment is Defective* – The act of a guardian will be valid even if his appointment is defective, if it was performed with respect to a person who did not know, and was not required to know, of such defect.

96. *Validity of Contract Entered into Prior to Court Approval* – Where a contract subject to court approval is entered into, the minor or ward and the other party will be viewed as having entered into a contract between them which is contingent upon the grant of approval by the court within a reasonable period of time.

97. *Joint Legal Acts of Parents and Guardians* – The provisions of sections 18, 19 and 46 Legal Capacity and Guardianship Law 5722–1962 will apply to joint legal acts of parents and guardians.

98. *Preservation of Laws Regarding Capacity to Perform Act* – The provisions of this Chap-

---

[5] Chapter Two in the Fourth Sub-Part (sections 487 through 496).

terdo not apply to the competence of a person for the transactions that establish or change his personal status.

Chapter Three: Agency

99. *What is Agency* – (a) Agency is the power of one person (in this Chapter – the agent) to perform a legal act on behalf of another person (in this Chapter – the principal).

(b) Any legal act can be performed by agency, unless by reason of its essence, its conditions or pursuant to legislation, it must be personally performed.

100. *A Person's Agent is Like Himself* – A person's agent is like himself, and the agent's act, knowledge and intent entitles or binds, as the case may be, the principal.

101. *Capacity of the Agent* – A person is competent to serve as an agent for a legal act that he has sufficient understanding to perform, however with regard to his rights and obligations, the Chapter dealing with capacity to perform a legal act and Legal Capacity and Guardianship Law 5722–1962 shall apply.[6]

102. *Creation of the Agency* – (a) Agency is created by authorization of the principal. The authorization shall be given by notice from the principal to the agent or to the person with respect to whom the legal act is performed (in this Chapter – the third party).

(b) A third party is entitled not to recognize the transaction of an agent unless a written authorization is presented to him and he is provided with a copy of it.

103. *Scope of Agency* – (a) The agent is authorized to perform any act which is reasonably required for the performance of the agency; however, he may not represent the agent in proceedings before a court, a tribunal or an arbitrator, arrive at a compromise or perform a transaction without consideration, unless he was expressly authorized to do so.

(b) An agent is authorized to perform any urgent and unforeseen act reasonably required for safeguarding the interests of the principal with respect to the agency.

104. *Sub-Agency* – An agent may not appoint another agent with respect to his agency, except with the authorization of the principal or for an act as set forth in section 103(b).

105. *Unauthorized Transaction* – (a) Where a person has acted as the agent of another person without authorization from him or in excess of his authorization, the other person may, subject to the provisions of subsection (b), ratify the transaction retroactively; a retroactive ratification will have the effect of authorization in advance, however it will not derogate from a right that was acquired in good faith and for consideration prior to the ratification.

(b) Where a third party did not know, and he was not required to have known at the time of the performance of the act, as described in subsection (a), that it was done without authorization or in excess of the authorization, and as long as he does not know of the ratification of the transaction, he may choose to operate in one of the following ways –

(1) to view the one who performed the transaction as a party to the transaction and to give him a reasonable opportunity to carry out the transaction;

(2) to rescind the transaction and to claim damages from the one who performed the transaction for the harm caused him as a result of the absence of authorization or the act in excess of such authorization.

(c) One who performs an act may demand from the third party that he notify him of his choice as set forth in subsection (b); if the third party did not notify him of his choice

[6] Chapter Two of this Part (the Third Part), sections 84 through 98.

within a reasonable time after receipt of the demand, he is viewed as one who chose to rescind the transaction.

(d) The third party and the one who performed the act may demand of the person in whose name the act was performed to notify them as to his position regarding the act; if such a demand was transmitted, that person may confirm the act that was performed in his name after the fact, as set forth in subsection (a), if he gives notice to that effect within a reasonable time after receipt of the demand.

106. *Transaction on Behalf of a Corporation* – A corporation may ratify an act performed on its behalf prior to its establishment, and the provisions of section 105 will apply.

107. *Hidden Agency* – If, at the time of the act, the third party did not know, and was not required to know, of the existence of the agency or the identity of the principal, the act of the agent shall bind the principal and the agent jointly and severally and shall benefit only the agent; however, the principal may assert for himself the rights of the agent with respect to the third party, provided that this does not violate a contract, legislation or the essence of the right.

108. *Fiduciary Duty of the Agent* – One who has taken upon himself to act as an agent owes a fiduciary duty to the principal.

109. *Remedies for Breach of Fiduciary Duty* – Where the agent performed an act with respect to a third party in breach of his fiduciary duty, and the third party knew of the breach of duty, the principal may invalidate the act; there is nothing in this provision to derogate from any other remedy given to the principal with regard to the third party.

110. *Property that the Agent Received* – Property, benefit or profit that the agent has received in consequence of the agency is held by him as a trustee for the principal.

111. *Reimbursement of the Agent* – The principal shall reimburse the agent for reasonable expenses that he incurred and for the reasonable obligations that he undertook for the purpose of the agency.

112. *Termination of the Agency* – (a) An agency ends with any one of the following:

(1) notification of its cancellation from the principal or the agent;
(2) when the principal or the agent dies or is of restricted capacity;
(3) the principal or the agent is declared bankrupt, and if it is a corporation – decided on voluntary liquidation or a liquidation order was issued with respect to it.

(b) The provisions of subsection (a) shall not apply if authorization was given to insure the rights of another person or of the agent himself, and their rights are contingent upon performance of the subject of the agency.

(c) As long as the agent did not know, and was not required to know of the termination of the agency, he is entitled with respect to the principal to regard the agency as continuing to exist.

(d) Where the third party did not know, and was not required to know of the termination of the agency, he is entitled to regard the agency as continuing to exist; if the agent knew or was required to know of its termination, the third party is entitled to chose between regarding the agency as continuing or the alternatives set forth in section 105(b).

(e) The agent is entitled to demand of the third party that he notify him of his choice as set forth in subsection (d); where the third party did not give notice of his choice within a reasonable time from receipt of the demand, he is treated as a third party who chose to renounce the act.

113. *Multiple Principals and Agents* – (a) Where the principal gave one authorization to several agents, there is a presumption that they are to act jointly.

(b) Where several principals have given an authorization, there is a presumption that the agent is to act on the joint authority of all of them together.

Part Four: Obligations

Sub-Part One: General Provisions Regarding Obligations

Chapter One: Completion, Fulfillment and Expiration of Obligations

114. *Source of Obligations* – An obligation is created pursuant to law or to a contract.

115. *Identity of the Obligor* – An obligation may be performed by one who is not the obligor, unless according to its substance or conditions or pursuant to legislation, the obligor must personally fulfill it.

116. *Time for Performance* – (a) An obligation pursuant to a contract must be performed within a reasonable time from its creation; if the obligor was required to perform the obligation within a particular period of time, he may set the time for its performance within that period of time.

(b) The obligor will give the obligee notice, a reasonable amount of time in advance, regarding the date that the obligation will be performed as set forth in subsection (a).

117. *Early Fulfillment* – An obligation may be performed before the deadline, providing that such early performance will not prejudice the rights of the obligee and that the obligor gave notice of such early performance a reasonable time in advance.

118. *Postponement of Deadline for Fulfilllment* – (a) The deadline for performance of an obligation is postponed –

(1) if timely performance was prevented because the obligee did not yet perform an obligation that he was required to perform first, or for another reason concerning the obligee – until such time as the hindrance has passed;

(2) if the parties were obliged to perform their obligations simultaneously (in this part – integrated obligations) – as long as the obligee is not ready to perform the obligation imposed on him.

(b) Where the deadline for the performance of the obligation has been postponed as set forth in subsection (a), the court may require the obligee to pay compensation to the obligor for the damages caused him due to the postponement, even if the obligee did not breach the contract as a consequence.

119. *Place of Fulfilling the Obligation* – (a) The obligor will perform the obligation at the obligee's place of business, and if he does not have a place of business or if the obligation is not connected to his business – at his place of residence.

(b) If the obligee changed his place of business or his place of residence after the date on which the obligation was created, the obligee will bear the additional expenses of performing the obligation in the new place.

120. *Fulfillment According to the Average* – An obligation to provide property or a service must be performed by providing property or service of an average kind and quality.

121. *Fulfillment in a Proper Amount* – The obligation to pay for property or service must be performed by payment of an amount that was appropriate according to the circumstances at the time the obligation was created.

122. *Fulfillment of the Obligation in Israeli Currency* – Where there is an obligation to

make a payment in Israel in a foreign currency and payment in such currency is prohibited by law, the payment shall be made in Israeli currency according to the exchange rate customary in transactions of that nature as it is known at the time of the payment.

123. *Expenses for Fulfillment of the Obligation* – The expenses incurred for the performance of the obligation will be borne by the obligor.

124. *Crediting Payment for One Obligation* – An amount paid for performing an obligation will be credited initially to the account of the expenses owing from the obligor with respect to the obligation and afterwards on account of the interest, and finally on account of the principle with the linkage differentials; in crediting the payment on account of the principle, the payment will be credited partially on account of the original principle and partially on account of the linkage differentials, consistent with the ratio between them.

125. *Crediting Payment for Several Obligations* – An obligor who owes several obligations to an obligee, is entitled to stipulate, at the time of the payment to the obligee, on account of which of the obligations the payment is to be credited; if he did not do so, the obligee may designate the manner of crediting the payment.

126. *Conditional Performance* – An obligation whose performance the obligor has undertaken with respect to the obligee in another obligation, or he has assigned him for this purpose a right against a third party, the obligor is not exempted from its performance if the other obligation, or the right that was assigned was not performed.

127. *Choice Between Two Alternative Obligations* – (a) In the case of alternative obligations, the obligor may choose the obligation that he will perform in a notice to the obligee within the time period established by the parties, and if no such time period has been established, within a reasonable period of time before the date of performance.

(b) Where the obligor did not choose which obligation to perform pursuant to subsection (a), the obligee may, upon notice to the obligor, choose which obligation the obligor will perform.

(c) Where the obligee had the right to choose, and he did not avail himself of it within the period of time established by the parties, and where there is no period of time within a reasonable time before the date for performance of the obligation, the obligor, in a notice to the obligee, may choose the obligation that will be performed.

128. *Offset* – (a) Monetary debts arising from one transaction that the parties owe to each other and the date for performance has arrived, may be offset against one another with notice of one party to the other party; and this is the rule regarding monetary debts that do not arise from one transaction, if they are debts of a fixed amount.

(b) An obligation whose performance is not subject to attachment may not be offset.

(c) The provisions of sections 124 and 125 will apply, with the necessary changes, to the performance of obligations by way of offset.

129. *Termination of Obligation* – An obligation is terminated, in each of the following events, *inter alia* -

(1) Performance of the obligation;
(2) Where it is void or becomes voided pursuant to law or contract;
(3) Merger;
(4) Waiver by the obligee;
(5) Frustration of an obligation arising from a contract.

Chapter Two: Assignment of Obligations

130. *Substance of Assignment* – Assignment is the transfer, pursuant to contract, of a right or a liability arising from an obligation, from one person (in this Chapter – the assignor) to another person (in this Chapter – the assignee).

131. *Applicability of the Chapter on Assignment Pursuant to Legislation* – The provisions of this Chapter will also apply, *mutatis mutandis*, to assignment pursuant to legislation of rights or liabilities arising from an obligation.

132. *Applicability of the Chapter on Pledge on Assignment by Means of Encumbrance* – The provisions of the Chapter on pledges will apply to assignment by means of encumbrance.[7]

133. *The Assigned Right* – The assignment of a right arising from an obligation may apply to the assignment in its entirety or partially, and this is the case with regard to a conditional right, a future right or a right that is not for a fixed amount.

134. *Assignment of Right by Obligee* –(a) An obligee may assign his right without the consent of the obligor, unless the transferability of the right has been limited by contract, legislation or due to the nature of the right.

(b) Where part of the right has been assigned, the obligor is entitled to be indemnified for the expenses incurred by him as a result of the splitting of the right.

135. *Completion of Assignment of a Right* – (a) Assignment of a right is completed on the date agreed upon by the assignor and the assignee.

(b) Assignment of a right that has not been created will be completed only after the right has been created.

136. *Assignment of Auxiliary Rights* – The assignment of a right also transfers to the assignee any guarantee that was given in order to insure it as well as any other right auxiliary to the assigned right, on the condition that they are transferable; the assignor will, upon demand by the assignee, perform the acts necessary in order for the transfer to vest with the assignee a right which has the same force as that of the right held by the assignor.

137. *Preservation of Claims of the Debtor Against the Assignee* – (a) The assignment of a right does not change the right or its conditions.

(b) A claim by the debtor against the assignor regarding the right assigned may be asserted by the debtor against the assignee.

(c) A claim of the debtor against the assignor that is not with regard to the right assigned may be asserted by the debtor against the assignee only if the grounds for such claim existed prior to the debtor's knowledge of the assignment.

138. *Defense of the Debtor in the Case of Assignment of a Right* – (a) Where the debtor has fulfilled his obligation toward the assignor before the assignor notified him of the assignment or before the written assignment by the assignor was presented before him, the debtor is excused from his obligation, unless he acted in bad faith.

(b) Where the debtor fulfilled his obligation to the assignee after the assignor notified him of the assignment or after the written assignment by the assignor was presented before him, the debtor is excused from his obligation even if the right has not been transferred to the assignee, unless he acted in bad faith.

139. *Assignment of the Obligation by the Debtor* – A debtor may assign his obligation, in

---

[7] Chapter Three of Sub-Part Two of Part Five (sections 628 through 668). A proposal for a new version of the Pledges Law is integrated into the Explanatory Notes.

part or in whole, if he has received the consent of the creditor to the assignment, except if the obligation is one whose transferability has been limited by legislation.

140. *Guarantee or Pledge not Given by the Debtor* – Where the obligation was guaranteed by a guarantee or by a pledge that was not given by the debtor, the assignment of the obligation terminates the guarantee or the pledge, unless the guarantor or the owner of the pledged property consented to the assignment.

141. *Preservation of Claims of the Assignee Against the Creditor* – (a) The assignment of an obligation does not change the obligation or its conditions.

(b) The claim of an assignor against the creditor regarding the obligation that was assigned may be asserted by the assignee against the creditor.

Chapter Three: Multiple Debtors and Creditors

Article One: General

142. *Applicability of the Chapter on Multiple Debtors and Creditors* – The provisions of this Chapter are applicable where there are two or more debtors who are liable for the same obligation or where there are two or more creditors regarding the same obligation.

143. *Debtors and Creditors in one Obligation* – Debtors who are obligated regarding the same obligation may be jointly liable, severally liable or liable jointly and severally.

Article Two: Multiple Debtors

144. *Presumption of Obligation Jointly and Severally* – Where more than one debtor is liable for the same debt, there is a presumption that they are jointly liable.

145. *Demand for Performance from Debtors Liable for One Obligation* – The creditor may demand performance of the obligation, entirely or in part, from all of those obligated for the same debt as one, or from each debtor separately, on the condition that they not fulfill more than the entire obligation.

146. *Vacating or Canceling the Obligation of Debtors* – (a) Where debtors are jointly or jointly and severally liable for an obligation pursuant to a contract, and the obligation of one of them is rescinded or becomes void, the obligation of the others will be voided at the rate of participation that they were entitled to receive from that debtor had his obligation not been rescinded or become void; if the liability of the other debtors was conditioned, pursuant to agreement, the circumstances or the substance of the obligation, on the performance of the obligation that was rescinded or became void – the liability of the others will be canceled.

(b) Notwithstanding the provisions of subsection (a), if some or all of the other debtors knew, or should have known, at the time the contract was entered into, of the grounds for the invalidity or rescission of the liability as set forth in that subsection, the other debtors will be liable for the entire amount of the obligation and will be entitled to the full rights with regard to the creditor; however, if the creditor also knew or should have known, at the time the contract was entered into, of such grounds, the provisions of subsection (a) will apply, and the court may obligate each party to indemnify the opposing party for the harm caused to him as a result of his reliance on the contract.

(c) If the grounds for the rescission or invalidity of the obligation was a defect in the competence or the representation of one of the debtors, there is a presumption that the other debtors knew or should have known of the defect, unless the contract pursuant to which the debt was created was entered into in the course of business of the creditor, and that the creditor did not know and had no obligation to know of it.

147. *Discharge for some of the Debtors* – (a) Where debtors are severally liable and the creditor discharges one of them from his obligation, in whole or in part, this discharge

shall not discharge the others, unless such intent may be inferred from the discharge; a discharge of one of the debtors that does not discharge the other debtors derogates from the right of participation of the other debtors with regard to him, only if it was given in the framework of an arrangement in good faith between the creditor and the debtor who was excused.

(b) Where debtors are liable jointly or jointly and severally, and the creditor discharges one of them from his liability, in whole or in part, the other debtors are discharged at the rate of the said discharge, unless another intention may be inferred from the discharge; however, the discharge of one of the debtors that does not entitle the other debtors does not derogate from their right of participation from the debtor who was discharged.

148. *The portion of debtors liable for the same debt* – There is a presumption that where debtors are liable for the same obligation they are liable in equal parts.

149. *Division of Burden Among Debtors* – Where there are more than two debtors and it is not reasonably possible to receive repayment from one of the debtors, the other debtors will be responsible for his part according to their relative liability for the debt.

150. *Right of Participation from Debtor* – A debtor who has fulfilled more than his share in the debt is entitled to participation from the other debtors according to their relative shares in the debt.

151. *Claims of the Debtor who has Paid the Debt* – Where a debtor has fulfilled the debt even though there was a claim that would excuse the debtors from fulfilling it, he is not entitled to participation from the other debtors; however, if the debtor who fulfilled the debt had a personal claim against the creditor that was not available to the other debtors, and if he fulfilled the debt in good faith, this does nothing to derogate from his right to participation.

Article Three: Multiple Creditors

152. *Presumption that Creditor Is Alone* – There is a presumption that creditors who are entitled to have one debt fulfilled (in this Article – co-creditors) are creditors severally.

153. *The Share of Co-Creditors in a Debt* – Co-creditors are entitled to fulfillment of the debt in equal amounts.

154. *Applicability of Chapter on Co-Ownership of Property to Co-Creditors* – The provisions of the Chapter dealing with co- ownership of property[8]will apply, subject to the provisions of this Chapter, *mutatis mutandis*.

155. *The right of Co-Creditor to Demand Fulfillment of the Debt* – Where co-creditors are creditors severally, each creditor is entitled to demand fulfillment of the debt from the debtor, on the condition that no more than the full debt be fulfilled; where the co-creditors are joint creditors, they are entitled to demand fulfillment only jointly.

156. *The Right of the Debtor to Fulfill the Debt* – Where co-creditors are creditors severally, the debtor is entitled to fulfill the debt with regard to any of the creditors, according to his choice, as long as a judgment has not been rendered in favor of a particular creditor; if the creditors were joint creditors, the debtor must fulfill the debt only with respect to all the creditors together.

157. *The Right of a Creditor to Discharge from a Debt* – (a) A creditor is not entitled to discharge the debtor from the debt without receiving the consent of the other co-creditors.

(b) There is nothing in the provisions of subsection (a) to derogate from the right of a

[8] Chapter Four in Sub-Part One of Part Five (sections 589 through 611).

creditor to discharge the debtor from that creditor's relative share in the debt; the discharge of the relative share in the debt will be applicable to that share with respect to the relationship between the rest of the co-creditors and the debtor.

158. *Conditioning Right of Partner Creditor on Act* – Where the right of the partner creditors is conditioned upon their performance of an act, the performance of the act by one of them will obligate and entitle the other creditors.

159. *Revocation of Contract for Breach by Co-Creditor* – Where a contract is breached by a debtor, each one of the co-creditors pursuant to the contract is entitled to avail himself of the right to revoke the entire contract pursuant to the provisions of the sub-part dealing with remedies for the breach of an obligation.[9]

160. *Personal Claim Against One of the Creditors* – (a) The personal claim of a debtor against one of the co-creditors does not derogate from the right of the other creditors to demand fulfillment of the debt.

(b) The personal claim of a debtor against one of the co-creditors as set forth in subsection (a) does not derogate from the right of that creditor to participation, pursuant to the provisions of section 162, from the creditors regarding whom the debt has been fulfilled.

161. *Claim of Set-Off Of a Debtor Against a Creditor Partner* – (a) A debtor is entitled to fulfill his debt as set forth in section 156, through means of a set-off as against a debt that the debtor is entitled to from one or more of the creditors.

(b) If the debt is fulfilled by means of a set-off, the remainder of the co-creditors are entitled to participation from the creditor against whom the set-off was performed, pursuant to the provisions of this Chapter.

162. *Participation from the Co-Creditor* – (a) Where the debt has been fulfilled with regard to a creditor in an amount greater than his share in the debt, the remainder of the creditors are entitled to participation from him at the rate of their share in the debt.

(b) A creditor who is bound to participate regarding others holds what he received in trust for such creditors.

Sub-Part Two: Special Provisions for Contracts

163. *Good Faith in Negotiations* – (a) Contract negotiations must be carried out in good faith.

(b) One who breaches the obligation of good faith set forth in subsection (a) will compensate the other party for the damage caused to him as a result of the negotiations or making of the contract.

Chapter Two: Making of Contract

164. *Mode of Making Contract* – A contract is made by way of offer and acceptance in accordance with the provisions of this Chapter.

165. *Offer to Enter into Contract* – A person's proposal to another person constitutes an offer, if it attests to the offeror's resolve to enter into a contract with the offeree and is sufficiently particular so as to enable the contract to be concluded by acceptance of the offer. A proposal includes a proposal to the public.

166. *Withdrawal of Offer* – (a) The offeror may withdraw the offer by notice to the of-

[9] Sub-Part Six in this Part (Part Four) (Sections 520 through 575).

feree, provided that the notice of withdrawal is delivered to the offeree before he has given notice of acceptance.

(b) Where the offeror has declared that the offer is not rescindable or has set a time for its acceptance, he may not withdraw it after it has been delivered to the offeree.

167. *Lapse of Offer* – The offeror's offer lapses when either one of the following occurs:

(1) The offeree has rejected it;
(2) The deadline for its acceptance has passed;
(3) The offeror or the offeree has died or has been declared to be of limited legal capacity or a receivership order has been given against him and if it is a corporation – it has decided upon voluntary dissolution or a dissolution order has been given against him, on the condition that a notice of acceptance has not been given. However, the offer will not lapse according to this paragraph if the offeror is not permitted to withdraw his offer as set forth in section 166(b).

168. *Acceptance* – Acceptance shall be by notice by the offeree delivered to the offeror, attesting to the offeree's resolve to enter into the contract with the offeror in accordance with the offer.

169. *Manner of Acceptance* – (a) Acceptance may be in any manner in which a legal transaction is performed pursuant to the provisions of section 76, unless a particular manner of acceptance is implied in the offer.

(b) A declaration by the offeror that the absence of a response on the part of the offeree will be considered acceptance is of no effect.

170. *Presumption of Acceptance* – Where an offer is for the exclusive benefit of the offeree, there is a presumption that he accepted it, unless he notified the offeror of his rejection of the offer within a reasonable time after he knew of the offer.

171. *Timeframe for Acceptance* – (a) The offeree may accept the offer within the time fixed for acceptance in the offer, and if no timeframe has been fixed – within a reasonable period of time.

(b) Where an offeree gave timely notification of his acceptance but his notice was delivered to the offeror late for a reason not dependent upon the offeree and unknown to him, the contract is regarded as having been made unless the offeror notified the offeree of the rejection of the acceptance immediately after the notice of acceptance was delivered to him.

172. *Late Acceptance or Acceptance with Variations* – Acceptance of an offer after it has lapsed, or acceptance that includes an addition, a limitation or some other variation of the offer will be considered a new offer.

173. *Withdrawal of Acceptance* – The offeree may withdraw his acceptance by notice to the offeror, provided that the notice of withdrawal is not delivered to the offeror after the notice of acceptance has been delivered to him or after he became aware of the acceptance by way of conduct.

Chapter Three: Rescission of Contract and Defective Contracts

Article One: Void Contracts

174. *Invalid Contract* – (a) A contract the making, contents or goal of which is illegal or contrary to public policy is void.

(b) The Court may relieve a party, in whole or in part, from the duty to restore what he received pursuant to the contract, and to the extent that one party has fulfilled his obligation according to the contract, it may require the other party to fulfill his corresponding obligation, in whole or in part.

175. *Contract made for Appearance* – A contract made merely for appearance is void. This provision shall not affect a right acquired by a third party who relied on the contract in good faith.

Article Two: Rescission of Contract Because of Defect in Free Will

176. *Mistake and Deceit* – In this Article –

"Mistake" – Whether a mistake of fact or of law, except a mistake regarding the advantageousness of the transaction.

"Deceit" – Including non-disclosure of facts by the other party that he was required, by law, custom or the circumstances to disclose.

177. *Rescission of Contract Due to Mistake* – (a) Where a person has entered into a contract due to a mistake and it is reasonable to assume that but for the mistake he would not have entered into it, and the other party knew or should have known this, that person may rescind the contract. If the other party did not know and need not have known of the mistake, the Court may, upon application of the mistaken party, rescind the contract for special cause, and it may require the mistaken party to compensate the other party for the damage caused to him in consequence of making the contract.

(b) Notwithstanding the provisions of subsection (a), mistake is not a ground for rescission of the contract if the contract can be carried out by correcting the mistake and prior to the rescission of the contract the other party notified the mistaken party that he is prepared to carry out the contract after such correction.

178. *Rescission of Contract Due to Deceit* – Where a person has entered into a contract in consequence of a mistake resulting from deceit practiced on him by the other party or by another person acting on behalf of the other party, he may rescind the contract.

179. *Duress* – (a) Where a person has entered into a contract in consequence of duress – by force or threats – applied to him by the other party or someone acting on his behalf, he may rescind the contract.

(b) Where a person has entered into a contract in consequence of duress – by force or threats – applied to him by a third party who did not act on behalf of the other party, and the other party knew or should have known of such duress, that person may rescind the contract. Where the other party did not know of the duress and need not have known of it, the Court may, upon application of the party acting under duress, rescind the contract, for special grounds, and it may require the party acting under duress to compensate the other party for the damages caused him in consequence of entering into the contract.

(c) A warning given in good faith regarding the exercise of a right will not be considered a threat for the purposes of this section.

180. *Extortion* – (a) Where a person has entered into a contract due to the other party or someone acting on his behalf taking advantage of his distress, mental or physical weakness or inexperience, and the terms of the contract are less favorable than what is customary, to an unreasonable degree, he may rescind the contract.

(b) Where the terms of the contract were unfavorable than what is customary to an unreasonable degree for one of the parties, and at the time the contract was entered into that side was dependent upon the other party, there is a presumption that the party has grounds to rescind the contract pursuant to subsection (a).

Article Three: Rescission and Voiding of Contract, General Provisions

181. *Mode of Rescission* – Rescission of a contract shall be by notice by one party to the

other party as set forth in section 83; where the ground for rescission were duress or extortion – within a reasonable time after becoming aware that the duress has ceased.

182. *Severing of Contract* – Where a contract is severable and the ground for the invalidity or the rescission relates only to one part thereof, that part alone shall be void or voidable. However, if it is reasonable to assume that a party to the contract would not have entered into the contract but for that part, the entire contract is void or voidable, as the case may be, and the party entitled to rescind may choose to rescind only the part to which the ground for rescission relates, in place of rescission of the entire contract.

Chapter Four: Contracts of Limited Justiciability

183. *Gambling, Lottery or Betting Contract* – (a) A gambling, lottery or betting contract under which a party may win some benefit, the winning being dependent on fate, guesswork or a chance occurrence more than on understanding or ability, does not give rise to grounds for enforcement or for payment of damages.

(b) The provisions of this section shall not apply to gambling, a lottery or betting regulated by law or for the conduct of which a permit has been issued under any law.

184. *Contract for Giving Marks* – Where under any contract a mark, title, prize or the like is to be given according to a decision or evaluation by one of the parties or a third party, such decision or evaluation shall not be the subject of court proceedings.

Chapter Five: Form and Contents of Contract

185. *Form of Contract* – Where a law or contract provides that a condition for the validity of a contract is a particular form and such condition was not fulfilled, yet the contract was performed in full or in its substantive part, the performance of the contract shall take the place of the requirement regarding its form.

186. *Contents of Contract* – The contents of a contract may be whatever is agreed upon by the parties.

187. *Interpretation of Contract* – (a) A contract shall be interpreted in accordance with the intention of the parties as it may be inferred from the contract and the circumstances.

(b) Where a contract is subject to various interpretations, an interpretation upholding its validity is preferable to an interpretation according to which it is void.

(c) Expressions and stipulations in a contract that are customarily used in contracts of that kind shall be interpreted in accordance with the accepted meaning in such contracts.

(d) Where a contract that is subject to various interpretations, and one party to the contract had greater control in drafting the stipulations of the contract, a interpretation that is detrimental to him is preferable to an interpretation that is beneficial to him.

(e) Sections 2, 4 through 8 and 10 of the Interpretation Law, 5741–1981[10]and Section 257 of the Evidence Ordinance [new version], 573–1971[11]will apply *mutatis mutandis* to the interpretation of a contract unless this is inconsistent with the context.

188. *Supplementing Particulars According to Custom* – Particulars not determined by or under the contract shall be in accordance with the practice obtaining between the parties or in the absence of an accepted practice between the parties, in accordance with the

---

[10] *Sefer Ha-Hukim* 5741, p. 302.

[11] *Dinei Medinat Yisrael* [*Nusach Chadash*] 18, 421.

practice customary in contracts of that kind. Such particulars shall be considered as having been agreed upon between the parties.

189. *Clerical Error* – (a) Where a clerical error has occurred, the content of the contract will be regarded as its content after the correction of the error and each party may demand correction of the contract accordingly.

(b) A clerical error is not a ground for rescission of the contract.

190. *Contract for an Unfixed Period of Time* – Where a contract is for an unspecified period of time, each party is entitled to terminate the contract with prior notification to the second side within a reasonable period of time.

191. *Extension of Contract for a Fixed Period of Time* – Where a contract for a fixed period of time that has expired was extended by the parties without providing the period of time for which it is extended, the extension shall be for a reasonable period of time and the same stipulations applicable to the original contract will continue to apply, *mutatis mutandis*.

192. *Mutuality of Obligations* – (a) Where the time for the performance of the obligation of one party to a contract is later than the time for the performance of the main obligation of the other party, the performance of the obligation shall be contingent upon the performance of the obligation of the other party.

(b) Where there is a reasonable apprehension that a party will not perform a main obligation and the time for performance has not yet arrived, the other party to the contract may demand delivery of a reasonable guarantee for the performance and he is entitled to delay the performance of his obligation until delivery of the guarantee.

193. *Conditional Contract* – (a) Parties may agree that the validity of the contract shall be dependent upon the fulfillment of a condition (in this Chapter – suspensory condition), or that the contract will cease upon the fulfillment of a condition (in this Chapter – resolutory condition).

(b) Where a contract is contingent upon the agreement of a third party or a permit pursuant to legislation, there is a presumption that the receipt of such agreement or permit is a suspensory condition to the contract.

(c) A party to a contract contingent upon a suspensory condition is entitled to remedies to prevent its breach even before fulfillment of the suspensory condition.

(d) Where a suspensory or resolutory condition was not fulfilled within the period fixed therefore, or where no period has been fixed, within a reasonable period of time after making the contract, the following provisions shall apply –

(1) In the case of a suspensory condition – the contract is void;

(2) In the case of a resolutory condition – the condition is void.

194. *Prevention of Suspensory Condition and Causation of Resolutory Condition* – (a) Where the contract was subject to a suspensory condition and one party prevents fulfillment of the conditions, such party is not entitled to rely on the non-fulfillment.

(b) Where the contract was subject to a resolutory conditon and one party causes fulfillment of such condition, such party is not entitled to rely on such fulfillment.

(c) The provisions of this Section will not apply where the condition is something that, according to the contract, the party was entitled to do or not to do, or if a party prevented the fulfillment of the condition or caused its fulfillment in good faith.

Chapter Six: Frustration of Contract

195. *Definitions for the Chapter on Frustration* – In this Chapter –

"A new circumstance" – a factual or legal circumstance that happened after the contract was entered into;

"A frustrating event" – any of the following:

(1) The occurrence of a new circumstance that makes the performance of the obligation of a party to the contract impossible, illegal, or fundamentally different from what was agreed upon by the parties;

(2) The occurrence of a new circumstance that renders the realization of the purpose of entering into the contract impossible;

"A suspending event" – a frustrating event that occurs temporarily.

197. *Lapse due to a Frustrating Event* – Where a contract has lapsed pursuant to the provisions of section 196(a), the obligations pursuant to such contract shall lapse and the Court may order each party to compensate the other party for reasonable expenses that he incurred or reasonable obligations that he undertook in order to fulfill the contract.

198. *Tolling of the Contract* – (a) Where a suspending event has occurred, the contract will not lapse, however the parties are entitled to refrain from fulfilling their obligations pursuant to the contract throughout the period that it occurs. Where the time for fulfilling the obligation falls within the period in which the suspending event occurs, or within a short time after it has ended, the time period for its fulfillment will be postponed for a reasonable time.

(b) Where the fulfillment of an obligation is postponed pursuant to subsection (a), the Court may require one party to the contract to compensate the other party as set forth in section 197 for expenses that he incurred or reasonable obligations that he undertook due to the postponement.

199. *Results of Tolling* – Where the postponement of fulfillment of the obligation has caued the fulfillment of the contract to be fundamentally different from its fulfillment at the agreed-upon date, the contract and the obligations according to it will lapse and the provisions of sections 196 and 197 will apply.

200. *Approximate Fulfillment due to a Frustrating Event* – Where a frustrating event has occurred, yet it is possible to fulfill the frustrated obligation in an approximate manner, and the creditor demands such fulfillment, the provisions of this Chapter will not apply and the obligation will be fulfilled in such approximate manner.

201. *Partial Frustration or Tolling* – Section 182 will apply, *mutatis mutandis*, to the frustration of a contract where the cause of the frustration relates only to a portion of the contract.

Chapter Seven: Contract in Favor of a Third Party

202. *Conferment of Right* – An obligation assumed by a person pursuant to a contract in favor of a person who is not a party to the contract (in this Chapter – the beneficiary) confers on the beneficiary the right to demand fulfillment of the obligation in accordance with the contract if the intention of the parties to confer this right on him is apparent from the contract.

203. *Repudiation of Right by the Beneficiary* – The beneficiary's right to demand fulfillment of the obligation becomes void retroactively if he informs one of the parties to the contract of the repudiation, within a reasonable time after one of the parties informed him of the right.

204. *Annulment of Beneficiary's Right by the Parties to the Contract* – (a) The parties to a contract may change or annul the right of a beneficiary by changing the contract, as long as neither of the parties has informed the beneficiary of his right according to the contract.

(b) Notwithstanding the provisions of subsection (a), if the beneficiary was accorded a right without compensation, the parties may annul the right even after one of them notified the beneficiary of his right if the conditions set forth in section 235 are fulfilled, *mutatis mutandis.*

(c) In the case of an obligation to be fulfilled in consequence of a person's death – by virtue of an insurance contract or membership in a pension or provident fund or on some other similar ground – the creditor may, by notice to the debtor or by a will of which notice is given to the debtor, terminate the beneficiary's right or replace him with another beneficiary, even after the beneficiary has been informed of his right.

205. *Claims against Beneficiary* – Any claim available to the debtor against the creditor regarding the obligation is also available to the debtor against the beneficiary.

206. *Creditor's Right to Demand Fulfillment of the Obligation* – The beneficiary's right does not derogate from the creditor's right to demand from the debtor the fulfillment of the obligation in favor of the beneficiary.

Sub-Part Three: Special Contracts

Chapter One: Sales Contract

Article One: General Provisions

207. *Essence of Sales Contract* – A sales contract is a contract between a seller and a buyer for the transferring of property in exchange for payment of a price.

208. *Applicability of the Chapter on Exchange of Property* – The provisions of this Chapter shall apply, *mutatis mutandis*, on the exchange of property for other property.

Article Two: Obligations of the Parties

209. *The Seller's Obligations – Delivery and Transferring* – The seller will deliver the property and will transfer the ownership of it to the buyer.

210. *Seller's Fulfillment of the Obligation to Deliver* – (a) The seller fulfills his obligation to deliver the property by making it available to the buyer.

(b) The obligation to make property that has not been set aside available is fulfilled by the seller setting aside such property.

(c) Where it is agreed that the seller will take care of the transport of the property, the obligation of delivery will be fulfilled upon delivery of the property from the transporter to the buyer.

211. *Delivery and Transfer of Components and Accessories* – The seller will deliver and will transfer ownership of the components and accessories that were installed in the property and that are necessary for its use.

212. *Place of Fulfilling the Obligation of Delivery* – (a) Delivery of the property shall occur in the place of business of the seller, and if he has no place of business, at his place of residence.

(b) Where it is agreed upon that the seller will take care of transporting the property, delivery shall take occur at the place agreed upon with the seller.

213. *The Buyer's Obligations – Payment and Acceptance* – The buyer will pay the seller the price of the property and will accept it.

214. *Time of Payment* – The buyer will pay the price when the property is delivered.

215. *Delivery and Acceptance of Documents* – The provisions of this Chapter regarding the delivery and acceptance of the property are also applicable to the delivery and acceptance of documents relating to the property.

216. *Interconnected Obligations* – The seller's obligation to deliver the property and the buyer's obligation to pay the price of the property are interconnected obligations.

217. *Transfer of Ownership of Moveable Property* – The ownership of moveable property is transferred to the buyer at the time agreed upon by the parties. In the absence of agreement, the ownership is transferred at the time of delivery of the moveable property to the buyer.

218. *Discrepancy of Property* – (a) The seller will transfer the property to the buyer in such condition that it is in compliance with what was agreed upon between the seller and the buyer.

(b) Discrepancy of the property includes, *inter alia*, delivery of –

(1) Part of the property or a quantity different from that agreed upon;

(2) Property that is different, including property whose description or type is different from what was agreed upon;

(3) Property that is not of the quality or does not have the characteristics necessary for its normal or commercial use or its use for a special purpose as can be inferred from the agreement. For this purpose, if at the time the sales contract was entered into, the seller knew the purpose for which the property was acquired, it will be regarded as a special purpose as inferred from the agreement.

(4) Property that from the perspective of type, description or characteristics is not consistent with the model or sample that the seller presented to the buyer, unless the seller notified the buyer at the time the contract was entered into of such discrepancy;

(5) Property that is not packaged as is customary, in packaging that can preserve it.

219. *Compliance of Property with Standards* – Where the seller performed the sale as part of a business and the property is subject to binding standards pursuant to legislation, the buyer will comply with the provisions of such legislation.

220. *Stipulation of Exemption in Sales Contract* – A stipulation exempting the seller from liability for discrepancy or limiting such liability is void if the seller knew or should have known of the discrepancy at the time the contract was entered into and did not notify the buyer of it.

221. *Buyer's Knowledge of Discrepancy* – The buyer may not rely on the discrepancy of the property if he knew of it at the time the contract was entered into.

222. *Buyer's Reliance on Discrepancy* – (a) The buyer is not entitled to rely on the property's discrepancy –

(1) If he did not notify the seller of it within a reasonable time after he discovered it or he should have discovered it, with a reasonable description of the discrepancy. This provision will not apply to a discrepancy which the seller knew or should have known of.

(2) If he did not give the seller a reasonable opportunity to examine the property.

(b) Notwithstanding the provisions of subsection (a), the buyer is entitled to rely on the discrepancy if, and to the same extent that, the non-fulfillment of the duties enumerated there did not result in any injury to the seller.

223. *Rescission of Contract Due to Discrepancy in Moveable Property* – The buyer may not rescind the sales contract for moveable property because of discrepancy if he notified the

seller of the discrepancy more than two years after the date of delivery of the property even if he did not discover it and was not expected to discover it within that time period.

224. *Sale Subject to License or Permit* – Where the seller has performed a sale as part of his business and the business in sales or the sale itself was subject to a license or permit pursuant to legislation, the seller must act according to the provisions of such legislation.

225. *Extra Quantity* – Where the seller delivered property to the buyer in a quantity greater than that agreed upon, and the extra quantity could be separated without undue expense or effort, the buyer is not entitled to rescind the contract for such discrepancy, however he may notify the seller within a reasonable time from the acceptance of the property that he does not accept the extra quantity. If he did not so notify, the buyer will pay the seller for the extra quantity according to the agreed upon rate.

226. *Rights in Property* – The seller will transfer the rights in the property to the buyer free of encumbrances, liens, or any other right of a third party.

227. *Notification of Rights of a Third Party in the Property* – The seller will notify the buyer of every claim of right of a third party within a reasonable time from the day when he knows or should know of such claim.

228. *Assumption of Risk of Loss* – (a) Where the property was lost or damaged after the seller did what was required to deliver it and before the buyer accepted it, the buyer is exempt from his obligation.

(b) Notwithstanding the provisions of subsection (a), the buyer is not exempt from his obligation if the loss of or damage to the property was not a result of the seller's negligence, after the seller did what was required to deliver it and the buyer breached his duty to accept it.

(c) Where it is agreed that the buyer will take care of the transportation of the property and the seller delivered the property to the transporter, the buyer is not exempt from his obligation if the property is lost or damaged after it is delivered to the transporter due to a reason that is not within the responsibility of the seller.

Chapter Two: Gift Contract

229. *Essence of Gift Contract* – A gift contract is a contract between the giver of the gift and the recipient of the gift for the transfer of property without consideration, including transfer by way of a waiver of rights.

230. *Applicability to Other Laws* – The provisions of this Chapter shall apply, *mutatis mutandis*, to every contract that does not provide for consideration.

231. *Time of Transfer of Gift* – The transfer of a gift may be immediate or in the future.

232. *Presumption of Acceptance of Offer* – There is a presumption that one who has been offered a gift will accept it, unless he notified the offeror of his rejection of the offer within a reasonable time after the offer was made known to him.

233. *Gift to an Fetus* – A fetus is competent to accept a gift, and he is entitled to demand fulfillment of the obligation even if the giver of the gift died within the 300 days preceding his birth.

234. *Requirement of Writing in an Obligation to Give a Gift* – The obligation to give a gift requires written documentation expressing the intention of the one undertaking the obligation to give the gift.

235. *Rescission of Obligation to Give a Gift* – (a) One who has made a commitment to give a gift may rescind that commitment under any one of the following conditions –

(1) The receiver of the gift did not change his situation in reliance upon the obligation, provided that the one who obligated himself to give the gift did not waive his right to rescind such obligation in writing;

(2) The rescission is justified in view of the unseemly conduct of the receiver of the gift toward the obligor or a member of his family;

(3) The rescission is justified due to a substantial deterioration of the obligor's financial situation.

(b) Where the obligation to give the gift was given by means of a contract for the benefit of a third party, the creditor and the debtor will be entitled to jointly exercise the right of rescission as set forth in subsection (a).

236. *Breach of Obligation to Give a Gift* – The obligor to give a gift is not liable for non-performance of the obligation unless such non-performance was caused by his negligence.

237. *Obligation to Give a Gift Of Property Set Aside for Such Purpose* – Where the obligor set aside property as a gift at the time the gift contract was entered into, such property will be given in the same condition it was in at that time. If at the time such contract was entered into, the obligor knew that there was a discrepancy in the property, as that term is used in section 218(b), he shall notify the receiver of the gift of such discrepancy at the time the contract is entered into.

[Option:[12] To add an additional subsection

(b) Where the obligor did not set aside property for a gift as set forth in subsection (a), the provision of section 120 shall not apply to this obligation.]

238. *Gift as Obligation and Conditional Gift* – (a) A gift contract can be conditioned upon the fulfillment of a condition, or it can obligate the receiver to do or to refrain from doing an act with respect to the gift.

(b) Where the receiver of a gift breached his obligation to do or to refrain from doing an act as set forth in subsection (a), the giver of the gift or the beneficiary, as set forth in section 202, is entitled to remedies pursuant to the Subpart dealing with remedies for breach of an obligation.[13] The Attorney General or his representative may also demand enforcement of the obligation, if the matter affects the public interest.

239. *Gift Contract for an Unfixed Period of Time* – Where the gift contract is for an unfixed period of time as set forth in section 190, the gift contract will lapse with the death of the giver or the receiver of the gift.

240. *Transfer of Ownership in a Gift of Moveable Property* – The ownership of a gift that is moveable property transfers to the recipient with delivery of the gift to him or with the delivery of a document that entitles him to receive it, and if the gift was in the possession of the recipient – in a notice of the giver of the gift to the recipient regarding the giving of the gift.

---

[12] *Option*: It is suggested to consider a clarification, in subsection (b), that the obligation of the giver of a gift to give non-particular property will refer to property of poor quality and not of average quality.

[13] Subpart Six in this Part (Part Four) (sections 520 through 575).

Chapter Three: Contractorship Contract and Service Contract

Article One: Contractorship Contract

241. *Essence of Contractorship Contract* – A contractorship contract is a contract for compensation between a client and a contractor for the performance of work on property without the existence of an employer-employee relationship regarding such work.

242. *Applicability of the Sales Chapter on Provision of Material by the Contractor* – Where the performance of work involves provision of materials that the contractor will provide pursuant to the contract or in accordance with the circumstances, the provisions of the chapter regarding a sales contract,[14] will apply, *mutatis mutandis*.

243. *Contractor's Obligation – Performance and Delivery* – The contractor will perform the work on the property and will deliver the property to the client.

244. *Fulfillment of Obligation of Delivery by the Contractor* – The contractor fulfills the obligation of delivery of the property on which the work was performed by making it available to the client.

245. *Place for Fulfillment of Obligation to Perform Work* – The contractor will perform the work at his place of business, unless according to its nature it must be performed elsewhere.

246. *Place for Performance of Obligation to Deliver the Property* – The delivery of the property on which the work was performed shall be performed at the place where the work was done.

247. *Client's Obligations to Pay and Accept the Property* – The client will pay the contractor the compensation for performance of the work on the property and will receive the property as stated.

248. *Time for Fulfillment of Obligation of Acceptance of the Property* – The client will accept the property on which the work was done within a reasonable time after the contractor notified him that the work on the property was completed and made the property available to the client.

249. *The Time for Fulfillment of Obligation to Pay* – The client will pay the contractor the compensation for the performance of the work when it is completed by the contractor. Where the work was performed on property that the contractor is obligated to deliver to the client, the client will pay the compensation upon delivery of the property.

250. *Place for Fulfillment of Obligation to Pay* – Compensation that must be paid at the time of completion of the work or at the time of delivery of the property on which the work was done, will be paid in the place in which the work was done or in the place where the property was delivered. Where the parties agreed on payment at another time – the payment of the compensation will be at the contractor's place of business and if he has no place of business, at his place of residence.

251. *Additional Work and Changes to Work* – (a) The client is entitled to direct the contractor to perform additional work or changes in the agreed upon work, provided that the performance of the additional work or the performance of changes as stated is necessary for fulfilling the purpose of the contractorship contract and it does not exceed to a substantial extent, with respect to its type and scope, the agreed upon work. Where the client has so directed, the contractor is entitled to object to performance of the additional work or the changes in the work for reasonable cause.

(b) The time for performance of additional work or for making changes to the agreed upon work and the compensation for such performance will be decided upon taking into

[14] Chapter One in Subpart Three in this Part (Part Four) (sections 207–228).

consideration the timeframe and the compensation agreed upon between the parties with respect to the performance of the agreed upon work.

252. *Discrepancy in Performance of the Work* – The contractor will perform the work on the property as agreed between him and the client and the provisions of section 218 will apply to this matter, *mutatis mutandis*, and subject to the provisions of this Article.

253. *Compliance of Work with the Standards* – Where the contractor performed the work as a part of his business and binding standards apply to the performance of the work pursuant to legislation, the contractor will act in accordance with such legislative provisions.

254. *Stipulation of Exemption in a Contractorship Contract* – The provisions of section 220 will apply, *mutatis mutandis*, to a stipulation exempting a contractor from liability for discrepancies or limiting his liability for such discrepancies.

255. *Discrepancies for which the Client is Responsible* – The contractor is not liable for a discrepancy caused by property, a plan or a directive given by the client, or for another cause that the client is responsible for, unless the contractor knew or should have known about the discrepancy in the property, the plan, the directive or the other cause, and he did not notify the client within a reasonable period of time from the date when he knew or should have known of it.

256. *Reliance of Client on Discrepancy* – Section 222 will apply, *mutatis mutandis*, to the reliance of the client on a discrepancy pursuant to this Article. In addition to the duties enumerated in that section, the client must give the contractor a reasonable opportunity to correct the discrepancy or to do the work over, to the extent that this is reasonable under the circumstances.

257. *Correction of Discrepancy by the Client* – Where the correction of the discrepancy is urgent, such that it cannot be demanded of the client that he wait for the correction to be performed by the contractor, the client may correct the discrepancy even without notifying the contractor of such correction.

258. *Work Subject to Qualification, Permit or License* – Where the contractor performed the work as part of his business and the performance of the work was subject to qualification, license or permit pursuant to legislation, the contractor will act in accordance with the provisions of such legislation.

259. *Assumption of Risk of Loss of the Work or the Property on which it was Performed* – (a) Where the work or the property on which the work was performed is lost or damaged after the contractor completed the work and made it available to the client and before the client received it, the client is exempted from his obligation.

(b) Notwithstanding subsection (a), the client is not exempted from his obligation if the work or the property on which it was performed was lost or damaged –

(1) not as a result of the contractor's negligence and after the client breached his obligation to accept it;

(2) due to a reason originating with the client, including the property, plan or directive that the client gave, unless the contractor knew or should have known of this reason and he did not notify the client of it within a reasonable time after it became known to him.

260. *Assumption of Risk of Loss Of Property Provided by the Client* – (a) Nothing in the provisions of section 259 shall derogate from the contractor's obligation to safeguard the property that the client provided as set forth in section 264. However, if the client breached his obligation to accept the property, the contractor will be considered a gratuitous bailee.

(b) If the property that the client provided to the contractor was lost or damaged after the contractor completed the work and made the property on which it was performed available to the client, the client is entitled to compensation only for the value of the property that was lost or the decrease in value of the property that was damaged.

261. *Fulfillment of Contractor's Obligations by Sub-Contractor* –

(a) The contractor (in this Article – the chief contractor) may fulfill his obligation through another person (in this Article – the sub-contractor), unless pursuant to the contractorship contract, or due to the circumstances or the substance of the work, he must perform the work personally.

(b) Where the contractor fulfilled his obligation through a sub-contractor, the client is not thereby excused from his obligations to the contractor.

262. *Supervision of Contractor over Sub-Contractor* – The chief contractor will personally supervise the performance of work by the sub-contractor unless under the contractorship contract, the circumstances or the substance of the work, the contractor is permitted to perform the work through another person without supervising such performance.

263. *Wages of Sub-contractor* – (a) Where the client paid the chief contractor compensation for the work performed by a sub-contractor, the compensation will be considered to be held by the chief contractor in trust for the benefit of the sub-contractor.

(b) Where the chief contractor breached his obligation to pay the sub-contractor's wages to him, the client may pay part or all of the compensation to the sub-contractor, provided that he notified the chief contractor accordingly a reasonable period of time in advance.

(c) Where the client paid part or all of the compensation to the sub-contractor as set forth in subsection (b), he is entitled to restitution from the chief contractor of the sum that he paid, unless the contractor had reasonable grounds to object to the payment of the compensation.

(d) Where the client did not notify the chief contractor of the payment of the compensation as set forth in subsection (b), the contractor will deduct the value of the damage he incurred due to the lack of notice from the sum to which the client is entitled.

264. *Safeguarding the Client's Property* – Where the contractor had to keep the client's property in order to perform the work, the contractor will be considered, for this purpose, as a bailee for hire, where the safekeeping of the property is the main reason for the possession.

Article Two: Contract for Services

265. *Substance of Contract for Services* – A contract for services is a contract between a client and the provider of services for the rendering of any service for remuneration, where there is no employee employer relationship regarding such service.

266. *The Provider's Obligation to Make an Effort* – The provider of the service will take all reasonable measures in order to achieve the result that the contract intended to achieve. Where the provider of services acted in such a manner, the failure to achieve the agreed-upon result will not, in itself, be considered as a breach of his obligations.

267. *Personal Performance by the Provider of the Service* – (a) The provider of the service will personally fulfill his obligations, unless according to the nature of the service, he may fulfill some or all of them through another person.

(b) The provider of service who may fulfill his obligations through another person will personally supervise the rendering of the service by that person.

268. *Obligation of Fidelity of the Provider of the Service* – The provider of the service owes fidelity toward the client, if this is justified considering the kind of the service at issue.

269. *Fee for the Service* – The client will pay to the provider of the service the fee for the performance of the service.

270. *Time for Payment for the Service* – The fee will be paid to the provider of the service at the time of completion of the service.

271. *Place of Payment for the Service* – A fee which is to be paid at the time the rendering of the service is complete will be paid in the place where the service was rendered. Where the parties have agreed on payment at another time the fee will be paid at the place of business of the provider of the service, and if he has no place of business, at his place of residence.

272. *Compliance of the Service with Standards* – Where the service was rendered through a business and binding standards apply to the rendering of the service pursuant to legislation, the provider of the service will act according to such legislative provisions.

273. *Service Requiring Qualifications, Permit or License* – Where the service was rendered through a business and the provision of the service requires certain qualifications, a license or a permit pursuant to legislation, the provider of the service will act in accordance with the provisions of such legislation.

274. *Safeguarding the Property of the Client* – Where the rendering of services required the provider of the service to keep property of the client, the provider of service will be considered, for this matter, to be a bailee for hire, where the safeguarding of the property is the main purpose of the possession.

Chapter Four: Brokerage Contract

275. *Substance of Brokerage Contract* – A brokerage contract is a contract between a broker and a client, in exchange for broker's fees, for the purpose of making a connection between the client and a third person, with the purpose of a contract being entered into between the client and that person.

276. *The Client's Obligation to Inform the Broker* – Where a contract is entered into between the client and the third person, the client will so inform the broker. Where the contract is contingent upon a suspensory condition, the client will notify the broker of the fulfillment of the condition, upon its fulfillment.

277. *Payment of Broker's Fees* – (a) Where the brokerage activity resulted in a contract between the client and the third person, the client will pay broker's fees to the broker.

(b) Where the client received information from the broker regarding the third person's desire to enter into a contract, there is a presumption that it was the action of the broker that resulted in the making of the contract with the client. However, if the client knew of the third person's desire to enter into a contract before he received such information from the broker, there is a presumption that the broker's action did not cause the making of the contract.

278. *Scope of Payment of Broker's Fees* – The client's obligation as stated in section 277(a) to pay broker's fees will apply even if one of the following exists:

(1) A contract was entered into between the client and the third person, which is different in form from the contract which was the purpose of the brokerage contract.

(2) A contract was entered into between a person to whom the client passed on information that he received from the broker regarding the third person's desire to enter into a contract, and that third person.

279. *The Right to Brokerage Fees in Special Cases* – (a) Where the contract between the client and the third person is rescinded due to a defect in its formation, the broker will

not be entitled to broker's fees. Where the client is responsible for the defect that led to the rescission of the contract, the broker will be entitled to broker's fees unless he knew of the defect at the time the contract was entered into.

(b) Where the contract between the client and the third person is contingent upon a suspensory condition, the broker is not entitled to broker's fees unless the condition is fulfilled. Where the contract is contingent upon a resolutory condition, this does not derogate from the broker's right to his fees.

(c) Where the client and the third person agreed, after the contract was entered into between them, to rescind it or to refrain from performance of it, this does not derogate from the broker's right to his fees.

(d) Where the making of the contract between the client and the third person, its contents or its object is illegal or contrary to public policy and the broker knew or should have known of this at the time the contract was entered into, he is not entitled to broker's fees, unless the court has ruled otherwise.

(e) Breach of the contract between the client and the third person does not derogate from the broker's right to his fees, even if the contract was rescinded because of the breach.

280. *Amount of Broker's Fees* – none

281. *Time for Payment Of Broker's Fees* – The client will pay broker's fees to the broker at the time the contract is entered into between the client and the third person. Where the contract was contingent upon a suspensory condition, the client will pay the broker's fees when the condition is fulfilled.

282. *Brokerage for Two Parties* – (a) The broker may enter into a brokerage contract with the third person as well, provided that he notified the client and the client consented to this.

(b) Where the broker entered into a brokerage contract with both of the parties to the contract, he is entitled to a brokerage fee from each of them.

283. *Obligation of Exclusivity* – Where the client undertook to refrain from entering into a brokerage agreement with another broker regarding the same matter, the broker will owe fidelity to the client.

Chapter Five: Lease

284. *Substance of Rental Contract* – A lease is a contract between a lessor and a lessee to transfer, in exchange for payment of rent, the right to possess and to use the property on a non-permanent basis.

285. *Application of the Chapter to Sub-Rentals* – The provisions of this Chapter will apply, *mutatis mutandis*, to sub-leases. In this matter the main lessee will be considered the lessor and the sub-lessee will be considered the lessee.

286. *The Landlord's Obligation – Delivery of the Leased Premises* – The lessor will transfer the leased property to the lessee.

287. *Fulfillment of Obligation to Transfer* – The lessor will fulfill the obligation to transfer the leased property by making it available to the lessee.

288. *Place for Fulfillment of Obligation to Transfer the Leased Property* – (a) The transfer of the leased property will be fulfilled in the place where the leased property is located at the time the contract is entered into.

(b) Section 212(a) will apply, *mutatis mutandis*, when it is agreed that the leased property will be delivered by a transporter.

289. *Prohibition on Disturbing the Use of the Leased Property* – The lessor will permit the

lessee to use the leased property in accordance with the agreement between them during the period of the lease, and neither he nor another on his behalf will disturb such use.

290. *The Lessor's Obligation to Repair Defects* – (a) The lessor will repair anything in the leased property or in property that serves such property and that creates an actual disruption to the normal use or the agreed upon use between the lessor and the lessee of the leased property (in this Chapter – defect) after he has received a demand from the lessee to do so. For this purpose, it makes no difference if the defect was present at the time the leased property was delivered to the lessee or if it developed after the delivery.

(b) The lessee is entitled to demand that the lessor replace the property rather than repair it, if it is moveable property and the repair of the defect would entail unreasonable disturbance of the use of the leased property or property that serves such leased property.

(c) Where the leased property or the property that serves such property is moveable property, the lessor may fulfill the obligation set forth in this section by replacing the leased property, at his expense, with similar property, if this is reasonable under the circumstances.

(d) The provisions of this section shall not apply in each of the following cases –

(1) The lessee is liable for the defect as a bailee pursuant to the Chapter dealing with safeguarding property;[15]

(2) Under the lease contract or according to the custom in such circumstances, repair of the defect is not imposed on the lessor;

(3) The property was leased in a perpetual lease.

291. *Payment of Rent* – The lessee will pay rent to the lessor.

292. *The time for Payment of Rent* – Where rent was set at a fixed sum for fixed periods of time, the lessee shall pay the rent at the outset of each period.

293. *Designated Use of the Leased Property* – The lessee will use the leased property as agreed upon in the lease contract. However, if the parties did not agree that such use was to be the exclusive use, the lessee may use the leased property for other purposes, provided that such use will not damage the leased property or burden the lessor beyond what was agreed.

294. *Examination and Repair of the Leased Property* – The lessee will enable the lessor or someone acting on his behalf to examine the leased property and to carry out repairs in it at any reasonable time, provided that the lessor notifies the lessee of such a reasonable period of time in advance, and minimalizes, to the extent possible, the disturbance of the lessee.

295. *Changes in the Leased Property* – (a) The lessee may not make any changes in the leased property, unless he received the lessor's agreement to the changes.

(b) Notwithstanding the provisions of subsection (a), a lessee under a perpetual lease may make changes in the leased property, that do not result in a decrease of the value of the property, provided that he returns the leased property at the end of the term of the lease in accordance with the provisions of section 303.

296. *Discrepancy in the Leased Property* – The lessor will deliver the leased property when it is compatible to the agreement between him and the lessee. The provisions of sections 218(b) and 221 shall apply, *mutatis mutandis*, and subject to the provisions of this Chapter, to a discrepancy in the leased property, regardless of whether the source of the discrepancy in the leased property is in the property itself or its surroundings.

---

[15] Chapter one in Subpart Five in this Part (Part Four) (sections 498 through 510).

297. *Stipulation of Exemption* – A stipulation exempting the lessor from liability for a discrepancy or limiting his liability is subject to the provisions of section 220, *mutatis mutandis.*

298. *Reliance of the Lessee on the Discrepancy* – Section 222 will apply, *mutatis mutandis,* to a discrepancy pursuant to this Chapter. In addition to the duties set forth in that section, the lessee must give the lessor a reasonable opportunity to correct the discrepancy, to the extent that is reasonable under the circumstances.

299. *Repair of Defect or Discrepancy by the Lessee* – (a) The lessee is entitled, at any time, to repair by himself a defect or discrepancy in the leased property for which the lessor is responsible, and to demand indemnity from the lessor for his reasonable expenses, provided that he gave the lessor a reasonable opportunity to examine the leased property and to repair the defect or the discrepancy as set forth in section 298, and the lessor did not do so. Where the repair of the defect or the discrepancy is urgent, such that the lessee cannot be required to wait for their repair by the lessor, the lessee may repair the defect or the discrepancy even without giving the lessor such reasonable opportunity.

(b) Notwithstanding the provisions of subsection 295(a), the lessee is entitled to repair by himself, at any time, a defect which the lessor is not responsible to repair, provided that he gave the lessor a reasonable opportunity to repair the defect.

300. *Suitability of Rights in the Leased Property* – The lessor will deliver the rights to possess and to use the leased property, free of any right of a third party that impinges upon the rights of the lessee and will abstain from the creation of such rights throughout the period of the lease. The provisions of sections 296 through 298 will apply to the first clause of this section.

301. *Assumption of Risk of Loss of the Leased Property* – Section 228 will apply, *mutatis mutandis*, to the risk of loss of the leased property.

302. *Beginning of the Rental* – The period of the rental will begin with the delivery of the leased property to the lessor.

303. *Return of the Leased Property upon Termination of the Rental* – (a) With the end of the period of the rental, the lessee will return the leased property to the lessor, free of any person or property, except property of the lessor used for purposes of the leased property.

(b) Where the lessee returned the leased property as set forth in subsection (a), the lessor will accept the leased property.

(c) Where the leased property was moveable property, the lessee will return it to the lessor at the place where the leased property was delivered to the lessee.

304. *Return of Leased Property in which Changes have been made* – (a) Where the lessee made changes in the leased property with the consent of the lessor, the lessee is entitled to choose between returning the leased property in its condition after the changes were made or restoring the leased property to its previous state and returning it as it was before the changes were made. Where the lessee chose to return the leased property as it is after the changes were made, he is not entitled to compensation for the changes he made.

(b) Where the lessee made changes in the leased property without receiving the consent of the lessor, the lessee will restore the leased property to its previous state, and will return it to the lessor as it was before the changes were made, provided that the lessor demanded that it be returned in such a state. Where the changes were installation of fixtures on leased immovable property as that term is used in section 717, the provisions of the Chapter on construction and planting on another's land[16] will apply.

305. *Guarding of Leased Property* – The lessee will be considered a bailee for hire where the purpose of safeguarding the leased property is subordinate to the main purpose of the possession.

Chapter Six: Borrowing Contract

306. *Substance of Borrowing Contract* – A borrowing contract is a contract between a lender and a borrower for the transfer, without compensation, of the right to possess and to use the property temporarily.

307. *Applicability of Provisions on the Chapter on Borrowing* – Sections 285 through 289, 294, 295, 300, 302 and 303 will also apply, *mutatis mutandis*, to borrowing.

308. *Termination of Borrowing Contract* – The lender may terminate the borrowing contract by notice to the borrower within a reasonable time in advance, even after the borrowed item has been delivered to the borrower, where one of the following exists –

(1) One of the conditions set forth in section 235(a);

(2) The borrower has died, or an order of liquidation or receivership in bankruptcy proceedings has been given against him, or he has been declared bankrupt;

(3) The borrowed item is needed by the lender due to circumstances that did not exist when the borrowing contract was entered into.

309. *Discrepancy of Borrowed Item* – Sections 296 through 299 will apply, *mutatis mutandis*, to the discrepancy of a borrowed item, however, the lender will not bear liability due to such discrepancy unless the discrepancy was caused by his negligence.

Chapter Seven: Contract to Permit the Use of Another's Property

310. *Substance of Contract to Permit Use* – none.

311. *Applicability of the Chapter on Leasing and the Chapter on Borrowing to the Right to Borrow* – none.

312. *Protection of Right of Use Against a Third Person* – none.

Chapter Eight: Guarantee Contract

Article One: General Provisions

313. *Substance of Guarantee Contract* – A guarantee contract is a contract in which a person undertakes (in this Chapter – the guarantor) to fulfill another person's obligation (in this Chapter – the debtor) towards a creditor.

In this regard, the term "obligation" includes a part of such obligation, a future obligation, a variable obligation, a renewable obligation, an unspecified obligation and a conditional obligation.

314. *Creation of Guarantee* – (a) A guarantee is created pursuant to a contract.

(b) Notwithstanding the provisions of subsection (a), a guarantee may be created pursuant to an order of an authority by means of delivery of a letter of guarantee to the authority; the provisions of this Chapter shall apply to such a guarantee.

315. *Independent Undertaking to Indemnify* – The provisions of this Chapter, with the exception of sections 314, 323, 324(a)(1) and 325, shall not apply to an independent un-

---

[16] Chapter Two in Subpart Three of Part Five (sections 717 through 723).

dertaking of a person to indemnify a creditor for the non-fulfillment of the debtor's obligation towards the creditor.

316. *Scope of Guarantee* – The guarantor is not liable for an obligation greater or more onerous than the debtor's obligation.

317. *Accompanying costs* – The guarantor is also liable for other obligations charged against the debtor due to non-fulfillment of the guaranteed obligation, including linkage differentials, interest, expenses, damages and restitution and all of these obligations shall be treated in the same way as the guaranteed obligation.

318. *Variation of Guaranteed Obligation* – (a) An increase in the guaranteed obligation does not affect the guarantor's obligation.

(b) A decrease in the guaranteed obligation discharges the guarantor to the same extent that the debtor is discharged.

(c) Where any other variation occurs in the guaranteed obligation, the guarantor's obligation is varied accordingly. However, if the variation caused actual prejudice to the guarantor's rights, the guarantor is discharged from fulfilling the guarantee unless it can be fulfilled without the variation and the guarantor notified the creditor of his desire to do so within a reasonable time after he knew of the variation.

319. *Guarantor's Defenses* – (a) Any plea the debtor has against the creditor regarding the obligation is also available to the guarantor.

(b) Where the debtor has a claim of a set-off against the creditor arising from the transaction relating to the guaranteed obligation, the guarantor also has the right to give notice of the set-off, and he may give such a notice even over the objection of the debtor.

320. *Guarantor's Liability* – The guarantor and the debtor are jointly and severally liable.

321. *Demand to Fulfill first from the Debtor* – (a) The creditor may not demand that the guarantor fulfill his guarantee without first demanding that the debtor fulfill his obligation and waiting 30 days for the fulfillment of the obligation by the debtor.

(b) The provisions of subsection (a) will not apply in any one of the following circumstances:

(1) The debtor has died, was declared of limited capacity or an order of receivership was given against him in bankruptcy proceedings;
(2) Where the debtor is a corporation – a liquidation order was given against it;
(3) A demand to the debtor as set forth in sub-section (a) involves unusual difficulties.

322. *Discharge of Guarantor* – (a) Where the creditor has caused the non-fulfillment of the guaranteed obligation, the guarantor is discharged.

(b) Where the creditor has caused the expiration of the security given to secure the guaranteed obligation, and damage is thereby caused to the guarantor, the guarantor is discharged to the amount of such damage.

323. *Guarantor's Right to Indemnification* – The debtor will indemnify the guarantor for expenses that he incurred or obligations undertaken by him for the purpose of fulfilling the guaranteed obligation, plus reasonable expenses that the guarantor incurred thereby.

324. *Limitations to the Guarantor's Right to Indemnification* –

(a) The guarantor is not entitled to indemnification from the debtor in any of the following situations:

(1) The guarantee was given without the debtor's consent; there is nothing in this provision to derogate from the guarantor's right pursuant to the chapter dealing with unjust enrichment;[17]

(2) The guarantor fulfilled an obligation whose validity was defective as to the capacity or representation of the debtor;

(3) The guarantor might have been discharged from fulfilling the guaranteed obligation on the strength of a claim available to the debtor against the creditor regarding the obligation, and the guarantor did not raise the defense despite knowing of its existence.

(b) The provisions of subsection (a)(3) shall not apply where the guarantor notified the debtor, prior to fulfilling the guaranteed obligation, of his intention to do so, and the debtor did not make an application to the court within a reasonable time after receiving the notice, to prevent the fulfillment of the obligation by the guarantor.

325. *Remedies Before Fulfilling theGuarantee* – Before fulfilling the guarantee and in order to ensure his right of indemnification, the guarantor is entitled to all of the remedies given to the creditor in order to ensure the fulfillment of the guaranteed obligation not yet due for payment.

326. *Guarantor for Guarantor* – Where a person has undertaken, *vis a vis* the creditor, to fulfill the guarantee of the guarantor, the guarantor's guarantee with respect to the creditor shall be like a guaranteed obligation, both for the purpose of the relations between that person and the creditor and for the purpose of the relations between that person and the guarantor.

327. *Rescission of Guarantee of Future Obligation* – (a) Where a guarantor has undertaken to fulfill an obligation that does not yet exist, and as long as the obligation does not exist, the guarantor may rescind his guarantee by written notice to the creditor, to the debtor and to the other guarantors, provided that he did not receive compensation for his undertaking.

(b) Where the guarantor has rescinded his guarantee as set forth in subsection (a), and as a result damage was caused to the creditor, the guarantor shall compensate the creditor for such damage.

(c) The creditor will, pursuant to the demand of the guarantor, transmit to him details regarding the other guarantors, for the purpose of giving notification as set forth in subsection (a).

(d) (1) The provisions of subsections (a) and (b) may not be conditioned upon, except to the benefit of the guarantor.

(2) Notwithstanding the provisions of clause (1), the guarantor may condition upon the provisions of subsection (a) with another guarantor.

Article Two: Guarantee of an Individual

328. *Definitions for Article on Guarantee of Individual* – In this Article –

"Creditor" – one who gives loans in the normal course of his business, even if this is not his main occupation;

"Individual guarantor" – one who is not a corporation, and is not the spouse or partner of the debtor, regardless of whether the partnership is registered or not; where the debtor is a corporation, one who has an interest in the corporation will not be considered an individual guarantor. For these purposes, the term "one who has as interest in the corpo-

[17] Chapter Two of Subpart Four of this Part (Part Four) (sections 487 through 496).

ration" is as the term "one who has an interest" in the corporation is defined in the Securities Law, 5728–1968;[18]

"Protected guarantor" – One of the following –

(1) An individual guarantor, who in a contract of guarantee between him and the creditor, a sum that does not exceed 60,000 NIS[19] is specified;

(2) An individual guarantor, who in a contract of guarantee between him and the creditor, a sum that does not exceed 500,000 NIS[20] is specified, provided that the guaranteed obligation is intended for the purchase of rights in an apartment to serve as the residence of the debtor, his adult children or his parent.

329. *Applicability of the Provisions of the Article on Guarantee of an Individual* – The provisions of this Article will apply to a guarantee that an individual guarantor gave to a creditor, regardless of what it is called, including an independent obligation for indemnification according to its meaning in section 315.

330. *Precedence of this Article over the Bills Ordinance* – The provisions of this Article will apply notwithstanding the provisions of section 57 of the Bills Ordinance.

331. *Update of Amounts of Protected Guarantee* – The amounts specified in the definition of "protected guarantor" in section 328 will be updated on 1 January of each year, according to the rate of increase of the index last published before that date as opposed to the last published index before 1 January of the previous year; for this purpose, "index" is the Consumer Price Index published by the Central Bureau for Statistics.

332. *Guarantee For a Fixed Amount* – (a) An individual guarantor is a guarantor only for the amount specified in the guarantee contract and for the additions as set forth in section 336.

(b) Where a fixed amount is not specified in the guarantee contract, the guarantor is discharged from his guarantee.

333. *Duty of Disclosure to the Individual Guarantor* – (a) The creditor will disclose to the individual guarantor, prior to entering into the guarantee contract, all of the following details, as set forth in the contract between the creditor and the debtor:

(1) the amount specified in the contract between the creditor and the debtor (in this Article – the principal);

(2) the annual interest rate, in a calculation that takes into account interest on interest in accordance with the repayment date;

(3) the period of the obligation, the amounts of repayment of the principal and the interest and the repayment schedule;

(4) where the interest is variable – the rate of interest at the time the contract is entered into, taking into account interest on interest in accordance with the repayment date at the time the contract is entered into, and the mechanism for variation;

(5) whether the principal or the interest is linked, and the basis of the linkage;

(6) additions that were provided for pursuant to section 336(a)(4);

(7) the rate of interest for late repayment as well as any charge to the debtor for non-fulfillment of the guaranteed obligation.

(b) In addition to the details enumerated in subsection (a), prior to entering into a

---

[18] *Sefer HaHukim* 5728, p. 234.

[19] The amount will be corrected during the legislative process.

[20] The amount will be corrected during the legislative process.

guarantee contract, the creditor will disclose the following details to the individual guarantor;

(1) whether the guarantor is an individual or a protected guarantor;

(2) the number of guarantors and the guarantor's relative share of the obligation;

(3) whether the guarantee is a guarantee for an existing obligation or for an obligation replacing an existing obligation;

(4) the rate of interest as defined in section 336(a)(2).

(c) The disclosure of the details set forth in subsection (a) (1), (3) and (4) shall be as they are updated to the date on which the guarantee contract was entered into.

(d) The disclosure of the details in subsection (a) regarding a guarantee for a future obligation shall be as they are known to the creditor at the time the guarantee contract is entered into or as they can be ascertained at such time.

334. *Consequences of Non-Disclosure to an Individual Guarantor* – (a) Where the creditor did not disclose to the individual guarantor the details set forth –

(1) in section 333(a)(1) – the guarantor is discharged from his guarantee if at the time the contract was entered into there was a significant difference between the amount of the guarantee and the amount specified in the contract between the creditor and the debtor;

(2) in section333(a)(2) – the individual guarantor will carry out his guarantee according to the minimum rate of interest customary in contracts of the same kind;

(3) in section 333(a)(4) – the individual guarantor will carry out his guarantee according to the minimum rate of interest customary in contracts of the same kind;

(4) in section 333(a)(3), (5), (6) or (7) and in section 333(b)(2) – the individual guarantor shall perform his guarantee according to his intention when the guarantee contract was entered into;

(5) in section 333(b)(1), (3) or (4) – the individual guarantor is discharged from his guarantee.

(b) Where the creditor proved that the individual guarantor knew any detail of the details enumerated in section 333, subsection (a) will not apply with respect to that detail.

335. *Transmittal of Copy of Guarantee Contract to Individual Guarantor* – (a) Before a creditor signs a guarantee contract with an individual guarantor, he will transmit a copy of the contract and will give him a reasonable opportunity to peruse it before he signs it, and will give him a signed copy after the contract is signed.

(b) A creditor will transmit a copy of the contract between him and the debtor to the individual guarantor, upon his request.

336. *Additions to the Amount of the Guarantee of an Individual Guarantor* – (a) In addition to the amount specified in the guarantee contract, an individual guarantor guarantees only the additions as set forth here:

(1) linkage differentials and interest that do not exceed the amount agreed upon between the creditor and the debtor;

(2) interest due to late repayment, provided that the rate does not exceed 0.4 of a percent above the interest provided for in the contract between the creditor and the debtor where repayment is timely (hereinafter in this clause – the original interest); where the original interest was variable interest, the computation

shall be done according to that interest as it changes from time to time, with an addition that shall not exceed 0.4 of a percent of the original interest rate;

(3) expenses as ruled upon by the court or by the head of the Execution of Judgments Office;

(4) an addition as provided by the Minister of Justice in consultation with the Governor of the Bank of Israel.

(b) An individual guarantor will be liable for the addition set forth in subsection (a)(2) only for the period of time after the 15 days from the day on which he received notice of the non-fulfillment of the obligation as set forth in section 337.

337. *Notice of Non-Fulfillment by the Debtor* – (a) Where the debtor did not fulfill his obligation, the creditor will give notice of the non-fulfillment to the individual guarantor within 90 days from the day on which the debtor was obligated to fulfill the obligation; where the creditor does not so notify, the guarantor will be discharged to the extent of the damage caused to him as a result.

(b) In the notice pursuant to subsection (a), the creditor shall set forth the content of the provisions pursuant to subsection (d)(2) and (3) and sections 338 and 340.

(c) The Minister of Justice may, in consultation with the Governor of the Bank of Israel, establish the kind and amount of obligations regarding which the creditor is exempted from notifying the guarantor of the non-fulfillment of the obligation as set forth in subsection (a).

(d) (1) Where the creditor requested early repayment of a loan that was to be repaid in installments, due to late repayment, he shall give notice of such to the individual guarantor at least 15 days in advance; where the creditor did not so notify, the guarantor will not be obligated to make early repayment.

(2) Where the individual guarantor notified of his desire to repay the loan in installments, he may repay the loan according to the conditions of the loan and the conditions of the spacing of payments as set forth in the contract between the creditor and the debtor, and this will not derogate from his rights as a protected guarantor.

(3) Where the guarantor did not give notice of his desire to repay the loan as set forth in clause (2) within 15 days from the day on which he received the creditor's notice as set forth in clause (1), the creditor may demand early repayment of the obligation.

(e) The notice of a creditor pursuant to subsections (a) and (d)(1) will be sent in registered mail to the address that the guarantor provided to the creditor; the manner for transmitting a notice of the individual guarantor pursuant to subsection (d)(2) will be set forth in regulations.

338. *Action Against Debtor First* – (a) A legal action will not be filed against a protected guarantor until both of the following are fulfilled:

(1) A judgment was rendered against the debtor;

(2) The Chairman of the Execution of Judgments Office confirmed that all of the proceedings of execution of judgments were undertaken in order to receive repayment from the debtor, including proceedings to realize the mortgage on his residence or to realize the pledge on his rights in a residence, all of this as is reasonable under the circumstances.

(b) Notwithstanding the provisions of subsection (a), a legal action may be filed against a protected guarantor for the fulfillment of his obligation in either of the following circumstances –

(1) the debtor has died, was declared to be of limited capacity, a receivership order was given regarding him in a bankruptcy proceeding or he has permanently left the country; where the debtor was insured by a mortgage or pledge, this exception will not apply unless the Court or the head of the Execution of Judgments office, as applicable, has found that reasonable efforts were made to locate the debtor or to realize the mortgage or the pledge;

(2) where the debtor was a corporation – if a receivership or liquidation order was issued with regard to him.

(c) Where a legal action was filed against a debtor, the creditor will serve notice to each protected guarantor, and each guarantor will be permitted to join the action.

(d) For the purposes of this section, "filing of a legal action" includes demand for payment in full or in part of the debt, setoff, or realization of any relief available to the creditor against the protected guarantor.

339. *Continuation of Debt Collection by Guarantor* – Where the protected guarantor fulfilled his guarantee, in whole or in part, he will be considered as a creditor for the purposes of debt collection processes that the creditor initiated against the debtor, and he may continue such processes.

340. *Multiple Protected Guarantors* – (a) Protected guarantors are equally liable towards the creditor.

(b) Where there are also guarantors who are not protected guarantors for the same debt, the share of each protected guarantor will be calculated according to the total number of guarantors.

(c) Where the amount specified in the guarantee contract of the protected guarantor is less than his share pursuant to subsections (a) or (b), that guarantor will not be liable beyond the amount specified in his guarantee contract; this provision will not affect the share of the remainder of the guarantors.

341. *Scope of Guarantee of Individual Guarantor* – Nothing in the provisions of this Article shall derogate from the provisions of section 317(a).

342. *Prohibition of Conditioning on Guarantee of Individual* – Regardless of the provisions of any legislation, in a guarantee pursuant to this Article, the provisions of this Article and of sections 318, 319, 322 and sections 325, 490(b) and (c) cannot be conditioned upon, except for the benefit of the individual guarantor.

342a. *Regulations for the Article Involving Guarantee of Individual* – The Minister of Justice may, with the consent of the Constitution, Law and Justice Committee of the Knesset, promulgate regulations regarding the application of this Article, including –

(1) Establishing additional details that the creditor must disclose to the individual guarantor;

(2) Establishing the ways of disclosing the details that the creditor is obligated to disclose to the individual guarantor pursuant to section 333;

(3) Establishing the method of presenting the information set forth in section 333(a)(3);

(4) Establishing the additions that an individual guarantor guarantees pursuant to section 336(a)(4);

(5) Establishing an exemption from the notification requirement pursuant to section 337(c);

(6) Establishing procedures for the continued collection of the debt pursuant to section 339.

Chapter Nine: Insurance Contract

Article One: Provisions Applicable to Every Kind of Insurance

Subarticle One: Insurance Contract

343. *Substance of Insurance Contract* – An insurance contract is a contract between an insurer and an insured that obligates the insurer, in exchange for insurance payments, to pay insurance benefits to the beneficiary upon the occurrence of the insurance event.

344. *Policy* – (a) Where an insurance policy has been made, the insurer must deliver a document signed by the insurer which details the rights of the parties and their obligations (in this Chapter – policy), unless it is customary with respect to that type of insurance not to issue a policy.

(b) As long as the policy has not been delivered to the insured, the conditions regarded as being consented to by the parties will be the accepted conditions in that type of insurance provided by the same insurer, as they were submitted to the Superintendent of Insurance, pursuant to section 16 of the Supervision on Insurance Businesses Law, 5741–1981[21], or as they were submitted or permitted, as relevant, pursuant to section 40 of that law, unless the parties agreed upon a deviation from those conditions.

345. *Duty to Emphasize Limitations in the Policy* – A condition or exception to the insurer's liability or the scope of such liability will be set forth in the policy near the subject to which it pertains, or it will be written with special emphasis; a condition or exception that is not set forth in accordance with this provision may not be relied upon by the insurer.

346. *Attachment of Copy of Response to Policy* – Where the insurance policy refers to a written response from the insured party to a question posed to him by the insurer, a copy of the response will be affixed to the policy; if the response is not affixed to the policy, the insurer is not entitled to rely on it.

347. *Provision of Copies of the Policy* – (a) The insurer shall deliver copies of the policy and of the responses of the insured affixed to it as set forth in section 346 to the insured and the beneficiary, in accordance with the request of the insured.

(b) The insurer shall deliver copies as set forth in subsection (a) to the beneficiary, in accordance with his request.

(c) In this section, "beneficiary" means a beneficiary who is a partner, directly or indirectly, in the payment, in full or in part, of the insurance premiums, and also a person whose life is insured or who is insured against accident, illness or disability.

348. *Non-Delivery of Details To Insured* – Notwithstanding the provisions of sections 346 and 347, the insurer in life insurance, or accident, illness or disability insurance shall not transmit to the insured who is not the one whose life is insured or is not the one who is insured for accidents, illness or disability, details regarding the health of the one whose life is insured or who is insured for accidents, illness or disability; non-transmission of such details will not derogate from the insurer's right to rely on the response, a copy of which was not affixed to the policy, pursuant to section 346.

349. *The Insured's Duty of Disclosure* – (a) Where the insurer presented to the insured prior to entering into the contract, whether by means of a form proposal of insurance or by some other means, in writing, a question which may affect the willingness of a reasonable insurer to enter into the contract at all or to enter into it under the conditions contained therein (in this Chapter – a material matter), the insured must make a full and honest response to it in writing.

---

[21] *Sefer HaHukim* 5741, p. 208.

(b) A sweeping question that connects various matters without differentiating between them, does not require a response as set forth in subsection (a) and the failure to respond will not be regarded as non-disclosure pursuant to section 350, unless the question was reasonable at the time the contract was entered into.

(c) Concealment of a material matter with the intent to deceive is regarded as giving a response that is not full and honest.

350. *Consequences of Non-Disclosure by the Insured* – (a) Where a response to a question in a material matter was not full or honest, the insurer may, within 30 days from the day on which he had knowledge of this, rescind the insurance contract by written notice to the insured.

(b) Where an insurance event occurred before the contract was rescinded pursuant to subsection (a), the insurer will pay reduced insurance benefits at a relative rate, that is the relation between the insurance premiums that were paid as acceptable to the insurer according to the true situation and the agreed upon premiums; however, the insurer is exempt from paying in any one of the following situations –

(1) the response was given with intent to deceive;
(2) a reasonable insurer would not have entered into such a contract, even with higher insurance premiums, if he had known the true situation.

(c) Where the insurer rescinded the contract pursuant to subsection (a), it will return the insurance premiums for the period of time after the rescission, after deduction of its expenses, to the insured, unless the insured acted with intent to deceive; where the insurer is discharged from paying insurance benefits pursuant to section (b)(2), the insurer will also return to the insured the insurance premiums that the insured paid for the period of time until the rescission, after deduction of its expenses.

351. *Notice by Insured of Incorrect or Incomplete Response* – Where it became known to the insured that a response that he gave in a material matter was incorrect or incomplete, and the true situation will substantially increase the insurer's risk, the insured will immediately notify the insurer in writing of such and the provisions of section 361 will apply, *mutatis mutandis*, to such situation.

352. *Negation of Insurer's Remedies* – The insurer is not entitled to the relief set forth in sections 350 and 351 in either of the following, unless the response that was not complete, honest or correct was given with intent to deceive –

(1) it knew or should have known the true situation at the time the contract was entered into, or it caused the response to be not complete, honest or correct;
(2) the fact with respect to which the response was given that was not complete, honest or correct, ceased to exist before the insurance event occurred, or it did not affect its occurrence or the liability of the insurer or its scope.

353. *Term of Insurance* – (a) In the absence of another agreement, the term of insurance begins with entering into the insurance contract and ends at midnight at the end of its last day.

(b) Where a term of insurance was agreed upon and the insured proposed to the insurer, in writing, at least 30 days before the end of the period, to extend the insurance for the period of time specified in his proposal, the insurer will be deemed to have agreed to the extension if it did not notify otherwise to the insured in writing, within 15 days from the delivery of the proposal, of his rejection.

(c) Where there is a condition that at the end of the agreed upon term the insurance policy will be automatically extended, the insurance policy will be extended each time for a term identical to the agreed upon term of insurance.

(d) Where the term of insurance was not agreed upon, each party may terminate the contract by written notice to the other party a reasonable period of time in advance.

354. *Time of Rescission O Insurance Contract* – Where one of the parties notified of rescission of the contract under its terms or pursuant to the provisions of this Chapter, the contract is rescinded at the end of 15 days from the day on which the notice of rescission was delivered to the other party; where the insurer rescinded the contract pursuant to the provisions of clauses (1) and (2) of subsection 350(b), the contract is rescinded on the date on which the notice of rescission is delivered to the insured.

Subarticle Two: The Beneficiary

355. *Beneficiary in an Insurance Contract* – (a) The insured is also the beneficiary if no other beneficiary was designated in his stead.

(b) Designation of a beneficiary shall be in such a manner as to permit his identification.

(c) As long as the insured event has not occurred, the insured may designate another beneficiary in his stead, by written notice to the insurer, and he may rescind the designation and designate another beneficiary; however the designation will be irrevocable if the contract or a written notice from the insured to the insurer so provides.

(d) A person may be designated as the beneficiary for a part of the benefits only.

356. *Status of Beneficiary in Insurance Contract* – (a) Where a beneficiary is designated who is not the insured, the beneficiary will be entitled to the insurance benefits.

(b) A claim available to the insurer against the insured will be available to him against the beneficiary as well. The insurer may setoff insurance premiums owed to him against insurance benefits to be paid pursuant to the same contract.

357. *Assignment, Encumbrance, and Attachment of Rights of Insured and Beneficiary* – (a) The designation of a beneficiary who is not the insured does not prevent the insured from assigning or encumbering his rights under the contract, or to prevent the insured's creditors from attaching such rights, provided that the insured event has not occurred. However, where the designation of the beneficiary was irrevocable, the assignment or encumbrance shall be subject to the beneficiary's written consent, and the creditors may not attach such rights.

(b) The right of the beneficiary may not be assigned, encumbered or attached as long as the insured event has not occurred, unless the designation of the beneficiary was irrevocable.

Sub-Article Three: Variations in the Risk

358. *Insurance Contract for Risk that has Lapsed* – (a) An insurance contract to cover a risk that at the time the contract was entered into had already passed, or for an insured event that at that time had already occurred, is void.

(b) Where the insured event became impossible after the contract was entered into, the contract lapses.

359. *The Insured's Right to Restitution* – Where the contract is void or rescinded as set forth in section 358, the insured will be entitled to restitution of the insurance premiums he paid, and if the contact lapsed as stated in section 358(b), the insured will be entitled to restitution for the period after the lapse.

360. *Duty to Notify of Material Change* – (a) The insured will notify the insurer in writing of any material change that has occurred, immediately upon becoming aware of it.

(b) In this Sub-Article, "material change" is any of the following –

(1) A change in a material matter as to which a question had been presented to the insured before the contract was entered into and the change, which will sub-

stantially increase the insurer's risk, occurred after the response to that question was given.

(2) A change that occurred after delivery of the policy to the insured, in a subject that was expressly stipulated to be a material matter.

361. *Consequences of Material Change* – (a) The insurer may rescind the contract by notifying the insured in writing within 30 days from the day it received the notice of the material change or from the day that it became known to him in another manner, according to the earlier of the two, provided that the insured event has not occurred.

(b) Where the insured event has occurred prior to the rescission of the contract pursuant to subsection (a) or a material change took place as to which the insured was required to serve notice prior to the occurrence of the insured event pursuant to sections 351 and 360, and no such notice was served and the material change became known to the insurer after the occurrence of the insured event, the insurer will pay reduced insurance benefits at a relative rate that is the ratio between the insurance premiums that would have been paid as customary with the insurer in the situation as it was after the change and the agreed upon insurance premiums. Notwithstanding this, the insurer will be discharged from such payment in one of the following situations –

(1) the insured's failure to notify pursuant to sections 351 and 360 was with intent to deceive;

(2) a reasonable insurer would not have entered into that contract, even with higher insurance premiums, if he had known that the situation was as it was after the change.

(c) Where the insurer rescinded the contract pursuant to the provisions of subsection (a), the insured is entitled to restitution of the insurance premiums that he paid for the time period after the rescission, unless the insured acted with intent to deceive; if the insurer was discharged from paying insurance benefits pursuant to subsection (b)(2), the insured is entitled to restitution of the insurance premiums that he paid for the period of time after the change.

362. *Denial of Remedies to an Insurer Regarding a Material Change* – The insurer is not entitled to that stated in section 361 in any of the following instances –

(1) the change ceased to exist before the insured event occurred or it did not affect its occurrence or the insurer's liability or the scope of such liability;

(2) the change was the result of steps taken with the insurer's consent;

(3) the change was the result of a measure taken in order to prevent serious physical damage or damage to property, provided that the insured notified the insurer in writing of the measure taken immediately after taking it or after he knew of them.

363. *Reducing Risk of Insurer* – Where the insurance premiums are fixed in view of circumstances that increased the insurer's risk, and after they were fixed such circumstances ceased to exist or to affect the insurer's risk, the insured is entitled to a reduction in the premium, after the insurer's reasonable expenses are deducted, for the period of time after he notified the insurer of the change, and to have them fixed at the level that would have been paid according to what is customary for that insurer at the time the premium was fixed in the absence of those circumstances.

364. *Measures to Reduce the Insurer's Risk* – Where a stipulation was made that the insured or the beneficiary must take a measure for the tangible reduction of the insurer's risk and this measure was not taken or was not taken within the allotted time, the provisions of sections 361 and 362 shall apply, *mutatis mutandis*.

Sub-Article Four: Insurance Premiums

365. *Date for Payment of Insurance Premiums* – (a) Insurance premiums will be paid when the contract is entered into or within a reasonable time afterwards, or if there is a provision for payments for fixed periods of time, at the beginning of each period.

(b) Where the insurance is for a number of years and the amount of the premium is set forth in the total sum, the premiums will be paid at the beginning of each insurance year.

366. *Late Payment of Premiums* – (a) Where the premium or part of it was not paid on time, and was not paid within 15 days after the insurer demanded, in writing, that the premium be paid, the insurer may notify the insured, in writing, that the contract will be cancelled at the end of an additional 21 days in the event that the premium is not paid during such additional period of time.

(b) Where a beneficiary was irrevocably designated, the insurer is not entitled to rescind the insurance contract, unless it gave the beneficiary notice, in writing, that the payment was overdue, and gave him an additional extension of at least 15 days beyond the extension provided for in subsection (a), and during such time the premium was not paid.

Sub-Article Five: Insurance Benefits

367. *Notice of Occurrence of Insured Event* – (a) When the insured becomes aware of the occurrence of the insured event, he shall notify the insurer immediately.

(b) When the beneficiary becomes aware of the occurrence of the insured event, he shall notify the insurer immediately of the occurrence of the event and his entitlement to benefits.

(c) Notification by the insured or the beneficiary pursuant to subsection (a) or (b) discharges the other from the duty to notify.

368. *Clarification of Insurer's Liability* – (a) Where notification has been transmitted to the insurer of the occurrence of the insured event and a written demand for payment of the insurance benefits (in this Sub-article – demand for payment of insurance benefits), the insurer must immediately take the necessary action to ascertain its liability.

(b) The insured or the beneficiary, as the case may be, will submit to the insurer, within a reasonable time after requested to do so, the information and the documents necessary in order to ascertain the liability, and if they are not in his possession, he will assist the insurer, to the extent he is able, to obtain them.

(c) Within 30 days from the day on which the insured or the beneficiary, according to the matter, carried out the requirements of subsection (b), the insurer will notify the insured and the beneficiary if it accepts or rejects the demand for payment of the insurance benefits, in whole or in part, with the reasons for such decision. In property insurance, as defined in section 399, the notice shall also contain the amount of insurance benefits owing according to the insurer's calculation.

369. *Prevention of Clarification of the Insurer's Liability* –(a) Where the duty pursuant to section 367 or 368(b) was not performed on time, and its performance would have enabled the insurer to mitigate its damages, it will not be liable for payment of insurance benefits except to the extent that it would have liable for such payment if the duty had been performed; this provision will not apply in either of the following situations –

(1) the duty was not performed or was performed late for good cause;
(2) the non-performance or late performance did not prevent or hinder the insurer from ascertaining its liability.

(b) Where the insured or the beneficiary intentionally performed an action that prevented or hindered the insurer from ascertaining its liability, it will not be obligated to pay the insurance benefits except to the extent that it would have been obligated if such action had not been performed.

370. *Fraud in Demand for Payment* – (a) The insurer is discharged from his liability where one of the following was done, with intention to defraud:

(1) the duty pursuant to section 367 or 368(b) was breached;

(2) an action as set forth in section 369(b) was done;

(3) the insured or the beneficiary submitted incorrect details to or concealed fact from the insurer regarding the insured event or the insurer's liability.

(b) Notwithstanding the provisions of subsection (a), the insurer will not be discharged from his liability if the fraud is not with respect to a material matter, or if it was not capable of having a real impact on the amount of the insurance benefits.

371. *Insured Event that was Caused Intentionally* – Where the insured or the beneficiary intentionally caused the insured event to occur, the insurer is discharged from his liability.

372. *Time for Payment of Insurance Benefits* – Insurance benefits will be paid within 30 days from the day that the insurer had the information and the documents necessary to ascertain its liability. However, where there is no dispute in good faith regarding the liability to pay any portion of the insurance benefits, such benefits shall be paid within 30 days from the day on which a demand for payment of the insurance benefits was submitted to the insurer, and they may be claimed separately from the other benefits.

373. *Linkage and Interest on Insurance Benefits and Premiums* – (a) Linkage differentials, as defined in the Adjudication of Interest Law, shall be added to the amount of insurance benefits from the day of the occurrence of the insurance event, and linked interest at the rate set forth in the definition of "linkage differentials and interest" in section 1 of the Adjudication of Interest Law from the end of 30 days from the day on which the demand for payment of insurance benefits was submitted to the insurer. Nothing in the provisions of this subsection shall derogate from the court's jurisdiction pursuant to the Adjudication of Interest Law.

(b) If insurance benefits are not paid on time in accordance with section 372, interest at the rate of 150% of the interest that the insurer is required to pay pursuant to the provisions of subsection (a) shall be added to the amount of benefits from said time and thereafter.

(c) Where the amount or part of the amount of insurance benefits was calculated according to their value on a date after the occurrence of the insured event, linkage differentials will be added to the amount of the benefits or part of them, as applicable, from such date only.

(d) The provisions of subsection (a) shall not apply to insurance benefits paid in foreign currency or in Israeli currency calculated in accordance with the value of a foreign currency. Interest at a rate set forth in accordance to section 4(a) of the Adjudication of Interest Law shall be added to such benefits beginning with the end of the 30-day period from the day on which the demand for payment of the insurance benefits was submitted to the insurer. Where the insurance benefits were not paid on time in accordance with the provisions of section 372, interest at the rate of 150% of such interest will be added from that date and thereafter.

(e) Linkage differentials and interest as set forth in subsection (a) shall be added to the amount of insurance premiums that the insurer is required to return to the insured or the beneficiary.

374. *Special Interest on Insurance Benefits* – (a) Where an insurer of personal insurance, that did not pay the insurance benefits that were not the subject of a dispute in good faith on the date on which he was required to pay them pursuant to the provisions of section 372, the Court may require it to pay special interest at a rate that shall not exceed triple the established interest set forth in the definition of linkage differentials and interest in section 1 of the Adjudication of Interest Law, which shall be calculated on the basis of such insurance benefits and on the linkage differentials that are added to such benefits pursuant to section 373, from the date that the insurer was required to pay the benefits until their actual payment. The special interest will be paid in addition to the interest set forth in section 373.

(b) In this section, "personal insurance" means life insurance, personal accident insurance, car (property) insurance, home and contents insurance, with the exception of liability insurance.

375. *Special Relief for Insured* – Where the insurer's liability or its scope was conditioned, pursuant to legislation or the insurance contract, on an act of the insured or the beneficiary, and the condition was breached, the Court may, if it was convinced that breach of the condition did not have a real effect on the existence of the liability and its scope, obligate the insurer to pay the insurance benefits, in whole or in part, if it found that doing so would serve the interests of justice under the circumstances of the matter.

376. *Reoccurrence of the Insured Event* – The insurer will pay the insurance benefits even if the insured event occurred more than once within the period of insurance, provided that it will not be obligated to pay a total amount that is greater than the sum of the insurance as defined in section 400.

377. *Period of Limitations Regarding Insurance Benefits* – The period of limitations for a claim for payment of insurance benefits is three years from the date the insured event occurred.

Sub-Article Six: Insurance Agent

378. *Insurance Agent* – In this Sub-Article, "insurance agent" means one who works as an insurance broker between insured parties and insurers.

379. *Agency Regarding Insurance Contract* – (a) An insurance agent will be regarded as the agent of the insurer for the purpose of negotiations towards entering into the insurance contract and regarding entering into the contract.

(b) The insurance agent's knowledge of the correct facts regarding a material matter will be considered as the insurer's knowledge with respect to the duty of disclosure at the stage of entering into the insurance contract.

380. *Agency Regarding Insurance Premiums* – An insurance agent who acted as a broker for the insurance or who is named in the policy as the insurance agent will be considered to be the agent of the insurer regarding the acceptance of insurance premiums unless the insurer notified the insured party, in writing, that the premiums should be sent to another person.

381. *Agency Regarding Delivery of Notices to the Insurer* – The insurance agent who acted as a broker for the insurance or who is named in the policy as the insurance agent will be considered as the insurer's agent regarding delivery of notices, information and documents of the insured party and the beneficiary to the insurer, unless the insurer notified the insured party and the beneficiary, in writing, that they should be sent to another person.

Sub-Article Seven: General Provisions

382. *Notice of Insurer, Insured and Beneficiary* – (a) The notice of the insurer to the in-

sured or to the beneficiary will be served according to the address last known to the insurer.

(b) The notice of the insured or of the beneficiary to the insurer will be served, according to the choice of the one providing the notice, to the insurer according to his business address, to the insurance agent, as set forth in section 381, or to another person in Israel whose address is provided in the policy or regarding whom the insurer notified the insured or the beneficiary in writing.

(c) If the insurer has no place of business in Israel and no address of another person in Israel was provided, the insurer is not entitled to rely on the fact that no notice was submitted by the insured or the beneficiary or that it was submitted late.

(d) In this section, "notice" includes information and service of documents.

383. *Exclusivity of Remedies* – Where the insurer is entitled to remedies pursuant to sections 350, 361, 366, 369 and 370, it will not be entitled to remedies pursuant to other legislation with respect to the matters dealt with therein.

384. *Prohibition of Conditioning in Insurance Contract* – (a) The provisions of sections 344 through 346, 364, 370, 371, 379(b), 380, 381 and 383 may not be conditioned upon.

(b) The provisions of sections 347 through 352, 353(c), 357, 360 through 362, 366 through 369, 372, 373, 377 and 382 may not be conditioned upon except to the advantage of the insured or the beneficiary.

Article Two: Life Insurance

385. *Substance of Life Insurance* – In life insurance the insured event is the death of the insured or of another or their reaching a specified age or another event in their life, with the exception of an accident, illness or disability.

386. *Insuring Another Person* – (a) Where the insured event was the death of another person who is not the insured, the insurance policy is contingent upon the written consent of that person, and if he is a minor or one of limited capacity, the consent of his guardian.

(b) The provisions of subsection (a) will not apply to a person belonging to a group of people whose lives are insured and whose composition is liable to vary within the period of the insurance, provided that the beneficiaries are those people or their heirs and the said person does not pay all or part of the insurance premium, and the beneficiaries are those people or their heirs.

387. *Beneficiaries in Life Insurance* – (a) Where the descendents of the insured are specified as the beneficiaries, without specifying their names, this shall also include a person born within 300 days after the occurrence of the insurance event.

(b) Where the beneficiary who is not the insured has died before the occurrence of the insured event, his descendents are entitled to the insurance benefits according to the rules of inheritance pursuant to the law. Where there are no such descendetns , or if the beneficiary waived his right before the occurrence of the insured event, the insured is entitled to the insurance benefits.

388. *Rescission of Life Insurance Contract* – (a) The insured may rescind the life insurance contract at any time by written notice to the insurer.

(b) Where a beneficiary who is not the insured is irrevocably designated and the insured rescinded the contract, the insured will immediately notify the beneficiary in writing, citing the provisions of this subsection, and the beneficiary may take over the contract through written notice to the insurer not later than 30 days from the receipt of the insurer's notice. Rescission of the contract will become effective within 30 days from the day of receipt of the insurer's notice if the beneficiary did not notify that he is taking over the contract.

(c) Where a beneficiary who is not the insured is irrevocably designated and the insurer rescinded the contract due to an action of the insured that does not constitute a ground for rescission pursuant to Article One, the beneficiary is entitled to take over the contract pursuant to the provisions of subsection (b).

389. *Conversion of Insurance and Redemption of Policy* – (a) An insured may notify the insurer in writing that he demands conversion of the insurance to paid-up insurance or redemption of the policy.

(b) Where the insured demanded conversion of the insurance to paid up insurance, the insurance benefits will be reduced, at the end of the continuous period for which insurance premiums were paid, in accordance with the amount provided for in the policy, and the obligation to pay insurance premiums will end at that time.

(c) Where the insured demanded redemption of the policy, the insurer will pay the redemption value set forth in the policy within seven days from the day that the demand was submitted, and the provisions of section 373 shall apply to this matter, *mutatis mutandis*.

(d) The insured may limit his demand to part of the insurance.

(e) Where a beneficiary who is not the insured is irrevocably specified, the insured's demand is contingent upon the written consent of the beneficiary.

390. *Conversion and Redemption Notwithstanding Rescission of Insurance Contract* – The rescission of an insurance contract by the insurer does not derogate from the right of the insured to redemption of the policy and such rescission due to non-payment of insurance premiums does not impinge upon the right to convert the insurance to paid up insurance, provided that the demand for conversion of the insurance is submitted within 30 days from the submission of the insurer's rescission notice.

391. *Policy as Loan Guarantee* – Where the insured pledged his redeemable rights pursuant to the policy to the benefit of the insurer as a guarantee for a loan that the insurer gave him and the loan was not repaid on time, the insurer will not setoff the loan from the redemption value of the policy, until the insurer has made a written demand from the insured to repay the loan within the period of time during which the insurer was required to pay the redemption value and the loan was not repaid within this period of time as well.

392. *Suicide of the Person whose Life is Insured* – Life insurance benefits are payable even if the person whose life was insured committed suicide, provided that one year passed from the date the policy was entered into.

393. *Taking Over Insurance Contract* – (a) Where a beneficiary who is not the insured is designated and the insured died, whereas the person whose life was insured is still alive, the insurer will provide written notice of such to the beneficiary, and within 30 days from the day of such notice the beneficiary may, through written notice to the insurer, take over the contract.

(b) Where a beneficiary who is not the insured is designated and the insured was declared bankrupt or a liquidation order was given with respect to him, the beneficiary may take over the contract as set forth in subsection (a), however, if his designation as the beneficiary was not irrevocable, the beneficiary will pay the redemption value of the policy at the time the order was given, to the bankruptcy trustee or the liquidator, as relevant.

394. *Prohibition to Rescind Life Insurance Contract* – The insurer may only rescind a life insurance contract in accordance with the provisions of this Chapter.

395. *Exception to Remedies Regarding Life Insurance* – (a) The insurer is not entitled to the remedies set forth in section 350 when three years have passed from the day the contract was entered into, unless the insured or the person whose life was insured acted with intent to defraud.

(b) The provisions of sections 351 and 360 through 362 shall not apply with respect to life insurance.

396. *Prohibition on Conditioning in Life Insurance* – (a) The provisions of sections 386, 393 and 395(b) may not be conditioned upon.

(b) The provisions of sections 388 through 392, 394 and 395(a) may not be conditioned upon other than to the advantage of the insured or the beneficiary.

Article Three: Accident, Illness and Disability Insurance

397. *Substance Accident, Illness and Disability Insurance* – In accident insurance, the insured event is an accident that happened to the insured or another, in illness insurance, an illness that he became ill with and in disability insurance, a disability with which he was affected.

398. *Applicability of Provisions on Accident, Illness and Disability Insurance* – (a) In accident, illness and disability insurance in which the insurer is required to pay insurance premiums according to a previously agreed upon rate, regardless of the amount of damage caused, the provisions of Article Two will apply, *mutatis mutandis*.

(b) In accident, illness and disability insurance in which the insurer is required to pay insurance premiums according to the amount of damage caused, the provisions of sections 386, 395(b), 396, 400, 405, 406 and 408 will apply, *mutatis mutandis*.

Article Four: Damage Insurance

Sub-Article One: Property Insurance

399. *Substance of Property Insurance* – (a) In property insurance, the insurer will indemnify for damage caused to the insured or the beneficiary as a result of the loss of or damage to the insured property.

(b) The insured property may belong to the insured or to another person.

400. *Scope of Liability in Property Insurance* – (a) Insurance benefits will be calculated in a manner that will place the beneficiary, to the extent possible, in the situation he was in had the insured event not occurred.

(b) The insurer's obligation to indemnify will be at the amount of the damage caused, provided that it will not exceed the amount it undertook to indemnify under the contract (in this Sub-article – amount of insurance). The amount of insurance, except the amount of insurance designated in a foreign currency or in Israeli currency linked to a foreign currency, will vary in accordance with the changes in the Consumer Price Index published by the Central Office for Statistics or another index so published that the parties agreed upon, between the index published shortly before the contract was entered into and the index published shortly before the occurrence of the insured event.

(c) The insurance contract shall not designate an insurance amount in a foreign currency or in Israeli currency linked to a foreign currency unless such currency is included in the list of foreign currencies promulgated by the Supervisor of Insurance for this purpose.

401. *Broadening of Liability in Property Insurance* – Insurance of property against a certain risk will cover, up to the amount of the insurance, damage caused to the property due to reasonable measures taken to save it from that risk.

402. *Excessive Insurance* – Where the amount of the insurance, at the time the contract is entered into or afterwards, is unreasonably higher than the value of the insured property, each party may, at any time during the period of the insurance, demand a reduction in the amount of the insurance to the value of property at the time of the demand. Where such reduction has been demanded, the amount of insurance will be reduced and the cost of the premiums will be reduced accordingly from the day of the demand.

403. *Double Insurance* – (a) Where property was insured against one risk by more than one insurer for overlapping periods of time, the insured must notify the insurers in writing immediately after the double insurance was entered into or became known to him.

(b) Where property was doubly insured and the sum of the amounts of insurance is unreasonably higher than the value of the property, the insured and each of the insurers may, at any time during the period of the insurance, demand reduction of the amounts of insurance to the value of the property at the time of the demand. Where a demand for reduction is made, the amounts of insurance shall be reduced, according to the ratio between them, and the cost of the premiums will be reduced accordingly from the day of the demand.

(c) In double insurance, the insurers are severally liable to the insured with respect to the amount of overlapping insurance.

(d) The liability between the insurers will be in accordance with the ratio between amounts of insurance.

404. *Insufficient Insurance* – Where the amount of insurance, at the time the contract was entered into, was unreasonably lower than the value of the insured property, the insurer's liability shall be reduced in a proportional amount that is the ratio between the amount of the insurance and the value of the property at the time the contract was entered into.

405. *Mitigation of Damages by the Insured or the Beneficiary* – (a) The insurer is not liable to pay insurance benefits for damage that the insured or the beneficiary could have prevented or mitigated, when the insured event occurred or afterwards, by taking reasonable measures. Where the insurer instructed the insured to take certain reasonable measures, the insurer will not be liable to pay insurance benefits for such damage if the insured did not take such measures within a reasonable period of time.

(b) Where the insured or the beneficiary, at the time the insured event occurred or afterwards, incurred reasonable expenses to prevent the damage or to mitigate it, or undertook reasonable obligations for this purpose, the insurer must to indemnify him, regardless of whether the damage was thereby prevented or mitigated or not. Where the expenses or the obligations were unreasonable, the insurer is liable for indemnification of the reasonable amount of expenditures under the circumstances. The duty to indemnify applies even if such amounts exceed the amount of the insurance.

(c) The provisions of this section will not apply to insurance where the parties agreed on an amount of indemnification as set forth in section 400(d).

406. *Substitution In Insurance Contract* – (a) Where, with respect to an insured event, the insured also had a right to compensation or indemnification by a third party, and such right was not pursuant to the insurance contract, this right is transferred to the insurer after it has paid the insurance benefits and at the amount of the benefits paid.

(b) The insurer may not use a right that has been transferred to him pursuant to this section in a manner that will infringe upon the insured's right to recover compensation or indemnification from the third party above the insurance benefits that he received from the insurer.

(c) Where the insured received compensation or indemnification from the third party that should have been paid to the insurer pursuant to this section, he must transfer them to the insurer. If he entered into a compromise, waived a right or did any thing else that derogated from the right transferred to the insurer, he must compensate the insurer for such derogation.

(d) The provisions of this section will not apply if the insured event was caused unintentionally by a person from whom a reasonable insured person would not claim compensation or indemnification, due to a family or employer-employee relationship.

407. *Nonpayment Insurance* – In insurance against the non-payment of a debt, the right of the insured against the debtor transfers to the insurer once the insurer has paid insurance benefits to the insured, in accordance with the amount of benefits paid, and the provisions of section 406(b) and (c) will apply, *mutatis mutandis*.

408. *Prohibition on Conditioning in Property Insurance* – The provisions of sections 400, 401, 403(a) through (c), 405 and 406 may not be conditioned upon except to the advantage of the insured or the beneficiary.

Sub-Article Two: Liability Insurance

409. *Substance of Liability Insurance* – Liability insurance obligates the insurer to indemnify the insured for a monetary liability that he is likely to owe to a third party. The insured event occurs on the day on which the ground of liability is created.

410. *Scope of Liability Insurance* – Where there is liability insurance, the insurer will also indemnify the insured for reasonable expenses necessary for defense in a lawsuit filed against him, even if the insurer's liability exceeds the amount of the insurance because of this, provided that the insurer's liability does not exceed the amount of the insurance plus an amount that is 20% of the amount of the insurance.

411. *Standing of Third Party in Liability Insurance* – (a) In liability insurance, the insurer may, pursuant to the demand of the third party to whom the insured is indebted, pay that third party the insurance benefits that the insured is obligated to pay to the insured, provided that he gave the insured written notice as set forth in subsection (b), and the insured did not object as set forth in that subsection. However, a claim that the insurer may assert against the insured may be raised by him against the third party as well.

(b) Where the third party demanded the insurance benefits from the insurer as set forth in subsection (a), the insurer shall notify the insured within 14 days from the day of the demand that if he does not notify it of his objection within 14 days, it will pay the insurance benefits to the third party.

412. *Bankruptcy or Liquidation of Insurer* – (a) If one of the following events occurs with respect to the insured by liability insurance and before or after it occurred the insured undertook a liability covered by the insurance *vis a vis* a third party, the rights of the insured *vis a vis* the insurer for that liability will not be among his assets, but rather will transfer to the third party and he may sue the insurer for such rights. However, a claim that the insurer may assert against the insured will be valid against the third party. The afore-mentioned events are as follows:

(1) the insured was declared bankrupt or arrived at a compromise or an accommodation with his creditors in bankruptcy proceedings;
(2) the insured died and an order was given for the administration of his estate in bankruptcy;
(3) the insured is a corporation with respect to which a liquidation order was given or a receiver has been appointed or a manager was appointed for its business or

factory, or it has made a decision for voluntary liquidation or it was dissolved, except if this was for the purpose of consolidation.

413. *Exception to Limitations in Liability Insurance* – In liability insurance, a claim for payment of insurance benefits is not prescribed as long as the claim of the third party against the insured is not prescribed.

414. *Exception to Transactions in Liability Insurance* – The transaction of the insured, the insurer, the trustee in bankruptcy, the liquidator, the receiver or the manager does not derogate from the rights of the third party pursuant to sections 411 and 412.

415. *Applicability of Provisions and Prohibition on Conditioning in Liability Insurance* – (a) The provisions of sections 400, 403, 405 and 406 will apply to liability insurance, *mutatis mutandis*, and they may not be conditioned upon, with the exception of section 40(d), other than to the advantage of the insured or of the third party.

(b) The provisions of sections 410 through 413 may not be conditioned upon.

Article Five: Miscellaneous

416. *Exception to Applicability of the Chapter on Insurance Contract* –

(a) (1) The provisions of this Chapter, with the exception of section 406, will not apply to secondary insurance;

(2) The provisions of this Chapter, with the exception of section 406, and 412 will not apply to marine and aerospace insurance;

(b) The Minister of Justice, with the consent of the Constitution, Law and Justice Committee of the Knesset, may set forth, in an order, types of transactions as to which some or all of the provisions of this Chapter shall not apply.

Chapter Ten: Standard Contracts

417. *Purpose of Uniform Contracts Chapter* – The purpose of this Chapter is to protect customers from unfair conditions in standard contracts.

418. *Definitions for Standard Contracts Chapter* – In this Chapter –

"the Tribunal" – the Standard Contracts Tribunal as defined in the Standard Contracts Law (Standard Contracts Court) …[22];

"standard contract" – version of contract some or all of whose conditions are set forth in advance by one of the parties for its use in many contracts between it and people of unspecified identity or number;

"customer" – one to whom a provider proposes a contractual arrangement between them pursuant to a standard contract, regardless of whether he is receiving or providing something;

"condition" – condition in a standard contract, including a condition referred to in it as well as any other condition that constitutes part of the contractual relationship, except a condition upon which the supplier and the customer specifically agreed for the purpose of a particular contract.

419. *Unfair Condition and its Invalidation* – The court or the Standard Contracts Tribunal may invalidate or change, in accordance with the provisions of this Chapter and after it has examined the entirety of the conditions of the contract and the circumstances of the matter, the condition in a standard contract that infringes upon the rights of customers, or gives an unfair advantage to the supplier that is liable to lead to an infringement of the rights of the customer (in this Chapter – an unfair condition).

---

[22] Here there will be a reference to a law that is outside of the proposed law in which provisions regarding the Standard Contracts Tribunal will appear (see also section 850).

420. *Presumption of Unfair Condition* – There is a presumption that each of the following conditions is an unfair condition –

(1) a condition that discharges the supplier, fully or partially, from liability that would be imposed upon him pursuant to legislation in the absence of such condition or a condition that unreasonably limits the liability that would be imposed on the supplier were it not for such condition;

(2) a condition that gives the supplier an unreasonable right to rescind the contract or to suspend or postpone the performance of the contract, or to change the material obligations of the contract;

(3) a condition that gives the supplier the right to transfer his responsibility to a third party;

(4) a condition that gives the supplier the right to establish or to change a price or other material obligations imposed on the customer, unless the change is due to circumstances that are not in the control of the supplier;

(5) a condition that unreasonably obligates the customer, to resort to the supplier or another person, or that restricts in another manner the customer's freedom to contract or not to contract with another person;

(6) a condition that abrogates or restricts a right or a remedy available to the customer according to law, or a condition that unreasonably restricts a right or remedy available to the customer under the contract, or a condition that makes such a right or remedy contingent upon an unreasonable requirement or on giving notice within an unreasonable period of time or in an unreasonable manner;

(7) a condition that imposes the burden of proof on the customer where such burden would not have been imposed upon him were it not for such condition;

(8) a condition that abrogates or restricts the customer's right to raise certain claims before the courts, with the exception of a reasonable arbitration agreement;

(9) a provision that conditions upon a legal provision regarding the judicial forum or a condition that gives the supplier an exclusive right to choose the judicial or arbitration forum in which the dispute will be clarified;

(10) a condition that sets forth that a dispute will be dealt with in arbitration, where the supplier has a better opportunity than the customer to influence the conditions of the arbitration; in this clause, "conditions of the arbitration" include the ruling of the arbitrators, the place of arbitration, the conditions of arbitration, the manner of conducting the arbitration and the procedural rules of the arbitration.

421. *Void Conditions in Standard Contract* – (a) A condition that abrogates or restricts the customer's right of recourse to the courts is void.

(b) A condition that partially or fully discharges the supplier from the liability imposed upon him pursuant to legislation for bodily injury or for a malicious deed is void.

**sec. 422–427 were dropped from the final version of the code

428. *Petition to Court to Invalidate an Unfair Condition* – (a) The Attorney General or his representative, or the one appointed for consumer protection pursuant to the Consumer Protection Law, 5741–1981[23], or any consumer organization or public authority that was named in regulations, as well as any consumer organization that the Minister of Justice

[23] *Sefer HaHukim* 5741, p. 248.

approves for a specific purpose, may submit a petition to the Tribunal to invalidate or to alter an unfair condition in a standard contract.

(b) The Minister of Justice may establish conditions for the submission of such a petition by a consumer organization or a public authority as set forth in subsection (a).

(c) The respondent in a petition for invalidation is the supplier who proposes entering into, or who intends to propose entering into a standard contract and anyone whom he sees fit to summon as a respondent; any representative organization of suppliers or any other entity interested in the petition may join as a respondent provided that the Tribunal has approved the joinder.

429. *Invalidation or Alteration of an Unfair Condition by the Tribunal* – (a) Where the Tribunal has found that a condition is unfair, it will invalidate the condition or alter it in order to nullify the unfairness.

(b) Where the Tribunal invalidated or changed a condition, it may give any order to ensure the fulfillment of its decision; for the purposes of carrying out orders and contempt of court, an order of the Tribunal is like a District Court order in a civil matter.

430. *Effect of Invalidation or Change of Unfair Condition by The Tribunal* – (a) Where the Tribunal invalidated a condition – the condition will be considered void in every contract even if it was entered into before the date its decision was rendered;

(b) Where the Tribunal changed a condition – the condition will apply, as changed, in every contract even if it was entered into before the date its decision was rendered however, the invalidation or change will not apply to obligations that have been fulfilled under the contract before the date of the decision.

(c) Notwithstanding the provisions of subsections (a) and (b), the Tribunal may rule that the invalidation or the change will also apply to contracts entered into before the date its decision was rendered and with respect to which not all of their obligations have been fulfilled; however, the invalidation or change will not apply to obligations that have been fulfilled under the contract before the date of the decision.

431. *Invalidation and Change of Unfair Condition by Court* – (a) Where, in a proceeding between a supplier and a customer, the Court found that a condition is unfair, it will invalidate or change the condition in order to do away with the unfairness, provided that it examined the entirety of the contract's conditions and their circumstances, including special circumstances of the matter adjudicated before it.

(b) In this section, the terms "supplier" and "customer" include their successors pursuant to legislation or under the contract.

432. *Notice Regarding Claim of Unfair Condition* – If an claim of an unfair condition in a contract entered into pursuant to a standard contract is raised in judicial proceedings, the court will notify the Attorney General of such.

433. *Concurrent Hearing Regarding Unfair Condition* – (a) The holding of a hearing regarding a standard contract before the Tribunal does not derogate from the jurisdiction of the court to adjudicate a claim of an unfair condition in a contract that was entered into pursuant to the standard contract that was before the Tribunal, as long as the Tribunal has not rendered a decision in the matter.

(b) Nothing in the holding of a hearing before a court regarding a claim that a condition in a contract entered into pursuant to a standard contract will prevent the Tribunal from considering the standard contract or any of its conditions; however, the Tribunal may postpone the hearing before it, pending the rendering of a decision by the court.

434. *Exceptions to The Applicability of the Standard Contracts Chapter* – The provisions of this Chapter will not apply to any of the following –

(1) a condition that establishes the monetary compensation that the customer or the supplier will pay for the subject of the transaction;
(2) a condition that complies with legislation;
(3) a condition that complies with conditions set forth in an international accord that Israel is a party to;
(4) a collective agreement pursuant to the Collective Agreement Law, 5717–1957,[24] regardless of whether it was submitted for registration pursuant to such law, including another collective arrangement, provided that it was made in writing and that rates of wages are set forth therein.

Chapter Eleven: Property Relation Agreement

435. *Substance Of Property Agreement* – A property agreement is an agreement between spouses that regulate the property relations between them; the provisions of the Property Relations Between Spouses Law, 5733–1973[25] will apply to such an agreement.

Sub-Part Four: Non-Voluntary Obligations

Chapter One: Torts

Article One: Torts Liability

436. Definitions to the Torts Chapter – In this Chapter –

"employee" – one of the following:
(1) A person integrated into the organizational system of the activities of another, but not within the framework of an independent business of his own;
(2) One whose work is under the complete control of another; "employer" – one who employs an employee, and he himself is not an employee in the same organizational entity.

437. *Torts and Applicability to Provisions in Other Legislation* – (a) The acts set forth in Articles Four and Five are torts.

(b) The provisions of this Article, Articles Two and Three and section 534 will also apply to the provisions set forth in other legislation regarding causing damage unlawfully.

438. *Right to Remedy in Torts* – One who suffered injury as a result of a tort (in this Chapter – the one entitled) is entitled to the remedy pursuant to the provisions of the subpart dealing with remedies for the breach of an obligation[26], from the person liable for the tort.

439. *Tort Liability* – (a) Tort liability is liability for damage caused by wrongful conduct or liability for the conduct itself.

(b) Wrongful conduct will be viewed as causing damage where both of the following exist:
(1) the wrongful conduct was the actual cause of damage; in this section, "actual cause" means the cause without which the damage would not have been however, if the damage was caused by more than a single wrongful conduct, each of them will be viewed as the actual cause; and

---

[24] *Sefer HaHukim* 5717, p. 63.

[25] *Sefer HaHukim* 5733, p. 267.

[26] Subpart Six in this Part (Part Four) (sections 520 through 575).

(2) the process by which the damage was caused and the damage were within the category of risk that the tort was meant to redress.

(c) Regarding the category of risk referred to in subsection (b)(2), the kind of liability and the protected interest will be examined, as well as the following:

(1) the reasonable expectation of the type of process of causing the damage and the type of damage as a cumulative result of the wrongful conduct;

(2) the degree of the contribution of the wrongful conduct to the increase of the risk of causing damage;

(3) the degree of culpability of another party, or of the injured party in the wrongful conduct that was the actual cause of the damage;

(4) the degree of culpability in the wrongful conduct of the one who caused the damage.

439A. *Liability for damage that cannot be attributed to the action of a specific malfeasor* – Where the court recognized the wrongful conduct of a several malfeasors and is unable to determine which of them was the actual cause of the damage, each one of the malfeasors shall bear the entire or partial liability for the damage, as the court shall determine.

440. *Personal Liability for Wrongful Conduct* – (a) A person bears personal liability in torts for a wrong if he committed it himself or through another or knowingly participated in its commission by way of abetting, counseling, procuring, commanding or authorizing it.

(b) A corporation bears personal liability in torts for a wrong a person committed acting as a functionary of the corporation; however, the provisions of this subsection do not derogate from the tort liability of such person.

441. *Employer's Liability as Principal* – An employer bears tort liability according to the laws of agency for a wrong committed by his employee in the course of his employment.

442. *Liability of Principal* – One who engages the services of an agent who is not his employee and is not a contractor, to perform an act, bears tort liability as the principal for a tort committed by the agent in the course of performing such act.

442A. *Obligors in one obligation in torts* – In torts, obligors are liable in one obligation, as referred to in section 76, upon the fulfillment of one of the following:

(1) the damage for which they are liable (hereinafter in this section referred to as "the damage") was caused following a wrong for which all the obligors are responsible either because of joint participation in its execution or pursuant to the provisions of sections 367 to 369;

(2) all or part of the damage was caused as a result of the wrongful conduct of each of the obligors and no reasonable basis existed under the circumstances to divide the responsibility among them;

(3) each of the defendants was found fully liable for the damage under section 366

443. *Death of Malfeasor Before the Damage has Given Rise to Cause of Action* – Where damage is caused as the result of a tort committed by a person and that person dies before the damage has been actualized, for the purposes of this Chapter, the cause of action that would have existed against him for the tort if he had died after the damage had been actualized is viewed as if it existed against him before he died.

Article Two: Exceptions to Liability

444. *Action Pursuant to Legislation* – In an action brought due to a tort, with the exception of negligence, it shall be a defense that the act complained of was performed in accordance with the provisions of legislation or that it was performed within the scope of legal authorization or it was performed in accordance with a belief, in good faith, that it was within the scope of such legal authorization.

445. *Lack of Control* – A person shall not bear liability in torts for the commission of an act if he did not have the choice between committing or refraining from such action due to a lack of control over his movements with respect to that action; the provisions of this section shall not apply where the one performing the tort voluntarily brought himself to said state of lack of control.

446. *Act of Rescue* – A person shall not bear liability in torts due to a reasonable act that he performed in order to protect himself or another from bodily injury or injury to health, freedom or property, provided that the relation between the reasonable damage that reasonably would have been caused by the act and the damage that reasonably would have been prevented by the act was reasonable.

447. *Assumption of the Risk* – A person shall not bear tort liability if the injured party knew of and assessed the expected risk to him and he willingly exposed himself or his property to the risk while prepared to bear the consequences of such risk himself.

448. *Strike and Closeout* – A person shall not bear tort liability for an act committed in the framework of a legal strike or lockout, provided that the act was carried out in the natural and direct course of the strike or lockout; this provision shall not apply with respect to an act that caused bodily harm.

449. *Liability in a Judicial Proceeding* – (a) A person who performs a judicial function, including an arbitrator, shall not bear tort liability for an act done in performing his judicial function.

(b) A party to a legal action, his counsel or a witness, shall not be liable in torts for an act done in good faith in or for a legal proceeding.

450. *Act of War* – none

451. *Injury Caused in the Course of Military Service* – none

452. *Death Caused During Military Service* – none

Article Three: Immunities[27]

453. *Definitions for Immunities Article* – In this Article –

"State employee" – includes an arm of the State and any person who, under State auspices, holds a public position pursuant to legislation, including those serving in the Israel Defense Services, in the Israel Police, in the Prison Service and in the other security organizations of the State, except a contract holder;

"employee of a public authority" – includes an arm of a public authority and every person who, under auspices of the authority, holds a public position pursuant to legislation, except a contract holder;

"public employee" – includes a State employee or an employee of a public authority, as the case may be;

"public authority" – includes a local authority and every corporation established by law enumerated in the First Schedule.

---

[27] Legislative proposal to amend the Torts Ordinance (No. 9) (Liability of Civil Servants), 5760–1999, dealing with this subject. is pending before the Constitution, Law and Justice Committee of the Knesset.

454. *Immunity of Public Employee* – (a) An action shall not be filed against a public employee for an act that he did while fulfilling his position in the State or the public authority, as applicable, giving rise to the tort liability; this provision shall not apply to such an act done with malicious intent and in abuse of authority.

(b) Nothing in the provisions of subsection (a) shall derogate from the liability of the State or of the public authority pursuant to sections 441 and 442 and pursuant to any legislation.

455. *Action Against a State Employee* – (a) Where an action was filed against a State employee for an act that he did while performing his function for the State, the plaintiff shall serve notice of such on the State.

(b) (1) Where such an action as referred to in subsection (a) is filed, the action shall be dismissed with respect to the State employee where both of the following are fulfilled:

(a) The State gave notice to the Court, within the deadline for filing an answer, that it acknowledges that the State employee's act that is the subject of the action was done in performance of his function for the State, or that commission of the act is denied;

(b) The State requested, in the notice pursuant to sub-clause (a) to dismiss the action against the State employee.

(2) A notice pursuant to clause (1)(a) is considered to be an answer, and it will be submitted only with the approval of the Attorney General or one whom he authorized for such purpose.

(3) Notwithstanding the provisions of clause (1), the action against a State employee will not be dismissed if the Court ruled in a preliminary proceeding, at the request of the plaintiff, that the act of the State employee, which is the subject of the action was not done in the performance of his job.

(c) (1) Where the State submitted a notice as set forth in subsection (b)(1)(a), the action will be regarded as if it was filed against the State pursuant to its liability for the act of the State employee pursuant to sections 441 or 442, and the act of the State employee will be regarded as having been done in the performance of his job.

(2) Where the State employee remains a party to the action, and the Court ruled that the act that is the subject of the action was not done in the performance of his job, the provision of clause (1) will not apply.

(d) (1) Where the State did not submit a notice as set forth in subsection (b)(1)(a), and the State employee argued that the State is liable, the State will be joined as a defendant to the action and the Court will rule, in a preliminary proceeding, whether the employee's act that is the subject of the action was done in the performance of his job.

(2) Where the Court ruled, in a preliminary proceeding, that the State employee did the act in the performance of his job, the action will be dismissed against him and the provisions of subsection (c)(1) will apply, and with respect to an answer, the filing deadline will apply from the day on which the claim was dismissed against the State employee; where the Court ruled in a preliminary proceeding, that the State employee did not do the act in the performance of his job, the action against the State shall be dismissed.

456. *Action Against Employee of Public Authority* – (a) Where an action was filed against an employee of a public authority for an act done in the performance of his job in the public authority, the plaintiff will serve notice of the action on the public authority.

(b) (1) Where an action was filed as set forth in subsection (a) and one of the parties to the action, or the public authority, argued that the public authority is liable, the public authority shall be joined as a defendant, and the Court will rule, in a preliminary proceeding, whether the act of the employee of the public authority was done in the performance of his job.

(2) Where the Court ruled, in a preliminary proceeding, that the employee of the public authority did the act in performance of his job, the Action will be dismissed against him and the provisions of section 455(c)(1) will apply, *mutatis mutandis*, and regarding the filing of an answer, the time for its filing will be determined from the day the claim was dismissed against the employee of the public authority.

(3) Where the Court has ruled, in a preliminary proceeding, that the employee of the public authority did not do the act in performance of his job, the claim will be dismissed against the public authority.

457. *Joinder of Public Employee as a Defendant to an Action* – A public employee may join as a defendant in an action that was filed against the State or a public authority, as pertinent, for an act for which he would bear tort liability of his own were it not for the provision of section 454(a), or in order to preserve, notwithstanding the provisions of sections 454 through 456, his standing as a defendant in an action filed against him.

458. *Regulations with Respect to the Article on Immunities* – The Minister of Justice may promulgate regulations regarding the carrying out of the provisions of sections 455 through 457, including procedural rules and special deadlines.

459. *Compensation and Indemnification of the State or the Public Authority* – Where the public employee acted in gross deviation from proper conduct, the State or the public authority, according to the matter at hand, is entitled, notwithstanding the provisions of section 454 –

(1) to compensation from him, if the public employee did an act that gives rise to tort liability;

(2) to indemnification from him, in an amount that the Court shall determine, if the State or the public authority was found to be liable for the act done by the employee.

460. *Alteration of Addendum* – The Minister of Justice, with the consent of the Constitution, Law and Justice Committee of the Knesset, may, by order, alter the first addendum.[28]

Article Four: General Wrongs

461. *Negligence* – (a) Negligence is a negligent act causing damage to a person towards whom the malfeasor owes a duty not to act negligently under the circumstances.

(b) Acting negligently is doing an act, including an act done intentionally, that a reasonable person would not have done under the circumstances.

(c) The duty not to act negligently as set forth in subsection (a) is imposed on a person with respect to anyone whom a reasonable person should have foreseen would be likely to be harmed as a result of the negligent act, provided that imposition of liability on the

[28] The placement of section 5A of the Civil Torts (Liability of the State) Law, 5712–1952, and its integration into the legislation will be considered.

said person is justified, fair and reasonable, taking into account the relationship of the parties and the public interest in the imposition of such liability, including the fear of impeding desired activities.

462. *Exception to Liability Regarding a Trespasser* – none

463. *Breach of Statutory Duty* – The breach of a statutory duty is the non-fulfillment of a duty imposed on a person pursuant to statute, whose purpose is to protect people of the same type as the injured party, where the breach caused damage to the injured party of the kind or nature against which the statute was designed to protect.

Article Five: Special Wrongs

Sub-Article One: Assault

464. *Assault* – Assault is the knowing use of force against the person of another, whether directly or indirectly, without his consent, or a real threat to use force as stated.

465. *Defense in an Action for Assault* – In an action for assault, the defendant will have a defense if either of the following is fulfilled –

(1) the defendant, without malice, used reasonable force and he had a reasonable basis to believe that it was immediately necessary for the good of the plaintiff, and before using the force he could not, under the circumstances, obtain the consent of the person lawfully appointed over the plaintiff; where the plaintiff had a temporary or permanent mental illness or impairment and there was a reasonable basis to assume that illness or impairment prevents him from arriving at informed consent, the defendant will be considered as one who could not, under the circumstances, receive the consent of the plaintiff;

(2) the defendant used force in the manner and the circumstances in which he was entitled to use force pursuant to section 582.

Sub-Article Two: False Imprisonment

466. *False Imprisonment* – False imprisonment is the unlawful and knowing deprivation of a person's liberty for any period of time, by physical means or by a show of authority.

467. *Defense in an Action for False Imprisonment* – In an action brought in respect of false imprisonment, the defendant shall have a defense if either of the following is fulfilled:

(1) the plaintiff had a temporary or permanent mental illness or impairment, and the defendant had reasonable grounds to assume that the deprivation of his liberty was necessary in order to protect the plaintiff or another, provided that the deprivation of freedom was not done with malice;

(2) the plaintiff is a minor and the defendant, who is the minor's guardian, deprived the plaintiff of his liberty temporarily only, for the period of time reasonably necessary for the purpose of correcting the plaintiff.

Sub-Article Three: Trespass

468. *Trespass* – (a) Trespass on property is one of the following, that is done unlawfully:

(1) deprivation of or interference with another's possession of property, or his right to possess it;

(2) damage to another's property.

(b) A third party's claim to a right in property shall not constitute a defense for the defendant in an action by the possessor.

469. *Defense in Trespass Action* – none

470. *Negligence as a Condition for Compensation* – A person shall not owe compensation for the tort of trespass unless there was negligence on his part.

Sub-Article Four: Nuisance

471. *Public Nuisance* – A public nuisance is an unlawful act that endangers the life, safety, health or property of the public, or that constitutes an obstruction to the public in the exercise of some common right.

472. *Action for Public Nuisance* – No action shall be brought in respect of a public nuisance except by one who has suffered monetary damage due to it.

473. *Private Nuisance* – A private nuisance is the actual disturbance of the reasonable use or enjoyment of land by the possessor thereof, considering its location and type.

474. *Prevention of Support of Neighboring Land* – Where any land provides support to neighboring land, the doing of any act that prevents or denies such support constitutes a prevention of support.

475. *Negligence as a Condition for Compensation* – A person shall not owe compensation for a wrong pursuant to sections 471 through 474, unless there was negligence on his part; however, the Court may, if it finds special reasons to do so, order that the person make compensation even if he was not negligent.

Sub-Article Five: Causing Breach of Obligation

476. *Causing Breach of Obligation* – (a) Causing a breach of obligation is when a person knowingly and without sufficient justification causes another not to fulfill his obligation to a third party.

(b) For the purposes of this section, the relationship created by marriage shall not be considered an obligation.

Sub-Article Six: Product Liability

477. *Definitions for the Sub-Article on Product Liability* – In this sub-article –

"manufacturer" – one who, for commercial purposes, deals in the manufacture or assembly of products, including –

(1) one who purports to be the manufacturer of the product, by lending his name, trademark or in any other manner;

(2) an importer who imported a product manufactured abroad to Israel for commercial purposes;

(3) the supplier of a product, when its manufacturer in Israel or its importer cannot be readily identified;

"manufacture" – will be interpreted according to the definition of "manufacturer";

"product" – moveable property, including a component, raw material, product packaging, products fixed to real property, buildings, electricity and other kinds of energy marketed to consumers after being hooked up to property.

478. *Applicability of Sub-Article on Product Liability* – This sub-article shall not apply to –

(1) livestock, poultry and fish;

(2) other unprocessed agricultural products; for this purpose, cleaning, sorting, ripening, storage and refrigeration will not be considered processing.

479. *Manufacturer's Liability* – (a) A manufacturer shall compensate one who has suffered bodily injury (in this Sub-article – the injured party) as a result of a defect in a product it manufactured, regardless of whether the manufacturer was at fault.

(b) Where the injury was caused by a defective component, both the manufacturer of the product and the manufacturer of the product shall be liable; where the injury was caused by defective raw material, both the manufacturer of the product and the manufacturer of the raw material shall be liable.

(c) Where the manufacturer in Israel or the importer of a product cannot be readily identified, its supplier shall be discharged from liability pursuant to this law, if, within a reasonable time after being requested to do so, it provided information to the injured party according to which he could locate the manufacturer, the importer or the supplier from which it bought the product, including the complete address of their places of business.

480. *Substance of Defect in a Product* – (a) A product is defective in each of the following cases:

(1) a particular product is different from the product as it was planned to such an extent so as to create an unreasonable safety risk;
(2) the planning, design or manner in which the product is meant to be used creates an unreasonable safety risk;
(3) the product was not accompanied by warnings or instructions for care and use that are necessary under the circumstances for its safe use, or such warnings or instructions are not appropriate in view of the risk inherent in the use of the product.

(b) There is a presumption that the product was defective if the general circumstances of the case are more consistent with a conclusion that it was defective than with a conclusion that it was in proper condition.

481. *Exceptions to Liability for Product Defects* – A person shall not bear liability pursuant to this sub-article where one of the following pertains –

(1) the defect that caused the injury came into being after the product left his control; where the manufacturer proved that a particular product passed reasonable safety checks before leaving its control, there is a presumption that the injury to the injured party was caused by a defect that came into existence afterwards;
(2) according to the level of scientific and technological development in existence at the time the product left its control, a reasonable manufacturer could not have known that there was a defect in the product as set forth in section 480(2) or (3);
(3) the product left the manufacturer's control against the manufacturer's wishes, and it took reasonable measures to prevent its leaving its control and to warn the public of the risk inherent in the product.

482. *Compensation for Injury from Defective Product* – (a) Notwithstanding the provisions of section 543, in computing the compensation pursuant to this sub-article due to loss of earnings and loss of earning potential, income in excess of three times the average domestic wages, according to the Central Bureau for Statistics on the eve of the ruling with respect to compensation, will not be taken into account. Where the compensation is exempt from income tax, the injured party's losses will be computed on the basis of his income after the deduction of the income tax applicable to him at the time of the ruling, provided that the reduction for such deduction of income tax does not exceed 25 percent of the income according to which such compensation was computed.

(b) Notwithstanding the provisions of section 542, compensation pursuant to this sub-article for damage that is not monetary damage will not exceed NIS 50,000;[29] The Justice Minister may, with the consent of the Constitution, Law and Justice Committee of the Knesset, increase such amount. The amount will be linked to the consumer price

[29] The amount will be updated in the course of the legislative process.

index that the Central Bureau for Statistics publishes from the day this law is enacted by the Knesset or from the day the amount is increased, as the case may be.

(c) The Minister of Justice may, with the consent of the Constitution, Law and Justice Committee of the Knesset, set forth standards in regulations for the calculation of the compensation referred to in subsection (b).

483. *Limitation Regarding Liability for Defective Products* – (a) The period of limitation for an action pursuant to this sub-article is three years.

(b) An action shall not be filed pursuant to this sub-article beyond ten years from the end of the year in which the product left the manufacturer's control.

484. *Prohibition of Conditioning Regarding Liability for Defective Products* – A condition discharging one from liability or limiting his liability pursuant to this sub-article is void; there is nothing in this provision to derogate from the manufacturer's right to indemnification from another, provided that he shall not indemnify himself from one to whom the product arrived for his personal, family or home use.

Article Six: Transfer of Burden of Proof

485. *Res Ipsa Loquitor* – Where injury was caused by property over which the defendant had complete control, the circumstances of the case have not been sufficiently clarified, and it seems that the general circumstances of the incident are more consistent with the conclusion that the injury was caused by the product due to a risk that the defendant created through negligence than with the conclusion that he was not negligent, the defendant will have to prove that the injury was not caused due to his negligence. In this regard, there is no difference if the ground of the action against the defendant is a tort of negligence or another tort.

486. *Injury Caused by a Dangerous Thing* – (a) Where injury was caused by a thing that is dangerous by its nature or due to the escape of a thing likely to cause injury by its escape, and the defendant had control over the dangerous thing, or over the thing that escaped immediately prior to its escape, the defendant has the burden of proof to show that he was not negligent in failing to prevent the injury; for this purpose, it makes no difference if the grounds of the action against the defendant is a tort of negligence or another tort.

(b) In this section, "a dangerous thing" includes poisonous substances, water, explosive substances, flammable substances, harmful radiation, electricity, fire, wild animals or an animal known to be dangerous.

Chapter Two: Unjust Enrichment

487. *The Principle of Restitution* – (a) One who received a benefit (in this chapter – the beneficiary) from another person (in this chapter – the benefactor), without having been entitled to it, will return the benefit to the benefactor.

(b) It is immaterial whether the benefit is derived from an act of the beneficiary, an act of the benefactor or in some other manner.

488. *Applicability of the Chapter on the Duty of Restitution* – The provisions of this chapter shall also apply to obligations to make restitution set forth in other chapters of this law, subject to the provisions of those chapters.

489. *Grounds for Restitution* – Without derogating from the generality of the provision of section 487, the beneficiary will return to the benefactor a benefit that he received because of one of the following –

(1) an unlawful act towards the benefactor;

(2) an act of the benefactor that transferred the benefit to the beneficiary –

(a) due to mistake, deceit, coercion or extortion;
(b) due to a ground that was invalid, void or rescinded;
(c) according to the request or with the consent of the beneficiary when the beneficiary knew or should have known that the benefactor expected compensation.

490. *Restitution Due to Fulfillment of the Obligation On Another* – (a) The benefactor will be entitled to restitution if there is an obligation imposed on the beneficiary towards a third party (in this section – the debtor), without his being obligated for it towards the beneficiary, unless the beneficiary had good cause to object to the existence of the obligation or part of it.

(b) A pledge or other right given to a creditor to guarantee the obligation that has been fulfilled shall be transferred to the benefactor in order to ensure his right to restitution from the beneficiary, to the extent that the creditor will not be harmed thereby.

(c) Where a pledge or other right as set forth in subsection (b) has been transferred, the parties must, upon request of the benefactor, take necessary action in order that the transfer will vest a right in the benefactor of equal validity as the creditor's right.

(d) The benefactor is not entitled to restitution of anything other than what he gave for fulfillment of the obligation.

491. *Safeguarding of Another's Interests* – (a) Where a benefactor performed an act in good faith and reasonably, so as to safeguard the life, physical wellbeing, health, dignity or property of the beneficiary, without his having been obligated to do so pursuant to contract, the following provisions shall apply to him –

(1) where the benefactor incurred, or undertook to incur expenses in connection to such act, the beneficiary shall indemnify him for his reasonable expenses, including his obligation to a third party;
(2) where property damage has been caused to the benefactor due to the act, the Court may order the beneficiary to pay him compensation;
(3) the Court may set an appropriate wage for the benefactor.

(b) Regarding subsection (a), one whose property was used to safeguard those stated values is regarded as one who performed an act in order to safeguard them.

(c) A beneficiary who objected, or who had a good reason to object, to the act or the use of property as stated, or to the amount of expenses that the benefactor incurred or obligated himself to incur, is not obligated to compensate or indemnify unless the act or the use of property was lawfully done in order to safeguard the life, physical well being or health of the beneficiary.

492. *Manner of Restitution* – Restitution shall be in kind; where restitution in kind is impossible or unreasonable, it shall be by restitution of the value.

493. *Calculation of Restitution* – Restitution for to the benefit shall be established, *inter alia*, in consideration of the following –

(1) the profit that the beneficiary derived, taking into consideration his contribution to the profit;
(2) the amount appropriate to pay for the use that the beneficiary made of the benefit;
(3) regarding the restitution of value, the intention is to the market value of the benefit.

494. *Rule of Substitution* – Where a person has become entitled to property or to a right *vis a vis* a third party (in this chapter – substitute) which was substituted by property, in

which the benefactor had a right, that was lost, damaged or transferred, the following provisions shall apply –

(1) if the benefactor was the owner of the property – the beneficiary must restore the substitute to the benefactor; as long as the substitute is not restored, the substitute will be considered to be held in trust for the benefactor;
(2) where the benefactor had a non-proprietary right in the property – the benefactor's right in the property becomes a right in the substitute; as long as the benefactor's right in the substitute has not been transferred, the right will be regarded as held in trust for the benefactor.

495. *Substitution for Performance* – Where the performance of the obligation has become impossible and thus there is a right to compensation or indemnification from a third party, the debtor must transfer the right, or what he received for the obligation, at the value of the obligation, to the creditor. Prior to such transfer, the obligation or what was received shall be regarded as held in trust for the creditor.

496. *Denial of Restitution* – The Court may discharge the beneficiary of the duty to make restitution of the benefit, in whole or in part, where one of the following is fulfilled –

(1) the benefit did not involve any loss to the benefactor;
(2) the beneficiary has a moral right to the benefit;
(3) the beneficiary changed his situation in good faith in reliance on the benefit;
(4) the benefit was lost, damaged or transferred to another and the beneficiary acted in good faith; this does not derogate from the provisions of section 492;
(5) the benefit was given to the beneficiary without his consent and he did not derive any advantage from it;
(6) the beneficiary is of limited legal capacity, and his obligation to make restitution is inconsistent with the purpose of the limitation of his capacity;
(7) restitution of the benefit is not in the public interest.

Chapter Three: Maintenance[30]

497. *Substance of Obligation of Maintenance* – An obligation of maintenance is a person's obligation to provide maintenance to another person pursuant to the provisions of any law, including the provisions of the Law for the Amendment of the Family Law (Maintenance), 5719–1959.

Sub-Part Five: Other Obligations

Chapter One: Bailment

498. *Safekeeping* – A bailee is one who safeguards property lawfully, not by virtue of ownership.

499. *Substance of the Obligation to Safeguard* – A bailee is liable towards the one for whom he holds the property (in this chapter – the property owner), in accordance with the provisions of this chapter.

500. *Bailee without Compensation* – (a) A gratuitous bailee is a bailee who derives no benefit from the safekeeping.

(b) A gratuitous bailee is liable for loss or damage to the property if it was caused by his negligence.

---

[30] The proposed chapter is undergoing examination in the Ministry of Justice

501. *Bailee for Hire* – (a) A bailee for hire is a bailee who receives compensation or derives some other benefit from the bailment, and he is not a borrower.

(b) A bailee for hire, in a case in which the safeguarding of the property is the primary purpose of the bailment, is liable for loss of or damage to the property, unless it was caused due to the occurrence of circumstances in which a contract would have lapsed pursuant to section 196.

(c) A bailee for hire, in a case in which the safeguarding of the property is incidental to the primary purpose of the bailment, is liable for loss of or damage to the property, if it was caused due to his negligence; if the property is lost or damaged, the bailee must prove that he was not negligent.

502. *Borrower* – (a) A borrower is a bailee who holds the property in order to use it or to enjoy it in some other fashion, without giving any consideration for this.

(b) A borrower is liable for loss of or damage to the property regardless of the reason for such loss or damage.

503. *Liability of Hotel Owner* – (a) In this section –

"hotel" – including a place used for hospitality as a business, as well as the facilities and services that the hotel places at the disposal of its guests; "hotel owner" – including one who manages a hotel; "guest" – one who is provided with a place to sleep in a hotel.

(b) Regarding property that a guest has brought and that is in the hotel, the hotel owner is like a bailee for hire where the safeguarding is the primary purpose of his possession.

(c) If the property is money, securities or other valuables, subsection (b) will not apply unless the guest informed the hotel owner of them and transmitted them, in accordance with his request, for safeguarding, or deposited them in accordance with the customary arrangement in the hotel.

(d) The hotel owner is discharged from his liability pursuant to this section if he was not notified of loss of or damage to the property within a reasonable time after the guest knew or should have known of it.

504. *Urgent and Unanticipated Actions in Bailment* – A bailee may perform any urgent and unanticipated act reasonably necessary to safeguard the interests of the owner of the property in connection with the subject of the bailment as if the owner of the property had given him a power-of-attorney to do so.

505. *Bailee's Notice of Expected Damage* – Where it became known to the bailee that the property was likely to be damaged or lost, he shall notify the owner of the property of this within a reasonable period of time, or shall take reasonable measures in order to so notify him even if he is not liable for the damage or loss pursuant to sections 500 through 502. If he did not do so, he will be liable for the loss of or damage of the property notwithstanding the provisions of such sections, to the extent that the notice would have allowed the owner of the property to prevent it.

506. *Exception to Liability of Bailee* – Where property is lost or damaged due to a defect in it at the time it was given to the bailee, or due to normal wear and tear, and the loss or damage was not caused by the bailee's negligence, the bailee will not be liable for the loss or damage.

507. *Liability of Bailee who Exceeded the Terms of the Bailment* – A gratuitous bailee or a bailee for hire, who materially breached a condition from among the conditions of the bailment has the liability of a borrower, as long as such breach continues.

508. *Indemnification of Bailee* – (a) The owner of the property shall indemnify a gratuitous bailee and a bailee who holds a pledge or other security, for the reasonable ex-

penses he incurred and the reasonable obligations that he undertook due to the bailment.

(b) The owner of the property shall indemnify any bailee for the expenses he incurred and the obligations he undertook as a result of the act he performed as set forth in section 504.

509. *Property that the Owner did not Recover from the Bailee* – Where the bailee took reasonable measures to transmit the property in his possession to the owner of the property, but the owner of the property was not found or did not accept the property, the bailee may request the Administrator General to issue instructions with respect to the property and will not be liable for the loss or damage of the property if he acted in good faith pursuant to the instructions of the Administrator General. If the bailee was a bailee for hire or a borrower, his liability for loss or damage of the property and his right to indemnification shall be as that of a gratuitous bailee, even if he did not request instructions from the Administrator General.

510. *Secondary Bailee* – (a) Where the bailee fulfilled his obligation through a secondary bailee, the acts of the secondary bailee are regarded as those of the bailee and the secondary bailee is also liable towards the owner of the property to the same extent that he is liable toward the bailee.

(b) The provisions of subsection (a) will apply regardless of whether the transmission of the property was done with consent of the owner of the property, provided that there is nothing in them to derogate from the bailee's liability pursuant to section 507 or to any other legislation.

Chapter Two: Fiduciary Duty

511. *Substance of Fiduciary Duty* – A fiduciary duty is the duty of a person (in this chapter – the one owing the duty), towards another (in this chapter – the entitled) to fulfill his duty diligently, skillfully, with devotion and without negligence, and to act in good faith in the interest of the entitled and not in his own interest.

512. *Sources of Fiduciary Duty* – A fiduciary duty is created by law, contract or according to the circumstances.

513. *Fiduciary Duty According to the Circumstances* – A fiduciary duty is created by the circumstances, *inter alia*, where one of the following is fulfilled –

(1) the interests or property of the entitled are deposited with the one owing the duty with the consent of the one owing the duty, or pursuant to legislation, for their safeguarding or management for the benefit of the one entitled.

(2) the entitled deposited with the one owing the duty information, with the consent of the one owing the duty or pursuant to legislation, with the entitled relying reasonably on the one owing the duty not to transfer it to another and not making use of it for a purpose other than the purpose for which it was deposited;

(3) the one owing the duty provides service of a personal nature, dependent, due to its character, on the reliance of the one entitled on the integrity and fairness of the one owing the duty.

514. *Personal Performance of the Obligations of the One Owing the Duty* – The one owing the duty will fulfill his obligations and perform his duties personally, however he may be assisted by another person in so doing.

515. *Prohibition of Conflict of Interest* – The one owing the duty shall not be in a position of conflict of interest.

516. *Prohibition of Receiving Benefit* – The one owing the duty shall not receive any benefit from a third party with respect to the performance of his obligations.

517. *Disclosure by the One Owing the Duty* – The one owing the duty will provide the entitled with any material information and documents regarding the fulfillment of the obligations imposed upon him, provided that giving them to the entitled is reasonably necessary.

518. *Duty of Confidentiality of the One Owing the Duty* – The one owing the duty will not transmit to another information given him by the entitled or by a third party, for the purpose of fulfilling the obligations imposed upon him, or information that reached him due to fulfilling such obligations, and he will make no use of such information other than for the purpose of fulfilling his obligations.

519. *Condition of Discharge in Fiduciary Duty* – A condition discharging the one owing the duty from liability for an act that has not yet been carried out shall be void in either of the following –

(1) where the condition is a sweeping condition;

(2) where the condition discharges the one owing the duty from an act that constitutes a breach of the fiduciary duty with malicious intent.

Sub-Part Six: Remedies for Breach of Obligation

Chapter One: General

520. *Definitions for Sub-Part Remedies for Breach of Obligation* – In this sub-part –

"enforcement" – regardless of whether it is in an order or an injunction, including an order for repayment of a monetary debt and an order to amend or remove the consequences of the breach.

"fundamental breach" of contract –

(1) a breach that results in the injured party being substantially denied that which he would have been entitled to expect under the contract, unless the party who breached the contract could not have anticipated such a result at the time the contract was entered into, and in the circumstances under which the contract was made.

(2) a breach that, according to the terms agreed upon under the contract, is a fundamental breach; however, a condition in a contract that provides in a sweeping manner that various breaches shall be fundamental is invalid unless it was reasonable at the time the contract was entered into;

"wages" – including income from a business, from work or from an occupation;

"dependents" – descendants of the deceased, his spouse, his parents and his grandparents, his brothers and sisters, and any other person who is a member of his household.

521. *Obligation to Abstain from Torts* – For the purposes of this subpart, the obligation to abstain from a tort is regarded as an obligation.

522. *Right to Remedies* – Where an obligation has been breached, the injured party is entitled to the remedies granted to him pursuant to this sub-part from the one who breached.

Chapter Two: Enforcement of Obligation

524. *Right to Enforcement* – (a) The injured party is entitled to enforcement of the obligation, except in the case that one of the following exists –

(1) the obligation cannot be fulfilled;

(2) the obligation is to perform or receive personal work or services;

(3) fulfillment of the enforcement order requires an unreasonable amount of supervision under the auspices of the Court or the Execution of Judgments Office;

(4) enforcement of the obligation would be unjust under the circumstances;

(5) enforcement of the obligation contravenes the character of the obligation.

(b) The provision of subsection (a)(4) shall not apply to either of the following –

(1) a monetary debt under contract, provided that the injured party fulfilled his obligations under the contract that entitle him to payment of the debt, without the breaching party having objected to the performance of the obligations;

(2) an obligation to refrain from infringing upon a right in land or moveable property, unless the Court found that there are special reasons for acting otherwise.

525. *Approximate Enforcement* – Where the injured party was not entitled to enforcement of the obligation pursuant to the provisions of section 524, the Court may, upon petition of the injured party, order approximate enforcement of the obligation, provided that this shall not change the substance of the obligation and shall not cause injustice to the breaching party; approximate enforcement shall be treated like enforcement.

526. *Deadline for Enforcement* – The Court may set forth in the enforcement order the date for fulfilling the enforcement of the obligation, which shall be later than the date upon which the order was rendered.

527. *Conditions for Enforcement of an Obligation* – The Court may condition the enforcement of the obligation on conditions that are necessary due to the circumstances of the matter.

Chapter Three: Rescission of Contract due to Breach

528. *Rescission of Contract due to Fundamental Breach* – Where there was fundamental breach of the contract, the injured party is entitled to rescind the contract.

529. *Rescission of Contract due to Breach that is not Fundamental* –

(a) Where there was a breach of the contract that was not fundamental, the injured party is entitled to rescind the contract, after he has given the breaching party a reasonable extension of time in which to fulfill the contract and the breaching party did not fulfill the contract within the extended time period.

(b) Subsection (a) shall not apply if the rescission was unjust under the circumstances, provided that the breaching party objected to the rescission within a reasonable time after receiving notice of the rescission.

530. *Rescission of Contract that can be Separated into Parts* – Where the contract is severable and one of its parts was breached, the provisions of section 182 shall apply.

Chapter Four: Compensation

Article One: Purpose of Compensation and Standard of Distancing the Damage

531. *Compensation for Damage* – The injured party is entitled to compensation from the breaching party for the damage caused him due to the breach and its consequences.

532. *Purpose of Compensation* – The purpose of compensation for a breach is to put the

injured party, to the extent possible, in the position he would have been in were it not for the breach.

533. *Remoteness of Damage due to Breach of Contract* – Compensation for breach of contract as set forth in section 531 will be made only for damage that the breaching party anticipated or should have anticipated at the time the contract was entered into, as a likely result of the breach.

534. *Remoteness of Damage due to Tort* – Compensation for a tort, as set forth in section 531 will only be made for damage that was likely to be caused in a natural manner in the normal course of things and that was directly caused by the wrongdoing of the breaching party.

Article Two: Additional Provisions Regarding Compensation

535. *Mitigation of Damages* – (a) The breaching party is not obligated to pay compensation for damage that the injured party could have prevented or mitigated with reasonable efforts.

(b) Where the injured party incurred reasonable expenses to prevent or mitigate the damage or undertook reasonable obligations for this purpose, the breaching party must indemnify him for them, regardless of whether or not the damage was prevented or mitigated; if the expenses or obligations were unreasonable, the breaching party is obligated to indemnify him for the reasonable amount under the circumstances.

(c) The provisions of this section will not apply to augmented compensation, compensation without need to prove damages and agreed upon compensation as set forth in Article Four of this chapter.

536. *Actions of the Injured Party that Aggravated the Damage* – Where the injured party took reasonable steps to prevent or mitigate the damage and such steps aggravated the damage to the injured party in comparison with his damage had he not taken such steps, the breaching party shall be liable to compensate him for this damage as well.

537. *Contributory Negligence* – Where an injured party's negligence has contributed to the damage caused to him, the court may deduct a sum from the compensation due to the injured party in an amount that the court finds appropriate in accordance with the extent of the injured party's contribution to the damage. Section 439 will apply to the question of causation of the damage by the injured party, *mutatis mutandis*.

538. *Deduction of Benefits from the Right to Compensation* – Benefits that the injured party was directly entitled to as a result of the breach shall be deducted from the compensation due him, subject to the provisions of any legislation.

539. *Capitalization of Compensation for Financial Damage* – (a) A one-time payment of compensation for financial damage that will be caused in the future shall be capitalized and the capitalization shall be calculated on the basis of three percent annual interest.

(b) The Minister of Justice, with the approval of the Finance Minister, may issue an order to change the interest rate set forth in subsection (a).

540. *Calculation of Wage of Injured or Deceased Person* – In establishing the wage of an injured or deceased person for the purposes of this chapter, the wage shall be calculated without deduction of taxes and other compulsory payments paid according to law.

541. *Calculation of Compensation by way of Estimate* – Where the court found that the amount of damage caused to the injured person has not been proven, it may award damages by way of estimate, provided that it was convinced that it was reasonable under the circumstances that damage was caused, but there is no reasonable possibility to establish the amount.

Article Three: Compensation for Bodily Injury

542. *Compensation For Bodily Injury* – An injured party to whom bodily injury was caused is entitled to compensation for each of the following:

(1) damage to his earning abilities;

(2) expenses for bodily injury, including medical care, assistance, rehabilitation, aid from a third person, machinery, accessories and movement aids.

(3) damage that is not monetary damage including –

(a) pain and suffering associated with bodily injury, including loss of enjoyment of life;

(b) shortened life expectancy.

543. *Compensation for Damage to Earning Ability* – Compensation for damage to earning ability of an injured person shall be in an amount consistent with the monetary damage caused or to be caused in the future in fact, as a result of his decreased earning ability after the breach, in comparison with his earning ability had the breach not occurred.

544. *Calculation of the Compensation for Shortened Life Expectancy* – Where the life expectancy of an injured person has been shortened due to the breach, the injured party shall be entitled, during his lifetime, to compensation for the monetary damage that his descendents are liable to suffer as a result thereof, throughout the period of shortened life expectancy, according to the degree of dependency on the deceased during that period; the Court may issue instructions in this matter as it shall deem proper to ensure the interests of the dependents.

Article Four: Compensation for Death

545. *Compensation to the Estate for Death of Injured Party* – Where a person has died, the estate is entitled –

(1) to the compensation to which such person would have been entitled had he not died, however, it is not entitled to compensation for the impairment of the deceased's earning ability for the period after his death;

(2) to compensation for the burial costs of the deceased, including mourning costs.

546. *Rights of the Deceased's Dependents* – Where a person has died due to a breach, and that person, had he not died, would have been entitled to compensation because of the breach, his dependents are entitled to compensation for the monetary damage that they suffered or will suffer in the future due to his death, according to the degree of dependency on the deceased.

547. *Calculation of Compensation to Dependents* – In calculating compensation to dependents of the deceased, the court shall not consider the chances of the surviving spouse to find another spouse.

548. *Bereavement Compensation to Relatives of Deceased* – (a) Each of the relatives of the deceased is entitled to bereavement compensation in the amount of one-third of the ceiling on compensation for damages that are not monetary damages, pursuant to section 4(a)(3) of the Compensation to Victims of Road Accidents Law, 5735–1975.[31]

(b) In this section, "relative" – each of these:

(1) spouse;

(2) parent;

(3) the deceased's children, including those born after his death.

(c) The amount of compensation to all of those entitled pursuant to this section, shall

[31] *Sefer HaHukim* 5735, p. 234.

not exceed double the amount that is the ceiling on compensation for damages that are not monetary damages as set forth in subsection (a).

Article Five: Periodic Payments

549. *Compensation in Periodic Payments* – The court may order that compensation for monetary damage caused due to bodily injury will be paid, in whole or in part, in periodic payments.

550. *Securities for the Guarantee of Periodic Payments* – (a) The court may order that suitable securities be given to guarantee the periodic payments.

(b) The Minister of Justice may promulgate regulations in this matter.

551. *Linkage of Periodic Payments to the Index* – The obligation to pay compensation in periodic payments will be linked to the Consumer Price Index that is published by the Central Bureau of Statistics beginning from the date the decision was rendered by the Court, unless the Court ordered linkage to another index.

552. *Increase or Decrease of Periodic Payments* – (a) Where the Court ordered compensation in periodic payments, the Court may, upon petition of one of the parties –

(1) order an increase in the periodic payments if it found that there has been a significant change in the circumstances that formed the basis for the decision regarding periodic payments;

(2) to rule on the decrease or termination of periodic payments if it found that there was an radical change in the circumstances that formed the basis for such decision.

(b) A petition as set forth in subsection (a) shall not be submitted prior to the passing of one year from the date the previous decision with regard to compensation was rendered, unless the court permitted this for special cause.

553. *Death of Injured Party After Award of Periodic Payments* – Where the injured party died after he was awarded periodic payments, the estate is entitled to a one-time payment in the amount of the periodic payments that have not yet been paid, after capitalization.

554. *Conversion of Periodic Payments* – The court may, at any time, convert periodic payments to a one-time payment.

555. *Contract Regarding Periodic Payments that were Awarded* – Where the parties entered into a contract that changes the amounts of the periodic payments or the time of payments, after they were awarded, such contract is subject to court approval.

Article Six: Amelioration of Damage

556. *Substance of Amelioration of Damages* – Amelioration of damages means the expenses incurred or service rendered in order to correct bodily injury, to prevent aggravation of the injury or additional injury or to lessen the injured party's suffering, including support given to the injured party for his upkeep and that of his household, as is necessitated due to the injury and, if the injured party died, such support that was given to a person entitled to compensation from the breaching party as a result.

557. *Assignment of Benefactor's Rights* – (a) Where damage has been caused to the injured party due to a breach and his damage was ameliorated by a benefactor, the rights of the injured party to compensation are transferred to the benefactor in a sum equal to the ratio between the amount of the amelioration of the damage and the total damage, provided that such sum does not bring about an increase in the amount of compensation that would have been awarded but for the amelioration.

(b) With regard to this article it is immaterial whether the source of the amelioration is a statutory obligation, a contractual obligation, or a voluntary act.

558. *Benefactor's Right* – (a) The right accorded to the benefactor pursuant to this arti-

cle is for expenses, wages for services or payment for the purpose of support, provided that they are reasonable.

(b) Wages paid to an employee who has been found to be unfit to work, or to the dependents of an injured party shall be considered to be a reasonable expense, provided that they are not greater than the wages that would have been paid to the injured party had bodily injury not been caused to him.

559. *Ensuring the Right of the Benefactor* – An injured party who received a benefit or who is entitled to receive a benefit due to injury on the basis of which he filed an action for compensation, shall give notice of the filing of such action to a benefactor to whom rights have been transferred pursuant to section 557.

560. *Exception to Amelioration of Damages* – (a) The following payments shall not be considered as amelioration of damages and shall not be taken into account in setting the amount of compensation –

(1) insurance benefits, with the exception of insurance benefits paid by a corporation that insures only its members;

(2) sums that the injured party is required to return to the benefactor.

(b) This section will apply, subject to the provisions of the chapter regarding insurance contracts.[32]

Article Seven: Compensation for Property Damage

561. *Compensation for Damage that cannot be Reasonably Repaired* – Where the owner or possessor of property incurred damage due to the loss of property, or damage to the property that cannot be repaired in a reasonable manner, he is entitled to compensation for each of the following –

(1) expenses for the acquisition of property identical to that which was lost or damaged, including auxiliary expenses; where identical property cannot reasonably be acquired, the injured party shall be entitled to expenses for the acquisition of property similar to that which was lost or damaged, including auxiliary expenses;

(2) the necessary expenses for making the property acquired suitable for the intended use, as set forth in clause (1);

(3) loss with respect to the benefit that the injured party could have derived from the property, including the loss of proceeds and profits.

562. *Compensation for Damages that can be Reasonably Repaired* – (a) Where the owner or possessor of property incurred damage due to damage to the property, and the damage can be repaired in a reasonable manner, he is entitled to compensation for each of the following –

(1) expenses for the repair of the property, its installation and making it suitable for renewed use, including auxiliary expenses, provided that the compensation pursuant to this clause shall not exceed the decrease in value that was prevented by the repair;

(2) the decrease in the value of the property, which shall be calculated as the difference between the value of the property prior to the damage and its value after it was repaired;

(3) loss with respect to the effectiveness that the injured party could have derived from the property in the past, including the loss of proceeds and profits.

(b) An injured party shall not be entitled to compensation pursuant to the provisions

[32] Chapter Nine in Subpart Three of this Part (Part Four) (sections 343 through 416).

of subsection (a) in a sum that exceeds the sum to which he would have been entitled had the provisions of section 561 been applicable to him.

Article Eight: Compensation for Non-Monetary Damage

563. *Non-Monetary Damage* – Where non-monetary damage has been caused, and such damage is not the result of bodily injury, the court may award damages to him for such damage in an amount that it finds appropriate under the circumstances.

Article Nine: Compensation for Non-Monetary Damage

564. *Enhanced Compensation* – none

565. *Compensation for Breach of Monetary Obligation* – Where a monetary obligation has been breached, the injured party is entitled to compensation for the amount of the payment that is in arrears, without the need to prove damages, from the day of the breach until the day that payment is made, in the amount of the linkage differential and the interest pursuant to the Adjudication of Interest Law, unless the court has ordered a different amount.

566. *Compensation for Breach of Duty Regarding Property or Service* – Where a duty to provide or to receive property or services was breached, and the contract was rescinded due to the breach, the injured party is entitled to compensation in the amount of the difference between the consideration set forth in the contract for the property or the services and the value of the property or the services on the day the contract was rescinded, without the need to prove damages.

567. *Exception to Compensation without Proof of Damages* – The provisions of sections 565 and 566 do not derogate from the injured party's right to compensation pursuant to other provisions of this chapter, however, if there was no consideration for the duty, or the consideration was unreasonable, the Court may decrease the amount of compensation to the injured party to the amount of compensation provided for in sections 565 and 566.

568. *Agreed Upon Compensation* – (a) Where the contract sets forth the amount of compensation for a breach, the injured party is entitled to the compensation set forth, without proof of damages (in this article – agreed upon compensation).

(b) Amounts paid by the breaching party to the injured party prior to the breach will be considered agreed upon compensation, provided that the parties agreed at the outset that if the contract is breached such amounts will be forfeited to the benefit of the injured party.

569. *Exception to Agreed Upon Compensation* – (a) The court may reduce the amount of agreed upon compensation if it was set without any reasonable regard to the damage that could have been foreseen as a reasonable result of the breach at the time the contract was made.

(b) Where the contract provides for agreed upon compensation, such provision does not, in and of itself, derogate from the injured party's right to claim compensation pursuant to other provisions of this chapter, or any other remedy for the breach in place of such agreed upon compensation.

Chapter Five: Restitution

570. *Restitution for Rescission of Contract* – (a) Where a contract has been rescinded due to its breach, each party must restore to the other party whatever he received pursuant to the contract, and if restitution in kind is impossible or unreasonable – to pay him the value of what he received.

(b) Notwithstanding the provisions of subsection (a), the injured party may choose to restore value to the breaching party even if restitution in kind is possible and reasonable; similarly, the injured party may demand payment of value of what he received rather than restitution in kind.

571. *Application of Unjust Enrichment Chapter to Restitution* – The chapter on Unjust Enrichment shall apply to the right to restitution, subject to the provisions of this chapter.

Chapter Six: Remedies for Anticipated Breach

572. *Right to Remedies for Anticipatory Breach* – Where an obligated party indicates his intention not to perform his obligation or where it is clear from the circumstances that it is nearly certain that there will be a breach, the injured party shall be entitled to all of the remedies set forth in this subpart, *mutatis mutandis*; however an order for enforcement of the obligation shall not be made that instructs that the obligation be performed at a date earlier than the date agreed upon for performance.

Chapter Seven: Additional Remedies

573. *Tolling of Performance of Obligations* – Where there has been a fundamental breach of a contract, the injured party is entitled to suspend the performance of his obligations until the breaching party performs his obligations.

574. *Remedy of Reduction* – (a) Where an obligation to make property or a piece of work suitable has been breached, the injured party is entitled to make a deduction from the consideration, provided that the breaching party was first given a reasonable opportunity to correct the deviation but he did not correct it within a reasonable period of time.

(b) Where the injured party paid the consideration for the property or the work, he is entitled to restitution of the sum that he would have been entitled to deduct pursuant to subsection (a), had he not paid the consideration.

(c) The deduction from the consideration for the property or work shall be calculated in accordance with the amount by which the value has been reduced due to the deviation, as opposed to the value were it not for the deviation; the value of the property or of the work shall be determined according to its value at the time the contract was entered into.

575. *Preventive Order* – (a) Where the court gave an enforcement order it may, if it deems it appropriate –

(1) issue an order requiring the breaching party to pay a sum that it determines for each day on which the breaching party has not complied with the enforcement order (in this section – the preventive order);

(2) provide for the beginning date of the preventive order and it may provide that the beginning date shall be a date later than the date that the enforcement order was issued.

(b) The issuance of a preventive order does not derogate from the validity of an enforcement order.

Part Five: Property

Sub-Part One: Provisions Regarding All Property

Chapter One: General Provisions

576. *Definitions for the Part on Property* – In this part –

"apartment" – a room or compartment, or a number of rooms or compartments, that were intended for use as a residence, a business or for another purpose, that constitute a complete and separate unit.

"possessor of property" – regardless of whether he has direct control of the property or the direct control of the property is vested with a person who possesses the property under his auspices;

"Inspector" – one appointed pursuant to section 117 of the Land Law and in whose area of jurisdiction the property in question is located;

"land registers" – as that term is used in section 123 of the Land Law.

577. *Validity of Property Right* – A property right is valid with respect to any person.

578. *Rights in Property Pursuant to Law* – There are no rights in property except as provided by law.

579. *Property Transaction* – A transaction in property is the granting of a right in the property in accordance with the wishes of the grantor, except in the case of inheritance in accordance with a will.

Chapter Two: Protection of Property Right

580. *Demand for Surrender of Property* – Where a person has unlawfully taken possession of property, the owner of the property, one who is entitled to possess it and one who possessed it at the time may demand its surrender from such person.

581. *Protection of Use of Property* – The owner of property, or one who possesses or uses it is entitled to demand from anyone who has no right to possess or use it, to refrain from any act that constitutes an interference with the use of the property.

582. *Availing Oneself of Remedies* – (a) The one who possesses property may use a reasonable degree of force in order to prevent trespassing upon it or the unlawful denial of his control of the property.

(b) Where a person has unlawfully seized property, one who possesses the property at that time may use a reasonable degree of force within fifteen days of the day of the seizure in order to take it from the one who seized it.

583. *The Right of the Possessor of Property to Restitution* – (a) One who removed property from the possessor without being entitled to do so pursuant to the provision of section 582(b) shall return it to the possessor.

(b) The provision of subsection (a) shall not prevent the court from adjudicating the rights of the parties mentioned in that subsection simultaneously, and it may regulate the possession of the property as it deems just and under the conditions as it may view as proper, pending a decision regarding their rights.

Chapter Three: Competition of Rights

584. *Granting of Property Rights* – A person may not grant rights in property that exceed his rights in such property unless provided otherwise in legislation.

585. *Acquisition Inconsistent with Prior Right in theProperty* – In acquiring a right in property as set forth below, the right transfers to the one acquiring it when it is free of any prior right in the property and any encumbrance –

(1) in the acquisition of ownership of moveable property- if the one who acquired the ownership in the property acquired it from one who deals in the sale of property of the same kind as the property in question, and the sale was in the normal course of his business, in good faith and for consideration;

(2) in the acquisition of property that is settled land – if the one who acquired the right in the property did so in good faith, for consideration and in reliance on the registration in the land registers, even if such registration was incorrect; for this purpose, "settled land" means land that was registered after settlement pursuant to the Land (Settlement of Title) Ordinance [New Version], 5729–1969;[33]

(3) in an assignment of right – if the assignee acquired the right in good faith and for consideration and the assignor or or the assignee informed the debtor of said assignment before he was informed of a prior assignment or prior encumbrance, as the case may be.

586. *Conflicting Acquisition from an Authority* – Where a property is sold by court, the Execution of Judgments Office or another authority pursuant to law, the ownership is transferred to the one who has acquired it free of any prior right or encumbrance.

587. *Redemption of Property from the one Acquiring it* – Where a right in property has been acquired as set forth in sections 585 and 586, the previous owner of the right may, within one year from the date of acquisition, redeem it from the one who acquired it, or the one who acquired it from such acquirer without consideration, by paying its value at the time of redemption, unless a material change occurred to the property during that time period; the one who redeems a right in property pursuant to this section shall indemnify the acquirer for the expenses incurred by him with respect to the acquisition of the right.

588. *Conflicting Rights with Respect to Property* – (a) Where a person has undertaken to bestow a right in property, or he is required to do so pursuant to law, and before the right has been transferred to the one entitled (in this chapter – the first entitled person), he undertook a conflicting transaction with regard to another person (in this chapter – the second entitled person), the right of the first entitled person shall prevail; however, if the second entitled person acquired the right in good faith and for consideration – his right prevails.

(b) Notwithstanding the provisions of subsection (a), where the property that is the subject of the commitment is land and the first entitled person negligently failed to register a cautionary note in the land registers, the right of the second entitled party shall prevail if he registered such a cautionary note in good faith and for consideration.

(c) The provisions of this section shall apply, *mutatis mutandis*, in each of the following –

(1) where the commitment or the obligation pursuant to law with respect to the first entitled party is to refrain from bestowing a right in the property;

(2) where the undertaking to the second entitled person was given in breach of a duty imposed upon a trustee toward a beneficiary pursuant to the conditions of the trust.

---

[33] *Dinei Medinat Yisrael, Nusakh Chadash*, p. 293.

588A. *Conflicting attachment* – (a) Where a person has undertaken to bestow a right in property to another person or is required to do so pursuant to law, and before the right has been transferred to the one entitled, an attachment was placed on the property that conflicts with the right of the first entitled person, the right of the first entitled person shall prevail.

(b) The provisions of subsection (a) shall not apply to undertakings without consideration upon fulfillment of the one of the conditions specified in section 182, *mutatis mutandis*.

Chapter Four: Joint Ownership of Property

Article One: Joint Ownership Relationships

589. *Joint Ownership of Property* – Where property is owned by several owners, the ownership of each of them, according to his share, extends over the whole of the property.

590. *Applicability of the Chapter on Property Right that is not Ownership* – The provisions of this chapter shall apply, *mutatis mutandis*, to rights in property that are not ownership, when they are of a number of people.

591. *Size of Share of Joint Owners* – The shares of each joint owner in property is presumed to be equal.

592. *Joint Ownership Contract* – (a) A joint ownership contract is a contract between joint owners in property regarding the management and use of the property, and regarding their rights and obligations with respect to the property.

(b) In the absence of other provisions in the joint ownership contract, the provisions of sections 594 and 596 through 599 shall apply.

593. *Validity of Joint Ownership Contract* – A joint ownership contract is also valid with respect to a person acting pursuant to a power-of-attorney of a joint owner, and with respect to a person who becomes a joint owner after the contract has been entered into (in this section – a third party), as detailed herein –

(1) with respect to property that is land, and the joint ownership is in a right that is subject to registration in the land registers – if the joint ownership contract was registered in the land registers; where the joint ownership contract was not so registered, it will be valid with respect to a third party who knew of it;

(2) with respect to moveable property or a right – if a third party knew of or should have known of the contract.

594. *Majority Decision In Joint Property* – (a) The owners of the majority of the shares in the jointly owned property may determine all matters relating to the ordinary management and use of the property.

(b) A joint owner who considers himself aggrieved by a determination pursuant to subsection (a) may apply to the court for instructions in the matter, and the Court shall order as it deems appropriate; this subsection shall apply notwithstanding any provision in the joint ownership contract.

(c) Any determination regarding a matter outside of the scope of ordinary management and use requires the consent of all of the joint owners.

595. *Court Instructions Regarding Management and Use of Property* – In the absence of a determination pursuant to section 594, the court may give instructions regarding the management or use of the joint property.

596. *Rights of Individual Joint Owner* – (a) Subject to sections 592 through 595 and instructions given pursuant to those sections, each joint owner may, of his own accord –

(1) make reasonable use of the property, provided that he does not prevent the reasonable use of another joint owner interested in such use;
(2) transfer his rights in the property or effect any transaction with respect thereof;
(3) do all that is reasonably necessary to prevent damage to the property and to protect the ownership, possession or use thereof;
(4) perform any urgent and unanticipated act for the proper maintenance and management of the property.

(b) A joint owner shall give notice regarding an act pursuant to subsection (a)(2) as set forth below –
(1) to the one to whom rights have been transferred – regarding the existence of the joint ownership contract and its terms, if there is such a contract -prior to carrying out the transaction;
(2) to the other joint owners – of carrying out the act as soon as possible after it was carried out.

(c) A joint owner shall notify the other joint owners of his intention to act pursuant to subsection (a)(3) or (a)(4) prior to carrying out the act, insofar as this is possible; where it cannot be done and the joint owner has carried out the act, he shall notify the other joint owners of it as soon as possible.

(d) A stipulation in a joint ownership contract that denies or restricts any right referred to in subsection (a)(2) shall be valid for a period of no more than five years.

597. *Right to Proceeds* – A joint owner is entitled to a share in the proceeds of the property, in accordance with his share in the property.

598. *Expenses of the Joint Ownership of the Property* – A joint owner shall bear the necessary expenses for the proper maintenance and management of the joint property in accordance with his share in the property.

599. *Payment for Use* – A joint owner who has used the joint property shall pay suitable fees for such use to the other joint owners, in accordance with their shares in the property.

Article Two: Severance of Joint Ownership

600. *Right to Claim Severance of Joint Ownership* – (a) Each joint owner is entitled to demand the severance of the joint ownership, at any time.

(b) A stipulation denying or restricting the right to severance is not valid for a period exceeding five years.

601. *Manner of Severance* – (a) The severance of joint ownership shall be in accordance with a contract between the joint owners; a contract for the partition of the land itself is subject to the certification of the Inspector that the partition is in conformity with the provisions of the Planning and Construction Law or any other relevant legislation.

(b) Where there is no contract between the joint owners, the severance shall be by court order in accordance with sections 602 through 606.

602. *Severance of Joint Ownership by Partition or Sale* – (a) Where there is no legislative barrier to partition and partition will not cause substantial loss to any of the joint owners, the court shall issue a severance order requiring the partition of the property and it may require a joint owner to make equalization payments to another joint owner and to determine the amount of the payment and its conditions, including the ways of ensuring such payment; where the property is land – the court may order the creation of an easement in the property and may order that the easement be registered.

(b) (1) Where there is a legislative barrier to partition of the property or its partition will cause a substantial loss to one of the joint owners, the court shall, in the severance order, order that the property be sold and the division of proceeds of the sale; sale of the property shall be in the manner in which encumbered property of the same kind is sold in execution of judgment proceedings, unless the court saw fit to order a different manner of sale.

(2) Where one of the joint owners attached fixtures to land and the joint ownership of such land is severed by sale as set forth in clause (1), and the price obtained in the sale is lower than the price that would have been obtained in a sale of the land without the fixtures, the joint owner who attached the fixtures shall pay the difference between the two prices to the other joint owners according to their shares. Where the price obtained from the sale of the land exceeded the price that would have been obtained from the sale without the fixtures, the joint owner who attached the fixtures is entitled to reimbursement of his investment in the fixtures from the other joint owners pursuant to the provisions of the Unjust Enrichment chapter.[34]

(c) With respect to moveable property, the court may order the severance of the joint ownership in ways other than those set forth in subsections (a) and (b).

603. *Winding-up by way of Conversion into Condominium* – (a) Where the joint property consists mainly of a house eligible for registration as a condominium, the court may, after receiving the Inspector's opinion, order the severance of the joint ownership by way of registration of the house in the Register of Condominiums and the allocation of apartments in it to the joint owners according to their shares. The provisions of section 602(a) shall apply regarding equalization payments.

(b) A severance order in the manner described in subsection (a) may also be issued pursuant to the application of the owners of apartments whose total area does not comprise half of the area of the owners of apartments in the buildings.

604. *Severance in Special Cases* – (a) Where legislation prevents the partition of jointly owned land in kind, or where such partition is unreasonable (in this section – prevention of partition) regarding one of the owners only, and such owner has land abutting the jointly owned land and he agreed that his share shall be joined to the abutting land, the land shall be partitioned accordingly.

(b) Where partition of the land is prevented with regard to all of the joint owners, however it will be possible to carry out the partition if some of the joint owners take their shares jointly, and such joint owners have agreed to do so, the land shall be partitioned accordingly.

(c) Where partition of the land is prevented with regard to some of the joint owners, the other joint owners may retain the land jointly among themselves or may partition it among themselves according to their relative shares in the property, unless they agreed otherwise, provided that they pay to the other joint owners the value of their shares in the land if it had been sold as set forth in section 602(b).

605. *Severance of Joint Ownership Of Spousal Residential Apartment* – Where the court issued a severance order regarding joint property that is the apartment of a couple used by them as a residence or the rights in such an apartment, it will not order execution of the order and the sale shall be delayed, as long as it is not convinced that the minor children of the couple and the spouse who has custody of them have, together, another living

[34] Chapter Two in Subpart Four in Part Four (sections 487 through 496).

arrangement suitable to their needs, including a temporary living arrangement suitable to their needs, for a period of time as shall be determined.

606. *Requests of Joint Owners Regarding the Joint Ownership* – (a) The Court will, to the extent possible, take into consideration the request of some of the joint owners to maintain the joint ownership between them and other requests of the joint owners or some of them.

(b) Where a joint owner installed fixtures to jointly owned land, in the order for severance of the joint ownership, the court shall, to the extent possible, determine the parcel of the owner who installed the fixtures so that it includes such fixtures.

607. *Management and Use Pending Severance* – Where an application for severance has been filed, the court may make a temporary order regarding the management and use of the property pending completion of the severance proceedings.

Article Three: Shared Boundaries

608. *Shared Boundaries* – (a) Notwithstanding the provisions of section 613(b), walls, fences, trees, fixtures and the like on the boundary between abutting pieces of land (in this article – boundary fixtures), are presumed to be jointly owned by the owners of such land.

(b) Each of the land owners may use the boundary fixtures for the purpose for which they were installed, and he must participate in the necessary expenses in order to maintain them in proper condition, according to the ratio agreed upon between them, and where there is no such agreement, in equal parts, unless the extent of the use of each of the owners of the land of the boundary fixtures was different.

609. *Severance of Jointly Owned Boundary* – Notwithstanding the provisions of section 600, a joint owner is not entitled to demand severance regarding the boundary fixtures.

610. *Produce that has Fallen from Plants Near the Boundary* – If fruit of trees or other vegetation that grows on or near the boundary has fallen

(1) into the neighboring land it belong to the neighbor;

(2) into a public place it is ownerless.

611. *Vegetation that has Spread* – Where the branches or roots of trees or other vegetation that grow on or near the boundary have spread into the area of the neighboring land, and this may cause damage to such land or interfere , to a substantial extent, with the use or enjoyment of the land, the owner or the possessor of the neighboring land may demand that the owner of the vegetation or his joint owners of the boundary remove the growth that has spread into said area. Where the demand was not complied with within a reasonable period of time, the owner or possessor of the neighboring land may himself remove what has spread into the area of land and demand that the owner of the vegetation or his joint owners of the boundary, as is the case, reimburse him for the reasonable expenses he incurred for this purpose.

Sub-Part Two: Property Rights

Chapter One: Ownership

612. *Ownership* – Ownership is a permanent right to possess and to use property, a right to its proceeds, to destroy it and to do anything with respect to it and any transaction regarding it, subject to restrictions pursuant to legislation or contract.

613. *Area of Land Ownership* – (a) Ownership of land applies to the entire depth beneath the surface of the land that can be practically exploited and it extends to the air-

space above the land that can be practically exploited, subject to laws regarding passage through such airspace and regarding water, petroleum, mines, quarries and the like.

(b) Land ownership also extends to that which is built or planted on it and to any other thing permanently fixed to it.

Chapter Two: Rental and Borrowing

614. *Lease* – Lease is the right that is conveyed for consideration to possess and use property on a non-permanent basis.

615. *Tenancy* – Tenancy is the lease of land for a period of more than five years.

616. *Long-Term Tenancy* – Long-term tenancy is the lease of land for a period of more than twenty-five years.

617. *Registration of Lease of Land* – (a) Notwithstanding the provisions of sections 712 and 713, the lease of land for a period of not more than ten years does not require registration in the land registers.

(b) The provisions of subsection (a) shall not apply to a lease that is one of the following:

(1) a lease for a period of time that will expire more than ten years from the day the lease agreement was entered into;

(2) a lease with respect to which there is an option to lease or a stipulation allowing extension of the term of lease for an aggregate term of more than ten years, or an extension for an aggregate term that will expire more than ten years from the day the lease was entered into.

618. *Registration of lease Exempt from Registration* – A lease that does not require registration may be registered with consent of the parties.

619. *Requirement of Writing for an Obligation to Lease* – (a) Notwithstanding the provisions of section 714, an obligation to lease land for a term of not more than five years does not require written documentation.

(b) Subsection (a) shall not apply to a lease containing an option to extend its term for an aggregate term that exceeds five years.

620. *Completion of Granting Leasing Rights* – (a) The granting of leasing rights in a property that is not land or in land where the lease does not require registration, is completed at the time and in the manner to which the parties agreed; in the absence of another agreement, granting the lease of rights is completed as set forth below –

(1) with respect to property that is not land – at the time that the property is made available to the lessee;

(2) with respect to property that is land, where the lease does not require registration – at the time that the possession is given to the lessee, or at the time the right is registered, whichever is earlier.

(b) The granting of a right of lease in land, where the lease requires registration, is completed upon registration as set forth in section 712.

621. *Transactions Regarding Rights in Lease* – (a) A lessee may not perform transactions in his right without the consent of the lessor.

(b) Notwithstanding the provisions of subsection (a), a lessee whose right was registered in the lands register is entitled to encumber his right in a mortgage or in an easement even without the lessor's consent.

622. *Refusal of Lessor to Perform Transaction* – (a) The lessor shall not refuse to give his consent to the performance of a transaction by the lessee in his right, as set forth in sec-

tion 621(a), other than for just cause and he may not set forth unreasonable conditions for the granting of his consent to perform the transaction.

(b) Where the lessor of a lease of property that is not land has refused to consent to the transaction, in violation of the provisions of subsection (a), the court may permit the transaction under conditions it shall determine.

(c) Where the lessor of a lease of land has refused to consent to the transaction, in violation of the provisions of subsection (a), the lessee may perform the transaction despite the lessor's refusal and the court may permit the transaction under conditions it shall determine, notwithstanding what is set forth in the lease contract.

623. *Transfer of Lessee's Obligations* – The provisions of sections 621 and 622 will also apply to assignment of obligations of the lessee to another person, provided that he transfers his right in the lease together with said obligations.

624. *Right of Lessee with regard to Third Party* – (a) Once the right in the lease has been conferred upon the lessee, the right is valid with respect to any person.

(b) The lessor may confer his right in the leased property to another (in this section – the acquirer); once he has done so, the rights and obligations of the lessor pursuant to the lease contract and pursuant to any law, whose time for performance is after the completion of the conferment of the rights, are viewed as assigned to the acquirer even if the acquirer did not know of the existence of the lease.

(c) A claim that the lessee has against the lessor due to non-performance of obligations imposed on the lessor before the completion of the conferment of the right will continue to be valid against the acquirer.

Article Two: Borrowing

625. *Borrowing* – Borrowing is a right that is conferred without consideration, to possess and use property on a non-permanent basis.

626. *Applicability to Borrowing* – The provisions of sections 617, 620 and 624(a) shall also apply, *mutatis mutandis*, to borrowing.

627. *Transactions in Right to Borrow* – A borrower is not entitled to perform a transaction in his right, including providing another with the right to use the property or joint use with another of the property, unless the lender consents.

Chapter Three: Pledge

Sections 628 through 668 – a proposal for a new version of the Pledge Law is integrated in the Explanatory Notes.

Chapter Four: Lien

669. *Definitions for the Chapter on Lien* – In this chapter –

"property" -immoveable and moveable property including documents, monies and securities as defined in the Securities Law, 5728–1968;

"possession" – including possession by a person, who is not the debtor, on behalf of the creditor.

670. *Lien* – Lien is the right of a creditor, pursuant to legislation, to attach property in his possession as a guarantee for the performance of an obligation whose time of performance has arrived.

671. *Realization of Attached Property* – The owner of the lien is entitled, pursuant to a court order, to realize the attached property pursuant to the provisions of the chapter on pledges.[35]

672. *Validity of Lien* – A lien is valid with respect to any person.

673. *Demand to Perform the Obligation Prior to Delay* – A creditor is entitled to attach property as set forth in section 670 only if prior to the attachment or immediately upon its commencement, he delivered a demand to the debtor that sets forth in reasonable detail the substance of the obligation, the source of the obligation and its amount.

674. *Creditors Entitled to Detain* – The following creditors shall be entitled to a lien as detailed below:

(1) the agent – regarding the principal's property that came into his possession in the wake of the agency, for the purpose of insuring the performance of the principal's obligations to him as a result of the agency.

(2) the seller – regarding property that is the subject of the sales contract, for the purpose of insuring the performance of the buyer's obligations towards him in the wake of the sale;

(3) the buyer – regarding property that is the subject of the sales contract, for the purpose of insuring performance of the seller's obligations towards him in the wake of the sale;

(4) the contractor – regarding property that is the subject of the contractorship contract and regarding property that the client delivered into his possession for the performance of his work, for the purpose of insuring the performance of the client's obligations towards him in the wake of the contractorship;

(5) the provider of services – regarding property that the client delivered into his possession for the performance of rendering service, for the purpose of insuring the performance of the client's obligations towards him in the wake of the service;

(6) the bailee – regarding property that is the subject of the bailment, for the purpose of insuring the performance of the property owner's obligations towards him in the wake of the bailment; for this purpose "property owner" is as that term is used in section 499;

(7) one injured as a result of a breach of contract -regarding property of the breaching party that came into his possession as a result of the contract, for the purpose of insuring the performance of the breaching party's obligation towards him in the wake of the breach;

(8) the trustee – regarding property of the trust property, for the purpose of insuring his fee and expenses in the wake of the trust.

675. *Termination of Lien* – Where the creditor has willingly taken the detained property out of his possession, the delay is terminated.

676. *Conflicting Interests to the Lien* – (a) Where a person who is not the debtor has rights in property that conflict with the lien and arose prior to it, these rights will prevail over the rights of the owner of the lien.

(b) The provisions of subsection (a) shall not apply to the lien of a contractor or provider of services as set forth in section 674(4) or (5) regarding the property that is the subject of the contractorship or regarding property that the client delivered to the pos-

---

[35] Chapter Three in Subpart Two of Part Five (sections 628 through 668). The proposal for a new version to the Pledge Law is integrated in the Explanatory Notes.

session of the service provider for the purpose of providing the service, provided that the contractor or the service provider performed with the property the act of contracting or service, as applicable, and did so in good faith.

677. *Provision of Alternative Guarantee for the Attached Property* – The debtor is entitled to release the detained property against the provision of another reasonable guarantee; if the debtor provided such guarantee and the creditor did not release the property, the lien shall be terminated.

678. *Detained Property that can be Severed* – Where the value of the detained property is greater, to an unreasonable extent, than the value of the obligation, and the attached property could be severed, the debtor is entitled to demand the release of the part of the property that is greater, by such extent, than the value of the obligation.

Chapter Five: Trust

Article One: Creation of Trust, Appointment of Trustee and Termination of his Term

679. *Trust* – A trustee is the owner of property who is obligated to act with respect to such property for the benefit of a person (in this chapter – the beneficiary) or for another purpose.

680. *Sources of Trust* – A trust is created by law, by a contract with the trustee or according to a unilateral trust instrument (in this chapter – trust instrument) in which the creator of the trust expresses his desire to create a trust, and determines its property, purposes and conditions.

681. *Trust Instrument* – A trust instrument shall be one of the following:

(1) a document signed by the creator of the trust before a notary;

(2) the will of the creator of the trust, even if it does not name a particular heir, excluding an oral will;

(3) a directive to make a payment for the purposes of section 147 of the Succession Law, 5725–1965.[36]

682. *Beginning of Trust* – The beginning of the trust shall be at the time the control of the trust property is transferred to the trustee.

683. *Proceeds of the Trust Assets* – The proceeds of any trust property, or something for which trust property has been exchanged, will also be trust property.

684. *Distrainment of Trust Assets* – The trustee's creditors are not entitled to receive repayment from the trust property except for debts imposed with respect to such property, or arising out of trust activities.

685. *Appointment of Trustee* – (a) In a trust created pursuant to a contract or a trust instrument, the trustee shall be appointed by the creator of the trust.

(b) A trustee shall not be appointed as set forth in subsection (a) in the trust instrument, or according to it, except with his consent.

686. *Court Appointment of Trustee and Temporary Trustee* –

(a) Where a trustee was not appointed as set forth pursuant to the provisions of section 685, or a trustee was appointed but he is not carrying out his functions, the court may appoint a trustee for a term and under the conditions that it shall set forth.

(b) *Court Appointment of Trustee and Temporary Trustee* – Where a trust was created pursuant to a trust instrument that is a will, and the will did not provide for the trustee, the

---

[36] *Sefer HaHukim* 5725, p. 63.

administrator of the estate shall serve as the trustee pending appointment of a trustee by the court.

687. *Qualifications to Serve as Trustee* – (a) A minor, one who has been declared to be of limited capacity, one who is bankrupt, and a corporation that has decided on liquidation or with respect to which a liquidation order has been issued, are not qualified to serve as trustees.

(b) The beneficiary of a trust is qualified to be a trustee of it, provided that a sole beneficiary shall not be a sole trustee.

688. *Termination of Tenure of Trustee* – (a) A trustee may resign by written notice that will be delivered a reasonable time in advance to the one who is authorized to appoint a trustee for that trust; where there are several trustees, the trustee will also deliver the notice to the other trustees.

(b) Notwithstanding the provisions of subsection (a), the resignation of a sole trustee or a court-appointed trustee is not effective, unless the resignation was approved by court, and from the date set forth in such approval.

(c) In a trust created pursuant to contract or trust instrument, the creator of the trust may dismiss the trustee if the conditions of the trust so permit.

(d) The court may dismiss a trustee if he did not fulfill his duties properly or if the court saw fit to do so for some other reason.

689. *Transfer of Ownership in Trust Property* – Where the position of trustee has been vacated for any reason, or he has ceased to act, or his qualification to serve as trustee has ended, the ownership of the trust property is transferred to the trustee who is appointed in his place; in a trust in which there is more than one trustee, the ownership is transferred to the other trustees.

Article Two: Management of Trust

690. *Holding Trust Property* – The trustee shall hold the trust property separately from other property, or in another manner that allows for them to be distinguished from one another.

691. *Registration of Acts with regard to Trust Property* – Where any acts in respect of property included in trust property requires registration in a register maintained pursuant to legislation, the trustee may notify the person in charge of the register of the existence of the trust and such person shall enter an appropriate notation in the register.

692. *Trustee's Duties* – (a) A trustee owes fiduciary duty to the beneficiary.

(b) A trustee shall preserve, manage and develop the trust property and shall act to achieve the purposes of the trust.

(c) A trustee shall hold or invest the trust funds that are not necessary for its on-going needs in a manner conducive to the preservation of the principal and the production of proceeds. The Minister of Justice may promulgate regulations governing the ways in which trust monies may be invested, in general or according to kinds.

(d) A trustee is authorized to do all that is necessary to fulfill his duties.

693. *Accounts and Reports Regarding the Trust* – (a) The trustee shall keep accounts regarding all the affairs of the trust.

(b) The trustee shall render a report on the affairs of the trust once a year and upon termination of his tenure, and to the creator of the trust upon his request, and shall provide any further information to the beneficiary and to the creator of the trust according to their reasonable request.

694. *Remuneration and Expenses of Trustee* – In the absence of another agreement, a trustee is not entitled to remuneration for fulfilling his duties, unless the fulfillment of

such duties is part of his business, however, the Court may award him remuneration if it found that the extent of his duties as trustee so necessitates.

(b) A trustee is entitled to indemnification for reasonable expenses that he incurred and for obligations that he reasonably undertook in consequence of fulfilling his duties.

(c) A trustee may deduct his compensation and expenses from the trust property.

695. *Several Trustees* – (a) In a trust that has more than one trustee –

(1) the trustees shall act pursuant to agreement among all of them; where there is a disagreement, they shall act in accordance with the directions of the Court;

(2) in a matter that does not allow delay, each of the trustee may act on his own authority;

(3) the trustees shall be liable, jointly and severally for their actions, with the exception of a trustee who opposed an act or did not know of it;

(4) if the place of one of the trustees has become vacant for any reason, or if a trustee has ceased to act or he is no longer qualified to act as a trustee, the remaining trustees must act immediately to fill his place and to continue fulfilling their duties insofar as the matter may not be delayed, and the provisions of section 689 shall apply.

(b) The act of one of the trustees that was done for consideration with regard to a person who acted in good faith shall be valid even if it conflicts with the provision of subsection (a)(1).

696. *Trustee's Liability* – (a) A trustee is liable for the damage caused to the trust property or to the beneficiary in consequence of a breach of his duty as a trustee. Regarding the liability of a trustee for the loss of or damage to trust property, the trustee shall be regarded as a bailee and the beneficiary as the owner of the property.

(b) The trustee is not liable for an investment of trust monies that was carried out in accordance with regulations promulgated by the Minister of Justice pursuant to the provisions of section 692(c).

(c) The trustee shall bear no liability if he acted in good faith according to the directions of the court as set forth in section 700.

(d) The court may discharge a trustee from liability where he did not act as part of his business, if he acted in good faith for the purpose of fulfilling his duties.

697. *Prohibition on Trustee from Acquiring a Benefit* – (a) A trustee shall not acquire for himself or any of his relatives any property of the trust or any right in such property, and shall not derive for himself or any of his relatives any other benefit from the property or activities of the trust, and shall do nothing involving a conflict of interests between the trust and himself or any of his relatives.

(b) In this section, "relative" of a trustee means –

(1) his spouse;

(2) a parent, grandparent, descendant, sibling of the trustee or of his spouse;

(3) spouse of one of those mentioned in clause (2);

(4) a partner of the trustee or of one of those mentioned in clauses (1) through (3);

(5) a corporation in which the trustee or one of those mentioned in clauses (1) through (3) hold five percent or more of a particular kind of the means of control;

in this section, "holding" and "means of control" –

as defined in the Banking (Licensing) Law, 5741–1981.[37]

(c) Notwithstanding the provisions of subsection (a), the court may approve in advance any of the acts mentioned there, if it found that such act is in the interest of the trust.

(d) Where the trustee or one of relatives is a beneficiary, nothing in subsection (a) shall be construed to derogate from his rights as a beneficiary.

(e) Where one of the acts mentioned in this section has been done without the prior approval of the court – the act is void unless it was done with regard to a person who is not a trustee or a relative mentioned in subsection (b)(1) and (2) and such person gave consideration for the act and acted in good faith.

698. *Restriction Upon Transferability of the Beneficiary's Rights* – The right of a beneficiary may not be assigned or attached except with court approval or if the terms of the trust permitted this.

699. *Prohibited Profit of Trustee* – A profit that a trustee has derived unlawfully, in consequence of the trust, shall be treated as part of the trust property.

700. *Court Directions To Trustee* – (a) A trustee may apply to the court for directions in every matter connected to the fulfillment of his duties.

(b) The court may, at any time, issue directions to a trustee in any matter relating to the carrying out of his duties, and any other direction that it considers necessary for the efficient management of the trust.

701. *Application to Court with respect to Trust* – A trustee, a beneficiary, the creator of the trust and any interested person may apply to the court regarding any matter pertaining to this chapter. The Attorney General or his representative may initiate any proceeding under this chapter, and enter an appearance and plead in such a proceeding, if he considers it to be of public interest.

702. *Declaration of Existence of Trust Pursuant to Trust Instrument* – Where property is managed as a trust created pursuant to a trust instrument, but there is no trust instrument regarding it, the court may declare the existence of a trust and to define its purposes, property, conditions and date of commencement.

Article Three: Alteration and Rescission of Trust

703. *Alteration of Trust* – (a) The court may alter or rescind any of the provisions of the trust if there has been a material change in the circumstances that justifies doing so and the alteration or rescission conforms with the intent of the creator of the trust.

(b) The court may permit a trustee to make use of trust property to provide for the vital needs of a beneficiary or his dependants, even if such use represents a departure from the terms of the trust.

(c) The creator of the trust that was created pursuant to a trust instrument or a third party may, at any time, add to the trust property.

704. *Termination of Trust* – The court may terminate a trust if it determines that its purposes have been achieved or cannot be achieved.

705. *Property of a Trust that has been Terminated* – Where the trust has been terminated and the provisions of the trust do not stipulate what is to be done with its property, the court may, in accordance with the provisions of the trust and the intent of its creator, prescribe what is to be done with them and order their transfer for purposes that it determines. Where the court did not find such purposes, the trust property shall be returned to the creator of the trust.

---

[37] *Sefer HaHukim* 5741, p. 232.

706. *Alteration and Revocation of Trust Under Terms of Trust Instrument* – (a) The creator of a trust by a trust instrument may not alter the provisions of the trust, derogate from its property or revoke it, after the commencement of the trust, unless he reserved the right to do so in the trust instrument or the beneficiary has consented thereto or the court has approved same.

(b) Nothing in the provisions of this section shall derogate from the right of the creator of the trust by a trust instrument to revoke the creation of the trust before its commencement, pursuant to the laws governing the revocation of a will or the laws for revocation or alteration of a direction for payment for the purposes of section 147 of the Succession Law, 5725–1965.

Article Four: The Public Trustee

707. *The Public Trustee* – (a) The Minister of Justice shall appoint a public trustee; notification of the appointment shall be published in *Reshumot.*

(b) The public trustee can act as a trustee of trusts.

(c) The court may appoint the public trustee as sole trustee even in trusts which have more than one trustee according to their terms.

708. *Representation of Beneficiary by the Public Trustee* – Where by reason of his age, state of health or a mental or physical defect, a beneficiary is not able to assert his rights and he has no guardian, the public trustee may represent him *vis-a-vis* the trustee.

709. *Measures to Safeguard Trust Property* – Where a trust does not have a trustee or the trustee is unable to act, the public trustee shall take measures as he sees fit to safeguard the trust property and the rights of the beneficiary.

Article Five: Miscellaneous Provisions

710. *Inapplicability of Trust Chapter* – none

Sub-Part Three: Special Provisions Regarding Land

711. *Definitions for the Sub-Part Special Provisions Regarding Land* – none

Chapter One: Transactions in Land

712. *Registration in the Land Registries* – A transaction in land requires registration in the land registries; the transaction is completed upon registration and the time at which the Registrar approves the transaction for registration is regarded as the time of registration.

713. *Transaction not Completed by Registration* – A transaction in land requiring registration, which did not culminate with registration is regarded as a commitment to effect a transaction.

713A. *Force of proof of registration* – (a) Registration in the land registers in respect of settled land as defined in section 508 shall constitute clear proof of its contents, however such proof shall not derogate from the provisions of sections 93 to 97 of the Land (Settlement of Title) Ordinance [New Version], 5729–1969.

714. *Requirement that Transfer of Right in Property be in Writing* – A commitment to effect a transaction in land, as well as the assignment of a right to receive a right in land and a commitment to make such an assignment, require written documentation that reflects the agreement of the parties to enter into a contract.

715. *Wholeness of the Proprietary Unit* – (a) A transaction in land extends to the land together with all of the parts over which the ownership extends pursuant to section 613, and a transaction as to a portion of a registered unit of land is invalid.

(b) Notwithstanding the provisions of subsection (a), a transaction in land is a valid transaction, even if it was carried out as to a portion of a registered unit of land, as specified below –

(1) lease or borrowing of land for a period of time that does not exceed 100 years; in this regard, a lease or borrowing agreement that accords the lessee the option to extend the period of the lease to a total period that exceeds 100 years is regarded as a lease or borrowing agreement for a period of time that exceeds 100 years.

(2) the granting of an easement in land.

716. *Restriction of Transferability in Land* – Where the contract or the articles of a condominium restrict the owner of an interest in land from effecting a transaction in his right, and ten years have passed since the commencement of the restriction, the court may permit the transaction to be effected notwithstanding the restriction, under the conditions it shall determine.

Chapter Two: Building and Planting on Another's Land

717. *The Option of the Owner of Land Regarding Fixtures* – (a) Where a person has erected any structure or planted any trees or permanently connected something else on the land of another without being entitled to do so by law or pursuant to a contract with the owner of the land (in this chapter – the person who erected), the owner of the land has the option to retain the fixtures or to demand from the person who erected them to remove them and to return the property to the condition it was in previously; where the fixtures were erected on jointly owned land, the right of the joint owner to demand the removal of the fixtures prevails over the right of another joint owner to retain them.

(b) Where the person who erected the fixtures has demanded in writing from the owner of the land that he exercise his option pursuant to subsection (a), and the owner of the land has not exercised it within six months from the receipt of the demand, he is regarded as one who has chosen to retain the fixtures.

(c) Where the person who erected the fixtures acted in good faith and the land owner is not interested in retaining the fixtures, and there is no justification for the removal of the fixtures under the circumstances, the court may require the land owner to do one of the following, under the conditions it determines:

(1) require the land owner to buy the fixtures from the person who erected them;

(2) require the land owner to sell or lease the land to him, and in respect of a person who erected them and believes in good faith that he is a long-term lessee of the land – to lease the land to him for a period that he believed was the leasehold period; in this matter, the provisions of section 721(b) shall apply, *mutatis mutandis*.

718. *Retention of Fixtures on Property Subject to Long Term Lease* – Where the land is leased in a long-term lease, the option set forth in section 717 shall belong to the long-term lessee and the provisions of sections 719 and 720 shall apply, *mutatis mutandis*; however, the long-term lessee is not entitled to choose to retain the fixtures if the retention of the fixtures on the leased land conflicts with the lessee's obligations to the lessor.

719. *Choice to Retain the Fixtures* – Where the land owner has chosen to retain the fixtures, he must indemnify the one who erected the fixtures for the expenses he incurred in erecting the fixtures, with the addition of linkage differentials according to the Consumer Price Index as published by the Central Bureau for Statistics beginning with

the day the fixtures were erected, or he must pay him the value of the fixtures at the time the choice was made, according to the lower of the two amounts.

720. *Choice to Remove Fixtures* – (a) Where the land owner demanded that the fixtures be removed, the one who erected the fixtures must remove them within a reasonable period of time; if he did not do so, the land owner may remove them at the expense of the one who erected them.

(b) Where the fixtures were removed, as set forth in subsection (a), they will be transferred to the ownership of the one who erected them; however the land owner may collect from the fixtures repayment due him for the removal.

721. *The Erector's Right to Buy the Land* – (a) Where the fixtures were erected on unsettled land, the one who erected them may acquire the land through payment of its value without the fixtures at the time of payment, unless such acquisition will cause damage to the land owner that cannot be compensated by such payment for it, provided that all of the following have been fulfilled;

(1) at the time the fixtures were erected the one who erected the fixtures believed in good faith that he was the owner of the land.

(2) the expenses that the one who erected the fixtures incurred at the time they were erected exceeded the value of the land without the fixtures at that time.

(b) (1) The expenses of acquiring the land pursuant to this section, including fees and compulsory payments that must be paid in connection with the transfer of the property, but excepting compulsory payments due for the period preceding the erection of the fixtures will be levied on the one who erected the fixtures;

(2) Payment of the Land Appreciation Tax will be levied on the land owner, however the court may provide that they shall be imposed, in whole or in part, on the one who erected the fixtures; in this matter –

"Land Appreciation Levy" shall have the same meaning as in the Planning and Construction Law;

"Sales tax" and "Land Appreciation Tax" shall have the same meaning as inthe Land Taxation (Appreciation, Sale and Purchase) Law, 5723–1963.[38]

(c) The provisions of subsection (a) shall also apply, *mutatis mutandis*, to one who erected fixtures and believed in good faith that he was a long-term lessee of the land; one who erected fixtures as stated may demand that the owner of the land lease him the land in a long-term lease for the period of time that he believed was the period of the lease.

(d) The right pursuant to this section of the one who erected the fixtures prevails over the rights of the land owner pursuant to section 717.

(e) The right of the one who erected the fixture pursuant to this section is also valid *vis a vis* one who comes in the place of the land owner.

722. *Applicability to Erection of Fixtures on Jointly Owned Land* – The provisions of this section shall apply, *mutatis mutandis*, in a case in which a joint owner erected fixtures on jointly owned property, without being entitled to do so according to law or according to the contract with the other joint owners.

723. *Registration of a Right Pursuant to the Chapter on Building and Planting on Another's Land* – Where the one who erected fixtures chose to acquire the right in the land pursuant to the provisions of this chapter, the acquired right shall be transferred to the ownership of the one who erected the fixtures upon its registration in the land registers.

---

[38] *Sefer HaHukim* 5723, p. 156.

Chapter Three: Condominiums

Article One: General Provisions

724. Definitions for the Condomium Chapter – In this chapter –

"house" – a permanent structure, including the land upon which it is built;

"condominium" – one of the following, that is registered in the Register of Condominiums and which has jointly owned property:

(1) a house in which there are two or more apartments;

(2) two or more houses in each of which there is at least one apartment and the houses were erected on a parcel or parcels of land which cannot be partitioned in such a way that each house will stand on a separate parcel of land;

(3) two or more houses with common installations;

"owner of residential unit" – regarding a residential unit that was leased in a long-term lease – the tenant in a long-term lease or the sub-tenant in a long-term lease, as applicable, unless the lease contract provides that for the purposes of this chapter he will not be regarded as the owner of the apartment;

"common property" – all of the parts of the condominium, except the apartments, including the permanently connected installations that are within the area of a particular apartment, which are intended to serve all or most of the apartment owners;

"condominium articles" – or "articles" – as defined in section 729.

Article Two: Residential Units and Common Property

725. *The Share of the Residential Unit in the Common Property* – (a) Each apartment owner in a condominium has a unspecified share in the common property of the house.

(b) The size of the share in the common property as set forth in subsection (a) shall be according to the relation of the area of the apartment to the area of all of the apartments in the condominium, unless the articles provide for a different share size.

(c) The Minister of Justice may promulgate regulations setting forth rules for calculating the area of the apartment as set forth in subsection (b).

726. *Transactions in Common Property* – (a) An apartment in a condominium shall be a separate unit for the purposes of ownership, rights and transactions, however the conferment of a right in the apartment shall apply to the share in the common property that the owner of the apartment owns.

(b) Notwithstanding the provisions of subsection (a), it is permissible to lease, lend or grant an easement in an apartment for a period not to exceed five years without conferring the same right in the common property.

(c) The provisions of the chapter dealing with jointly owned property[39] shall not apply to the common property, except for sections 596(a)(1), (3), (4) and (c) as well as the provisions of section 722.

(d) A transaction or conferment of another right in the share of the owner of an apartment in the common property separately from a transaction or other act with respect to the apartment is invalid. The provision of this subsection shall not prevent, upon consent of all of the owners of residential units:

(1) enlargement or diminishment of the area of land which is part of the common property;

(2) leasing or lending of a certain part of the common property or the conferment of an easement in it.

---

[39] Chapter Four in Sub-Part One in this part (Part Five) (sections 589 through 611).

727. *Changes and Repairs to Residential Units* – (a) The owner of an apartment may not make changes or repairs to the apartment that constitute a material disturbance of the reasonable use of the common property or endanger or are likely to endanger its existence or alter or are likely to alter its value, unless he received prior consent from the general assembly of the owners of the apartment; for this purpose, "injury to the common property" includes injury to the external proper and uniform façade as it was upon completion of construction.

(b) The owner of an apartment may not make changes or repairs to the apartment that constitute a material disturbance of the reasonable use of another apartment or that endanger or are likely to endanger its existence or that are likely to change its value, unless he received the prior consent of the owner of the other apartment for such changes or repairs.

(c) The owner of an apartment may make any other change or repair of his own accord.

728. *Linkage of Common Property to a Residential Unit* – (a) The apartment owners may stipulate in the articles that a certain part of the common property will be linked to a particular apartment, provided that this shall not pertain with respect to stairways, shelters, elevators or installations intended for the use of all of the owners of the apartments.

(b) For the purposes of this Article, the area of a part that has been linked to a apartment shall be considered part of the area of that apartment in the amount provided for in the articles, or in the absence of such a provision, in the amount that the Supervisor shall decide upon under the circumstances.

(c) A part that was linked to an apartment shall no longer be considered part of the common property, and it shall be considered as part of the apartment to which it was linked. However, the owner of that apartment may, if there is no other provision in the articles, transfer such a part, separately from his apartment, to the owner of another apartment in the condominium, even without the consent of the other apartment owners, provided that the provisions of section 145 of the Land Law have been fulfilled.

Article Three: Management of the Condominium

729. *Articles of Cooperative House* – (a) A condominium shall be managed according to the articles that regulate the relations between the apartment owners and their rights and obligations with regard to the condominium.

(b) The articles will be promulgated or amended by decision of the general meeting of the apartment owners on the basis of the vote of a majority of apartment owners who own at least two-thirds of the common property, however,

(1) rights or duties of apartment owners shall not be set forth, nor shall payments be imposed, of a kind or in an amount not set forth in this Part, except with their consent;
(2) a particular part of the common property shall not be linked to a specific apartment, except with the consent of all of the apartment owners.

(c) For the purposes of subsection (b), "apartment owner" includes a long-term tenant in a residential unit and a long-term sub-tenant in a residential unit.

730. *Transfer of Part of Residential Unit* – none

731. *Registration of Articles of Cooperative House* – (a) The articles and any change in them may be registered in the Condominiums Register.

(b) Articles that were registered as set forth in subsection (a) are valid with respect to one who has acquired ownership of an apartment in a condominium after the registration of the articles. The articles or any change in them that have not yet been registered bind those who were apartment owners at the time they were set forth as well as any other person who became an apartment owner later, if he knew of the articles.

(c) A provision in the articles regarding the manner of maintenance and use of the common property will also be binding upon a person in the name of the owner of the apartment.

(d) Articles may be registered even while the entire condominium is owned by one person.

(e) The model rules in the Second Appendix shall be regarded as the articles that were registered by the apartment owners where articles were not registered pursuant to subsection (a), or regarding a specific matter concerning which there is no provision in the articles that were registered.

732. *Expenses for Maintenance of the Common Property* – (a) An apartment owner shall contribute to the expenses necessary for the proper maintenance and management of the common property and to ensure the services mandated by law or customary, according to his share in the common property, unless the articles provide for a different rate of contribution.

(b) The Supervisor shall establish the part that the apartment owner to which part of the common property has been linked shall contribute to the expenses due to such linkage.

(c) Notwithstanding what is set forth in subsection (a), the apartment owner shall not be required, for a specific part of the common property that was linked to his apartment or for a part that is external to his residential unit, that constitutes part of the apartment according to its registration, to contribute to the necessary expenses for heating water or for heating the premises and for the proper maintenance of the central system for heating water or heating the premises, if such part is not connected to the central system as set forth unless the articles provide otherwise.

(d) In this section "proper maintenance" means preserving the condition of the common property as it was at the time the construction was completed, including changes that were carried out afterwards with the consent of the apartment owners.

733. *The Cooperative House Committee and its Authority* – (a) In each condominium there shall be a committee that manages the common property and acts pursuant to the provisions of the articles.

(b) The committee is the agent of the apartment owners regarding everything concerning the proper maintenance and management of the common property and ensuring the services required pursuant to legislation or accepted according to custom, as set forth in section 732, and it is authorized in such matters to enter into contracts and to be a party in any legal proceedings and any other negotiations in the name of the apartment owners.

734. *Establishment of the Cooperative House Committee* – (a) The committee shall be established pursuant to the provisions of the articles and shall act in accord with the decisions of the general meeting.

(b) With the registration of the house in the Register of Condominiums, the Supervisor who gave the registration order shall appoint a provisional committee for that house until the first committee is established according to the articles. The provisions of subsection (c) will apply, *mutatis mutandis*, to the appointment of the committee and the fixing of its remuneration.

(c) Where a condominium committee was not established pursuant to the provisions of the articles or the committee that was established is not functioning, the Supervisor may appoint a committee for that house from among the apartment owners and where there is no practical possibility to do so – even from those who are not among the owners; similarly, the Supervisor may fix remuneration for the committee that shall be paid by the apartment owners, as part of the expenses, after he has given the apartment owners the opportunity to state their arguments.

(d) Where the articles state that the committee shall be chosen by the apartment owners in the general meeting, the Supervisor shall not exercise his authority pursuant to the provisions of subsection (c) until after he has convened a general meeting for that purpose and a committee was not chosen, or he has come to the realization that convening a general meeting, as provided, is impractical.

(e) A committee appointed by the Supervisor pursuant to the provision of this section, shall for all purposes be considered a committee that was established pursuant to the provisions of the articles in accordance with the provisions of this section.

735. *General Meeting in a Cooperative House* – (a) The general meeting of the apartment owners may, in accordance with the articles, make decisions regarding the management and use of the common property; the decisions of the general meeting shall be registered in the register of resolutions.

(b) The decision of the apartment owners that was arrived at in accordance with the articles shall bind every apartment owner; such decision that was registered in the register of resolutions shall also bind one who becomes an apartment owner after the decision was passed. Where the decision dealt with the manner of maintenance and use of the common property, the decision shall also bind one acting on behalf of the apartment owner.

(c) Where the articles of a condominium have provisions regarding the holding of a general meeting of the apartment owners and the meeting was not convened on time in accordance with the provisions of the articles, the Supervisor may convene it and prescribe its agenda. The provisions of the articles shall apply to a meeting convened as stated and it will be considered a general meeting that was convened in accordance with the articles.

736. *Register of Resolutions in a Cooperative House* – The committee shall keep a register of decisions, as set forth in section 735, and it shall be open, at any reasonable time, for inspection of any apartment owner and anyone assuming his place.

737. *Management of the Common Property by a Provider of Maintenance* –

(a) (1) The apartment owners may provide, in the articles or in a decision by a majority of apartment owners who own two-thirds of the common propertythat the management and proper maintenance of all or most of the common property, shall be carried out by one whom the apartment owners contract with forsuch purpose (in this section – a provider of maintenance).

(2) The decision regarding entering into a contract with a specific provider of maintenance, or his replacement shall be made by the apartment owners who own more than one-half of the common property.

(b) The remuneration of the maintenance provider is considered an expense that the apartment owners are required to contribute to, as set forth in section 732(a).

(c) The duties imposed on a treasurer pursuant to section 15 of the model articles in the second appendix, with respect to keeping accounts and certification of such accounts and imparting information to the apartment owners shall apply to the provider of maintenance.

738. *Jointly Acquired Property* – The provisions of this chapter shall also apply, *mutatis mutandis*, to property acquired jointly by apartment owners for the purpose of the proper maintenance and management of the common property.

739. *Condominium Consisting of Buildings or Wings* – (a) In this section "a housing complex" means a condominium consisting of several buildings or wings each of which has a separate entrance or installations.

(b) Where the apartment owners in a housing complex have provided, in the articles, that all or part of the common property that is within the area of a building or wing shall be linked to the apartments in that building or wing, or that the maintenance and management of such common property shall be separate, the obligation to contribute to the expenses and management of the common property in accordance with the provisions of section 732, shall apply only to the apartment owners in that building or wing with respect to the common property in that building or wing. The apartment owners may set forth in the articles that separate general and committee meetings shall be held regarding that building or wing.

(c) In the absence of a provision in the articles as set forth in subsection (b), the Supervisor may direct that a housing complex shall be managed as set forth in subsection (b), if he is impressed that the circumstances justify doing so; where the Supervisor has so directed, he will determine portions of the common property to which subsection (b) shall apply.

(d) Nothing in the provisions that a housing complex shall be run as set forth in subsection (b) shall derogate from the provisions of the law applicable to common property in such a house, whose maintenance and management have not been severed.

Article Four: Provisions Regarding Certain Installations and Services

740. *Installations and Pipes in a Cooperative House* – (a) Installations or pipes in a cooperative building that were intended for the use of a specific apartment only, shall constitute part of that apartment regardless of whether they are located inside the apartment or they are outside of the apartment. If the installations are within the area of another apartment, the owner of the apartment which the installations were intended to serve may enter the other apartment in order to take care of their proper maintenance, after prior coordination with the owner of the other apartment.

(b) Subject to the provisions of any law, installations or pipes in a condominium that were intended for the use of all or some of the apartment owners, with the exception of a container, meter or regulator that can be disconnected, shall constitute part of the common property.

(c) A provision in the articles or in a contract that conflicts with subsections (a) or (b) is void, unless it is to the advantage of the apartment owners.

741. *Installment of a Solar Heater* – (a) In a condominium the roof of which is sufficient to hold a number of solar heaters equal to the number of apartments in the house, an apartment owner may, subject to the provisions of subsection (b), install a solar water heater (in this section – solar heater) in a reasonable place on the roof of the condominium without the consent of the other apartment owners, and to install in a reasonable manner the installations connected to the solar heater and the pipes for the conduct of the water to his apartment, provided that all of the following are fulfilled:

(1) he notified the other apartment owners of his intention to install a solar heater a reasonable amount of time in advance;
(2) he received a permit for the installation pursuant to the Planning and Construction Law, and fulfilled the conditions of the permit;

(3) on the day the permit mentioned in clause (2) was given, the place upon which the solar heater is to be installed did not serve, throughout a reasonable period of time, the owners of the apartment any purpose, agreed upon, whether by decision of the apartment owners or by their conduct, and it was not intended on said day to be used for any purpose pursuant to the articles of the condominium;

(4) installment of the installations shall be done in a manner that limits, to the extent possible, any damage to the façade of the building.

(b) In a condominium the roof of which is not sufficient to hold a number of solar heaters equal to the number of apartments in the house, an apartment owner may not install a solar heater as set forth in subsection (a) if another apartment owner objects to the installment prior to its performance.

(c) Where the Supervisor found that an apartment owner unreasonably objected to the installment as set forth in subsection (b), or conditioned his consent on unreasonable conditions, the Supervisor may permit the installment of the solar heater under the conditions that he shall determine.

(d) A certificate signed by the engineer of the Local Council for Planning and Construction shall serve as evidence that the roof of the condominium is sufficient or insufficient for a number of solar heaters equal to the number of apartments in the house; in said certificate the engineer shall state how many solar heaters may be accommodated on the roof.

742. *Disconnection from the Central Heating System* – (a) An apartment owner may, at his expense, disconnect his apartment from the central system for heating water or heating the apartment (in this section – the central system), without the consent of the other apartment owners, provided that if the central system integrates heating water and heating the apartments, he may not disconnect from just one of those services. Nothing in this provision shall derogate from the provision of section 727.

(b) The Minister of National Infrastructure shall set forth, with the approval of the Constitution, Law and Justice Committee of the Knesset, what constitutes disconnection for the purposes of this section, what are the conditions allowing disconnection and in what conditions it will be carried out.

(c) Disconnection as set forth in subsection (a) shall not derogate from the rights of the apartment owner in the central system from which he disconnected, and it shall not discharge him from bearing the necessary costs of proper maintenance of the system.

(d) The Minister of Justice, upon consultation with the Minister of National Infrastructure and with the approval of the Constitution, Law and Justice Committee of the Knesset, shall establish directives regarding payment of costs as set forth in subsection (c) that the apartment owner who disconnected from the central system shall pay, as well as his share in the on-going costs for the operation of the central system, bringing into consideration the amount of increase of such costs that is caused to the other residents due to the disconnection.

743. *Adjustments for a Person with a Disability* – (a) In this section –

"a person with a disability" – as defined in the Equal Rights for Persons with Disabilities Law, 5758–1998;[40]

"the Commission" – The Equal Rights for Persons with Disabilities Commission, as used in the Equal Rights for Persons with Disabilities Law, 5758–1998;

---

[40] *Sefer HaHukim* 5758, p. 252.

"physician" – a licensed physician pursuant to the Physicians Ordinance [new version], 5737–1976.[41]

(b) An apartment owner who is a person with a disability, or a member of his family who lives with him is a person with a disability or a person who is renting the apartment from him is a person with a disability, may, subject to the provisions of subsections (c) and (d), make adjustments in the common property as set forth pursuant to the provisions of subsection (h) (in this section – the adjustment), provided that all of the following have been fulfilled:

(1) where carrying out the adjustment requires work or a use that requires a permit pursuant to the Planning and Construction Law – the apartment owner has received the permit pursuant to such law and fulfilled the conditions of the permit;

(2) a physician, physiotherapist or occupational therapist has certified, by signing the form that the Minister of Justice has decided upon pursuant to the provision of subsection (h), that carrying out the adjustment, as he has specified, is necessary for the person with the disability, due to his disability, for the purpose of his safe and independent access to the apartment or the common property that serves it;

(3) the adjustment does not prevent the other apartment owners from reasonable use of the common property, and the adjustment shall be done in a manner that minimizes, as much as possible, injury to the other apartment owners and to the façade of the house;

(4) the apartment owner shall pay for carrying out the adjustment;

(5) the apartment owner or someone acting on his behalf delivered, not later than forty days before the date of performance of the adjustment, a detailed written notice to the condominium committee regarding the intent to carry out the adjustment and its nature; if there is no house committee, the notice shall be delivered to each apartment in the cooperative house.

(c) The carrying out of the adjustment requires the consent of the other apartment owners in the condominium according to the majority necessary pursuant to the provisions of subsection (h), unless it was determined that pursuant to the provisions of that section the performance of the adjustment does not require such consent.

(d) Where the Supervisor found that an apartment owner unreasonably opposed the adjustment or conditioned his consent upon unreasonable conditions, and he decided to permit the carrying out of the adjustment, his decision shall be in place of the consent of the owner of that apartment for the purposes of subsection (c).

(e) The condominium committee, as well as an apartment owner who views himself as aggrieved from the carrying out of the adjustment, may file a claim with the Supervisor within 30 days from the day of receipt of the notice described in subsection (b)(5); the submission of the claim shall not prevent the carrying out of the adjustment, unless the Supervisor has directed otherwise; the Supervisor may, for special cause, extend the deadline for filing the claim pursuant to this subsection.

(f) An apartment owner who carried out the adjustment shall bear all of the on-going costs necessary for the proper maintenance of the product of the adjustment. However, if the product of the adjustment is intended to serve all or most of the apartment owners, all of the apartment owners shall bear such costs.

---

[41] *Dinei Medinat Yisrael*, new version 30, p. 594.

(g) The general meeting may decide that with the end of the need for the adjustment, including a case in which the person with the disability has ceased to live in the apartment, the apartment owner must remove the adjustment, restore the situation to its former condition, and bear all of the attendant costs; a decision pursuant to this subsection must be made not later than 90 days from the date on which the need for the adjustment ended.

(h) The Minister of Justice shall set forth, after consultation with the Commission and with organizations that deal with promoting the rights of persons with disabilities, and with the approval of the Labor, Welfare and Health Committee of the Knesset –

(1) the adjustments which do not require the consent of the other apartment owners in the condominium in order to carry them out;

(2) the adjustments which require the consent of the majority of the apartment owners in the cooperative house in order to carry them out;

(3) the adjustments which require the consent of the apartment owners who own sixty percent of the apartments in the condominium in order to carry them out;

(4) a certificate form of a physician, a physiotherapist or an occupational therapist regarding the need for the adjustment.

744. *Change of Gas Provider* – (a) In a condominium in which there is a system for providing gas, through which gas is provided to two or more apartments (in this section – central gas system), the apartment owners who purchase gas through the central gas system may decide on the termination of all of the contracts that were signed with the gas provider or through it, and to contract with another gas provider in order to purchase gas from it or through it.

(b) A decision as set forth in subsection (a) requires the written consent of more than half of the apartment owners who purchase gas through the central gas system.

(c) Where the gas provider was changed as set forth in subsection (a), an apartment owner to whose apartment gas is provided through the same central gas system may not install a separate installation for the provision of gas to his apartment.

745. *Operation of Elevator as a Sabbath Elevator* – (a) In this section –

"Sabbath Operating Mechanism" – as defined in the Installment of Sabbath Elevators in Public and Residential Buildings (Provisions and Legislative Amendments) Law, 5761–2001;[42]

"Sabbath elevator" – an elevator in which there is a Sabbath operating mechanism and regarding which the provisions of subsection (b) are fulfilled.

(b) In a cooperative building in which some or all of the apartments are used for residential purposes, and in which there is more than one elevator that serves such apartments and in one of the elevators there is a Sabbath operating mechanism, any apartment owner may demand that the elevator in which there is a Sabbath operating mechanism shall be operated as a Sabbath elevator.

(c) The Minister of Justice shall set forth the times of operation of the Sabbath elevator, taking into consideration, *inter alia*, the number of people requesting its operation and their needs.

(d) Notwithstanding what is set forth in subsection (b), all of the apartment owners in a condominium may decide upon the operation of a Sabbath elevator during certain hours.

---

[42] *Sefer HaHukim* 5761, p. 519.

(e) The apartment owners demanding the operation of the Sabbath elevator shall bear the costs of its maintenance and operation stemming from the operation of the elevator as a Sabbath elevator.

(f) The payments that the apartment owners shall make pursuant to this section shall be in accordance with the ratio between the floor area of each apartment and the floor area of all of the apartments whose owners make such payments.

(g) For the purposes of this section, in a housing complex according to its meaning in section 739, each building or wing shall be regarded as a condominium.

(h) The provisions of Chapter Six, Article Four of the Land Law shall apply to the hearing pursuant to this section before the Supervisor, *mutatis mutandis.*

Article Five: Changes in the Common Property and the Building Rights

746. *Definitions Regarding Changes in Common Property* – In this Article –

"enlargement" – enlargement of the area of an existing apartment in a condominium regarding which a building permit may be obtained pursuant to a valid plan;

"building rights" – rights to build in a condominium according to a valid plan within the meaning of that term in Chapter Three of the Planning and Construction Law.

747. *Changes in Common Property and Building Rights* – (a) Notwithstanding the provisions of section 729, or section 11(b) of the model articles in the second appendix, those who are the owners of at least three-quarters of the apartments and at least two-thirds of the common property linked to their apartments may reach a decision regarding taking out certain parts from the common property and linking them to a particular apartment that is used as a residence in order to build for the purpose of enlarging that apartment and may also make a decision regarding the division of the necessary building rights for this purpose according to the share of the apartment owner in the common property, subject to what is set forth in subsection (c) (in this section – the enlargement decision).

(b) An enlargement decision shall not be made if it may impinge upon the relative building rights of another apartment owner for expansion pursuant to this article, unless the apartment of the other apartment owner cannot be expanded in accordance with his share in the common property.

(c) Where an expansion decision has been made, the apartment owner who wishes to expand his apartment and whose apartment can be expanded to an extent that is relatively greater than his share in the common property, shall pay, at the time of the expansion decision, equalization payments to the owner of the apartment whose apartment cannot be expanded according to his share in the common property.

(d) Where the apartment owners did not agree upon the amount of the equalization payments, such payments shall be determined by a real property assessor, who shall be appointed by consent.

(e) The expenses of the assessment shall be paid by the apartment owners in accordance with their share in the common property, before the expansion decision was arrived at.

(f) An expansion decision shall not be made will deny an apartment owner a reasonable possibility to build a sukkah in any part of the common property, if he customarily did so before the decision.

748. *Claim Because of Expansion of an Apartment in a Cooperative House* – (a) The owner of an apartment who objects to a decision that was made as set forth in section 747(a) and who claims material injury to his rights, as well as an apartment owner who desires the appointment of a real property assessor in the absence of consent as set forth in section

747(d) and an apartment owner who disagrees with the finding of the assessor as set forth in that section, may file a claim with the Supervisor.

(b) The claim shall be filed within 30 days from the day the decision was made, and if the apartment owner was not present at the time the decision was made, within 30 days from the day the decision was delivered; the Supervisor may extend the deadline for filing the claim for special cause.

(c) The provisions of Article Four of Chapter Six of the Land Law shall apply to the hearing before the Supervisor, *mutatis mutandis*.

(d) Where the Supervisor found that the right of an apartment owner has been materially infringed, or that the real property assessor was mistaken in his ruling, it may instruct that the decision that was made be voided, changed or made contingent upon conditions, as he sees fit, whether by making equalization payments or in another manner, and he may give instructions regarding the registration regulations in the Land Registration Office as that term is used in section 115 of the Land Law.

(e) The filing of a claim with the Supervisor shall not in itself constitute grounds for a delay in carrying out the expansion, unless the Supervisor has directed otherwise.

749. *Improvement of Common Property* – (a) The apartment owners who own at least two-thirds of the apartments in the condominium may decide in a general meeting to improve the common property (in this section – improvement), provided that all of the following have been fulfilled:

(1) where the improvement requires a permit pursuant to the Planning and Construction Law – it is possible to obtain such a permit.

(2) the improvement can be carried out in a manner that shall not cause substantial damage to another apartment or to the common property including to the façade of the house.

(b) (1) The apartment owners who decided on the improvement shall bear the costs of carrying it out and they may agree that only some of them shall bear such costs.

(2) All of the apartment owners shall contribute to the costs of maintenance of the improvement and the costs of operating it, as the case may be; where the imposition of the obligation to contribute to the costs is unreasonable, an apartment owner who objected to the improvement shall not be obligated to pay such costs.

(3) The payments that the apartment owners shall bear pursuant to this subsection shall be in accordance with the relation between the floor area of each apartment and the floor area of all of the apartments whose owners are making those payments.

750. *Installation of Elevator* – (a) Apartment owners who own at least two-thirds of the apartments in a condominium may decide in a general meeting to install an elevator in the common property, provided that all of the following are fulfilled:

(1) a building permit to install the elevator can be obtained pursuant to the Planning and Construction Law;

(2) the elevator can be installed in such a manner so as not to cause substantial damage to another apartment or to the common property, including the façade of the house.

(b) (1) Apartment owners who have decided to install an elevator shall bear the costs of the installation of the elevator, but they may agree that only some of them shall bear the costs as set forth.

(2) apartment owners on the ground floor shall not bear the costs of the installation of the elevator, even if they are among those who decided to install it.

(3) all of the apartment owners shall participate in the maintenance and operating costs of the elevator;

(4) in a condominium composed of a number of wings, each of which has a separate entrance, the apartment owners in that entrance shall participate in said costs.

(5) The payments to be made by the apartment owners pursuant to this subsection shall be according to the ratio between the floor area of each apartment and the floor area of all of the apartments whose owners bear such payments.

(c) (1) The apartment owners may, with the consent of all of the apartment owners, set forth in agreed upon articles that the provisions of this section shall not apply to them.

(2) Nothing in this section shall derogate from the special provision in the agreed articles regarding the installation of an elevator.

(d) (1) The Supervisor may direct that a decision made pursuant to this section be voided, changed or be made contingent upon conditions, including compensation, if he found that the right of an apartment owner has been materially infringed as a result of the decision.

(2) The provisions of Article Four of Chapter Six of the Planning and Construction Law shall apply to a hearing pursuant to this section before the Supervisor, *mutatis mutandis*.

(e) (1) The apartment owners who have decided to install an elevator as set forth in subsection (a) may decide that the apartment owners who do not participate in the costs of the installation shall not be authorized to use the elevator; where it has been so decided, the apartment owners who are not authorized to use the elevator shall not bear the costs of its maintenance and operation, notwithstanding the provisions of subsection (b).

(2) Notwithstanding the provisions of clause (1), an apartment owner who is not authorized to use the elevator may notify the house committee at any stage after the decision that he is joining those who participate in the costs of the installation and in the costs of the maintenance and operation of the elevator; with the giving of such notice and payment of his relative share of the costs of the installation, and if the elevator was renovated, the costs of the renovation as well, to the apartment owners who bore the costs, or to those who have come in their stead, the apartment owner may use the elevator; where the apartment owner used the elevator without being permitted to do so, he shall be deemed to have notified the house committee that he is joining those who participate in the costs, as specified in this clause.

751. *Restoration of Cooperative House that was Destroyed* – (a) Where a condominium has been totally or completely destroyed, and the apartment owners who own at least three-quarters of the common property (in this section – the restorers) decided to rebuild the house in a manner similar to its original structure, or to repair it, each apartment owner shall bear the costs pertaining to his apartment, and the owners of all of the apartments shall participate in the costs pertaining to the common property, each one according to his share in the common property linked to his apartment.

(b) If an apartment owner has refused to participate in the rebuilding or repair of the condominium as set forth in subsection (a), upon application of the restorers, and after he is convinced that the condominium cannot be rebuilt with regard to the other apartments only, the Supervisor may order the apartment owner to transfer his right in the apartment to another person, whom the apartment owner shall designate, who will take his place for the purpose of such rebuilding or repair, within a time period that the Supervisor specifies, that shall not be less than six months.

(c) If an apartment owner did not transfer his right as set forth in subsection (b), the Supervisor may, upon request of the restorers, order the transfer of the right to another person who shall be proposed by the restorers, and in the absence of such a proposal – to whomever the Supervisor shall decide upon. The Supervisor may also order the registration of such right on the name of that person after the value of the right is paid to the apartment owner or deposited with the Supervisor.

(d) Where the parties did not agree upon the value of the right as set forth in this section, the Supervisor shall determine its value pursuant to the request of the restorers or of the apartment owner.

(e) An application to the Supervisor to exercise his authority pursuant to this section, is like any claim before the Supervisor, and the provisions of Article Four of Chapter Six of the law shall apply.

752. *Conditioning Upon Provisions Regarding Changes in the Common Property* – (a) The apartment owners in a condominium may, with the consent of all of the apartment owners, establish in agreed articles, that the provisions of this Article shall not apply to them.

(b) Nothing in the provisions of this Article shall derogate from the special provision in the agreed articles regarding the expansion of an apartment or building rights.

Chapter Four: Houses that are not Registered as Condominiums

753. *Definitions for the Houses that are not Registered as Cooperative Houses Chapter* – In this chapter –

"house" – a permanent structure, including the land upon which it is build, in which there are two or more apartments, and it is not registered as a condominium;

"apartment owner" – one who pursuant to a written contract is entitled to be registered as the owner of an apartment in a house or one who is registered or is entitled to be registered, pursuant to a written contract, as a long-term tenant or a long-term sub-tenant. For the purposes of this Chapter, there is a presumption that the one in possession of an apartment in a house is the owner of the apartment;

"common property" – as defined in section 724;

articles of a condominium" or "articles" – as per its meaning in section 729.

754. *Applicability of the Provisions of the Cooperative Houses Chapter* – Sections 725(b) and (c), 726(c), 727, 728(b), 729(b), 731(e), 732 through 734(a) and (c), 735 through 749 and 752 shall apply to a house pursuant to this Chapter, *mutatis mutandis*.

754A *Articles* – A house shall be managed in accordance with the standard articles in the Second Schedule, *mutatis mutandis*.

755. *The First Committee* – (a) The Supervisor may appoint a provisional committee until the first committee shall be formed pursuant to the articles; the composition of the provisional committee shall be in accordance with the recommendation of the owners of at least half of the apartments; in the absence of such a recommendation, the Supervisor shall appoint a provisional committee from among the apartment owners who are in the house, and in the absence of a practical possibility to do so – not from among the apart-

ment owners, and he may decide upon remuneration to be paid to it by the apartment owners.

(b) The committee that was appointed pursuant to subsection (a) shall for all intents and purposes be considered a committee formed pursuant to the provisions of the articles.

756. *The Practice in the Absence of a Committee in an Unregistered House* – Where a committee has not been formed pursuant to the provisions of the articles, or the committee is not functioning, the Supervisor may appoint a committee for the house and the provisions of 755 shall apply, *mutatis mutandis*, to the appointment of the committee, setting its remuneration and its status.

757. *A House that has been Registered* – Where a house was registered in the Register of Condominiums after it was managed pursuant to the provisions of this Chapter, the following provisions shall apply to it:

(1) a right or obligation of the house committee on the eve of the registration shall become a right or obligation of the committee of the condominium formed after its registration;

(2) a legal proceeding in the wake of a dispute as set forth in section 72 of the Land Law, that was applied to it on the eve of the registration shall be continued and it shall be regarded, *mutatis mutandis*, as if it was filed pursuant to Article Four of Chapter Six of said law.

Chapter Five: Mortgage

758. *Mortgage* – A mortgage is a pledge of immovable property.

759. *Applicability of the Chapter on Mortgage* – Immovable property or a registered lease of immovable property shall not be pledged except by mortgage.

760. *The Right of the Mortgagor in the Mortgaged Property* – A mortgage does not derogate from the right of the owner of the immovable property to possess it, to use it and to make any transaction with regard to it.

761. *Different Levels of Mortgage* – Where immovable property was mortgaged with mortgages of different rank and one of them has been redeemed, the owner of the property may replace the redeemed mortgage with another mortgage of the same rank if the terms of the mortgage next in rank provides for such a right.

762. *Transfer of Mortgage* – (a) The mortgagee may transfer the mortgage, or part of it, to another person, together with all or part of the debt secured by it, without the consent of the owner of the property.

(b) Where the mortgage was transferred, and the debtor was not informed of the transfer, he is discharged by paying the debt to the former mortgagee.

763. *Redemption of Mortgage Before the Time for Repayment of the Debt* – The terms of the mortgage do not derogate from the right to redeem the mortgaged property prior to the date for payment of the debt according to the provisions of section [13(b) of the Pledges Law[43]].

764. *Deposit of Repayment in the Office* – If the owner of real property wants to repay what he owes on the mortgage and the mortgagee does not accept the repayment, the owner of the property may deposit the whole or part of what is due from him with the

---

[43] Chapter Three in Subpart Two in Part Five (sections 628 through 668). The proposal for a new version of the Pledges Law is integrated in the Explanatory Notes. The reference is to the section in the existing law.

Registrar and may request that the Register discharge the mortgage to the extent that it has been redeemed. The Minister of Justice may promulgate regulations with regard to this section.

765. *Realization of Mortgage* – Realization of a mortgage shall be in accordance with a court judgment or an order of the Head of the Execution of Judgments and in the manner set forth in section [18 of the Pledges Law[44]].

Chapter Six: Easements

766. *Easement* – (a) An easement is a charge on immovable property conferring a right of enjoyment (hereinafter – subject property) but not the right of possession of the property.

(b) An easement may be pursuant to law or according to a contract.

767. *Types of Easement* – (a) An easement may be for the benefit of any of the following –

(1) immovable property (in this Chapter – the dominant property);
(2) a particular person (in this Chapter – the one entitled);
(3) kinds of people;
(4) the public.

(b) An easement in immovable property shall be for the benefit of the owner of the dominant property or for the benefit of the long-term lessee of the dominant property.

768. *Content of the Easement* – (a) An easement may provide –

(1) that the owner or the long-term lessee of the dominant property or one for whose benefit the easement was given, is entitled to make certain use of the servient property or to derive some other benefit from it;
(2) that the owner of the servient property shall refrain from carrying out a specific act with regard to it.

(b) An easement for the benefit of property may also provide that the owner of the servient property –

(1) shall carry out a specific act with respect to it;
(2) is not entitled to prevent the carrying out of a specific act in the dominant property.

769. *Easement by Limitation* – (a) A person who has exercised a right capable of being an easement for a period of thirty consecutive years, acquires the easement and is entitled to demand its registration; the provisions of this subsection shall not apply to an easement the content of which is as set forth in section 768(a)(2) or 768(b)(1).

(b) Written notice by the owner of the servient property to the person who has made use of such a right as set forth in subsection (a), including notice to the public, of his objection to the use of the right, interrupts the period referred to in subsection (a).

(c) The period of use of a right that is suitable to be an easement for the benefit of immovable property, by one who came in the place of the original user, shall be consecutive to the period use of the original user.

770. *Period of Easement* – An easement is for an unlimited period of time unless a time period has been set in the terms of the easement.

771. *Transferability Of Easement* – (a) The transfer of an easement for the benefit of a

[44] Chapter Three in Subpart Two in Part Five (sections 628 through 668). The proposal for a new version of the Pledges Law is integrated in the Explanatory Notes. The reference is to the section in the existing law.

person or a class of people or for the benefit of the public requires the consent of the owner of the servient property. The provisions of section 622 shall apply, *mutatis mutandis*, regarding the refusal of the owner of the servient property to approve the transfer of the easement.

(b) The provisions of subsection (a) shall apply, *mutatis mutandis*, to the transfer of an easement, as set forth in that subsection, as a result of death.

772. *Rescission or Change of Easement* – The court may, upon application of an interested party or of the Attorney General or his representative, rescind an easement or change its terms, if it found it appropriate to do so due to the non-exercise of the easement during a prolonged period of time or due to a change of circumstances; the court may award damages to one who incurred damages due to the rescission or the change.

773. *Easement in Re-Partition or Unification of Property* – (a) Where the dominant or the servient property is partitioned, the easement shall be attached to the parcel to the benefit of or over which the easement existed, as the case may be.

(b) Where the dominant and servient property are unified, the easement is terminated.

774. *Easement Between Property of One Owner* – The fact that the dominant and the servient property belong to the same person does not preclude the creation of an easement or bring about the termination of an existing easement.

774A. *Undertaking to bestow easement* – In respect of the obligation to bestow an easement for consideration, the provisions of the Subpart Three of Part Three of Chapter Three: Rental Contract, and the provisions of the aforesaid subpart in Chapter Seven: Borrowing Contract, shall apply, *mutatis mutandis*, to the undertaking to bestow an easement without consideration[45].

774B. *Registration of easement* – The provisions of section 541 shall also apply to an easement, *mutatis mutandis*.

Chapter Seven: Preemption

775. *Preemption* – (a) Preemption is the right of a person (in this Chapter – the owner of the preemption) that an owner of immovable property shall not transfer his right to another, in whole or in part, unless he offered it first to the owner of the preemption.

(b) Where a right of preemption has been granted regarding transfer of ownership, the right shall also apply regarding a long-term lease of the property.

(c) A right of preemption may be pursuant to a contract or to law.

776. *Failure to Exercise Preemption* – Where the owner of a right of presumption has chosen not to exercise his right and the rights in the property have been transferred to a third party, the right of preemption shall be terminated.

777. *Applicability of Preemption with Regard to Substitute* – Notwithstanding the provisions of section 776, the owner of a right in immovable property and the owner of a right of preemption pursuant to a contract may make a stipulation that the right of preemption shall not be terminated upon transfer of the right in the property to a third party as set forth in that section, provided that if it is so stipulated, the right of preemption shall apply for a period not to exceed twenty-five years from the date on which the right was first transferred to a third party.

778. *Preemption Between Spouses* – (a) Where immovable property that is an agricultural farm or business jointly owned or leased in a long-term lease by spouses and jointly

---

[45] Sections 230 to 251 and 252 to 255, respectively.

managed by them, or a place that serves as their residence, each spouse has a right of preemption with respect to the share of the other spouse in such property.

(b) The provisions of subsection (a) shall also apply, *mutatis mutandis*, to spouses who are entitled to be registered as owners or long-term tenants of such property in that subsection.

779. *Preemption in Property of Heirs* – (a) Where immovable property is an agricultural farm and the right of ownership or long-term tenancy of it has passed by way of succession to several joint heirs, each heir has a right of preemption with respect to the portion of the other heirs in that property for a period of two years from the date that the succession order or the order for execution of the will is given; for this purpose "agricultural farm" means a unit the partition of which will damage its suitability as an agricultural farm that is likely to provide a livelihood for an agricultural family.

(b) In the course of the period of time set forth in subsection (a), each heir may register a right of preemption to his benefit as set forth in that subsection, for any additional period of time; if he did so, the heir shall have a right of preemption for the additional period of time that he registered.

(c) If the heirs did not exercise their right of preemption pursuant to subsection (a) or (b), and a third party acquired the part of one of the heirs, the remaining heirs shall have a preemption vis a vis the other heirs.

Article Two: Acquisition by Preemption

780. *Acquisition by Preemption* – (a) The owner of a right of preemption may, within 30 days from receipt of the offer as set forth in section 775, pay to the owner of the right in the property the price demanded together with any fee and other mandatory payment due from him with respect to the acquisition or to deposit it with the Land Registrar, and having acting thus, the parties are viewed as having consented to the transfer of the right in the property for the price demanded.

(b) If the owner of the right of preemption did not act as set forth in subsection (a), the owner of the right in property may, within six months from the end of the period set forth in that subsection, transfer the right as he desires, provided that he shall not transfer it for a price lower than or according to more beneficial terms than those set forth in the offer.

(c) Where there are two or more owners of a right of preemption, the owner of the right in the property shall make his offer to all of them; if all or some of them agreed to acquire the right in the property, they may act as set forth in this section, according to the share of each of them in the right of preemption; if one of them did not do so, his share shall accrue to the others, according to their shares.

Article Three: Applicability of Right of Preemption

781. *Applicability of Preemption Right – Transfer Without Consideration* – The right of presumption shall not apply to the conferment of a right without consideration or to the transfer by succession; however, the right of preemption shall not be terminated in such a case and shall apply with respect to the one receiving the right and his heirs.

782. *Applicability of Preemption Right – Transfer by Law* – none

Chapter Eight: Notes

783. *Registration of Cautionary Note due to Obligation* – (a) Where the Land Registrar is convinced that the owner of a right in immovable property registered in the Land Registry, of the nature of ownership, lease, borrowing, easement, right of preemption or mortgage, has undertaken in writing to effect or to refrain from effecting a transaction

in his right (in this Chapter – the person obligated), the Registrar shall register a note to such effect, upon the application of the person obligated or the one entitled under the undertaking (in this Chapter – the person entitled).

(b) Where a note was registered solely on the basis of the application of the person entitled, the Registrar shall notify the person obligated, as soon as possible, of the entry of the note.

(c) A cautionary note that was registered as stated in this section does not require registration in any other registry or ledger kept pursuant to legislation.

784. *Note on Need for Consent* – Where the Land Registrar is convinced that a transaction by an owner of a right in immovable property, as stated in section 783, requires the consent of a third party pursuant to legislation, court order or written undertaking, the Registrar shall register a note to that effect upon the application of such third party.

785. *Note on Restriction of Capacity* – Where it has been proven to the Land Registrar, by means of a court order or public certificate, that the legal capacity of the owner of immovable property or the owner of rights in immovable property as set forth in section 783 has been restricted pursuant to legislation, the Registrar shall register a note to that effect upon application of an interested third party or of the Attorney General or his representative; For this purpose, a "public certificate" is as defined in section 29 of the Evidence Ordinance [new version], 5731–1971.

786. *Note on the Basis of Court Order* – The court may order the registration of another cautionary note under the conditions it deems appropriate, and once the order is submitted to the Land Registrar he shall register the note in accordance with the order.

787. *Note on the Basis of Regulations* – The Minister of Justice may prescribe other regulations that the Registrar shall register, if he has found that it is necessary for the operation of legislation or in order to prevent a violation of legislation, and he may, in such regulations, provide for the manner of their registration and cancellation.

788. *Consequences of Registration of Note* – (a) Where a cautionary note has been registered pursuant to section 783, as and long as it has not been cancelled, a transaction that is inconsistent with the content of the note shall not be registered, except pursuant to court order or with the consent of the person entitled according to the note.

(b) If a note has been registered pursuant to sections 784 through 787, and as long as it has not been cancelled, a transaction that is inconsistent with the content of the note shall not be registered.

(c) A transaction that confers part of the immovable property, by way of ownership or long-term lease, to a local authority for the purpose of roads, sidewalks or widening of such, that is done according to a plan that was approved pursuant to the Planning and Construction Law, will not be regarded as a transaction that is inconsistent with a cautionary note, provided that thirty days before the registration of the transaction, a notice was sent to the person entitled according to the cautionary note.

789. *Force of Cautionary Note* – (a) Without derogating from the provisions of section 588, where a cautionary note has been registered and afterwards a lien is imposed on the right in immovable property that is the subject of the note or a receivership order in bankruptcy proceedings has been issued or a dissolution order against the owner of the immovable property or the owner of the right in the property or a receiver has been appointed for his property, and as long as the cautionary note has not been cancelled, nothing in all of this shall infringe upon the rights of the person entitled stemming from the obligation that is the subject of the note.

(b) Notwithstanding the provisions of subsection (a), a claim for the rescission of the transaction due to bankruptcy or liquidation that would have been available against the transaction, if it was completed by registration at the time the note was registered, shall be valid against such undertaking.

790. *Cancellation of Note* – (a) A note registered pursuant to sections 783 through 785 shall be cancelled pursuant to a court order, or if the Land Registrar is convinced that one of the following has been fulfilled:

(1) the interested parties consented to the cancellation;

(2) the grounds for the note no longer exist, provided that the Registrar notified the interested parties in advance of his intention to cancel the note, and gave them reasonable time to apply to the court.

(b) A note registered pursuant to section 786 shall be cancelled pursuant to a court order.

Chapter Nine: Cancellation of Attachments

791. *Limitation on Period of Validity of Attachment* – (a) When ten years have passed from the day upon which the attachment was registered, the Land Registrar may cancel it unless an order to extend its validity has been submitted for registration.

(b) If the Land Registrar decided to cancel an attachment at the end of the period set forth in subsection (a), he shall send a notice, at least forty five days prior to the erasure, to the person to whose benefit the lien was registered, to the extent that his address is known, or shall publish a notice in two daily newspapers.

Sub-Part Four – Special Provisions for Chattels

Chapter One: Chattels

792. *Definitions for Moveable Property Chapter* – In this Chapter, "chattels" includes property rights, to the extent that it is appropriate under the circumstances, *mutatis mutandis*.

793. *Connection or Intermingling of Moveable Property* – (a) If the chattels of one person has become connected or intermingled with the chattels of another person, to the point where they cannot be identified or separated, or separating them necessitates unreasonable damage or expense (in this Chapter – connected chattels), the connected chattels shall be jointly owned by the two people, each of them according to the value of the chattels immediately prior to their becoming connected.

(b) If the chattels of one person were the primary property and the chattels of the other person were subordinate, the ownership of the subordinate chattels shall be transferred to the owner of the primary chattels, and he will pay the owner of the subordinate chattels the amount that he became entitled to through acquisition of the subordinate chattels.

794. *Encumbrance of Connected Moveable Property* – (a) If the chattels of one of the joint owners as set forth in section 793(a) were encumbered immediately prior to the connection, the encumbrance shall apply to his share of the connected chattels.

(b) If the primary chattels as described in section 793(b) were encumbered immediately prior to the connection, the encumbrance shall also apply to the chattels the ownership of which was transferred pursuant to that section; if the subordinate chattels were encumbered, the encumbrance shall apply to the obligation that the owner of the primary chattels owes.

(c) Where a pledge has been substituted pursuant to this section, the parties shall do the acts necessary pursuant to the chapter on pledges,[46] according to the demand of the creditor, in order for the pledge to be enforceable with respect to other creditors of the debtor.

(d) For the purposes of subsections (a) and (c), a lien is regarded as an encumbrance.

(e) This section shall also apply, *mutatis mutandis*, to a case in which the chattels were under the ownership of one person immediately prior to becoming connected.

795. *Processing of Connected Chattels* – Sections 793 and 794 shall also apply, *mutatis mutandis*, when a person causes changes to chattels of another in the course of his work; in such a case, the value of the work shall be viewed as the value of the chattels.

796. *Abandonment of Chattels* – Ownership of chattels ends when their owner removes them from his control with the intention to abandon them.

797. *Gain from the Abandonment of Chattels* – Any person may, subject to any law, acquire chattels that are ownerless by taking possession of them with the intention of gaining entitlement to them.

Chapter Two: Restoration of Lost Property[47]

798. *Definitions for the Restoration of Lost Property Chapter* – In this Chapter –

"lost property" – chattels that their owner has lost or as to which it may be assumed that they left his control, under the circumstances;

"owner" with respect to lost property includes one entitled to possess the lost property.

799. *The Obligation to Return Lost Property* – (a) One who finds lost property and takes it (in this Chapter – the finder) must return it to its owner or notify the police of it promptly unless under the circumstances it may be assumed that the owner of the lost property has given up on it due to its negligible value.

(b) If the finder informed the police, he may deliver the lost property to the police, and must do so if the police so requested him.

800. *Lost Property in the Domain of Another* – (a) One who finds lost property in the domain of another must notify the owner of the domain of the lost property and deliver it to him upon his request. If the owner of the domain requested delivery of the lost property, the rights of the finder are acquired by him even if the finder did not comply with the request. If the owner of the domain did not request delivery of the lost property, the rights shall be those of the finder.

(b) The court may rule that the rights in lost property shall be divided equally between the finder and the owner of the domain, unless it deemed it appropriate to fix another rate of division.

801. *Lost Property Whose Owner was not Discovered* – (a) Where the finder notified the police of lost property pursuant to section 799 and the owner of the lost property was not discovered within four months from the day that he so notified the police, he will be the owner of the lost property.

(b) If the finder did not notify the police pursuant to the provisions of section 799 and the owner of the lost property was not discovered within four months after the police became aware that the lost property was found, the State shall be the owner of the lost

---

[46] Chapter Three in Subpart Two of this Part (Part Five) (sections 628 through 668). A proposal for a new version of the Pledge Law is integrated in the Explanatory Notes.

[47] The chapter is under consideration.

property; if the finder delivered the lost property to the police but did not demand its delivery to him within two months from the day on which he became its owner pursuant to subsection (a), the ownership of the lost property shall be transferred to the State.

(c) The Minister for Internal Security may, upon consultation with the Minister of Justice, decide that the provisions of this section shall not apply to valuable lost property or to lost property that may be assumed to be of special sentimental value to its owner, or to other special kinds of lost property, or that the provisions shall apply with extension of the time limits set forth or with other changes as shall be provided for in regulations.

802. *Sale of Lost Property* – (a) Where lost property is property likely to be ruined or to lose a substantial portion of its value or the costs of keeping it are unreasonable as compared to its value, or if it is an animal, the finder may sell it in a reasonable manner, as may the police if the lost property was delivered to it.

(b) The finder shall not sell the lost property as set forth until he has so notified the police a reasonable period of time in advance and the police did not request him to deliver the property to it.

(c) If the lost property has been sold, for the purposes of this Chapter, the price received for it shall come in its stead.

803. *Neglected Property* –(a) If property was deposited or left in a facility in which people stay, are hospitalized or visit, or in a similar place, and it was not requested within two months from the day that it was left or from the end of the period for which it was deposited, the property will be considered, for the purposes of the Administrator General Law 5738–1978,[48] as abandoned property as defined in that law.

(b) The provisions of subsection (a) shall not derogate from the terms of the deposit.

804. *Property of an Absentee* – The provisions of this Chapter shall apply, *mutatis mutandis*, to the chattels of a person whose whereabouts are unknown, or who died and his heirs are unknown, and the Administrator General or another who is so authorized did not receive them.

805. *Redemption of Lost Property* – (a) If the finder of lost property became entitled to it according to this Chapter, the former owner of the lost property may, within one year after such entitlement, redeem it from the one who became entitled by paying its value at the time of the redemption, unless a material change has occurred in the meantime.

(b) The provisions of subsection (a) shall also apply regarding a third party who acquired the lost property from the one who became entitled to it, unless the third party acquired the lost property for consideration and was unaware of the existence of the right to redeem it.

806. *Delegation of Functions and Authority* – The Minister of International Security may, with the consent of the Minister of the Interior, delegate the police's functions pursuant to this Chapter to a local authority that it authorized for this purpose; this delegation may by limited or contingent.

---

[48] *Sefer HaHukim* 5738, p. 61.

Part Six: Limitation Of Claims[49]

Chapter One: Definitions

807. *Definitions for the Limitations Part* – In this Part –

"area" – as defined in the addendum to the Extension of the Validity of the Emergency Regulations (Judea, Sumeria and Gaza Strip – Adjudication of Crimes and Legal Assistance), 5728–1967;[50]

"court" – judicial or quasi-judicial authority, excepting a religious court, including an arbitrator, and with respect to an action regarding a debt – including all of the following:

(1) a trustee who was appointed pursuant to the provisions of the Bankruptcy Ordinance [new version], 5740–1980;[51]
(2) a liquidator appointed pursuant to the Companies Ordinance [new version], 5743–1983[52], the Cooperative Societies Ordinance,[53] and the Non-Profit Organizations Ordinance, 5740–1980;[54]
(3) one who was appointed pursuant to the Companies Law, 5759–1999,[55] as the holder of a position in a compromise or arrangement process;

"action" – civil process before a Court.

Chapter Two: Principles of Limitation of Claims

808. *Limitation of Claim* – A claim for the enforcement of a right that any person has vis a vis another person (in this Part – a claim) is subject to limitation of claims.

809. *Action for a Claim that has Expired* – The court shall not entertain an action on a claim that has expired provided that the argument of limitation of claims was raised at the first reasonable opportunity after the action was filed; if limitation of claims was not argued at that time – the argument shall not be entertained.

810. *Effect of Limitation on a Right* – (a) Limitation of claims of a claim does not void the right itself, in the absence of any other provision in the legislation.

(b) Without derogating from the provisions of subsection (a), nothing in the provisions of this Part prevent the exercise of a right, through means other than a legal action, according to the provisions of any law, including collection processes.

Chapter Three: The Period of Limitation of claims and the Date of Limitation of claims

811. *Period of Limitation* – The period of limitation of claims of a claim is four years, unless it is been provided otherwise in this law or other legislation.

812. *Period of Limitation Regarding Claim by a Minor* – The period of limitation of a claim of a minor is seven years, but no more than four years from the day that he reached the age of majority; however the claim of a minor shall not be prescribed before he reaches the age of ten.

---

[49] This Part is undergoing a separate legislative process.

[50] *Sefer HaHukim* 5728, p. 20; 5756, p. 34.

[51] *Dinei Medinat Yisrael*, new version 34, p. 639.

[52] *Dinei Medinat Yisrael*, new version 37, p. 761.

[53] *Hukei Eretz Yisrael*, vol. 1, p. 336.

[54] *Sefer HaHukim* 5740, p. 210.

[55] *Sefer HaHukim* 5759, p. 186.

813. *The date of Limitation of Claim* – A claim shall be limited on the day on which the period of limitation that was set forth for it pursuant to the provisions of this law or other legislation ends; however, claims arising from the same cause of action shall be prescribed together, on the earliest date on which the period of limitation that was set forth for one of the claims has run.

814. *Claims Arising from the Same Cause of Action* – (a) Claims that are different from one another with respect to their facts, the rights whose enforcement is claimed, the law that establishes such rights or the relief requested – shall be considered, for the purposes of section 813, as claims arising from the same cause of action, if they are essentially identical so as to justify their limitation together at the time set forth in that section.

(b) Claims for compensation, that are different from one another only with regard to the damage for which the compensation is claimed, shall be considered claims arising from the same cause of action, as set forth in subsection (a).

(c) Notwithstanding the provisions of section 813, where the limitation has run on a claim for compensation for specific damage (in this subsection – earlier damage), the claim for compensation for later damage (in this subsection – later damage) arising pursuant to the provisions of subsection (a) from the same cause of action shall not run on the same day as the claim for the earlier damage, if all of the following are fulfilled:

(1) the plaintiff refrained, on reasonable grounds, from filing an action for compensation for the earlier damage;
(2) the later damage is substantially greater than the earlier damage;
(3) the plaintiff did not delay in filing an action for the later damage.

(d) For the purposes of this section, increase in the monetary value of specific damage shall not be considered to be other damage.

814a. *Causes of Action Created from an On-going Event* – Where a number of causes of action arise consecutively from an on-going event, the limitation shall run as to each cause of action in its turn.

815. *Beginning of the Running of the Period of Limitation* – The period of limitation of a claim shall begin to run on the day on which the cause of action was created, unless the running of the period was delayed pursuant to the provisions of Chapter Four in this Part.

816. *Claim Contingent upon Demand or Notice* – A claim contingent upon delivery of notice or demand from the plaintiff arises on the day the notice or the demand is delivered, or on the day on which a reasonable plaintiff would not have delayed delivery of the notice or of the demand, according to the earlier of the two.

817. None

Chapter Four: Tolling of Period of Limitation

818. *Grounds for Tolling of the Running of the Period of Limitations* – The running of the period of limitation of a claim shall be tolled when the parties to the claim are the original parties, as long as one of grounds for tolling as set forth below pertains:

(1) The plaintiff did not know, and did not need to know, a fact that constituted part of the cause of action, that is vital to the filing of the action; for this purpose –
   (a) The following facts, inter alia, shall be considered vital facts: the identity of the defendant, the act of the defendant that is the subject of the claim, the injury to the defendant that is the subject of the claim and the existence of a causal relationship between said act and said injury;

(b) knowledge of the law that establishes the right that is the subject of the claim shall not be regarded a vital fact;

(c) regarding a plaintiff who is a minor or a person who, due to a mental disability, whether temporary or permanent, is not capable of taking care of his affairs (in this section – a person with disability), the knowledge of the guardian will be viewed as the knowledge of the plaintiff;

(2) The plaintiff is a person with disability and a guardian was not appointed for him;

(3) the plaintiff is a minor who does not have a guardian;

(4) in a claim for bodily injury only – the plaintiff is a minor who has a guardian and both of the following have been fulfilled:

(a) the guardian refrained from filing an action as set forth, due to special circumstances that justify the tolling of the running of the period of limitations regarding the minor;

(b) the injury that will be caused to the minor if the running of the period of limitations is not tolled is significantly greater than the injury that will be caused to the defendant and to the public if the running of the period of limitations is tolled;

(5) The plaintiff is the guardian of the defendant or is is subject to his guardianship;

(6) The parties to the claim are married to one another; for these purposes, where a marriage was declared null ab initio, or where they were lawfully annulled, the parties shall be regarded as married until the date of the declaration that the marriage is void or until it is annulled, as is the case;

(7) The defendant is outside of Israel or the area, and as a result he was prevented from conducting the litigation in Israel or in the area, as is the case; for this purpose, purpose, "plaintiff" or "defendant" means –

(a) in a claim regarding property conferred on the Guardian of Property of Missing Persons pursuant to the Missing Persons Law, 5710–1950[56] or conferred on the Guardian of Property of Germans pursuant to the Property of Germans Law, 5710–1950[57] – the one who was the owner of the rights in the property immediately prior to the conferment;

(b) in a claim regarding property administered by the Administrator General pursuant to the Administrator General Law, 5738–1978[58] – the owner of the rights in the property immediately prior to the beginning of the management;

(8) The plaintiff refrained from filing an action because the defendant or someone acting on his behalf was intentionally misleading the plaintiff, applying force against him, threatening him or exploiting his distress; for this purpose "misleading" – includes by means of admitting to a right that is the subject of the claim or partial fulfillment of such right, or by way of concealing a vital fact as set forth in clause (1), from the plaintiff.

819. *Running of the Period of Limitations in Transfer of a Right* – (a) The transfer of a right that is the subject of the claim from the original plaintiff or the one who came in his stead

---

[56] *Sefer HaHukim* 5710, p. 86.

[57] *Sefer HaHukim* 5710, p. 266.

[58] *Sefer HaHukim* 5738, p. 61.

to another person (in this section – plaintiff by transfer), regardless of whether it was pursuant to legislation or contract, shall not, in itself, affect the running of the period of limitation of the claim.

(b) If the plaintiff was a plaintiff by transfer, the running of the period of limitation of the claim that he is a party to shall be tolled as long as one of the following grounds for tolling is fulfilled with respect to him:

(1) the grounds for tolling set forth in section 818(1), provided that the running of the limitation period of the claim has not yet started due to such grounds for tolling, as set forth;
(2) the grounds for tolling set forth in section 818(7) or (8);
(3) with respect to a plaintiff by transfer who is an heir – the grounds set forth in sections 818(2) through (6) as well.

820. *Running of Period of Limitations in Transfer of Obligation* – (a) The transfer of an obligation to fulfill a right that is the subject of a claim from the original defendant or one who replaces him to another person (in this section – the defendant by transfer), whether pursuant to legislation or contract, shall not in itself affect the running of the period of limitation of the claim.

(b) If the defendant was a defendant by transfer, the running of the period of limitation of a claim that he is a party to shall be stopped as long as one of the grounds for tolling set forth in section 818 is fulfilled with respect to him.

Chapter Five: Extension of the Period of Limitation

821. *Extension After End of Interruption* – Where the running of the period of limitation was tolled pursuant to the provisions of Chapter Four, the period of limitation shall not end prior to the expiration of six months from the day on which the grounds for the tolling ceased to exist.

822. *Extension Due to Absence from Israel* – (a) Where the plaintiff is outside of Israel or the area and he was consequently prevented from conducting the litigation in Israel or in the area, as is the case, for this reason and for additional conditions and circumstances that justify an extension of the period of limitation, the period of limitation shall not end until a year has expired from the day on which the plaintiff is in Israel or in the area, as is the case, or from the day on which such conditions and circumstances have ceased to exist, according to the earliest day.

(b) If the plaintiff and the defendant are outside of Israel or of the area, as is the case, and the plaintiff is prevented from conducting the litigation due to conditions and circumstances that justify extension of the period of limitation, the period of limitation shall not end before a year has expired from the day on which such conditions and circumstances have ceased to exist.

(c) In this section "plaintiff" and "defendant" are as defined in section 818(7).

823. *Extension Regarding Attendant Claim* – (a) Where an action was filed for a claim (in this section – original action and original claim), and the proceedings in the action have ended in such a manner that the plaintiff is not barred from filing another action for the original claim or an attendant claim, the period of limitations of the original claim or of the attendant claim, as is the case, shall not end until one year has passed from the day that the judgment in the original action became final.

(b) Where an application to amend the original action was filed in order to include in it an additional claim, and on the day the application was filed the period of limitation regarding the additional claim had already expired, the court shall not accede to the application, unless the additional claim was an attendant claim.

(c) In this section "attendant claim" – a claim with respect to which all of the following are fulfilled:

(1) it originates in the same event that gave rise to the original claim;
(2) the defendant is the defendant in the original claim or his successor;
(3) the period of limitation of with respect to it had not yet expired on the day the original action was filed;
(4) the defendant knew or should have known, due to the filing of the original action, of the possibility that an action would be filed against him due to the attendant claim, in addition to or in place of the original action.

824. *Extension due to the Court not Working* – Where the plaintiff could not file an action on a claim, due to an unexpected break in the course of the work of the court of jurisdiction, the period of limitation shall not expire until 60 days from the day on which the work of the court of jurisdiction was resumed.

825. *Extension due to Death* – Where a person died before the limitation ran on a claim available to him, the period of limitation of the claim shall not expire before the expiration of one of the periods of time detailed herein:

(1) six months from the day of the appointment of an executor of the estate;
(2) six months from the day that an inheritance order or an order to execute the will has been issued;
(3) two years from the date of death.

826. *Extension for Special Reasons* – (a) The court, as that term is used in the Courts Law [integrated version], 5744–1984[59], or the labor court as that term is used in the Labor Court Law, 5729–1969[60], may, upon application of the plaintiff and on special grounds, extend the period of limitations of a claim within its jurisdiction, provided that the plaintiff's application was submitted to the court or to the labor court, as is the case, and was served upon the defendant within the period of limitations.

(b) The extension of the period of limitations pursuant to the provisions of subsection (a) shall be for a very short period of time, as necessary under the circumstances.

(c) Where the plaintiff requested an extension of the period of limitations pursuant to the provisions of subsection (a), the period of limitations of the claim shall not terminate until 60 days have passed from the date of the court decision.

(d) The costs of the proceeding pursuant to this section shall be borne by the plaintiff, unless the court has ruled otherwise.

Chapter Six: Upper Limit on Limitations

827. *The Upper Period* – (a) Notwithstanding the provisions of this part, with the expiration of the period of the upper limit on limitations, the period of limitations on the claim shall have run, even if on such date the period of limitations has not yet expired.

(b) In this Chapter, "the period of the upper limit" – 25 years from the date of the act of the defendant that is the subject of the claim, however, in a claim the subject of which is medical treatment as defined in the Patient's Rights Law, 5756–1996,[61] the period of the upper limit shall be 18 years from the date of the act of the defendant that is the sub-

[59] *Sefer HaHukim* 5744, p. 198.
[60] *Sefer HaHukim* 5729, p. 70.
[61] *Sefer HaHukim* 5756, p. 327.

ject of the claim and if the act that is the subject of the claim was done on a date when the plaintiff was a minor, 22 years from the day of such act.

828. *Postponement and Extension of the Period of the Upper Limit* – (a) The running of the period of the upper limit shall not be postponed due to the grounds for the running of the period of limitations pursuant to the provisions of Chapter Four, other than for the grounds for tolling as set forth in section 818(8).

(b) The period of the upper limit shall not be extended due to an extension of the period of limitations pursuant to the provisions of Chapter Five.

829. *The Period of Upper Limit in a Claim for Participation or Restitution* – The period of limitation on a claim for participation or restitution due to an act of the defendant as to which the period of the upper limit has expired, shall expire, even if on this date the period of limitations has not yet expired.

Chapter Seven: Special Provisions Regarding Limitations

830. *Limitation Regarding Acquisition of Chattels* – (a) Where the period of limitations has run on a claim of the owner of chattels or the person entitled to possess them to receive such chattels from the person possessing them, and at least seven years have passed from the date on which said claim arose, the rights of the owner of the chattels or of the one entitled to possess them shall expire and shall be conferred upon the one possessing them, and the period of limitations with respect to any claim available to them against the possessor with regard to the possession of the chattels shall run, if it had not run previously.

(b) For the purpose of calculating the period of the limitations of a claim as described in subsection (a) and calculation of the period of seven years from the day on which the claim arose, as set forth in that subsection, the periods of possession of the various successor possessors shall be combined; nothing in the provisions of this subsection shall derogate from the provisions of Chapter Four.

831. None

832. *Limitations of Pledge and Mortgage* – (a) The limitations of claim of a creditor to realize a mortgage, or to realize a pledge for a right regarding immoveable property, shall be at the end of ten years from the date on which the period of limitations ran on the claim for the fulfillment of the obligation that the mortgage or pledge was given to insure.

(b) The limitation of a claim of a creditor to realize a pledge, that is not a pledge as set forth in subsection (a), shall be at the end of three years from the date on which the period of limitations ran on the claim to fulfill the obligation that the pledge was given to insure.

(c) Where the limitation ran on all of the claims to realize a pledge or a mortgage, the court shall order, upon application of the debtor, their cancellation and cancellation from the registry kept pursuant to law, and the court may order as stated upon application of another interested party; where the limitation ran with respect to some of the claims to realize the pledge or mortgage, the court may, upon application of the debtor or another interested party, order the correction of the registration of the pledge or the mortgage in such registry.

(d) For the purposes of this section, "pledge" – a pledge registered in accordance with law in the registry in which encumbrances are registered pursuant to law or a pledge deposited within the meaning of section 4(2) of the Pledge Law, 5727–1967.[62]

832a. *Limitations of a Claim after Conviction of a Sexual Offense against a Minor* – In a civil claim for which an action was filed pursuant to the provisions of section 77 of the Court Law [integrated version], 5744–1984,[63] against a person who was convicted of a offense from among those in section 354(a)(1) and (2) of the Penal Law, 5737–1977,[64] perpetrated against a minor, a plea of limitations shall not be entertained.

833. *Limitations Regarding Claim for Fulfillment of Ancillary Right* – The limitations with respect to a claim for the fulfillment of a right that is ancillary to another right shall run with the running of the limitations of the claim for the fulfillment of the other right if it has not run prior to that time.

834. *Limitations of Judgment* – (a) The period of limitations on a claim for the execution of a final judgment and of any other claim for the fulfillment of a right pursuant to such judgment is seven years.

(b) For the purposes of this section, a mortgage, a pledge as defined in section 832(d), and a note as defined in section 81a of the Execution of Judgments Law, 5727–1967,[65] shall not be considered to be a judgment.

835. *Limitations of a Claim for Declaratory Relief* – For the purpose of this Part, judicial proceedings for the granting of declaratory relief against another person is regarded as a claim for the fulfillment of a right against that person.

836. *Declaratory Relief on Limitations* – The court may give declaratory relief regarding the limitations of a claim within its jurisdiction; the declaration shall be valid against anyone who was a party to the proceeding.

837. *Limitations on Set-Off Claims and Counterclaims* – (a) Where a defendant has made a plea of set-off against the claim of a plaintiff, no plea of limitations against the claim on which the plea of set-off is based shall be entertained, unless both of the following are fulfilled with respect to such claim:

(1) its source is not in the event that gave rise to the plaintiff's claim;

(2) the limitations ran before the plaintiff's claim arose.

(b) Where the defendant has a counterclaim, whose origin is in the event that gave rise to the plaintiff's claim, no plea of limitations made on the part of the plaintiff shall be entertained.

837a. *Existence of Right after Limitations have Run* – Where a debtor fulfilled an obligation after the limitations ran on the claim for the fulfillment of that right, he will not be entitled to restitution on the sole basis that the limitations on the claim ran.

837b. *Declaratory Relief on Limitations* – The court may give declaratory relief regarding limitation of a claim that is within its jurisdiction; such declaratory relief will be valid *vis a vis* one who was a party to the action regarding the granting of such relief.

838. *Agreement Regarding Period of Limitations* – (a) The parties to a contract may agree on a period of limitations different from that set forth in this Part, provided that it shall not be less than one year.

(b) A contract for an agreement regarding the period of limitations shall be a separate written contract.

---

[62] *Sefer HaHukim* 5727, p. 48.

[63] *Sefer HaHukim* 5744, p. 198.

[64] *Sefer HaHukim* 5737, p. 322.

[65] *Sefer HaHukim* 5727, p. 116.

Chapter Eight: Preservation of Laws and Miscellaneous Provisions

838a. *Preservation of Laws Regarding Limitations on Actions Regarding Immoveable Property* – (a) Notwithstanding the provisions of this Part and subject to the provisions of subsections (b) and (c) and section 832, the provisions of the law that applied to the limitations on a claim regarding immoveable property prior to the effective date of this law shall continue to apply.

(b) On a claim on the basis of an obligation for the transfer of a right in immoveable property or regarding immoveable property, or the prevention of the transfer of such a right, the provisions of this law shall apply.

(c) Notwithstanding the provisions of subsection (b), the period of limitations on a claim on the basis of an obligation for either of the following is seven years:

(1) transfer of ownership or long-term lease in immoveable property;

(2) transfer of right of a transferor regarding a third party for the receipt of the ownership or long-term tenancy in immoveable property;

however, limitations shall not run on a claim for the enforcement of such an obligation if the possession of the immoveable property was transferred according to that obligation.

838b. *Preservation of Laws Regarding Limitations on a Claim Connected to the Holocaust* – A claim regarding damage caused as a consequence of the Holocaust, the limitations on which is earlier that the limitations according to the law that was applicable to it prior to the effective date of this law shall be prescribed pursuant to such law.

838c. *Dismissal of Action due to Delay* – This Part shall not derogate from the court's authority, pursuant to another law, to dismiss an action or to refuse to grant relief, due to delay or on other grounds connected to the date that the claim was raised.

839. *Effectiveness* – The provisions of this Part shall apply if there is no other explicit or implicit intent in any other law or legislation, regarding the matter dealt with in this Part.

840. *Regulations for the Limitations Part* – The Minister of Justice may promulgate regulations regarding, *inter alia*, the conferring of validity to the provisions regarding the calculation and length of the periods of limitation set forth in an agreement between Israel and another state, or in an international treaty that Israel is a party to, even if the provisions in such agreement or treaty conflict with a provision contained in this Part.

Sections 841–843 – none

Table of Concordance
(see the final paragraph of the preface to this volume)

The sec. in the current version	*The sec. in the former version*	*The sec. in the current version*	*The sec. in the former version*	*The sec. in the current version*	*The sec. in the former version*
1	1	96	29	124	58
2	2	97	30	125	59
3	3	98	31	126	60
4	4	98A	32	127	61
4A	5	99	33	128	62
5	6	100	34	129	63
none	6–74	101	35	130	64
75	7	102	36	131	65
76	8	103	37	132	66
77	9	104	38	133	67
77A	10	105	39	134	68
78	11	106	40	135	69
79	12	107	41	136	70
80	13	108	42	137	71
81	14	109	43	138	72
82	15	110	44	139	73
83	16	111	45	140	74
84	17	112	46	141	75
85	18	113	47	142	76
86	19	114	48	142A	77
87	20	115	49	142B	78
88	21	116	50	143	79
89	22	117	51	144	80
90	23	118	52	145	81
91	24	119	53	146	82
92	25	120	54	147	83
93	26	121	55	148	85
94	27	122	56	149	86
95	28	123	57	150	84

The sec. in the current version	*The sec. in the former version*	*The sec. in the current version*	*The sec. in the former version*	*The sec. in the current version*	*The sec. in the former version*
151	87	193	129	235	183
152	88	194	130	236	184
153	89	195	131	237	185
154	90	196	132	238	186
155	91	197	133	239	187
156	92	198	134	240	188
157	93	199	135	241	189
158	94	200	136	242	190
159	95	201	137	243	191
160	96	202	138	244	192
161	97	203	139	245	193
162	98	204	140	246	194
163	99	205	141	247	195
164	100	206	142	248	196
165	101	207	155	249	197
166	102	208	156	250	198
167	103	209	157	251	199
168	104	210	159	252	200
169	105	211	158	253	201
170	106	212	160	254	202
171	107	213	161	255	203
172	108	214	162	256	204
173	109	215	163	257	205
174	110	216	164	285	206
175	111	217	165	259	207
176	112	218	166	260	208
177	113	219	167	261	209
178	114	220	168	262	210
179	115	221	169	263	211
180	116	222	170	264	212
181	117	223	171	265	213
182	118	224	172	266	214
183	119	225	173	267	215
184	120	226	174	268	216
185	121	227	175	269	217
186	122	228	176	270	218
187	123	229	177	271	219
188	124	230	178	272	220
189	125	231	179	273	221
190	126	232	180	274	222
191	127	233	181	275	223
192	128	234	182	276	228

The sec. in the current version	*The sec. in the former version*	*The sec. in the current version*	*The sec. in the former version*	*The sec. in the current version*	*The sec. in the former version*
277	224	319	263	360	305
278	225	320	264	361	306
279	226	321	265	362	307
280	none	322	266	363	308
281	227	323	267	364	309
282	229	324	268	365	310
283	230	325	269	366	311
284	231	326	270	367	312
285	232	327	271	368	313
286	233	328	272	369	314
287	234	329	273	370	315
288	235	330	274	371	316
289	236	331	275	372	317
290	237	332	276	373	318
291	238	333	277	374	319
292	239	334	278	375	320
293	240	335	279	376	321
294	241	336	280	377	322
295	242	337	281	378	323
296	243	338	282	379	324
297	244	339	283	380	325
298	245	340	284	381	326
299	246	341	285	382	327
300	247	342	286	383	328
301	248	342A	287	384	329
302	249	343	288	385	330
303	250	344	289	386	331
304	251	345	290	387	332
305	252	346	291	388	333
306	253	347	292	389	334
307	254	348	293	390	335
308	256	349	294	391	336
309	255	350	295	392	337
310	none	351	296	393	338
311	none	352	297	394	339
312	none	353	298	395	340
313	257	354	299	396	341
314	258	355	300	397	342
315	259	356	301	398	343
316	260	357	302	399	344
317	261	358	303	400	345
318	262	359	304	401	346

The sec. in the current version	*The sec. in the former version*	*The sec. in the current version*	*The sec. in the former version*	*The sec. in the current version*	*The sec. in the former version*
402	347	447	376	489	413
403	348	448	377	490	414
404	349	449	378	491	415
405	350	450	none	492	416
406	351	451	none	493	417
407	352	452	none	494	418
408	353	453	379	495	419
409	354	454	380	496	420
410	355	455	381	497	421
411	356	456	382	498	422
412	357	457	383	499	423
413	358	458	386	500	424
414	359	459	384	501	425
415	360	460	385	502	426
416	361	461	387	503	427
417	143	462	none	504	428
418	144	463	388	505	429
419	145	464	389	506	430
420	146	465	390	507	431
421	147	466	391	508	432
427–422-	none	467	392	509	433
428	148	468	393	510	434
429	149	469	none	511	435
430	150	470	394	512	436
431	151	471	395	513	437
432	152	472	396	514	438
433	153	473	397	515	439
434	154	474	398	516	440
435	362	475	399	517	441
436	363	476	400	518	442
437	364	477	401	519	443
438	365	478	402	520	444
439	366	479	403	521	445
439A	367	480	404	522	446
440	368	481	405	523	447
441	369	482	406	524	448
442	370	483	407	525	449
442A	371	484	408	526	450
443	372	485	409	527	451
444	373	486	410	528	452
445	374	487	411	529	453
446	375	488	412	530	454

The sec. in the current version	*The sec. in the former version*	*The sec. in the current version*	*The sec. in the former version*	*The sec. in the current version*	*The sec. in the former version*
531	455	573	497	614	539
532	456	574	498	615	540
533	457	575	499	616	541
534	458	576	500	617	542
535	459	577	501	618	543
536	460	578	502	619	544
537	461	579	503	620	545
538	463	580	504	621	546
539	464	581	505	622	547
540	465	582	506	623	548
541	466	583	507	624	549
542	467	584	508	625	550
543	468	585	509	626	551
544	469	586	510	627	552
545	470	587	511	628	553
546	471	588	512	669	554
547	472	588A	513	670	555
548	473	589	514	671	556
549	474	590	515	672	557
550	475	591	516	673	558
551	476	592	517	674	559
552	477	593	518	675	560
553	478	594	519	676	561
554	479	595	520	677	562
555	480	596	521	678	563
556	481	597	522	679	564
557	482	598	523	680	565
558	483	599	524	681	566
559	484	600	525	682	567
560	485	601	526	683	568
561	486	602	527	684	569
562	487	603	528	685	570
563	488	604	529	686	571
564	462	605	530	687	572
565	489	606	531	688	573
566	490	607	532	689	574
567	491	608	533	690	575
568	492	609	534	691	576
569	493	610	535	692	577
570	494	611	536	693	578
571	495	612	537	694	579
572	496	613	538	695	580

The sec. in the current version	*The sec. in the former version*	*The sec. in the current version*	*The sec. in the former version*	*The sec. in the current version*	*The sec. in the former version*
696	581	736	620	774B	662
697	582	737	621	775	663
698	583	738	622	776	664
699	584	739	623	777	665
700	585	740	624	778	666
701	586	741	625	779	667
702	587	742	626	780	668
703	588	743	627	781	669
704	589	744	628	782	none
705	590	744A	629	783	670
706	591	745	630	784	671
707	592	746	631	785	672
708	593	747	632	786	673
709	594	748	633	787	674
710	none	749	635	788	675
711	none	750	634	789	676
712	595	751	636	790	677
713	596	752	637	791	678
713A	597	753	638	792	679
714	598	754	639	793	680
715	599	754A	640	794	681
716	600	755	641	795	682
717	601	756	642	796	683
718	602	757	643	797	684
719	603	758	644	798	685
720	604	759	645	799	686
721	605	760	646	800	687
722	606	761	647	801	688
723	607	762	648	802	689
724	608	763	649	803	690
725	609	764	650	804	691
726	610	765	651	805	692
726A	611	766	652	806	693
727	612	767	653	807	none
728	613	768	654	844	694
729	614	769	655	845	695
730	none	770	656	846	696
731	615	771	657	847	697
732	616	772	658	848	698
733	617	773	659	849	699
734	618	774	660	850	700
735	619	774A	661	851	701

The sec. in the current version	*The sec. in the former version*	*The sec. in the current version*	*The sec. in the former version*	*The sec. in the current version*	*The sec. in the former version*
852	none	854	703	855	none
853	702				